READING
from this
PLACE

READING
from this
PLACE

Volume 2

Social Location and
Biblical Interpretation
in Global Perspective

Fernando F. Segovia
and
Mary Ann Tolbert,
Editors

Fortress Press   Minneapolis

Cover design: Brad Norr Design
Interior design: ediType

The Library of Congress has catalogued Volume One as follows:
Reading from this place / Fernando F. Segovia and Mary Ann Tolbert, editors.
    p.   cm.
    Papers originally presented at conferences on Social Location and Biblical Interpretation and on Globalization and Theological Education, the first held at Vanderbilt University, Jan. 21–24, 1993.
    Includes bibliographical references and index.
    Contents: v. 1. Social location and biblical interpretation in the United States.
    ISBN 0-8006-2812-8 (v. 1 : alk. paper)
    1. Bible—Hermeneutics—Congresses. 2. Theology—Study and teaching—Congresses. 3. Bible as literature—Congresses. Religious pluralism—Christianity—Congresses. I. Segovia, Fernando F. II. Tolbert, Mary Ann, 1947– .
BS476.R42   1995
220.6′01—dc20

94–33208
CIP

ISBN 0-8006-2949-3 (v. 2 : alk. paper)

The paper used in this publication meets the minimum requirements of American National Standard for Information Sciences—Permanence of Paper for Printed Library Materials, ANSI Z329.48-1984.

Manufactured in the U.S.A.   AF 1–2949

99   98   97   96   95   1   2   3   4   5   6   7   8   9   10

To the memory of
GEORGE M. SOARES-PRABHU, S.J.,
radical thinker and genuine human being,
who met an untimely death in India
on July 22, 1995

Contents

Part Three
READINGS FROM EUROPE

Part Four
READINGS FROM LATIN AMERICA

Part Five
READINGS FROM NORTH AMERICA

Preface

The present volume represents the second phase of a multidimensional and multivolume project entitled "Reading from This Place: Social Location and Biblical Interpretation," whose background, contours, and aims were explained at length in the preface to the first volume, published by Fortress Press early in 1995. In effect, this second volume gathers together the papers presented at the international conference, which took place at the Vanderbilt Divinity School on October 21–24, 1993, and which was made possible by a generous grant from the Lilly Endowment. Unfortunately, two of the presentations made at the conference were not submitted as papers afterward and thus could not be included in this volume. Both were from African scholars, which accounts for the smaller representation from Africa in the volume itself. As with the first volume, the introduction and conclusion were written, the former by Fernando F. Segovia and the latter by Mary Ann Tolbert, after the conference and in the light of its presentations and proceedings. Like the first, this second volume is meant as an additional contribution to the fundamental question regarding the role of the interpreter in a radically changing world within biblical criticism—a world of increasing and irreversible diversity and pluralism, the world of the twenty-first century.

Acknowledgments

The editors would like to express their profound gratitude to all those individuals and institutions who have made this volume possible.

First, to the Lilly Endowment and Dr. Craig Dykstra, Vice President for Religion, for their unfailing support of the project and the generous funding that made possible bringing together all these individuals for the second and international conference entitled "Reading from This Place."

Second, to Dr. Joseph C. Hough, Jr., Dean of the Divinity School at Vanderbilt University, for his much-appreciated assistance in all the different areas and dimensions of the project.

Third, to Dr. Marshall Johnson, Editorial Director of Fortress Press, who backed the project from the very beginning; to the editorial staff of Fortress Press, especially Michael West and David Lott, who brought it to completion under their expert care and advice; and to Hank Schlau of ediType, for his superb editorial hand and acumen.

Fourth, to all the students in the area of New Testament and Early Christianity within the Graduate Department of Religion at Vanderbilt University whose kind participation and assistance proved so valuable during the course of the conference itself. Two deserve special recognition and gratitude: Mr. William Gregory Carey, who carried out the task of editing and formatting the papers for publication; and Mr. Francisco Lozada-Smith, who once again served as manager for the conference and whose close attention to detail and organization made this second conference another unqualified success.

Finally, to all those scholars and friends who graciously accepted our invitations and whose contributions to the project grace the pages that follow. To them we are specially indebted.

Contributors

Naim Ateek, St. George's Cathedral, Jerusalem.

Tereza Cavalcanti, Pontifícia Universidade Católica do Rio de Janeiro.

J. Severino Croatto, Instituto Superior Evangélico de Estudios Teológicos, Buenos Aires.

Peggy L. Day, the University of Winnipeg.

Paulo Fernando Carneiro de Andrade, Pontifícia Universidade Católica do Rio de Janeiro.

Lone Fatum, Institute for Biblical Exegesis, University of Copenhagen.

Hisako Kinukawa, International Christian University, Tokyo.

Archie C. C. Lee, the Chinese University of Hong Kong.

Temba L. J. Mafico (from Zimbabwe), Interdenominational Theological Center, Atlanta.

Néstor Míguez, Instituto Superior Evangélico de Estudios Teológicos, Buenos Aires.

Mercy Amba Oduyoye (from Ghana), General Secretariat, World Council of Churches, Geneva.

Teresa Okure, S.H.C.J., Catholic Institute of West Africa, Port Harcourt, Nigeria.

Pablo Richard, Departamento Ecuménico de Investigaciones, San José, Costa Rica.

Christopher Rowland, the Queen's College, Oxford University.

Luise Schottroff, Kassel Universität, Kassel, Germany.

Fernando F. Segovia, the Divinity School, Vanderbilt University, Nashville.

George M. Soares-Prabhu, Pontifical Athenaeum, Institute of Philosophy and Religion, Ramwadi, Pune, India.

Mary Ann Tolbert, Pacific School of Religion, Berkeley, California.

Elaine M. Wainwright, Catholic Theological Seminary, Banyo, Queensland, Australia.

Cultural Studies and Contemporary Biblical Criticism: Ideological Criticism as Mode of Discourse

_____ Fernando F. Segovia _____

I have argued elsewhere that the development of biblical criticism in the twentieth century can be plotted in terms of four different paradigms or umbrella models of interpretation, each with its own fairly distinctive mode of discourse and broad spectrum of interpretation.[1] I have further argued that these four paradigms find themselves at present, in the mid-1990s and thus already at the turn of the century, in competition with one another within the discipline, in what is perhaps best described as a state of seemingly stable if not actually permanent anomie.[2] Now, having already

---

1. See F. F. Segovia, " 'And They Began to Speak in Other Tongues': Competing Modes of Discourse in Contemporary Biblical Criticism," *Reading from This Place,* vol. 1, *Social Location and Biblical Interpretation in the United States* (ed. F. F. Segovia and M. A. Tolbert; Minneapolis: Fortress Press, 1995) 1–32. For a different plotting, with a focus on the Gospel of Mark and the author-role as leitmotif, see J. Capel Anderson and S. D. Moore, "Introduction: The Lives of Mark," *Mark and Method: New Approaches in Biblical Studies* (ed. J. C. Anderson and S. D. Moore; Minneapolis: Fortress Press, 1992) 1–22.

2. This characterization I borrow in part from the parallel plotting of anthropological studies from the 1950s through the early 1980s undertaken by S. B. Ortner ("Theory in Anthropology since the Sixties," *Comparative Studies in Society and History* 26 [1984] 126–66). With the 1960s, Ortner observes, the major paradigms in place in the 1950s gave way to a wide array of theoretical models, rendering communication itself within the field a forbidding if not altogether impossible enterprise, what she describes as a classic situation of liminality. (See, for example, 372: "The field appears to be a thing of shreds and patches, of individuals and small coteries pursuing disjunctive investigations and talking mainly to themselves...confusion of categories, expressions of chaos and antistructure....") That, I would argue, was not at all unlike what happened in biblical criticism in the 1980s, or approximately twenty years later. Interestingly enough, Ortner does point to a new key symbol in anthropological orientation (a focus on "practice" or "praxis" and the "agent" or "actor") that gave rise to a variety of theories and methods and that perhaps marked an initial movement in the direction of a new and emerging consensus. Despite clear similarities between such practice theory and the cultural studies I envision, I would make no such claims for the latter in biblical criticism. Not only do I not see any developing or forthcoming consensus in sight, but also I must confess that I find anomie neither inherently objectionable nor unattractive. On the impact of the 1960s on the humanities in general, see, for example, V. B. Leitch, *American Literary Criticism from the Thirties to the Eighties* (New York:

focused upon the first three paradigms involved in the plot, I should like to provide in this study an initial, overall characterization of the fourth paradigm, what I have chosen to call cultural studies or ideological criticism.[3] By way of introduction a brief recapitulation and further explication of the plot in question will prove most appropriate and useful.

Plotting Biblical Criticism

The proposed plot as I construct it includes a spatial and poetic dimension as well as a temporal and ideological dimension; further, there are three basic stages involving the largely sequential emergence and development of the critical paradigms in terms of a process of liberation and decolonization at work in the discipline.[4] As such, the plot reveals a fairly classic mold with regard to structure and movement. On the one hand, the plot does have a beginning, a middle, and an end: an existing state of affairs, unruffled and long-lasting, undergoes from within a situation of conflict and tension, ultimately giving way to resolution and a new state of affairs. On the other hand, besides this implicit sense of movement, the plot possesses an explicit sense of progress, whereby the beginning state of affairs is seen as changing throughout *for the better,* as the terms "liberation" and "decolonization" readily imply. At the same time, however, the plot also reveals a more contemporary, ironic mode with respect to content and argumentation. First, the resolution envisioned is quite open-ended and hence a sort of nonresolution: instead of a new consensus, multiplicity reigns. Second, the progress is not so much linear or monolingual but rather multidirectional and multilingual: a speaking in many tongues.[5]

The three stages in question proceed as follows. To begin with, a

---

Columbia Univ. Press, 1988) 366–407; S. Seidman, *Contested Knowledge: Social Theory in the Postmodern Era* (Oxford: Blackwell, 1984) 234–80.

3. I would emphasize the "initial" or tentative character of this description, insofar as it does not have, unlike the other three, the privilege of years of hindsight. I would certainly emphasize as well the constructive and perspectival nature of this description: this is an overview of the paradigm as I see it and practice it from my own vantage point and experience.

4. To be sure, the plot involves a rhetorical dimension as well, insofar as it represents an attempt on my part to persuade readers not only of its historical validity and heuristic value but also of the need for and benefits of the paradigm of cultural studies, where I would presently situate myself. Indeed, this essay is written not only from the point of view of a practitioner but also in the mode of cultural studies.

5. Thus, while inscribed in the logic and closure of modernism, the plot is also inscribed in the logic and openness of postmodernism: not only insofar as it sees itself in terms of "plotting" and thus admits theoretically and practically of any number of other such plottings but also insofar as the plot offered does in the end deconstruct itself, so to speak, presenting diversity both as a new and as a positive and welcome state of affairs. On the inescapable relationship of postmodernism to modernism, see especially L. Hutcheon, *The Politics of Postmodernism* (New York: Routledge, 1989).

thoroughly entrenched and dominant historical criticism (the first stage)—which had been firmly in place since, in effect, approximately the middle of the nineteenth century[6]—is rather swiftly displaced, beginning in the mid-1970s, by two different and largely unrelated movements: literary criticism and cultural criticism, each of which rapidly gains strength and sophistication through the 1980s and into the 1990s (the second stage). Subsequently, a number of developments within each of these two paradigms in the late 1980s gradually begin to point the way toward another such paradigm or umbrella model of interpretation, cultural studies or ideological criticism (the third stage), with a specific focus on both texts and readers of texts—real, flesh-and-blood readers.

On the one hand, literary criticism is eventually forced to wrestle with the fundamental issue of real readers on two counts: first, insofar as it gradually moves from an analysis of the formal features or elements of texts (narrative criticism) to an analysis of readers (intratextual readers, that is) and the reading process in the construction of meaning (reader-response criticism); second, insofar as it increasingly entertains the notion of multiple interpretations, whether based primarily on the text (via the polysemy of language) or on the reader (via the filling in of textual gaps).[7] On the other hand, cultural criticism is also brought to confront this crucial issue of real readers on two counts as well: first, in the light of the persistent emphasis of neo-Marxist interpretations on readers and readings as socioeconomic and ideological products; second, in the light of the turn toward readers and readings as sociocultural products in anthropological approaches.[8]

This gradual turn toward the reader on the part of both literary criticism and cultural criticism eventually brings biblical criticism face-to-face with the question of real, flesh-and-blood readers, and, in so doing, shifts it into

---

6. See, for example, R. F. Collins (*Introduction to the New Testament* [Garden City, N.Y.: Doubleday, 1983] 41–74, esp. 41–45]), who attributes the rise of such critical consensus in large part to the work and influence of F. C. Baur (1792–1860) and the success of the Tübingen school. See also in this regard J. Fitzmyer's spirited defense of historical criticism ("Historical Criticism: Its Role in Biblical Interpretation and Church Life," *Theological Studies* 50 [1989] 244–59), where the relationship between the historical-critical paradigm and the classical philology of the late eighteenth and nineteenth centuries is clearly and directly brought to the surface.

7. For recent accounts of the path of literary criticism, see E. Struthers Malbon and J. Capel Anderson, "Literary-Critical Methods," *Searching the Scriptures*, vol. 1, *A Feminist Introduction* (ed. E. Schüssler Fiorenza; New York: Crossroad, 1993) 241–54; D. M. Gunn, "Narrative Criticism," and E. V. McKnight, "Reader-Response Criticism," *To Each Its Own: An Introduction to Biblical Criticisms and Their Application* (ed. S. L. McKenzie and S. R. Haynes; Louisville: John Knox/Westminster, 1993) 171–95 and 197–219, respectively; E. Struthers Malbon, "Narrative Criticism: How Does the Story Mean?" and R. M. Fowler, "Reader Response Criticism: Figuring Mark's Reader," *Mark and Method*, 23–49 and 50–83, respectively.

8. For recent accounts of the path of cultural criticism, see M. A. Tolbert, "Social, Sociological, and Anthropological Methods," *Searching the Scriptures*, 255–71; Dale B. Martin, "Social Scientific Criticism," *To Each Its Own*, 103–19; D. Rhoads, "Social Criticism: Crossing Boundaries," *Mark and Method*, 135–61.

a very different model of interpretation with its own mode of discourse and theoretical spectrum. The end result, once again, is the existence of four competing paradigms within the discipline at one and the same time: not at all a new consensus, therefore, replacing the earlier one of historical criticism, but rather a situation of radical plurality (or perhaps a consensus about no consensus).

At the same time, besides such methodological and theoretical developments in the discipline, the proposed plot involves a crucial demographic and sociocultural development as well. Following a pattern at work not only across the entire disciplinary spectrum but also within theological studies itself, biblical criticism, which had remained since its inception largely, if not exclusively, the preserve of Western males—Western male clerics, to be more precise—begins to witness an influx of outsiders, individuals now making their voices heard for the first time: Western women; non-Western theologians and critics; and racial and ethnic minorities from non-Western civilizations in the West.[9]

Such individuals, to be sure, received their training almost exclusively in the academic institutions of the West, where historical criticism reigned supreme and where they were duly introduced to the fundamentals of the method at the hands of Western male scholars in their role as *Doktorvätern,* master researchers and teachers as well as founders of or links in all-important pedigree lines. As such, these outsiders were very much subject to the powerful centripetal and homogenizing forces of this training, with its emphasis on the classic ideals of the Enlightenment: all knowledge as science; the scientific method as applicable to all areas of inquiry; nature or facts as neutral and knowable; research as a search for truth involving value-free observation and recovery of the facts; the researcher as a champion of reason who surveys the facts with disinterested eyes. A further, fundamental—though much more implicit—dimension of this socialization, quite in keeping with the cult of modernity emerging from the Enlightenment, should be noted as well: the conviction that such training not only represented progress over against traditional interpretations of the

---

9. By "Western" civilization or culture I mean, following the proposal of S. P. Huntington ("The Clash of Civilizations?" *Foreign Affairs* 72 [summer 1993] 22–49, and idem, "If Not Civilizations, What? Paradigms of the Post-Cold War World," *Foreign Affairs* 72 [November/December 1993] 186–94), all those who view and identify with the West as their highest level of cultural grouping and broadest level of cultural identity. For Huntington, therefore, a civilization or culture encompasses both common objective elements (for example, language, history, religion, customs, institutions) and the subjective self-identification of people. In addition, civilizations may have subcivilizations; for example, the West itself is seen as comprised of two such variants: Europe and (Anglo/Francophone) North America. To be sure, like any highly abstract category, the concept is not without its problems. Thus, for example, an analysis of the construction of "the West"—its narrative elements of plot, characters, events, and so forth—within the West itself would reveal manifold and significant variations. Nevertheless, within the given framework of ideal types for cultures and civilizations, I find that it does have value for purposes of identification and comparison.

Bible (the triumph of light over darkness and reason over tradition) but also reflected the superiority of the West over against other cultures and civilizations (the hermeneutics of over/against and the white man's burden). In other words, historical criticism was perceived and promoted not only as the proper way to read and interpret the biblical texts but also as the ultimate sign of progress in the discipline, the offer of the (Christian) West to the rest of the (Christian) world and the means by which the backward and ignorant could become modern and educated.[10]

Despite this overwhelming academic socialization, many of these individuals slowly began to question the program and agenda of such biblical criticism, especially the construct of the scientific, objective, and impartial researcher—the universal and informed reader—operative in one form or another not only in historical criticism but also in the other two emerging paradigms; these individuals then also began to raise the radical question of perspective and contextualization in biblical criticism.[11] This growing insistence on the situated and interested nature of all reading and interpretation would bring additional, pointed, and unrelenting pressure on biblical criticism to come to terms with the question of flesh-and-blood readers, further pushing the discipline as a result into a quite different model of interpretation, with its own mode of discourse and interpretive spectrum.[12]

---

10. To be sure, a ready analogy can be drawn between the cultural ramifications of this assumption and its ramifications for gender: just as historical criticism represented progress and superiority vis-à-vis all other cultures, so did it embody the "masculine" traits of reason and objectivity vis-à-vis the "feminine" traits of emotion and subjectivity.

11. Not surprisingly, the very same phenomenon was taking place in the field of historical studies, a discipline constituted in the aftermath of the French Revolution; biblical criticism turned to historical studies for guidance and inspiration in the first half of the nineteenth century as it sought to come to terms with the Enlightenment, modernity, and the scientific method. On the significance of voices from the outside in historical studies, see the recent overview of historiography by J. Appleby, L. Hunt, and M. Jacob (*Telling the Truth about History* [New York: Norton, 1994] esp. 129–59 and 198–237), as well as the similarly recent overview of the question of objectivity in historiography by P. Novick (*That Noble Dream: The "Objectivity Question" and the American Historical Profession* [Cambridge: Cambridge Univ. Press, 1988] esp. 469–521). For the impact of outside voices on literary criticism, see V. B. Leitch, *Cultural Criticism, Literary Theory, Poststructuralism* (New York: Columbia Univ. Press, 1992) 83–103. For their impact on social theory in general, see N. B. Dirks, G. Eley, and S. B. Ortner, eds., *Culture/Power/History: A Reader in Contemporary Social Theory* (Princeton, N.J.: Princeton Univ. Press, 1994) esp. 3–45. For their impact on anthropology, see, for example, T. Asad, ed., *Anthropology and the Colonial Encounter* (New York: Humanities Press, 1973) and R. Rosaldo, *Culture and Truth: The Remaking of Social Analysis* (Boston: Beacon Press, 1989).

12. See, for example, from the perspective of Western women: E. Schüssler Fiorenza, *Bread Not Stone: The Challenge of Feminist Biblical Interpretation* (Boston: Beacon Press, 1984); idem, *Searching the Scriptures* (2 vols.; New York: Crossroad, 1993–94); C. A. Newsom and S. H. Ringe, eds., *Women's Bible Commentary* (Louisville: Westminster/John Knox Press, 1992); from the perspective of non-Western cultures, see R. S. Sugirtharajah, *Voices from the Margin: Interpreting the Bible in the Third World* (Maryknoll, N.Y.: Orbis Books, 1991); from the perspective of non-Western minorities in the West, see C. H. Felder, ed., *Stony the Road We Trod: African American Biblical Interpretation* (Minneapolis: Fortress Press, 1991). An analysis of the correlation between the raising of such voices and concerns

Thus, the long-standing project of the Enlightenment, as embodied in historical criticism and its emerging rivals, was ultimately being called into question, as were a number of attendant principles and notions: the character of biblical studies as *science* and the use of the *scientific* method; the nature of *history;* the possibility of *value-free* observation; the role of the *rational, disinterested* researcher; the notion of *progress.* In the process, historical criticism along with the new competing paradigms began to be analyzed (like the Enlightenment itself) in terms of perspective and contextualization, agenda and social location, inextricably tied as these were to the gender and origins of its practitioners—Western male clerics. In other words, the thoroughly Western and gendered character of the discipline lying just behind the scientific facade of the universal and informed reader began to be exposed and critiqued. In effect, reading and interpretation were no longer seen as value-free and disinterested but rather as thoroughly enmeshed in the public arena and thus as irretrievably *political* in character and ramifications, from the point of view of both the narrower meaning of this term (the realm of politics within the sphere of the sociocultural) and its broader meaning (the realm of power within the sphere of the ideological).

From within and without, therefore, on the basis of internal disciplinary developments as well as external sociocultural developments, biblical criticism was being pushed to take into account not only the texts of ancient Judaism and early Christianity but also the readers and interpreters of such texts—the twofold focus I have advanced as central to the emerging paradigm of cultural studies.[13] Such a plot I have described in terms of liberation and decolonization. This I do on two counts: first, with respect to models and strategies, insofar as a tightly controlling paradigm is displaced by enormous diversity in the theoretical and methodological realm; second, with respect to reader-constructs, insofar as the construct of the scientific and detached ideal reader as well as the faceless and nameless constructs of intratextual readers are displaced by enormous diversity in the sociocultural realm. As a result, the Western and gendered nature of the discipline, operating under the mask of objectivity and impartiality, is unveiled, and the issue of perspective and contextualization is brought to bear as much on the texts as on the real readers and interpreters of the texts. Such a dénouement, I would readily confess, represents for me, inscribed as I have been and continue to be in a variety of colonial realities

---

and the critical paradigms available and invoked would prove most valuable and remains a project for the future.

13. I should explain that by "biblical criticism" I mean not only criticism of the canonical texts, whether of Judaism or Christianity, but also criticism of all other texts surviving from ancient Judaism or early Christianity. I use the term "biblical criticism" throughout merely as a shorthand for such comprehensive studies and for lack of a better inclusive and concise term.

and discourses, a most welcome and attractive situation of liberation and decolonization, whereby other voices can now speak in their own tongues and no center controls the discourse. If the result be a situation of anomie, and I believe that it is, I find that neither regrettable nor deplorable but rather something to be welcomed and embraced.[14]

Cultural Studies: The Text as Construction

For this still emerging paradigm of cultural studies, then, real readers lie behind all models of interpretation and all reading strategies, all recreations of meaning from texts and all reconstructions of history; further, all such models, strategies, recreations, and reconstructions are seen as constructs on the part of flesh-and-blood readers; and all such readers are themselves regarded as variously positioned and engaged in their own respective social locations. Thus, different real readers use different strategies and models in different ways, at different times, and with different results (different readings and interpretations) in the light of their different and highly complex social locations. Consequently, for cultural studies a critical analysis of real readers and their readings (their representations of the ancient texts and the ancient world) becomes as important and necessary as a critical analysis of the ancient texts themselves (the remains of the ancient world), since these two critical foci are seen as ultimately interdependent and interrelated. In other words, all recreations of meaning and all reconstructions of history are in the end regarded as constructs or re-presentations: re-creations and re-constructions.

As such, cultural studies has recourse to a broad variety of theoretical frameworks and modes of discourse, ranging from the more traditional historical and theological discussion of historical criticism, to the more recent dialogue partners of literary criticism and cultural criticism, to the field of cultural studies as such.[15] Cultural studies within biblical criticism thus

14. In this regard, quite ironically, my evaluation of the present situation in biblical criticism is further inscribed in the text of modernity and its emphasis on freedom from the past. In other words, just as historical criticism gloried in the élan of freedom from religious tradition and dogmatism and as both literary criticism and cultural criticism rejoiced in the feeling of freedom from a critical stranglehold, so does cultural studies, as I envision it, rejoice and glory in the sense of liberation from the surface dehumanization of readers (the call for objectivity) and of decolonization from the underlying rehumanization of readers (the Westernization of all readers). Of course, the evaluation is also inscribed in the text of postmodernity, insofar as the operative concepts of liberation and decolonization call for a humanization of all readers, whether high or low, in the center or on the periphery, dominant or subaltern.

15. On cultural studies, see, for example, S. Hall, "Cultural Studies: Two Paradigms," *Media, Culture, and Society* (2 vols; Newbury Park, Calif.: Sage, 1980) 2:57–82; A. Easthope, *Literary into Cultural Studies* (New York: Routledge, 1991); L. Grossberg, C. Nelson, and P. Treichler, *Cultural Studies* (New York: Routledge, 1992); Leitch, *Cultural Criticism;* F. Inglis, *Cultural Studies* (Oxford: Blackwell, 1993).

seeks to integrate, in different ways, the historical, formalist, and socio-cultural questions and concerns of the other paradigms on a different key, a hermeneutical key, with the situated and interested reader and interpreter always at its core. As a result, a new mode of discourse, bearing its own analytical wherewithal and corresponding nomenclature, comes into play—a mode of discourse best characterized as *ideological,* given its central focus on contextualization and perspective, social location and agenda, and hence on the political character of all composition and texts as well as reading and interpretation. Such a mode of discourse is by no means monolingual but rather quite varied, profoundly polyglot, given the complex nature of social locations and agendas. In the end, a different model of interpretation begins to take shape, calling yet again for a very different type of reading and application on the part of its subscribers.

With this background in mind, I now proceed to an overview—again, I would stress, preliminary and tentative, given the absence of precious hindsight—of the basic principles I see as guiding and informing this umbrella model in biblical criticism. In so doing, I follow my earlier analysis of the other paradigms with respect to the categories of comparison employed: location of meaning; reading strategy; theoretical foundations; the role of the reader; theological presuppositions; and pedagogical implications.

1. *Location of Meaning.* The cultural studies model approaches the text as a construct, insofar as meaning is taken to reside not in the author of the text or the world behind the text (as postulated by both historical criticism and cultural criticism) or in the text as such (as postulated by literary criticism of the text-dominant variety) but in the encounter or interchange between text and reader. For the model, moreover, the reader in this interaction is seen primarily in terms of real readers rather than intermediate and formalistic reader-constructs (as in literary criticism of the reader-dominant sort), although the latter are not at all ruled out in the process of reading and interpretation.[16] Meaning emerges, therefore, as the result of an encounter between a socially and historically conditioned text and a socially and historically conditioned reader.

From this perspective, the text—no matter how approached, whether as medium or means, or by whom, whether oneself or others—is always looked upon not as an autonomous and unchanging object, as something "out there" with a stable meaning that precedes and guides/controls in-

---

16. Two points are in order. First, such reader-constructs (see the section below entitled "The Role of the Reader") would be explicitly identified as such, justified in terms of reading strategies, and acknowledged as constructions on the part of real readers, variously positioned and engaged in their respective social locations. Consequently, the readings produced through the use of such intermediate and formalistic reader-constructs, regardless of the goals and purposes adduced for their employment, are not seen as more neutral and objective productions but rather as thoroughly contextualized and ideological productions. Second, real readers themselves would ultimately have to be seen and analyzed in terms of constructs as well.

terpretation, but rather as a "text," as something that is always read and interpreted by real readers.[17] The text, therefore, may be approached and analyzed from a variety of angles.

First, it may be viewed as a medium, as a message between a sender and a receiver, an author and a reader. The focus would then lie on the text, with a corresponding emphasis on its artistic and/or strategic character and an examination of its formal aesthetic and/or persuasive features—the text as a literary and rhetorical creation. Second, it may be approached as a means, as evidence from and for the time of composition. The focus would then rest on the world behind the text (the world presupposed by, reflected in, and addressed by the text), with a corresponding emphasis on contextualization and perspective and an examination of its historical, sociocultural, and political dimensions—the text as a historical, cultural, and ideological creation. Third, it may be understood as a construct, as the result of interaction or negotiation between the text and its reader(s). The focus would then lie on the text as actually read and interpreted, with a corresponding emphasis on its various readings, whether historical or contemporary, and an examination of the contextualization and perspective of such readings—the text as a creation on the part of readers and interpreters.

In the end, however, whether the text is approached directly or indirectly, cultural studies remains keenly aware throughout of the fact that any reading and interpretation—any account of the text, whether in terms of its historical and theological, literary and rhetorical, sociocultural and ideological dimensions, by oneself or by others, in the present or in the past—constitutes a construction or re-presentation on the part of real readers: a re-*creation* of its meaning and re-*construction* of its context on the part of readers who read and interpret from within specific social locations and with specific interests in mind. For cultural studies, therefore, this character of the text as "text" ultimately makes a joint analysis of texts and readings of texts indispensable and imperative. There is never a text out there but many "texts."

2. *Reading Strategy.* In principle, in terms of theory, cultural studies would be as interested in layered as in holistic readings of the text. In other

---

17. Such a position need not deny altogether the existence of authorial intention (whether realized or intended), literary or rhetorical elements and features, and sociohistorical context or sociocultural scripts and codes. Self-reflection has taught me in no uncertain ways that, when writing or speaking or acting, I very often do so with certain goals and purposes in mind, which I then proceed to formulate in certain ways in the light of the context at hand and under the influence of a variety of sociocultural scripts and codes. At the same time, experience has taught me that there are usually many other goals and purposes at work— many other subtexts behind the texts—of which I am not aware at the time of acting, speaking, or writing. Experience has further taught me that any perception or rendering of such intentions, elements, context, and script of myself and the various "texts" I put forth— and hence of texts as well—always constitutes a reading and interpretation, contextualized and perspectival, that in the end reveal as much about myself and my "texts" (or about texts) as about my readers and interpreters.

words, both the largely vertical reading of historical criticism, that reading that is based on *aporias* and textual ruptures, and the largely horizontal reading of both literary and cultural criticism, that reading that is based on the unity and coherence of the text, are seen in terms of reading strategies and underlying theoretical models on the part of real readers. As such, the presuppositions and ramifications of such strategies and models become a primary focus of attention: Why is it that some readers see disunity in the text to the extent that a reading of it as it presently stands is deemed impossible, proceed to identify the seams and ruptures in question, and engage in an excavative sort of criticism whereby literary layers are sifted out and chronologically arranged for a proper reading of the text? Why do other readers find unity and coherence in the text as it stands, downplay or rule out altogether the presence of ruptures and seams, and opt for a horizontal type of criticism with an emphasis on literary anatomy and flow or social script and codes?

In practice, therefore, in its own approach to texts, cultural studies would neither rule out the presence of textual ruptures nor find it necessary to argue for unity and coherence. Indeed, it could very well argue, along the lines of deconstruction, that there are *aporias* in the text but that such *aporias* point not to conflicting literary layers but rather to a fundamental lack of unity or coherence in the text.[18] Any decision would be made ad hoc, as the occasion were deemed to require. In the end, however, regardless of the particular decision reached and applied with respect to the text in question, the result would be regarded as a "text," a reading and interpretation on the part of real readers, involving and thus calling for an analysis of contextualization and perspective: situated and interested flesh-and-blood readers arguing for disunity and incoherence as evidence for underlying literary strata, unity and coherence, or disunity and incoherence as evidence for ideological contradictions and implosion.

3. *Theoretical Foundations*. With cultural studies the spirit of positivism and empiricism—so prevalent in historical, literary, and cultural criticism—draws to a close. To begin with, the meaning of the text is no longer regarded as objective and univocal, nor is the critical approach employed in the analysis of the text presented as scientific in the sense of yielding, when rigorously formulated and applied, an accurate retrieval and recreation of such meaning. Similarly, the path of history behind the text also ceases to be

---

18. In other words, a deconstructive approach would also be seen in terms of reading strategies and underlying theoretical orientation on the part of real readers, bringing to the fore thereby, once again, the question of presuppositions and ramifications: Why is it that some readers look for inconsistencies and contradictions in the text so as to emphasize its disunity and incoherence? Further, why is such a strategy presented as a critical move against any and all totalizing ideologies and characterized as liberative? For deconstruction in biblical criticism, see S. D. Moore, *Literary Criticism and the Gospels: The Theoretical Challenge* (New Haven: Yale Univ. Press, 1989) 131–78; idem, "Deconstructive Criticism: The Gospel of Mark," *Mark and Method*, 84–102.

regarded as univocal and objective and thus open to scientific retrieval and reconstruction. For cultural studies the text has no meaning and history has no path without a reader or interpreter—without a creation of such a meaning and a construction of such a path from within a contextualized perspective; likewise, there is no critical approach without a critic—without a construction of methods and models out of a contextualized perspective.

Given its location of meaning in the interchange between text and reader (real reader, that is) and its view of the text not as something out there, both preceding and guiding/controlling interpretation, but as "text," as something that is always read and interpreted, cultural studies accepts a plurality of interpretations not only as a given but also as a point of departure for an analysis of texts and history. As such, it approaches the question of validity in interpretation as a problematic, since even the very criteria used for judgment and evaluation are seen not in essentialist terms, as universally valid and applicable at all times and in all places, across all models and social locations, but as themselves constructions on the part of real readers and hence as emerging from and formulated within specific social locations and agendas. For cultural studies, therefore, the concept of multiple interpretations is, in the end, much less circumscribed and much more open-ended than in literary criticism.

Consequently, cultural studies focuses on the variety of readings and interpretations of texts. As such, scholarship tends to be seen less as evolutionary and progressive, with serious aberrations and deviations along the way, and more as multidirectional and multilingual, reflecting different reading strategies and models at work on the part of real readers, whose contexts and interests call for critical analysis as well.[19] It should be pointed out in this regard that the critical situation envisioned is not necessarily one where "everything goes," since readers and interpreters are always positioned and interested and thus always engaged in evaluation and construction: both texts and "texts" are constantly analyzed and engaged, with acceptance or rejection, full or partial, as ever-present and even shifting possibilities. At the same time, that sense of sharp competition, of demolition and exposé, that has been at the heart of the discipline for so long (reflecting no doubt its primary context in both the male world and the capitalism of the West) yields as well to a realization that no final recreation of meaning or reconstruction of history is possible—beyond all perspective

---

19. This is not to say that there is no sense of evolution and progress at all. Indeed, I myself have recourse to categories that imply a measure of progress and development: liberation and decolonization. On the one hand, however, such categories are themselves presented as constructions on my part, as my concept of plotting has made amply clear. On the other hand, the evolution and progress envisioned have nothing to do with a final and definitive retrieval and unveiling, almost eschatological in character, of the stable meaning of the text or the given path of history; to the contrary, such progress and evolution are seen in terms of movement toward diversity and multiplicity, with a view of both meaning and history as decentered and polyglot.

and contextualization; that all recreations and reconstructions are productions—creations and constructions—on the part of real readers; that such readers are differently situated and engaged; and that all constructs call for critical analysis and engagement in a spirit of critical dialogue.

4. *The Role of the Reader.* It is the role assigned to the reader that, without doubt, most sharply differentiates cultural studies from the other competing paradigms in contemporary biblical criticism. For cultural studies the reader does not and cannot ever remain faceless: the reader is a real reader whose voice does not and cannot remain in the background, even if so wished and attempted, but is actively and inevitably involved in the production of meaning, of "texts" and history; who does not and cannot make any claims to objectivity and universality, but is profoundly aware of the social location and agendas of all readers and readings, including his or her own; and who does not and cannot argue for sophisticated training, of whatever sort, and the creation of corresponding ideal readers as essential for a correct and proper understanding of a text, but is keenly aware of the nature of all readings as "texts," whether high or low, academic or popular, trained or untrained.[20] Such a foregrounding of the reader's face and voice has immediate consequences for the critical task.

First, cultural studies calls for critical analysis of reading strategies. On the one hand, strategies are to be identified, with a broad variety of options regarding reader-constructs available: internal readers or readers "inscribed" in the text, such as narratees, implied readers, or implicit readers; external readers of a historical sort, such as original, intended readers and ancient, Mediterranean readers; external readers of a suprahistorical sort, such as first-time, naïve readers and sophisticated, ideal readers; external readers of a contemporary sort, whether considered as individuals or as social beings; any combination thereof. On the other hand, since all strategies are regarded as constructs, their use is also to be justified: What goals and purposes are served thereby? What are the presuppositions and ramifications of the approach adopted? Why are different strategies invoked at different times?

---

20. The argument is not, lest I be misunderstood on this score, that education and scholarship are unnecessary and superfluous. Indeed, I for one see both scholarship and education as vital for liberation and decolonization. It is no accident that a primary tool of the colonizer is either to deny formal education altogether to the colonized (What would it benefit them?) or to undertake it in such a way as to deny the social location and interests of the colonized (Let us make them in our image and likeness!). The argument rather is that education and scholarship—a high socioeducational level—represent no privileged access to the meaning of a text or the path of history, but are simply another constitutive factor of human identity affecting all reading and interpretation, and in this sense are no different from any other such factor. It should be clear how such a position is inscribed in both modernism and postmodernism: in the former, insofar as education and scholarship are regarded as most valuable and liberating; in the latter, insofar as they are also seen in terms of social context and ideology.

Second, cultural studies also calls for critical analysis of real readers—of those who lie behind, opt for, construct, and apply such strategies. Real readers are seen as neither neutral nor impartial but as inextricably positioned and engaged within their own different and complex social locations. For cultural studies, therefore, the contextualization and perspective of readers are seen as impinging, in one way or another, upon their readings and interpretations, thus calling for critical analysis of such social locations and agendas in terms of the various constitutive factors of human identity: sexuality and gender; socioeconomic class; race and ethnicity; sociopolitical status and affiliation; socioeducational background and level; intellectual moorings; socioreligious background and affiliation; ideological stance; and so forth. For cultural studies all these dimensions of human existence must be studied not only with regard to texts, their representation in texts, but also with regard to readers of texts and their readings, their representation in "texts."

Finally, cultural studies calls for critical analysis of all readers and readings, whether located in the academy or not, highly informed or not. In effect, the traditional distinction between high and low is collapsed thereby: the readings of, say, base Christian communities (*comunidades de base*) or marginalized social groups, such as millenarian groups, are regarded as being as worthy of analysis and critique as the readings emerging from prominent scholars following the latest intellectual movements. As such, the position of the critic ultimately emerges as much less powerful and authoritative, at least in principle. On the one hand, the critic ceases to be a necessary intermediary between texts and readers, since the critic also has to acknowledge a particular reading strategy or set of reading strategies based on certain theoretical frameworks as well as certain social contexts and interests. In other words, the critic is no less positioned and interested than any other reader. On the other hand, the critic, given the highly privileged socioeducational training received, is *presumably*—although experience often indicates otherwise—in a better position to articulate not only his or her reading strategy but also those of others. While the former position tends to diminish the highly powerful and authoritative role of the critic, the latter tends to perpetuate it. All in all, however, the open admission of contextualization and perspective does serve, in the end, to relativize and hence subvert the highly privileged education and position of the critic. In this regard, to be sure, a fundamental question regarding the role of the critic in society and the church comes immediately to the fore, a question that lies, however, beyond the scope of the present essay.

5. *Theological Presuppositions.* The model of cultural studies is no less theological than any of the other models, but it does call for radical openness in this regard as well. Besides the factors of sexuality and gender (the male nature of the discipline) and sociopolitical status and affiliation (the Western character of the discipline), a third factor has been highly

influential as well in biblical criticism: socioreligious background and af-filiation. In fact, the socioreligious matrix or ambit of the critic—his or her institutional, religious, and theological moorings—has been more ex-plicit or evident than any other factor as regards the recreation of meaning from texts, the reconstruction of history behind texts, and the use of crit-ical methodologies in relation to texts. Even when a critic pretended to the highest levels of objectivity and impartiality, his or her socioreligious identity proved unconcealable and undeniable in reading and interpreta-tion, with the representation of ancient texts and communities bearing the unmistakable stamp of the world of that critic.

For cultural studies the socioreligious factor—the question of belief sys-tems, their discourses and practices, and their relationship to ideological worldview and stance—is not and cannot be denied or put aside but rather must be brought out into the open and critically analyzed, not only in texts but also in the reading of texts. In other words, all recreations of mean-ing from texts, all reconstructions of history behind texts, and all critical models and methods used to approach texts are seen as profoundly reli-gious, whether by way of affirmation or negation, reflecting once again the contextuality and perspective of critics and readers.

On the one hand, therefore, cultural studies is interested in the deeply socioreligious character of texts: both the theological positions, conflicts, and developments present in texts and a comparative analysis of these in the light of other socioreligious traditions are seen as worth pursuing from a critical point of view, as an important dimension of the text's mean-ing and history. At the same time, on the other hand, cultural studies is also interested in the socioreligious matrix of real readers and hence in the relationship of interpretation to theology, howsoever conceived or articu-lated: as an exercise in the history of religions, divorced from the wider theological enterprise and yielding facts or data for the theologians to deal with in their respective contexts; as an exercise leading to a greater understanding of the text in its original setting—whether conceived along historical, literary, or cultural lines—and thus ultimately to a more in-formed hermeneutical appropriation of the text as the "Word of God" in the contemporary religious community; or as an exercise on the side of the oppressed and with liberation in mind, sifting from the text what is liberating and putting aside what is oppressive.

For cultural studies, therefore, all readers and critics are theologians, im-plicitly or explicitly, by way of negation or affirmation, and all approaches to the text are theological in one respect or another. It is, then, this sociore-ligious dimension of reading and interpretation that needs to be surfaced and examined, in terms both of belief systems and of their ramifications for ideological worldviews and stances. For cultural studies there is simply no escape from the socioreligious dimension. Moreover, given its fundamental conception of texts as constructs or "texts," there is not and cannot be *a* meaning for all readers at all times and in all cultures. No meaning can dictate and govern the overall boundaries and parameters of Christian life; in effect, such boundaries and parameters are radically problematized thereby.

6. *Pedagogical Implications.* The educational implications of cultural studies are radically different from those of the other three paradigms. A number of factors call for a complete rethinking and reformulation of biblical pedagogy, its discourse and practice, within theological education: the broad variety of interpretive models; the conception of all readings as constructions on the part of real readers; the emphasis on social location and perspective with regard to real readers; the view of the critic as being as contextualized and perspectival as any other reader of the text. Certain consequences of such a revisioning are immediately clear.

First, there can no longer be a demand for a common methodological approach and theoretical apparatus on the part of all readers, regardless of theological moorings or sociocultural contexts, in order to become informed critics. Diversity in methods and models has rendered such a call not only unworkable in practice but also and above all groundless in theory. Indeed, one could very well argue that what is now necessary to become an informed reader or critic is metatheory, a grasp of theory and its history, not only within the discipline itself but also across the disciplinary spectrum. Second, informed readings can no longer be perceived as hermeneutically privileged and hence inherently superior to uninformed or "popular" readings, since both modes of reading involve, in their own respective ways, contextualization and perspective on the part of real readers. In this regard the call for readers to become informed, to become critics, has to be reconceptualized as well. Finally, readers can no longer be called upon to put aside their "faces" and voices in order to become informed, but rather must be called upon to become self-conscious and self-critical regarding these in the process of reading and interpretation, that is, learn how to read not only texts but also themselves and their readings.

In the end, the long-established model of learned impartation and passive reception, carried on within a seemingly ahistorical and asocial vacuum, must yield to a model of self-conscious, highly critical, and global dialogue involving constant and ever-shifting impartation and reception. In so doing, the pedagogical model would follow closely upon the interpretive model, becoming in the process highly decentered (or multicentered) and multilingual.

Concluding Comments

Such, then, are the basic principles that inform and guide the paradigm of cultural studies. Following this overview of the model, I should like to conclude, as I did in the case of the other three paradigms, with some remarks on the consequences of this new paradigm for theory and methodology as well as culture and experience in the task of biblical criticism. In so doing, I make use once again of the fundamental themes of liberation and decolonization invoked and deployed in my plotting of the discipline—its past, its present, and its future.

First, from a methodological and theoretical point of view, cultural studies represents a further and profound liberating step in biblical criticism, insofar as it allows for a diversity of reading strategies and theoretical models, while calling for critical awareness and engagement regarding the grounding, application, and ramifications of all such models and strategies. Cultural studies does not argue for any one strategy or framework as the sole and proper entry into the text to the exclusion of all others, for a totalizing narrative as it were; it contemplates instead a creative use of historical, literary, and cultural perspectives and concerns. In so doing, cultural studies finds itself in conversation with a wide variety of disciplines and critical frameworks. It does regard, however, all strategies and models as constructs on the part of real readers and thus calls on all readers to be quite up-front regarding their reading strategies and theoretical frameworks as well as their social locations and agendas.

Second, from a historical and cultural point of view, cultural studies represents an even more profound and liberating step in biblical criticism, insofar as it moves well beyond diversity in the methodological and theoretical realm into diversity in the sociocultural realm. Cultural studies is interested in analyzing not only the social location and agendas of texts but also the social location and agendas of flesh-and-blood readers and "texts," their readings of texts. Since all reading strategies and "texts" are regarded as constructs on the part of real readers, the task of criticism is seen as encompassing both an analysis of culture and experience vis-à-vis texts and an analysis of culture and experience vis-à-vis their readers, in the fullness of their diversity. For cultural studies, therefore, all *exegesis* is ultimately *eisegesis:* interpretation and hermeneutics go hand in hand.

Through such a joint analysis of texts and "texts," readers and their readings, cultural studies moves well beyond the implicit and dominant Western moorings and concerns of the discipline to embrace the concerns and moorings of readers throughout the rest of the world, to let everyone speak in their own tongues and from their own place. With cultural studies, therefore, the process of liberation and decolonization in biblical criticism takes a crucial step. What happens when the inculturation of the critic as gendered and Western ceases? What happens, in effect, is what can be presently witnessed in the discipline and what takes place whenever any process of liberation and decolonization begins to prove successful: a situation of simultaneous celebration, wailing, and conflict. First, the outsiders rejoice over their new-found identity and history on the periphery. Second, the insiders wail over the decline of standards and "scholarship" represented by the center. Third, there is conflict: on the one hand, sharp and inevitable criticism of the center, of its discourse and practice (the what-have-you-done-to-us syndrome), by the outsiders; on the other hand, ready dismissal of the periphery, of its discourse and practice (the after-all-we-have-done-for-you syndrome), by the center.

At the same time, beyond the celebration, lamentation, and conflict, new and fundamental problems arise. To mention but a few: If no master narrative is to be posited or desired, how does one deal with the continued abuse of the oppressed by the oppressor, the weak by the strong, the subaltern by the dominant? If the ideal of the master teacher is to be put aside, how does one carry on the task of biblical pedagogy and theological education? If the critic is neither objective nor disinterested, what then becomes the role of the critic in society and religion? If biblical criticism is not to be regarded as scientific, nontheological, and nonreligious at heart, what then should be its relationship vis-à-vis the other classical theological disciplines and the so-called fields of religious studies? Anomie, to be sure, does have its price. A consideration of such issues must, however, wait for another occasion.[21]

A final comment is in order. I have argued that cultural studies calls for and demands dialogue, critical dialogue. I would also argue, however, that there should be no romantic illusions whatsoever about such dialogue. Were one to plot the discourse and practice of dialogue along an interpretive spectrum, the following three positions would readily come to mind: toward one end, the totalitarian position, whether of the left or the right, of no dialogue whatsoever, with dialogue seen as profoundly subversive; in the center, the liberal-humanist position of genteel dialogue—perhaps the most common position in both professional and graduate theological programs—in which the political questions of power and ideology are distinctly frowned upon and actively skirted as disruptive and politicizing, as undoing or not building "community"; toward the other end, the democratic and liberative position of critical dialogue, according to which all voices have a right to speak up, loud and clear, and no subject remains untouched, including that of power and ideology. I see cultural studies as fully ensconced within this latter end of the spectrum and thus as both a progeny of conflict and a progenitor of conflict: such dialogue is born out of conflict and engenders conflict. Such, I would add, is also the inevitable result and mode of a postcolonial world and a postcolonial biblical criticism.

---

21. In effect, the issue of pedagogy, of the critic as teacher, will be pursued from a broad variety of angles, both national and global, in the third and final volume of this project, *The Impact of Pluralism and Globalization on Biblical Pedagogy.*

Part One _____

Readings from Africa

1

The Divine Name Yahweh 'Ĕlōhîm from an African Perspective

_____ Temba L. J. Mafico _____

The divine name Yahweh has been studied by many scholars. Frank Moore Cross appropriately described the extent of the study done on the name as constituting "a monumental witness to the industry and ingenuity of biblical scholars."[1] In spite of the relentless scholarly scrutiny, however, the appellation Yahweh, particularly when it is compounded with epithets such as *'ĕlōhîm, yiśrā'ēl, 'ābôt,* and *ṣĕbā'ôt,* still bristles with lexical difficulties. The problem of the name persists because Western scholars have limited their study to a select number of cultures that attach great significance to the names given to children. While that perspective has shed some light on the possible meanings of the name Yahweh, my thesis in this essay is that the significance of the name Yahweh lies not in its meaning but rather in its function of unifying the tribal gods often referred to as the *'ĕlōhê hā'ăbôt* (gods of the fathers). Whether the etymology of Yahweh may ever be secured beyond doubt is another matter. However, there is much evidence to corroborate the fact that Yahweh is the first element of several names that form a sentence name.[2] F. W. Albright argues that some Canaanite divine names were originally longer sentence names. For example, the epithet of 'Al'iyān Ba'l was *'al'iyu qarrādīma qāriyêya ba-'arṣi malḥamati*. In *Corpus des tablettes en cunéiformes alphabétiques* 4.8.34 and 5.2.10, 18, the shorter form of the name, 'Al'iyu Qarrādīmam, is used. Cross confirms that even this short form is still a sentence name in its own right. Such name structures are also attested in African names. The best example is the clan name in a poem my father taught me as a child.

The poem is used by members of my clan to greet each other on special occasions. In his old age, my father used to beam whenever I greeted him by any element of that poem. It always revived his spirits and brought back

---

1. F. M. Cross, *Canaanite Myth and Hebrew Epic* (Cambridge, Mass.: Harvard Univ. Press, 1973) 61.

2. F. W. Albright, "Recent Progress in North-Canaanite Research," *Bulletin of the American Schools of Oriental Research* 70 (1938) 19, and idem, *Archaeology and the Religion of Israel* (Baltimore: Johns Hopkins Univ. Press, 1940) 195 n. 11.

the glorious memories of the past. It reconnected him with his ancestors, even if for only an instant. The poem is brief and reads like a proverb:

> Mapamba chihwe chirema
> Chinoremera varikure
> Vari pedo vechiita chokutamba nacho.
>
> [Mapamba, the heavy stone
> Which is too heavy for the distant ones,
> But those who live close to it play on it.]

I have come to realize that this poem is also used as the clan's heroic sentence name. It epitomizes the heroic attributes of the clan members, particularly in their past. This long, heroic sentence name was generally shortened to "Mapamba Chihwe Chirema" or simply to "Mapamba." Familiarity with the name's historical context has enabled me to identify many African names that are shortened sentence names.[3]

In addition to the similarities in their treatment of names, African and Near Eastern cultures parallel one another in the significance they give to the concept of *pars pro toto* (a part stands for the whole).[4] In Africa, children are taught not to pull their milk teeth and cast them away in public. The teeth are to be secretly disposed of, often with some ritual chant. Moreover, if one is hurt while walking on the road, one's main concern is to erase all traces of the blood. A person always fears that enemies might use that blood and inflict grievous harm on the blood's owner. By the same token, it is also believed that witches and wizards might use a person's hair, voice, name, footprint, or clothing to harm or kill their owner. It is believed that any part or aspect of individual persons bears their physiognomy or essence.

When I studied the history and religions of the ancient Near East, with special emphasis upon Israel, I was struck by the fact that these communities, like the African people, used the principle of *pars pro toto*.[5] This realization has given me some fresh insights into the study of the divine compound name Yahweh 'Ĕlōhîm, erroneously translated as "the LORD God."[6] I am amazed that scholars have devoted so much time to the name Yahweh while paying very little attention to its significance in the divine

---

3. For example, "Kurauwone" (literally, "Grow up and see") is often shortened to "Kura" or "Wone."

4. H. Frankfort et al., *The Intellectual Adventure of Ancient Man* (Chicago: Univ. of Chicago Press, 1946) 12–20.

5. Ibid. See my "The Ancient and Biblical View of the Universe," *Theology for Southern Africa* 54 (1986) 6.

6. The Christian interpretation of Yahweh 'Ĕlōhîm as "the LORD God" is grossly erroneous and misleading. This interpretation is caused by reading into the early history of Israel a monotheistic religion, a phenomenon that seems to have fully developed only in the postexilic era.

compound name Yahweh 'Ĕlōhîm and its implications for the religion of Israel.[7]

Yahweh: The New Name of God

Some of the elaborate etymological study of the name Yahweh done by F. M. Cross is relevant to our discussion. Cross pointed out that the name Yahweh was originally *yahû* or *yaḥi*, which became an element of a longer sentence name. He added that *yahû-* or *yaḥī-* should be translated as a causative verb in the imperfect and jussive form.[8] Thus, if this name was given to a child at a naming ceremony, the *yahû/yaḥi* element would have expressed a statement that "the (god) *yaḥī/yahû* brings (brought) life (being) to (so and so) or an indirect command: Let the (god) *yahû* (*yaḥī*) give life to (so and so)."[9] Cross went on to give examples of Akkadian names like Nabu-ušabši (Nabu has called [a child] into being) and Nabu-šabši (Call into being [a child], O Nabu). Sometimes the object of the verb is given, for example, Nabu-zēra-ušabši (Nabu has brought progeny into being) and Bēl-aḫa-ušabši (Bel has called a brother into being).[10] The jussive would therefore represent a petition, "Let (the named child) endure, O god (so and so)," or "Give life, O god (so and so)." Several Canaanite names, for example, *ḫa-ya-il/ḫayya-'il* (alphabetic *ḥy'il*), express the meaning "'Ēl

---

7. See, for example, A. Alt, "The God of the Fathers," *Essays on Old Testament History and Religion* (New York: Doubleday, 1967) 1–100; D. N. Freedman, "The Name of the God of Moses," *Journal of Biblical Literature* 79 (1960) 151–56; R. Abba, "The Divine Name Yahweh," *Journal of Biblical Literature* 80 (1961) 320–28; S. Mowinckel, "The Name of the God of Moses," *Hebrew Union College Annual* 32 (1961) 121–33; J. P. Hyatt, "The Origin of Mosaic Yahwism," *The Teacher's Yoke* (ed. E. J. Vaderman et al.; Waco, Tex.: Baylor Univ. Press, 1964) 85–93, and idem, "Was Yahweh Originally a Creator Deity?" *Journal of Biblical Literature* 86 (1967) 369–77; F. M. Cross, "Yahweh and the God of the Patriarchs," *Harvard Theological Review* 4 (1962) 225–59, and idem, *Canaanite Myth*, 13–76; J. C. de Moor, *The Rise of Yahwism: The Roots of Israelite Monotheism* (Bibliotheca ephemeridum theologicarum lovaniensium 9; Leuven: Leuven University Press/Peeters, 1990); M. S. Smith, *The Early History of God: Yahweh and the Other Deities in Ancient Israel* (San Francisco: Harper & Row, 1990).

8. Cross, *Canaanite Myth*, 65, esp. n. 76. See also T. N. D. Mettinger ("YHWH Sabaoth—The Heavenly King on the Cherubim Throne," *Studies in the Period of David and Solomon and Other Essays* [ed. T. Ishida; Tokyo: Yamaka-Shuppansha, 1982] 109–38), who argues that the name Yahweh may have been used as a generic appellative for a deity. If that is the case, he adds, then it could be used in a bound form as Yahweh Ṣĕbā'ôt. He supports his argument by citing an epithet Šamaš līmīma (Shamash of the thousand), which he found in one of the Amarna letters (*EA* 205.6). C. L. Seow (*Myth, Drama, and the Politics of David's Dance* [Atlanta: Scholars Press, 1989] 8–22) briefly reviews the works of several scholars who have studied the title Yahweh Ṣĕbā'ôt but offers no new insights.

9. Cross, *Canaanite Myth*, 63.

10. See K. L. Talqvist, *Assyrian Personal Names* (Helsinki: Societas Scientarum Fennica, 1914) 276; J. J. Stamm, *Die akkadische Namengebung* (Leipzig: S. Hirzel, 1939) 145, 148–49.

lives," or "'Ēl endures."[11] Cross supported his interpretation by noting that "in Canaan and in Mesopotamia the epithets of the gods describe them, male and female, as creators of heaven and earth, father or creatress of all creatures, gods and men, formers or progenitors of the world."[12] Since sentence names, of which South Canaanite Yahweh is a theophoric element, take objects in their verbal forms, Cross translated the phrase Yahweh Ṣĕbā'ôt as "Yahweh who creates the (divine) hosts," not "Yahweh (the LORD) of hosts."[13]

While Cross's study of the divine appellation is quite comprehensive, it also raises some questions. Scholars have disputed his assertion that Yahweh should be interpreted as a causal causative verb in the imperfect and jussive form. R. Abba, for example, has failed to find textual evidence to support Cross's hypothesis. He found that where the hiphil of the verb *hāyah* was expected it was the piel that was used instead.[14] While the lack of textual evidence makes it impossible to arrive at a definitive conclusion regarding the meaning of Yahweh, I am more inclined to regard Yahweh as a name derived from the verb *hāyāh* (to be). In the first-person singular, imperfect tense, the form would be *'ehyeh,* in this case referring to what the *'ĕlōhîm* of Israel were about to become. At any rate, the improbable etymology of Yahweh does not affect my goal of explaining what the compound name Yahweh 'Ēlōhîm implies for the early religion of Israel.

The fact that Yahweh appears in combination with *'ĕlōhîm, 'ĕlōhê hā'ăbôt, yiśrā'ēl,* and *ṣĕbā'ôt* shows that it was God's basic name, particularly during and after the exodus. Indeed, the thrust of this article is that the name 'Ēlōhîm and the alternate forms *'ĕlōhê hā'ăbôt* or *'ĕlōhê yiśrā'ēl* attest to Israelites' being polytheistic like the other nations of the ancient Near East. Albrecht Alt, in an essay on the god of the forebears, arrived at the same conclusion:

> It seemed that originally several distinct gods of this type [the gods of the fathers][15] must have existed side by side, before they were combined in the figure of the God of the Fathers and identified with the God worshipped by Israel in historic times; and we believed that there was evidence that the authors of the great compilations of sagas saw in this type of religion the characteristic and distinctive religion of their people's ancestors, in which only tribes closely related took part, and not the inhabitants of Palestine, or other nations.[16]

---

11. Cross (*Canaanite Myth,* 64) gives more details.
12. Ibid., 66. It appears more convincing to regard the names Yahweh and Ṣĕbā'ôt as two names in apposition to each other, as will be demonstrated below.
13. Ibid., 65.
14. See Abba, "Divine Name," 325.
15. Words in brackets are mine.
16. Alt, "God of the Fathers," 38.

In making this statement, Alt acknowledged that many scholars dismiss this position out of hand, preferring to explain the 'ĕlōhê hā'ăbôt as an "image of the national God of historical time," "transformed into a family god."[17] Alt challenged these scholars to explain why it was necessary to create such an image and to give it so much space in the patriarchal history.[18] Alt also attributed the injustice done to the early history of the religion of Israel to scholars who studied it on the basis of a later period of Israel's history.

Alt's argument is corroborated by A. Hunter, who, in his study of Ruth, realized that translators arbitrarily translate the term 'ĕlōhîm to refer to God. He pointed out that the "gratuitous imposition of capital letters [to 'ĕlōhîm, in chapter 1] in verse 16, tends to conceal what the balanced artistry of the story seeks to convey, that a real and meaningful parallel exists between Ruth, worshiper of Chemosh, and Naomi, worshiper of Yahweh."[19] His argument is further strengthened by the fact that Ruth refers to the 'ĕlōhîm in the plural, that is, wĕ'ĕlōhayik wĕ'ĕlōhay (your gods [will be] my gods). It is obvious, then, that in Moab, Ruth believed in a polytheistic religion of which Chemosh, like Yahweh, was the plenipotentiary deity.

Having weighed all the arguments put forward, I am more inclined to regard the term 'ĕlōhîm, in the compound name Yahweh 'Ĕlōhîm, as having originated as a generic term meaning "gods." This hypothesis is sustained by the fact that the same term is also used of the gods of the other nations, commonly known as the 'ĕlōhîm 'ăḥērîm (the other gods). The 'ĕlōhîm of the forebears were real to the tribes of Israel (Gen 35:1ff.). For this reason, the Israelites were not willing to abandon them. This tribal adherence to their 'ĕlōhê hā'ăbôt (the gods of the fathers) became a very divisive issue at a time when national unity was desperately needed to confront formidable enemies such as the Philistines. While the Israelite tribes could defeat the Canaanites, who normally faced them as individual city-states, the Philistines were more organized and were led by kings. Therefore, to promote unity among the tribes of Israel, the 'ĕlōhê hā'ăbôt were venerated as family members of the divine council presided over by Yahweh, the ruler of all the world (Gen 18:25; Isa 33:22).[20] The only gods who were forbidden to the Israelites were the 'ĕlōhîm 'ăḥērîm (the other gods), simply because they were the 'ĕlōhê nēkār (the foreign gods) (Joshua 24). Not only were the Israelites forbidden to venerate the 'ĕlōhîm 'ăḥērîm, but they were also not to adopt the customs of the other nations (Deut 7:1-4; cf. 1 Kgs

---

17. Ibid., 38–39.
18. Ibid.
19. A. Hunter, "How Many Gods Had Ruth?" *Scottish Journal of Theology* (1978) 435.
20. In traditional societies of Africa, as appears to be the case in Israel, the oldest person, or the hero, was accorded the highest rank at village councils. There is a parallel here with Yahweh, who was accorded the plenipotentiary position because of heroic military accomplishments against mythical dragons.

11:1-2). The Israelites could maintain their *'ĕlōhê hā'ăbôt* so long as these *'ĕlōhîm* remained members of the divine council under Yahweh. This sheds some new light on the relationship between Yahweh and 'Ĕlōhîm. The picture that emerges is as follows. Israel, as a nation, remained basically a tight confederation of clans and tribes. Each tribe appears to have continued to adhere firmly to its patron deities, that is, the gods of its ancestors. This, apparently, was a very divisive issue. To forge national solidarity, these *'ĕlōhîm* were later coalesced as members of the divine council, presided over by Yahweh. Yahweh, the divine warrior, was accorded the supreme position over all the gods of Israel following his victories over mythological dragons such as Leviathan, Rahab, and the twisting serpent (Isa 27:1). These mythological creatures were regarded by the Israelites as a threat to human existence, particularly to themselves (cf. Marduk vs. Tiamat; Baal vs. Mot and Yamm).

Several psalms portray Yahweh's rise from obscurity to the position of king of heaven and earth and head of the council of the gods. Psalm 89:6b-19 states:

> Let heaven confess your wonders, Yahweh,
> your faithful deeds in the council of the holy ones.[21]
> For who in the heavens compares with Yahweh?
> Who may be likened to Yahweh among the children of the gods [*bĕnê 'ĕlōhîm*]?
> The God terrible in the council of the holy ones,
> great and dreadful above all around him,[22]
> Yahweh, the hosts,[23] who is like you?[24]

Yahweh and the Principle of *Pars Pro Toto*

An appreciation of the principle *pars pro toto* facilitates the interpretation of the divine compound appellation Yahweh 'Ĕlōhîm and also some of the enigmatic biblical texts in which it is used. One such text is Exod 32:4-24. In discussing this text, Cross found it intriguing that when the Israelites

---

21. Yahweh's victories and benevolent deeds resulted in Yahweh's elevation to the position of head of the gods.

22. See "Our king is 'Al'iyān Ba'l, Our ruler, and there is no one above him" (*Corpus des tablettes en cunéiformes alphabétiques* 4.4.43–44; cf. 3.5.40–41).

23. Originally, this must have been Yahweh *'ăšer haṣṣĕbā'ôt* (Yahweh [who is the] armies), which was shortened to Yahweh ṣĕbā'ôt. Cross supposes that Yahweh ṣĕbā'ôt might have originated as *du yahwī ṣĕbā'ôt* (He who created the heavenly armies) or some other ancient Canaanite cultic, sentence-name forms (*Canaanite Myth,* 71). See also F. W. Albright's review of B. N. Wambacq, *L'Épithèt divine Jahwe Ṣĕbā'ôt: Étude philologique, historique et exégétique* (Bruges, Belgium, 1947), in *Journal of Biblical Literature* 67 (1948) 377–381.

24. Bible translations throughout this essay are mine. See also Ps 82:1–8, which shows how Yahweh, the head of the gods, may also pass punitive judgment upon the gods.

demanded of Aaron, "Rise, make us gods who will go before us" (*qûm 'ăseh lānû 'ĕlōhîm 'ăšer yēlĕkû lĕpānênû*), he responded by making them one golden calf.[25] But when he presented the bull to them he said: "These are your gods, Oh Israel, who brought you up from the land of Egypt" (*'ēlleh 'ĕlōhêkā yiśrā'ēl 'ăšer he'ĕlûkā mē'ereṣ miṣrāyim*) (Exod 32:4). Cross pointed out that this statement is a characteristic Yahwistic confession.[26] Further scrutiny revealed to him that a singular god is implied. He arrived at this conclusion by examining this text in conjunction with 1 Kgs 12:28. In the latter text, Jeroboam made two bulls, one for the sanctuary at Dan and the other for Bethel. When he dedicated them, he said: "Behold your gods who brought you up from the land of Egypt" (*hinneh 'ĕlōhêkā 'ăšer he'ĕlûkā mē'ereṣ miṣrāyim*). Cross found the phrase *hinneh* (or *'ēlleh*) *'ĕlōhêkā* to be ambiguous because, while it might be apt in 1 Kgs 12:28, it is the same phrase used by Aaron to refer to one bull in Exod 32:4. Cross pointed out that, although the bulls were supposed to be pedestals for the one god, the worshipers ended up worshiping both the deity and the bull. This resulted in the use of the term "gods."[27]

This text has baffled scholars like Cross because they have overlooked the principle of *pars pro toto* by which the one golden calf was, in essence, the very *'ĕlōhîm* (the gods) of Israel. The bull was not simply a symbol or a pedestal of the gods: it was regarded as the gods (or the progenitors) themselves because, being the pedestal(s), it was a part of the gods. Several biblical texts support the argument that the Israelites revered many gods.

In Joshua 24 a concerted effort to unite the Israelites by allegiance to Yahweh alone was attempted. Joshua tried hard to convince the Israelites to adopt Yahweh as their *'ĕlōhê yiśrā'ēl*.[28] He asked them to abandon the *'ĕlōhîm 'ăḥērîm*. These were explained as the gods whom the ancestors served from across the river, or those they had adopted in Egypt, or the gods of the Amorites in whose land they were then dwelling. Joshua labeled these gods the *'ĕlōhê nēkār* (the gods of the alien) (Josh 24:20). They should not be confused with the *'ĕlōhê hā'ăbôt* (the "gods of the forebears"), who later became Yahweh *'ĕlōhê yiśrā'ēl*, "Yahweh, the gods of Israel" (Josh 24:2). The children of Israel replied: "Far be it from us to abandon Yahweh to serve other gods because Yahweh (he) is our gods" (*ḥālîlâ lānû mē'ăzōb 'et-yhwh la'ăbōd 'ĕlōhîm 'ăḥērîm kî yhwh 'ĕlōhênû hû'*).

This response shows that the Israelites regarded *'ĕlōhê nēkār* as the *'ĕlōhîm 'ăḥērîm*. In Josh 24:19, Joshua himself revealed that his appeal to

---

25. Cross, *Canaanite Myth*, 73–74.
26. Ibid., 73.
27. Ibid., 73 n. 117.
28. The name Israel was also adopted at this time in order to unite the Israelites by both religious and genealogical bonds. This datum may also shed light on why the historicity of the patriarchs has been debated to no avail. The patriarchs appear to have been used to reinforce unity in Israel.

the Israelites to abandon the *'ĕlōhê nēkār* did not include the *'ĕlōhê hā'ăbôt*. Joshua's statement excluded the *'ĕlōhê yiśrā'ēl* because he himself identified Yahweh with the *'ĕlōhîm* in his warning to the Israelites: "You are not able to serve Yahweh because he is the holy gods" (*lō' tûkĕlû la'ăbōd 'et-yhwh kî 'ĕlōhîm qĕdōšîm hû'*). The people of Israel repeated their earlier statement that they would serve Yahweh "because Yahweh (he) is our gods" (*kî yhwh 'ĕlōhênû hû'*). Joshua then warned them that if they should abandon Yahweh and serve "foreign gods" (*'ĕlōhê nēkār*), Yahweh would bring great evil upon them. Joshua's speech did not in any way discourage the Israelites from worshiping their ancestral deities.

The principle of *pars pro toto* is also evident in 1 Kgs 18:20-40. The Israelites began to identify Yahweh with Baal because the attributes of both gods were similar.[29] Like Baal, Yahweh is depicted as riding on the clouds (Ps 104:3). Yahweh was further manifested through lightning, thunder, storm, earthquake, fire, and smoke, just like Baal (Ps 104:7, 32; 114:5-6; Isa 31:9b). The identification of Yahweh with Baal created a serious religio-political crisis in Israel. The crisis was caused not only by the Israelites' identification of Yahweh with Baal but also, and above all, by the fact that this identification would ultimately lead to the identification of the Israelites with the Canaanites. By becoming like the Canaanites the Israelites would lose their particularity as a people claiming to have been chosen by God among the nations.[30] The desire to remain separate from the other nations of Canaan was the major issue in the polemic against Baal. In the ancient Near East, a god could claim supremacy over the other gods only by demonstrating prowess in terms of great victories. This fact explains why the Israelites did not answer Elijah when he asked them: "How long will you limp along with two options? If Yahweh is the gods [*'im-yhwh hā'ĕlōhîm*], (then) follow him. If (the) Baal [*habba'al*], then follow him" (1 Kgs 18:21). The people did not answer Elijah. They would change their loyalty from Baal to Yahweh only if Yahweh could prove that he was different from and stronger than Baal. They needed more tangible evidence of Yahweh's might. Therefore, to convince the Israelites that only Yahweh should be their plenipotentiary deity, the religious crisis was resolved on Mount Carmel in a showdown between the two rival plenipotentiary

---

29. Cross ("Yahweh," 235) saw this identification as the coalescence or fusion of the gods into another deity. This fusion is even clearer when the concept of *pars pro toto* is taken into consideration. Yahweh had become Baal, and Baal had become Yahweh, in reality and essence, even though they remained separate from each other. Cross alludes to this view as well (230–32).

30. The campaign for the promotion of Yahwism is, in my opinion, the source of Israel's doctrine of election. This doctrine naturally led to Israel's belief in the *yôm yhwh* (the Day of Yahweh) (Amos 5:18–20), the day on which God would destroy all other nations except Israel, who would join God in a banquet. Amos turned the tables on Israel when he prophesied that on the Day of Yahweh the Israelites would be judged for their neglect of *mišpāṭ* (justice).

deities, Yahweh and Baal (1 Kgs 18:20-40).[31] Throughout the ancient Near East a deity who could answer the supplications of its prophet(s) was the only true and living deity. In other words, the gods earned the allegiance of the people by doing benevolent acts for their followers. Only the gods who could defend their own rights without human assistance were powerful gods who deserved worship. Therefore, no human being should try to defend God because God is capable of self-defense. This is the underlying argument of the contest between Baal and Yahweh (cf. Job 13:7-11). Furthermore, it is significant that Elijah's controversy with the Israelites about the gods did not deny the existence of the 'ĕlōhê hā'ăbôt. He challenged the Israelites to choose between Baal and Yhwh hā'ĕlōhîm (Yahweh the gods).[32] But the people would not respond to his question before they had seen some concrete evidence that Yahweh and Baal were two distinct deities and that only Yahweh was benevolent like their 'ĕlōhê hā'ăbôt. In the following discussion, the process by which Elijah was able to merge or identify Yahweh with the gods of the progenitors will become self-evident.

Yahweh versus Baal on Mount Carmel

In Elijah's time, the Israelites, like the Canaanites, strongly believed that Baal, among his other benevolent acts, caused rain and dew, which sustained their agrarian economy. That the Israelites had been straddling the fence for a long time with regard to their loyalty to both Yahweh and Baal is evident in Elijah's question: "How long will you limp along with two options?" (1 Kgs 18:21). Just as Joshua (Josh 24:15) had exhorted the Israelites to make a choice between Yahweh, the 'ĕlōhê hā'ăbôt (the gods of the forebears), and the 'ĕlōhîm 'ăḥērîm (the other gods), so Elijah confronts the Israelites with the choice between Yahweh, the 'ĕlōhîm, and Baal, the lord of the 'ĕlōhîm 'ăḥērîm.

That the Canaanites believed Baal was a living god is evidenced in an Ugaritic text that reads:

> kî ḥayya 'al'iyānu ba'lu
> kî'itê zubulu ba'lu 'arṣi.

---

31. The circumstances surrounding Gideon's destruction of Baal's altar in part resemble the contest between Yahweh and Baal on Mount Carmel (1 Kgs 18:25–33). Gideon's father defended his son by challenging the villagers that if Baal were a real god, he should be able to defend his own altar. If Baal could not defend his own altar, then he was not a god worth worshiping. This is the same argument used on Mount Carmel. Yahweh proved to be the real God by sending a miraculous fire that consumed Gideon's sacrifice (v. 21).

32. The article hā- before 'ĕlōhîm clearly shows that the 'ĕlōhîm were regarded as gods, and not as God. Normally, an article is not used before a proper noun.

[Indeed 'Al'iyānu Ba'l lives;
indeed Prince Lord of Earth exists.][33]

The stress in this couplet is on the life and existence of the god. Baal's life and existence were manifested through his manipulation of the elements: riding on the clouds; causing rain, thunder, lightning, fire, smoke, earthquakes; and so forth. These actions demonstrated that he was really alive.

As stated above, the separation of Yahweh from Baal was effected in a showdown between them on Mount Carmel (1 Kgs 18:20-40). The emphasis in the episode is on Yahweh as the living God. At Mount Carmel, Yahweh caused things to happen while Baal, in addition to his failure to cause dew or rain during the drought, was not able to respond to his prophets' supplication at the sacrifice.

To demonstrate this reality convincingly, Elijah announced in the name of Yahweh, the *'ĕlōhê yiśrā'ēl* (the gods of Israel), that there would be no rain or dew for several years: and it was so (1 Kgs 17:1). Baal was not able to reverse the decree of Yahweh. The intensity of the drought was underscored by the fact that it dried up even the brook Cherith, from which Elijah drank on Yahweh's advice (1 Kgs 17:7). If the drought affected the well-being of the prophet of Yahweh this much, then the followers of Baal, together with their livestock, must have fared far, far worse, a scenario the author allows the reader to imagine. With this as background, the narrative takes us to the top of Mount Carmel where Elijah and the prophets of Baal must demonstrate the active power of their respective gods in the presence of the Israelites.

The adherents of Baal were first to call on their gods to accept their sacrifice, which they had set on dry wood. But "There was no voice, and there was no one answering, and there was no one listening." The phrase is repeated twice to underscore the fact that the other gods—Baal, Asherah, and their host—were nothing but idols: they were not living gods.

After repairing the altar of Yahweh, Elijah called on the name of Yahweh, who was the *'ĕlōhê* of Abraham, Isaac, and Jacob (Israel). As the twelve tribes united and assumed the name Israel, so were the *'ĕlōhê hā'ăbôt* of all the twelve tribes coalesced with Yahweh, who became Yahweh, *'ĕlōhê hā'ăbôt*. Because Yahweh was the living God, a miraculous fire came from Yahweh. Israel called twice: "Yahweh, (he) is indeed the gods. Yahweh, (he) is indeed the gods" (Yahweh *hû' hā'ĕlōhîm,* Yahweh *hû' hā'ĕlōhîm*).[34] This response clearly shows that the Israelites finally realized that Yahweh, by the principle of *pars pro toto,* had become, in reality, the gods of their ancestors whom they had always trusted. By their response,

---

33. See *Corpus des tablettes en cunéiformes alphabétiques* 6.3.21; see also 6.3.3; 6.3.9. The vocalization is that of F. M. Cross (*Canaanite Myth,* 64).

34. As I have already pointed out (see n. 32, above), the article *hā-* provides strong evidence that the term *'ĕlōhîm* should be regarded as a generic noun for gods.

the Israelites agreed to abandon the *'ĕlōhîm 'ăḥērîm* (the other gods), but not the *'ĕlōhê hā'ăbôt* (the gods of the ancestors). They had accepted Yahweh because Yahweh had proved to be *hā'ĕlōhîm* (the gods). The Israelites coalesced their patron deities into Yahweh, who therefore became their god par excellence.

Conclusion

The Israelites worshiped Yahweh because they regarded Yahweh as the hero or senior deity among their *'ĕlōhê hā'ăbôt*. They were forbidden to identify Yahweh with Baal, the chief of the *'ĕlōhîm 'ăḥērîm*, simply because these "other gods" were "the gods of the foreigner," that is, the *'ĕlōhê nēkār* (Josh 24:20). As long as they worshiped Yahweh, who had become the gods of their forebears, the Israelites could not be accused of apostasy. The real purpose for the worship of Yahweh with the *'ĕlōhê hā'ăbôt* was the preservation of the Israelites as a particular people. If the tribes of Israel were left to worship the deities of their progenitors, this would generate tribal independence and rivalries. By merging the gods of the forebears with Yahweh, and by centralizing worship in Jerusalem, the unity of Israel was promoted and preserved.

The most appropriate period in the history of Israel for the beginning of this gradual merging of Yahweh and the *'ĕlōhîm* was that of the exodus. The tribes of Israel were continually exhorted to lay more emphasis on Yahweh, the unifying deity, than on the ancestral patron deities. The tribes of Israel welcomed this move as long as their acceptance of Yahweh did not deny the existence and importance of their clan and tribal gods. Moreover, because Yahweh was performing all the functions that the gods of their progenitors performed, Yahweh became, in essence, as benevolent as their gods.

An appreciation of the concept of *pars pro toto* in relation to Yahweh enables us to comprehend the designation of God as Yahweh 'Ĕlōhîm and Yahweh Ṣĕbā'ôt. Yahweh Ṣĕbā'ôt strongly appears to have referred to Yahweh who had become, in essence, the armies of Israel. In their military campaigns against the Canaanites, the Israelites believed that Yahweh was fighting for them. Yahweh was, therefore, Israel's *ṣĕbā'ôt*. The translation of Yahweh Ṣĕbā'ôt as "Yahweh of the armies" or "Yahweh of hosts" is problematic. Which armies are being referred to? What the Israelites meant by the title was that Yahweh had become the armies of Israel, the armies that fought for them during the conquest and the armies that would vanquish their present enemies. Yahweh Ṣĕbā'ôt therefore meant "Yahweh, the armies."

On the basis of this evidence, the compound divine name Yahweh 'Ĕlōhîm could be translated in several ways. Yahweh and 'Ĕlōhîm were two independent names in apposition to each other. Yahweh was, in this case, not a verb in the causative imperfect, but a name in apposition to 'Ĕlōhîm, the generic plural noun meaning "gods." This interpretation is supported by several biblical texts. In Gen 1:26-27 we read:

> Let us make man in our image, after our likeness.... So God created man in his own image, in the image of God he created him; male and female he created them.

In Gen 3:22, Yahweh 'Ĕlōhîm says:

> "Behold, the man has become like one of us, knowing good and evil; and now, lest he put forth his hand and take also of the tree of life, and eat, and live for ever"—therefore Yahweh 'Ĕlōhîm expelled them from the garden of Eden.

The redactor deliberately juxtaposed the Priestly story of creation in Genesis 1 with the Yahwist's story in Genesis 2 in order to attribute the creation of the world to the 'ĕlōhîm prior to Yahweh's assumption of the plenipotentiary position among the gods. The Priestly school, in its tendency to archaize, attributed the creation to the gods ('ĕlōhîm). In Genesis 2, to harmonize creation by the 'ĕlōhîm with creation by Yahweh, the redactor merged Yahweh with 'ĕlōhîm to produce the compound divine name, Yahweh 'Ĕlōhîm (see Josh 24:17a; 1 Kgs 18:39b). Thus, Yahweh 'Ĕlōhîm means "Yahweh is (the) gods." The term certainly did not mean "the Lord God," a very erroneous interpretation indeed.

2

Biblical Interpretation and the Social Location of the Interpreter: African Women's Reading of the Bible

_____ Mercy Amba Oduyoye ____

The Bible

The most precious common heritage of Christians all over the world and in all ages is the Bible. This rather trite truism may seem simple enough, but it is loaded with pitfalls. One could ask, for example: Which Bible? Whose interpretation? Does one have to have the whole of the Bible? At another level, although reading the Bible as individuals and in groups has been the tradition of some Christian communions, for others this "open Bible" represents a recent experience. A further set of questions could be raised around the fact that the Bible is a *book* to be read. Of what use is it if one cannot read at all or cannot read the language in which the Bible is presented? Such questions are very real in Africa, given its high level of illiteracy, which defeats even the heroic efforts at translation of the Bible Society. This essay on the use of the Bible in Africa has such questions as a backdrop.[1]

Muhammad described Jews, Christians, and Muslims as people of the Book. In fact, the Bible and reading became the distinguishing mark of Christians in West Africa in the early days of the nineteenth-century missionary enterprise. Later, when people began to distinguish between Protestantism and Roman Catholicism, they associated going to Bible class with the former and attending catechism with the latter. The "open Bible" of the Protestant is exemplified by the practice of the Harris Movement, which swept West Africa from Liberia to the Ivory Coast and was taken over by Wesleyan missionaries operating out of the Gold Coast (Ghana) at the time.

---

1. The Africa referred to in this essay excludes Mediterranean as well as Nilotic Africa, the location of the Christianity of the first millennium.

Churches that are part of this movement leave a Bible open and in a conspicuous place in order to symbolize its availability to all. It is said that by reading directly from the Bible and retelling the story of the salvation of humanity by God in Christ from the principalities and powers, the prophet Harris moved tens of thousands to forsake "their fetishes and to seek a higher religion," one that has *a book*. The book became the new idol, a carrier of the divine presence. This was the effect of the Bible as taught from the social location of Western missionaries evangelizing Africa, without regard for the sociocultural background of the audience.

The open Bible—together with prayers, dreams, and visions—continues to bring many to God-in-Christ through the African-instituted churches. This phenomenon is greeted with mixed feelings. For Roman Catholics in eastern Africa, for example, it has resulted in the church's keen interest in "small Christian communities" that attempt to appropriate the biblical message for themselves. This has led to attempts at co-opting and institutionalizing them. The spontaneous attraction to the Bible is also recognized as an opportunity for teaching. All Christian communions in Africa now recognize this need for "the church" to guide believers through the Bible.

With that as background, I should like to focus on the following five topics: (1) the Bible as a symbol of God's presence and protection; (2) the Bible and African religiocultural contexts; (3) the Bible as the main source of Christian theology in Africa; (4) reading the Bible from the context of African Christian women; and (5) an example of a Bible reading from an African cultural location.

The Bible as Symbol of God's Presence and Protection

The Bible has a special place in the hearts and homes of African Christians. The question is, How is it appropriated? A couple of stories will suffice to illustrate this. Living a rover's life, I am often behind in my assessment of how life in Ghana is changing. I was, thus, completely puzzled when I arrived at a sister's house and saw an open Bible in the cot of her newborn babe. "You have left your Bible here," I called. "No, it is deliberate; it will keep away evil influences." I was dumbfounded: the daughter of a Methodist pastor, with a doctorate in a discipline of the natural sciences, earned in a reputable U.S. university, using the Bible as a talisman! When I told this story in the course of a social occasion in Nigeria, a discussion ensued that revealed many more such uses of the Bible: Christian lawyers who keep a Bible on every shelf of their library; houses built with Bibles buried in their foundations and individuals buried with Bibles in their coffins; Bibles in cars that may never be read but whose presence proves comforting, a sort of Immanuel, or God-with-us.

The Psalms, although well known and well loved, also have a mystique all their own. Specific psalms are prescribed for specific circumstances. Some are to be said with a lit candle and a bowl of water for greater effectiveness as vehicles of petitions. Others, like Psalms 21 and 23, are to be memorized and repeated when danger lurks in one's path. Firm is the belief that the Bible speaks the truth and protects the innocent, so young people have recourse to the Bible as a key system for "divining" whenever a dispute arises, especially concerning petty pilfering and gossip. And of course in most of the English-speaking world of Africa, persons swear on the Bible to tell the truth in the courts of law.

There is also a use of the Bible as guide that involves reading. This we find among those who believe in using a verse a day to guide them. They open the Bible and take as the message from God whatever meets their eyes, often acting that day as much as possible in accordance with the message in question. More systematic individual and family readers make use of daily guides, which add comments, prayers, and hymns to Bible passages to facilitate daily devotions. Bible study groups usually focus on specific books and use a variety of forms, although most churches follow a lexicon developed by themselves, issued by their communion, or borrowed from other communions. Somehow or other, much of the Bible gets read in church.

The Bible is a popular book in Africa, peddled by colporteurs and sold in markets alongside other wares, sometimes even by Muslims. Its price fluctuates according to supply and demand. In many countries it is a best-seller, and in some it is the only book in the mother tongue. Passages, verses, and stories are alluded to in conversations, even by persons who have never stepped into a church. Creative literature written by Africans often quotes or alludes to the Bible.

Bible passages employed in these ways are, like any biblical text, to be studied with the social location of the authors in mind. Many Africans find that the Bible has a ring of truth about it, that its language, proverbs, and ideals of morality and justice are very close to the world they know and understand. It is one of the few books they own or have heard about, and many read it if they can. It may be the only religious book in which God speaks their language, since African-language Korans are few.

The stories I noted above about uses of the Bible in Africa could be compounded endlessly. These stories are not just anecdotes but realities that biblical scholars in Africa have to bear in mind when attempting to communicate their scholarly readings of the Bible.

The Bible and the African Religiocultural Context

Why do Africans find the Bible attractive? What's in it for them? In effect, Africans who study the Bible locate themselves within its history, its culture, its social structures, and its obvious assumption that the divine is a reality and is involved in the created order.

J. S. Mbiti provides an overview of this inadequately analyzed aspect of Christianity in Africa.[2] He points out that when black Africans are in direct conversation with the Bible, they experience an affinity with the culture of the Bible—what is "history" in the Bible corresponds to life as they live it. The Bible mirrors life, affirming and confirming African cultural, social, and religious life. For example, the Bible presents events and concepts that are echoed in the African colonial and neocolonial experience: in the takeover of land in Africa by immigrants from Europe; in Africa's economic life at a very basic stage; in migrations, settlements, and the struggle between the urban and the rural, the pastoral and agricultural; and in African ethnic strife and "tribalness." Similarly, the Bible's depiction of social arrangements of families and lineages; of royalty and birthright; of rules governing community interaction; and of caring for the stranger—all these are familiar to Africans as well, as are rules governing what one eats. A dramatic parallel in this regard involves the creation of nations out of ethnic communities and the tensions and challenges of that effort. The primal world of the Bible is thus alive in Africa today, as is exploitation by the global economic order.

In Africa people do not quibble about what they should learn from the Bible: the simple rules of life, ethical and moral, are life-enhancing. Where there is a conflict in the Bible, it is often a case of an old law versus a new law. Such dilemmas are not unknown in the corpus of African wisdom. When all else fails, we create new myths to replace oppressive African myths. In fact, at some points, where the Bible text is clearly a "text of terror" from the standpoint of what we understand to be the project of the living God, we may even need other texts. The Bible has become part of the received wisdom. For the African Christian as for the early white missionary, the Bible has become a standard for evaluating African religion, culture, and society. Since the Bible does not divorce religion from other aspects of life, Africans have felt at home with it. All of life is seen as a whole. Unfortunately, much of this acceptance follows the legalism of the missionary approach, which is still rampant even though the Western churches are under African leadership.

The universal history of Genesis 1–11 confirms several African myths of beginnings, which also seek to explain fundamental puzzles such as the unity and diversity of humanity, the immanence and transcendence of God, the human capacity for good and evil, and God's continued care in spite of human unworthiness. The Bible speaks of God and God's dealings with the world and involvement in human realities. It is the written source of theology, and it challenges, confirms, corrects, modifies, and reshapes the

---

2. J. S. Mbiti, *Bible and Theology in African Christianity* (Nairobi: OUP, 1989).

belief in God that informs Africa's own religion and causes those who read it to try a fresh approach to God, Christianity, and life. The Bible is the word of life.

At a consultation of Jewish scholars and African Christian theologians (Nairobi, November 1986), a statement was made that proved significant for me: "Scripture is not a European creation." Such a realization frees African Christianity from the insistence that it justify itself before the court of European and American judges. Both the attempts by Mbiti and others to show that Africans use the whole of the Bible and the view of Kwesi Dickson and others who point to the African predilection for the Old Testament are relevant here. We are accountable in our theology to God and to the people to whom we tell it.

If we are selective in Africa, we are not alone in this "sin." When one is being denied justice, the God of justice speaks with exceptional clarity from the pages of the Bible. Yet, as is true elsewhere, not all in Africa go to the Bible with ears and eyes keen to hear and see this God. So then in Africa too one finds a variety of theological emphases coming from the one Bible. African Christians are not alone in being Christocentric: Jesus Christ is our teacher and the example we follow for a life acceptable to God. We are also, to be sure, trinitarian monotheists, but what is unique about our religion is Jesus Christ. So we do need the New Testament and the Hebrew Bible. We need the whole Bible, including what is called the Apocrypha.

The Bible as Main Source of Christian Theology in Africa

African Christian theologians take the traditional Reformation view that the central source for theology is the Bible. Only when we have had the chance to read for ourselves can we begin the steps toward our own theologizing. For the churches instituted and led by black Africans, the Bible was the only written source for Christian theology, liturgy, and practice. They found in the Bible how God had spoken directly to Adam and Hagar, to Pharaoh through a prophet, and to Joseph through dreams and their interpretation; they found there the use of symbolism, the taking off of shoes, the blessing of water, and many other ritual approaches to religion. They also found sacrifices, healings, and appearances of spirit-beings. They understood theology in the Bible as people talking about their encounters with God. Praying is a real and dynamic encounter with God that has power to bring about what is desired. The Bible is used to construct types of ministries and to validate the roles of persons in the congregations.

Preachers and theologians who have a background in formal biblical studies do their theology from the open books of the life around them, the Bible, and other written sources. Theologies worth that name in Africa speak of a salvation that reconciles humanity to God and with creation and that brings a reign of justice, peace, and compassion on earth among human beings. The Kairos Document, which came out of South Africa, has been an open challenge to the historical theology that lies at the foundation of Western Christianity in Africa. It has recalled the story of Jacob and Esau: there is no reconciliation without repentance and restitution. The insistence on working for transformation as the required end of theologizing and as a further source of theology is a word for all Christians everywhere. African biblical scholars are conscious of being part of a faith community to which they are accountable for exposing the truth as they see it.

The narrative theologies exemplified by the sermons of Desmond Tutu and Allan Boesak, the speeches and healing sessions of Emmanuel Milingo together with the written theology of Jean-Marc Elá—these and all the other forms that see the God of the exodus and the gospel at work in Africa demonstrate the liberative use of the Bible in Africa. They have witnessed in the Bible the God who comes to rescue and who promises a future of righteousness and peace. It is this God of the Bible that African theology seeks to present, so that the people may praise and adore God and become partners in the struggles for God's future. Women sing of the exodus in Fanti lyrics, and the God of Moses who caused thousands to cross the river is praised as the God of compassion. Shoes are taken off to remind us of God's holiness and the sacredness of each place that God has given us. Reading the Bible, we are assured that God has not moved away from earth and has not withdrawn from human history, leaving us to our own clever devices. God's story has not been sold to humanity as the Akan folktale alleges; rather, the human situation is seen as infused with the story of God.

In the Bible we have found samples of the revelation of God through human history, reality, and experience. The Bible empowers us to proclaim God's will in the name of Jesus and through the power of the Holy Spirit. The Spirit that came mightily at Pentecost is alive and well and powerful in African Christianity—the Bible affirms this belief as the gifts of the Spirit are experienced in both dramatic and pragmatic modes. The Bible has brought a message of hope to Africa and African Christians; therefore, we hail and love the Bible. If one finds a Bible in a cot in Africa, one should know that it is a symbolic expression of God's continued presence in and care of the whole of creation, especially of those too weak to fend for themselves. In such a cot, then, lie the two loves of African sisters—God and humanity.

Reading the Bible from the Context of
African Christian Women

Women's Bible Study Groups

The story of "the Bible in the cot" should be taken together with the story of the Bible that is sung. The first women to appropriate the Bible in Africa heard it read and its stories retold. They met God in the narrative and transmitted their testimonies in "poetic theology," singing, praying, and commenting on the biblical events. These women—mostly farmers, traders, often marketing their own produce and products—also had crucial responsibilities in their families and the larger community. These were women with not a minute to spare, but they still found time for church and churchwomen's groups, where praying, reading, and sharing insights from the Bible were central.

They appropriated the Christian faith not only from sermons but also from listening to the Bible read by the few women who at that time could read. In Bible class there was opportunity to talk about what they had heard, something that they could not do when the Bible was preached as doctrine. In Bible class they had their faith strengthened and were blessed with courage for the journey. Such groups continue not only in rural Africa where the illiteracy rate is high but also in urban communities where people read the Bible for themselves. Reading the Bible as a community of believers has become a practice for empowering women.

It is not often that these groups move on to public issues, but there have been instances when the women have observed that their experience of particular aspects of church and/or society could not be the will of God. When they have judged certain situations to be unjust, these women have usually gone ahead to seek amelioration without politicizing the issue or seeking to enter a protest in the appropriate quarters. Women have taught other women, especially girls, to read. They have passed on survival skills, both economic and societal. Only on very rare occasions have African churchwomen challenged African culture, even when they have judged its practices to be inhuman and unjust. It is therefore important to call attention to the Presbyterian women of Kenya who, as far back as 1922, formed the Council of the Shield in order to resist female circumcision. This initiative later became the Presbyterian Women's Guild, a group offering courageous resistance to a practice woven into the very fabric of their community life. To sustain their resolve, they needed to stay close to the Bible. Through Bible study meetings and prayers, they learned to live as Christians in the wider community. Bible study groups in girls' boarding schools remain a valuable part of Christian women's culture in most parts of Africa. Nyambura

Njoroge's research, although focusing on ethics, deals extensively with the biblical concept that promotes women's dignity and humanity.[3]

Women Theologians

Although several of the African women with tertiary education in theology are in fields other than biblical studies, they all resort to the Bible in theologizing and in the construction of Christian ethics in the African context. The particular contexts of these women result in a reading of the Bible that varies as much from the perspectives of African male theologians as from those of the churchwomen discussed above. The churchwomen who are ordained and/or work directly in the institutions of their churches, especially in pastoral roles, also tend to approach the Bible somewhat differently than the women theologians working in academic situations. The critical approach to the Bible possible in a university context is deemed unsuitable in Bible study groups, especially in cases where there is no opportunity for continued contact. The context determines whether the Bible is to be read as shared sustenance, for meditation, as an aid to prayer, or as a source of solace. We concentrate here on Bible study as a written contribution from women seeking to understand or discover God's will for their particular circumstances. This rereading is empowered by the fact that within the Bible itself there is reinterpretation.

Certain aspects of life in Africa send women theologians to reread their Bibles. Everyone knows from the mass media that life in Africa can be ugly. In spite of this reality, we have evidence of how African women continue to say, "We dare to believe." Women theologians living in Africa, where the daily news sounds like Hebrew Bible narratives without the miraculous deliverances, still dare to believe in a God of love who delivers from adversity. As churchwomen memorized biblical events of deliverance, composed lyrics, and sang them in the midst of adversity, so women theologians write down their cries, confident that God hears and comes to deliver them. In the midst of internecine wars, the Bible is read for the affirmation of family and community as well as for a proper interpretation of hospitality in the African context. The experiences of shifting populations, famine, flood, and other disasters send women to the Bible in search of the God of love, the gracious one who blesses and nourishes the whole of creation. Women see affluence and poverty, misuse of political and economic power, the battle of religions in Africa, and they go to the Bible in search of a word from the God of justice.

In the midst of such conditions, the Bible has been a pivotal tool in the search for meaning. Women have brought their experience into Bible trans-

---

3. N. Njoroge, "The Woman's Child: The Institutional Locus for an African Women's Christian Social Ethic," Ph.D. diss., Princeton Theological Seminary, 1992.

lation seeking accuracy and inclusiveness. Finding dynamic equivalents in African languages to describe women and women's experience has been a challenge to Musimbi Kanyoro of Kenya, who picks up translations of concepts like "help," "wife," and "concubine" that tend to put a negative label on women and that are deduced even when they are not explicit in the text. In addition to the words used of women are the stories told about women in the Bible. Sarah, Tamara, Hannah, Ruth, and Elizabeth are used to validate the unrelenting search of African women for fertility: the message is that God will open the womb, so one must keep on trying and hoping and believing. The struggle between Rachel and Leah to bear sons and the fact that all "special" babies of the Bible are boys come in for a great deal of attention. Women thus seek for a word from God that validates them apart from their child bearing. They look for strong women of the Bible.

The lives of biblical women are reviewed from the perspective of their tenacity arising out of their faith in a God whose purpose for human beings is fullness of life. African women can thus center their thoughts on the salvation, love, and grace of God. Women who read the Bible for themselves or with other women are able to enrich and critique the selective repertoire chosen by men for women, a repertoire that focuses on the alleged inferiority of women and their alleged culpability as the source of sin and evil in the world. They begin to critique both culture and faith as taught and transmitted by men. Teresa Okure's scientific study of the Johannine corpus uncovers a profound meaning of mission and reinterprets the woman at the well in a way that will cause traditional missiologists to sit up and take notice.[4] Those who love to focus on the "embarrassing sex life" of the woman will need to take up their Bibles and read a little more carefully.

When African women who live under active and blatant patriarchy read the Bible, it touches their situation actively and directly. They see the horrors around them and gather courage to expose such horrors and to struggle against them. The affirmation of the dignity and humanity of women drawn from the Bible makes African women audacious. They no longer join in teaching girls to accept and defend their alleged inferiority. Women feel a strong and double affinity with those Gentiles whose admission into the household of God features prominently in the New Testament. In the midst of patriarchy African women seek to live beyond it because they can point to women in the Bible who lived beyond the patriarchy that surrounded them.

Okure points out the need to recognize human sinfulness as "cultural conditioning" and not "the dictate of God." This means that instead of the self-righteous dismissal of those different from us, what women learn from the Bible is that "what is not liberative cannot be of God." She validates these women's readings from their experience by means of a comparison

---

4. T. Okure, *The Johannine Approach to Mission* (Tübingen: Mohr, 1988).

with the response of the crowds to the teaching of Jesus. The crowds, argues Okure, recognized authority in the teaching of Jesus, not in that of the scribes. It is, therefore, quite in order for women to decide which scripture is authoritative. They can detect "what makes sense, what claims their lives and allegiance." When women read the Bible, they hear God affirming their search for community; they see God working through the disadvantaged; and they expect God to act to liberate African women, members of the disadvantaged of humanity. African women theologians like Okure, who have learned not to see biblical texts as normative, are learning to deal wisely with the book, for even with texts about the life and words of Jesus not all can be said to be culturally liberative.

Women theologians in Africa are open to the liberating and empowering themes of the Bible. The Bible has good news for women. The Bible studies of five women published as *Talitha, qumi!* all bring out the empowering elements in the chosen passages.[5] Freedom in Christ summarizes what they live even as they move in a largely oppressive cultural context. They are in tune with the method suggested and practiced by Okure when they reread Scripture, particularly those texts said to embody the eternal and divine will for women in creation, while recognizing that the Bible has both oppressive and liberative elements. While appropriating the liberative strand, the women theologians consistently struggle against the use of its elements for the victimization and marginalization of women. It is in so doing that they draw heavily on the interaction between Jesus and other characters of the New Testament, especially the women. Employing the contextual approach, women reread the stories and from them draw new and empowering meaning.

Musimbi Kanyoro, who coordinated the Bible study sessions at the September 1989 convocation that resulted in the book *Talitha, qumi!* observes: "During the Bible study sessions, it became clear to us that for women to find justice and peace through the texts of the Bible, they have to try and recover the women participants as well as their possible participation in the life of the text." She also proposes that women read the Scripture side by side with the study of cultures and learn to recognize the boundaries between the two. Her own study of Luke 8:40-46 includes role play, personal reflections, group reflections, and retelling the event from the perspective of the various actors, including that of the mother of the girl Jesus raised, a person who does not say a word during the entire proceedings.[6]

Justine Kahungu Mbwiti, studying John 4:1-42, begins by saying: "We have come into contact with this text of John, which is an interpretation of the life of Jesus. Our reading in faith is therefore an 'interpretation.' What

---

5. M. A. Oduyoye and M. Kanyoro, eds., *Talitha, qumi! Proceedings of the Convocation of African Women Theologians* (Ibadan: Daystar, 1990).

6. M. Kanyoro, "Daughter, Arise (Luke 8:40-46)," *Talitha, qumi!* 54–62.

meaning do we make for this day? What questions do we have to put to John?" Here too the response is one of faith seeking meaning and relevance from the biblical narrative.[7] For Okure, one meaning drawn from this biblical event is that if the woman at the well can be redeemed, so can all other sinners who encounter the Christ and engage in dialogue with Jesus through the Gospels. Both Kahungu and Okure underline the testimony of the woman to her own people, the whole village, not just the women and children.

The context of marginalization in the church, the demonization of women's sexuality in both church and society, and the crossroads of the gospel and African culture have all generated intensive Bible studies. Women's actual experiences are discussed in the context of the biblical text. Reflections on slavery, poverty, and lack of recognition have led to studies on how the Bible has been used to support injustices such as apartheid and the lack of adequate compensation for and recognition of women's economic participation. The underlying patriarchal ideology has been traced to African usages, biblical patriarchy, and the Westernization of African society. The Bible is seen by African women as a two-edged sword. On the one hand, it is used to support women's alleged inferiority, polygamy, levirate marriage, the focus on sons, the silence of women, and so on. On the other hand, the same book is seen as a source for resistance of sexual violence and the promotion of the dignity of the women. So like biblical women, African women sing God's victory; they demand justice in the name of God. Some create sisterhood to deal with women's disabilities, such as widowhood and single parenting, and confront structures of injustice with resistance and transforming actions.

The Bible is read by economically poor women and in the context of a poverty that is shared across the "classes"—a conclusion that African family traditions demand. The God of justice and power is seen in the Bible as the God of new life and transformation, and women challenge the church to be in mission to poor women. When women observe and describe the injustice perpetrated in church and society, they pronounce God's judgment and demand that the breaches in community be mended. The Bible is read from current history with little influence of traditional, historical, and doctrinal theology. The tools for biblical exegesis are used but not followed as unbending, once-for-all rules. Jesus is announcing a new way of living, and each generation has to listen to this message in its own context. One may learn from history, but African women claim the freedom not to see the received interpretation as a static deposit of faith. We read the Bible knowing that no one has the last word on the word of God.

We could characterize this appropriation of the Bible via one's own con-

---

7. J. Kahungu Mbwiti, "Jesus and the Samaritan Woman (John 4:1-42)," *Talitha, qumi!* 63–75.

text as a liberation method. Women are committed to fullness of life in Christ; therefore, they are involved in life-enhancing activities and courses. Reading the Bible, they bring all this experience with them and reflect on the word from God as it comes to them through the Bible. Women's contextual approach to the Bible is anchored in faith in the God who acts continuously in the affairs of creation. Hence, Judith Bahemuka writes: "Revelation is not only a process which began at the time of our ancestors and achieved its fullness in apostolic times, it extends to all history and will never cease."[8] From the Bible, generations have protested many forms of injustice. Today, when African women enumerate the "texts of terror" both in the Bible and in real life, they include cultural texts, racist texts, imperialistic texts, colonial texts, and neocolonial texts, but they continue to hold on to the Bible because in it, also, lie embedded the texts of divine love that empowers.

The primary social determinants of the majority of African women are that they are women and black. Gender discrimination knows no class boundaries. The women writers of Bible studies referred to here cannot be comfortably located in any affluent class. When they talk about poverty, they are not talking of poor cousins, for in Africa you are only as "rich" as family responsibility will allow you to be—and I mean the extended family.

In the very strong conservative and literalist African milieu in which we read the Bible, this liberation method is suspected as subversive, if not altogether unacceptable. We have chosen workshops and other community efforts to give support to one another and provide a forum for self-critique. We can never forget that we live in a religiously pluralistic continent and that our concerned critique of the church and rereading of the Bible may be construed as disloyalty to Christianity in its struggle to show itself as truly African. We also read the Bible as individuals looking for consolation and guidance and sometimes simply to enjoy the sheer beauty of its language and the vividness of its imagery and symbolism. Above all, as women in a continent where the majority of women do not read, we have a context of advocacy. The Bible is a source for the right to fullness of life for all who give and nurture life, and it is as such that women theologians read the Bible.

A survey of the small Christian communities who study the Bible in Kenya reported that most of the participants in these groups were women and children. In one of Nairobi's parishes, 76 percent of the membership of these communities were women.[9] Women's experience in both church and society makes them run to the Bible for consolation and affirmation.

---

8. J. Bahemuka, "The Hidden Christ in African Traditional Religion," *Jesus in African Christianity. Experimentation and Diversity in African Christology* (ed. J. N. K. Mugambi and L. Magesu; Nairobi: Initiatives, 1989) 1–16.

9. "Report on Consultation on Methods of Research to Find Out How the Bible Is

In 1987 women from Umtata in the Transkei of South Africa, of all ages, of different races and marital status, and having a wide variety of interests, commitments, and careers, constituted themselves into a women's theology group. They read the Bible together, discussed "matters of mutual concern," and committed to writing the studies they carried out in order to share them with other women and make them available to men as well.[10] The love of African women for the Bible has moved into a phase in which they consciously seek to share its message as they see it with others. Being South Africans, the Umtata women recognize that they are torn by race, class, culture, and gender, but also that they are united by many things. Indeed, women's common fears unite them: husbands who drink; husbands who are violent; children struggling with growing up; unemployed men around them; rape. One gets much the same list in Kenya and in Algeria. Women are joined together in the struggle to make life a bit more comfortable for those around them—they work eighteen hours a day and always do more than two jobs. They study the Bible together in the context of hope.

Women who read the Bible from the context of relative privilege, such as the professional women who met at the University of Calabar, Nigeria, in 1990, often pick up on the struggles of biblical women on behalf of others.[11] They want the heroines of the Bible to become models for their own struggle to be a liberative force in their communities. It is interesting to note that the Calabar conference was organized by women theologians in the context of the sociopolitical program called "Better Life for Rural Women," which was the brainchild of Mariama Babangida, the wife of the Nigerian head of state. To illustrate this reading of the Bible by African women, I turn now to the infancy narratives of Matthew's Gospel.

An Example of Reading from an African Cultural Location: The Annunciation to Joseph

The following is a reading of the Matthean infancy stories (Matthew 1–2) in the context of the challenge to the churches to stand in solidarity with women. The phrase "Ecumenical Decade: Churches in Solidarity with Women" has revealed a number of assumptions and ambiguities about what the church is understood to be. The most critical of these is the question: Are women not an integral part of the church? While in Africa some women have been baptized into the church, the vast majority have not.

Being Used in Small Christian Communities in Africa" (Karen-Nairobi, 1989). Sponsored and organized by the Catholic Biblical Centre for Africa and Madagascar (BICAM).

10. *Umtata Women's Theology Bible Study Series* (Pretoria: C. P. Powell Bible Centre, 1987).

11. R. Edet and M. Umeagudoso, eds., *Life, Women and Culture: Theological Reflections* (Lagos: African Heritage Research and Publications, 1990).

They do not belong to an institution called church nor even to the organized religion called Christianity; they have their own faith traditions. The "Ecumenical Decade" is asking for the church's solidarity with all women. A second question has to do with the traditional naming of the church in feminine terms, while the vast majority of the visible leadership (clergy) is made up of men who are themselves members of this female body. This state of affairs is much in focus because of the parallels it evokes with male-female relations in the human community in general and with certain images in Scripture.

In the Hebrew Scriptures the kinship of Israel and Yahweh is described in terms of marriage. Israel (a man's name) becomes the spouse of Yahweh. This relationship recalls the Canaanite religions in whose context Yahwism grew. Both the congregation of Israel (*qahal*) and the covenant assembly (*'edah*) are feminine in gender, thus reinforcing the femaleness of Israel in relation to Yahweh. This imagery is reproduced in the New Testament, where the kinship of Jesus the Messiah and the church is described by Paul in marital terms (Eph 5:21-33). Here again the gender of both *ekklesia* and *kuriakē* (kirk, church) is feminine. In the English language one also finds the custom of making the church female. So the church is female, while its rulers, the priests, are male. As Jesus the Messiah husbands the church and is its head, so we have been socialized to believe that it is an anomaly to have a woman as head of a church.

Further, Mary, the mother of Jesus, is sometimes called the prototype of the church, the first to believe that the kingdom of God was about to become a reality. She believed that God could dwell with people. She believed that the chains of the oppressive aspects of traditional community and human relations were about to be broken, that hierarchies would be no more, that the church, the gathering of God's people, would become truly human, and that the presence of God in this new human community would become truly palpable. Indeed, a bleeding woman would touch the garments of Immanuel and be healed. Mary believed that God would come among us and that the human community would be transformed into the fully gathered family of God. This faith of Mary makes her a symbol of the church; thereby another female image is painted.

This female image of the church has encouraged the leadership of the church (mainly male) to appropriate for themselves the headship. Sadly, then, the church of human experience is a male organization (of clergy and prominent laymen) that has to be called into solidarity with women. The church of experience cannot be described as com-passionate nor as being among the people of the world "as one who serves"—nor even as a father living and nurturing both daughters and sons as God does. Women's solidarity with the church is not reciprocated by the church. In the church as in the family, women's services are taken for granted and received without recognition. Why is this?

Reflecting upon the tardiness of some sectors of the church over the issues of the churches' "Ecumenical Decade," it has dawned on me that perhaps it has something to do with this marital image and the way marriage functions in many societies. I am suggesting that the dominant image of the church as a female ruled by the ordained (men) has affected even how we remember our gospel narratives. The "annunciation" in Luke has overshadowed that in Matthew. So I propose to take the events of the coming of Immanuel/God-with-us from the perspective of Joseph, the first man to accept that God would be with us in human form and the man who stood by the woman who was filled with the vision of what that world would look like.

Joseph's Dreams (Matt 1:18-25; 2:13-15; 2:19-21; 2:22-23)

In Matthew's narrative of the events surrounding the birth of Jesus the Messiah, the role of Joseph is highlighted, thus offering us an opportunity to see God's project with humanity in a holistic manner. The *annunciation* in Matthew is to *Joseph,* a man guided by dreams and visitations from God's angels. When we first meet Joseph, he is described as a son of David in a genealogy geared toward telling us why Jesus of Nazareth was called Son of David later in the narrative (1:1-17). Then follows the saga of the marriage that could not be consummated (1:18-25).

Mary and Joseph were planning to follow the traditional expectations of their culture and community to the effect that young people of marriageable age would get married and start a family. The reverse was an abomination. The story says that Mary was "found to be with child from the Holy Spirit" (v. 18). This explanation of the origin of the pregnancy could only have come from Mary herself. We know of only one other person who shared the secret, her cousin Elizabeth (Luke 1:39-45). Mary and Joseph were living in Galilee in a town called Nazareth. But when Mary accepted this marvel, she left to go to Judaea in the hills to see Elizabeth, for the angel had disclosed that she too was about to deliver a miracle-child. This type of solidarity of women has held the churches' "Ecumenical Decade" together until now. So now we turn to what the solidarity of the churches with women could look like, for, like Mary, many women are pregnant with a new vision of how to live as God's family and in God's world with God among us.

First Dream (Matt 1:18-25). The gossip about Mary's pregnancy got to Joseph. How, we are not told. But I prefer to imagine Joseph beaming at the sight of Mary, his would-be bride. The whole town is filled with the excitement of the anticipated wedding feast. They hope the wine will last the stipulated number of days. Joseph and Mary and their two families owe it to the town to provide the usual festivity. Joseph begins to rehearse

the coming public declaration of approval of their marriage and the blessing that Mary will be like a fruitful vine. "Wait a minute," says Mary, "I
have something to tell you." Imagine the painful story Mary had to tell, the
shock and disbelief on Joseph's face—the emotions, from anger to despair
and disappointment.

Joseph's world begins to crumble around him. Mary has deviated from
traditional expectations. As if that were not enough, she is making this out-
rageous claim—a child of the Holy Spirit indeed! Filled with their different
thoughts, they go their separate ways. For Joseph this is a nightmare. Tradition requires that all plans for the union be called off. Tradition demands
that he make a public example of this girl who has gone against the norms
of society. That night he tosses and turns. Joseph the righteous (Matthew's
description of him) agonizes. He suffers with Mary. She is just as distraught
and disappointed at the turn of events, if not worse.

The first question: How do I give up a person I love to be disgraced
before the whole community, maybe stoned to death (Nazareth was known
for that) or burned alive (as happens elsewhere)? Genesis 38:11-26 tells of
the response of Judah, Tamar's father-in-law, to the news that Tamar had
played the whore and was pregnant: "Bring her out, and let her be burned"
(v. 24). These drastic measures were necessary to ensure the purity of the
patriarchal line. Joseph's ancestry by the father's line included Abraham,
Zadok, David, Mattan, and his own father, Jacob. Mary is telling him the
name of the child she is carrying. He does not participate in the choice.

The second question: Can I call this "Immanuel" son of Joseph, when
he is in fact "son of the Most High"? Can I hand on my patriarchal line to
this Immanuel conceived of the Holy Spirit? Is the line begun by Abraham
to end with me? How do I face the family of Jacob? How do I explain the
link between Joseph son of Jacob and Jesus son of the Holy Spirit? The
discontinuity was too dramatic to pass over lightly. He turns over, wide-
eyed; that night was not going to be for resting.

Third question: How do I face my friends, the peer group, the whole
clan, and the whole of Nazareth? Am I now the laughingstock of the town?
(Joseph twists and turns.) I cannot stand being disgraced, and I cannot bear
having Mary disgraced. The way out?

Joseph the righteous responds differently from Judah, Tamar's father-in-
law. He will not bring her out. Better call off the marriage quietly. (Having
made this painful decision, Joseph falls into an uneasy sleep.) Joseph is
then visited by the divine solution to this human dilemma. How is tradition
transformed to respond to the will of God, the plan of God to live among
God's people? Joseph wants a middle way to conform to tradition only to
the extent that the new would not be hurt. God proposes radical solidarity.

The angel of God appears to him and says: "Joseph, son of David, do
not be afraid to take Mary as your wife, for the child conceived in her
is from the Holy Spirit" (v. 20). Joseph keeps these words in his heart

and resolves to act on them. I would like all men to put themselves in Joseph's place, walking around Nazareth facing insults and insinuations. Joseph stands by Mary; Joseph shares Mary's burden. Joseph enables Mary to carry through God's project. Joseph believes Mary's encounter with the Holy Spirit. He stands by her while the whole community wonders, What next? A major tradition is being undermined, and Joseph, son of David, is part of the new move. Imagine the tough journey to Bethlehem. From hotel to hostel to homes they search for accommodation. Joseph is sharing God's project. He is participating with Mary to facilitate God's project. Joseph is helping to look for a place where room could be made. The rest of creation too had been waiting, the stars and the animals are all awaiting the coming of God among creation. Joseph has to be midwife to Mary. Joseph has to provide the encouragement and comfort and security needed to bring "the new" out safely. Mary says, as in the Christmas carol:

> Joseph dearest, Joseph mine,
> help me cradle this child divine.

Joseph sits contemplating this vision of new life at his bosom, while Mary tries to rest from the task, excitement, and wonder of the birth of Immanuel, grateful for the silent and not-so-silent witnesses at the birth of the child of the Most High. Mary blesses God for giving her Joseph, the com-passionate.

Second Dream (Matt 2:13-15). As if this were not enough, this new life is the cause of a national crisis. This "new" brought in by a woman with the solidarity of a man must not be allowed to live. The event is a threat not only to religious and cultural traditions of the Jews but also to the political situation. So the angel of dreams visits Joseph again: "Get up, take the child and his mother, and flee to Egypt, and remain there." For the sake of this "son" of the Holy Spirit, Joseph is to become a refugee. He will have Mary and the baby to keep him company, but what happens to his carpentry shop? His contribution to Nazareth as a skilled person for the building of projects will be missed, and he will lose income. He will lose contact with friends, colleagues, and family. All for the sake of the "son" of the Holy Spirit and his (Joseph's) decision to stand in solidarity with Mary and her burden from God. So to Egypt the family goes—Jesus, Joseph, Mary—refugees in Egypt living out the meaning of solidarity.

Third Dream (Matt 2:19-21). Finally, the time comes to move back. The dream comes again: "Get up, take the child and his mother, and go to the land of Israel" (v. 20). But the family cannot stay in Israel for fear of Archelaus (v. 21), now reigning in Judaea.

Fourth Dream (Matt 2:22-23). As a result of another dream, the family sets off for Nazareth in Galilee. Here Joseph keeps all these things in his heart, and together with Mary they nurture the "son" of the Holy Spirit.

We began with marriage; here we see marriage as partnership. Here there is no master-servant relation that objectifies women. Here is love in action. Such total solidarity, empathy, co-laboring, companionship, and faith in the vision of a woman are what the "Ecumenical Decade" calls the churches to embark upon. First, the "Ecumenical Decade" calls upon the churches to learn to believe women have a new vision of what church and society could look like. Second, the churches are also called upon to reexamine their own and society's traditions and make room for the new to be born.

The Churches in Solidarity

There are churches that, like Joseph, have enough faith to stand by women against unbending traditions. These churches, like Joseph, are cradling the visions of the "Ecumenical Decade" and "making room" for their realization. In the first four years of the decade we have found men who, like Judah, the father-in-law of Tamar, are able to say: "The woman is right; I was wrong." Let us look for men who, like Joseph, love and respect the humanity of women and are therefore ready to grant that God works through women. The churches shall be in solidarity with women when, like Joseph, the angel of dreams visits them with the annunciation of the birth of the new life in God's kingdom. This I believe.

We have had happy experiences of churches in solidarity. We have also been faced with painful experiences of churches and persons who seem unable to relate to women, except in hurtful, patronizing, or demeaning ways. Thus, there are churches that do not feel able to leave the past and go to Egypt, that are unable to break with the old structures, that fear the new relationship of women and men that the "Ecumenical Decade" calls for, that are refusing to open themselves to dreams of the new, that are refusing to listen to God's messengers, that cannot even believe that women can be pregnant with the Holy Spirit and bring into being new visions and new perspectives, that have no room for women pregnant with new visions of a community of women and men.

Conclusion

Women reading the Bible in Africa are doing so in a context permeated by death and death-dealing forces. These women are not insulated from this context and therefore belong to the social and civic forces seeking to protect and nurture life, to guard and promote the dignity of the human person, and to ensure that neither human life nor the rest of creation is abused. As Christian theologians they bring a spirituality of struggle fueled by hope into this effort of African women. They hope the church will believe and act out the message of salvation. They hope the Spirit of God will move governments and traditional leaders to be just, compassionate, and respectful of human life and women's lives. They hope that in good time the fullness of God's presence will be realized in Africa.

3

Reading from This Place:
Some Problems and Prospects

Teresa Okure, S.H.C.J.

The issue of "reading from this place" deals with the relationship between the biblical text and the social location of the interpreter. The *text* is the Bible, the word of God, expressed in human language, by a human author to a human audience, in a given period of history, in the vast span of history covered by the Bible.[1]

By *social location* I understand the sum total of those human experiences that shape the lives of the persons connected with the Bible at three levels: (1) the level of the peoples in and of the Bible itself (those whose lives the Bible is concerned with), the primary level; (2) the level of the biblical authors and their respective audiences at various epochs of history, the secondary level; and (3) the level of the readers/interpreters of the Bible throughout the course of history up to the present day, the tertiary level. Thus in dealing with the Bible, these three social locations come into play, whether or not these are consciously addressed by the reader/interpreter. The total reality of these social locations includes culture, language, politics, economics, worldview, faith/creed, thought patterns, value systems, and geography, as well as such foundational locations as sex, race, and class.

By *interpreter* I understand simply anybody who reads/hears the text with a view to deriving from it a meaning for life. He or she could be rich or poor, black or white, scholar or nonscholar, married or widowed, employed or jobless, citizen or alien, a member of the church hierarchy or a layperson, one who reads the text alone or in community.

Any human life is lived in a concrete social location. Hence the total reality of this location in its several aspects affects and conditions the lives of the people concerned at all three levels mentioned above. It is entrenched in the lives of the people in and of the Bible, the primary level. For, as

---

1. See, further, R. E. Brown, *Critical Meanings of the Bible: How a Modern Reading of the Bible Challenges Christians, the Church, and the Churches* (New York: Paulist, 1981) esp. 1–22.

I observed in a previous study, in dealing with the Bible, it is important to remember that "in the beginning was the life and the word which expressed the life, not the book."[2] The book came at a later stage, in some instances, long after the life that it records. The total reality of the social location also influences the lives of the biblical authors and their respective audiences within their own living contexts. Hence the record of previous lives that they selectively interpreted and recorded in the book for the encouragement (*parenesis*) of their audience in turn bears the stamp and conditionings of their own respective social locations in all their dimensions. The same applies in the case of interpreters down through the ages. Since these human beings are also influenced and conditioned by the different aspects of their particular social locations, their interpretations or readings of the Bible necessarily bear the stamp of such influences, as happens in any human activity.

In sum, the influence of social locations on the biblical text at any given level—be it primary, secondary, or tertiary—is a fact of life. Seen in this light, the question of the relationship between the text and the social location of the interpreter is not simply a late twentieth-century issue, though the intense awareness of and focus on it may be. This observation is important if we are to see the current concern over the relationship between the interpreter and his or her social location in its proper perspective.

During the Renaissance and the Enlightenment, concern with the issue of social location with respect to the Bible centered on the first level, that of the primary characters in and of the Bible. I consider, for instance, the various works on the life of Jesus of Nazareth that were written at this period and the later studies on life in Palestine in the first century CE as different efforts to get in touch with the concrete social locations or life situations of the primary characters in and of the New Testament, with special reference to the Gospels.[3]

The historical-critical method that grew out of the Enlightenment carried the issue of social location further through its most cherished child, redaction criticism. In this regard, redaction criticism focused predominantly, if not exclusively, on the social location of the biblical authors as this influenced their interpretation of their sources. Though at its early stages redaction criticism saw these authors simply as compilers and editors of their oral and written sources, it later came to regard them as theologians whose interpretive compositions were influenced by their own social loca-

---

2. Paper presented at a workshop on biblical hermeneutics during the Third General Assembly of the Ecumenical Association of Third World Theologians (EATWOT), Nairobi, January 6–13, 1992.

3. The data on this can be found in most introductions to the New Testament. On the aims and objectives of the Enlightenment, see, for instance, P. Stuhlmacher, *Historical Criticism and Theological Interpretation of Scripture: Toward a Hermeneutics of Consent* (Philadelphia: Fortress Press, 1975).

tions and the theological needs of their respective Christian communities.[4] The history-of-religions approach (*Religionsgeschichte*) and the various studies on the New Testament background and environment supplied information on the religious thought patterns that could have influenced the biblical authors.[5] But the main focus in all this was the author/redactor and his social location. New Testament students are familiar with the way scholars believe that Matthew, for instance, was influenced by his Jewish background, and Luke by his Hellenistic background. More recent studies on the social setting of the New Testament have moved the question from the social location of the biblical authors to that of their audiences. In addition to the synthesis of these studies done by Carolyn Osiek, one should mention the works by Helmut Koester and Sean Freyne, to cite but a few.[6]

Today we have come full circle, as it were, by taking full cognizance of the influence that the social location of the interpreter plays on his or her search for meaning in the Bible. Thanks for this recognition is due for the most part to the theological efforts of Third World theologians (Latin American liberation theologians, black theologians of South Africa and North America, African and Asian theologians) in the richness and diversity of their own social locations in the different continents and to women across the globe who engage in feminist hermeneutics or reading the Bible from women's perspective.[7] As a result, it has become widely accepted that to do theology or a fully engaged reading of the Bible one has to address, if not start with, one's own consciousness of oneself. Even such traditional theological bodies as the Society for New Testament Studies felt it important to introduce a continuing seminar on reader-response to the Bible. A reading of the Bible that is not directly related to the social location of the reader is almost considered out of fashion.[8]

---

4. See, for details, E. Krentz, *The Historical-Critical Method* (Guides to Biblical Scholarship; Philadelphia: Fortress Press, 1975); and R. K. Harrison et al., eds., *Historical Criticism: Historical, Literary and Textual* (Grand Rapids: Zondervan, 1978).

5. Among the best known of these studies are C. K. Barrett, *The New Testament Background: Selected Documents* (New York: Harper and Row, 1956), and E. Lohse, *The New Testament Environment* (Nashville: Abingdon, 1974).

6. C. Osiek, *What Are They Saying about the Social Setting of the New Testament?* (Ramsey, N.J.: Paulist, 1985); H. Koester, *Introduction to the New Testament* (2 vols.; Philadelphia: Fortress Press, 1982) esp. 2:304–48 on Christianity in its encounter with its social world; S. Freyne, *Galilee from Alexander the Great to Hadrian: 323 B.C.E. to 135 C.E.* (Wilmington, Del.: Glazier, 1980), and idem, *Galilee, Jesus, and the Gospels: Literary Approaches and Historical Investigations* (Philadelphia: Fortress Press, 1988).

7. The publications of EATWOT along with the works of the Latin American liberation theologians furnish perhaps the most well-known and influential literature on this. See, in particular, S. Torres and V. Fabella, eds., *The Emergent Gospel: Theology from the Underside of History* (Maryknoll, N.Y.: Orbis Books, 1978); idem, *Doing Theology in a Divided World* (Maryknoll, N.Y.: Orbis Books, 1985); and R. Gibellini, ed., *Frontiers of Theology in Latin America* (Maryknoll, N.Y.: Orbis Books, 1979). The works by feminist theologians are too many to be listed.

8. See, for instance, J. Pobee and B. von Wartenberg-Potter, eds., *New Eyes for Reading* (Geneva: World Council of Churches, 1986), and M. Amba Oduyoye and R. A. Kanyoro,

Problems with This Approach

Exciting as this new approach is, it carries with it some major problems that need to be addressed. These problems center around the nature of the text itself as the life of a given people and as the inspired word of God. Raymond Brown has argued that the designation of the Bible as the word of God was not applied by the biblical authors to their work, except perhaps in the case of the prophetic books.[9] However, the canonical community did, and we have inherited the book as canonical from them. Another important source of the problem is the right of an author to his or her meaning. The primary meaning of any word or thought is that intended by the author/speaker. But once the word has been spoken or written, it becomes subject to as many interpretations as the audiences or readers that it encounters. It can then happen that the original meaning intended by the author becomes lost in the plethora of interpretations given to it by its audiences. Given the belief by most Christians that the Bible is the inspired word of God and that it has canonical status within the Christian community, how does one safeguard the authenticity of the meaning of the text and guard against subjectivism?

This question cannot be sufficiently addressed without recourse to the fundamental nature of the Bible itself, the purpose of its existence, and the purpose of its interpretation. Brown has taken pains to illustrate that the "literal sense" of the text, the meaning intended by the author, is different from the "canonical sense," the meaning given to it by the believing community that accepted it into the canon of Scripture.[10] Hence, if the first community had the right to give the text a meaning different from that of the author, so, it might be argued, do the community and individuals who read the Bible today. The problem with this line of argument is that the "literal sense" of the text is found only in its canonical form, as it is recorded in the biblical context. Nevertheless, the problem of what the text meant then and what it means now remains and is crucial for our present purposes.

I stated earlier in this essay that by the "interpreter" I understand anybody who reads the biblical text in order to discover a meaning for life. Such a reading implies that the reader is one who believes that he or she can discover life from the Bible. In other words, I am interested here not in any scientific or literary reading of the Bible that leaves the believer's life untouched by the exercise. I am concerned rather with a person who believes that the Bible is fundamentally the word of God, even though it has been expressed in human language with all its sociocultural and historical

eds., *The Will to Arise: Women, Tradition, and the Church in Africa* (Maryknoll, N.Y.: Orbis Books, 1992).

    9. Brown, *Critical Meanings*, 1–22.

    10. Ibid.

moorings. In this respect the question whether or not the Bible can be regarded as the word of God does not really arise. Such a question cannot be answered scientifically or objectively, but only relationally. It is a matter of faith, of one's relationship to God in faith. Readers who approach the Bible from this standpoint of faith, as the primary and secondary communities and individuals did, seek in it a message of God that can challenge, liberate, and energize their lives in their own social locations. Insofar as the text is to address life and life problems concretely, the influence of social location cannot be treated as a matter of indifference, nor can the tension between this social location and that of the canonical text be minimized.

Ironic as this may seem, the solution to the problem for me lies in the realization that the Bible is the word of God, in the sense that it embodies a divine message for humanity. Further, this God speaks not only in the social location of the biblical authors and their community but also in the different social locations of the interpreters. If God, who dwells beyond time and social location, wills the existence of each time and social location and wishes to address a living and abiding word to that social location through the biblical word, then the authentic meaning given by the modern reader who searches the Scriptures *in faith* for this divine meaning must also be willed by God. The God who speaks in the Scriptures is the same God who speaks in social locations in history. Believers who seek to hear this word—whether in the Scriptures or in a given social location— believe that they will find life in it. They are reminded that God's ways are not our human ways nor God's thoughts human thoughts (Isa 55:8). This word has an efficacy all its own that does not depend on human interpretations or social locations but that permeates and transcends such locations (Isa 55:10-12). It follows that no one social location can exhaust the possibilities of meaning of the divine word.

Given this reality, readers in any given age have the duty to seek to discover this abiding word of God as it applies to their own particular contexts. One sure way to do this is to seek to understand first the meaning that is embodied in the canonical text within its own canonical context, and this includes the social location of the biblical authors. If this is not done, one can hardly speak of claiming the meaning of the biblical text for one's context, nor can one dialogue with such a text, since one could organize one's life independently of it. If one regards the text as important, then one has a duty to understand first what the text says before applying or claiming its meaning for one's own context. The same Holy Spirit that inspired the canonical authors and their communities also inspires the reader who is willing to be led and guided by the same Spirit in the reading of the text. This is a matter of faith, not of logic.

First, therefore, the social location of the interpreter does not deprive the text of its fundamental (that is, divine) meaning. Rather, it furnishes the hermeneutical questions that are brought to the text in order to discover

new meanings latent in the text, as does the wise scribe (Matt 13:52)—
meanings that can challenge and give fuller life to the reader. The social
location cannot ask of the text answers to questions it never asked itself.
To be fruitful, reading from a given social location must be a faith exercise.
It is this faith that guarantees fidelity to the word of God spoken in the text.
As I have stated elsewhere, this last point is important. Insofar as the Bible
is the book of a faith community, spread across history, any reading that
lacks this faith dimension has missed its point or at best is incomplete.[11]

Second, the Bible is the book of the community of faith, the people of
God, not of individuals. The community aspect of the book applies at the
level of the primary and secondary characters of the text; it should also
apply at the tertiary level of the interpreters. In other words, the community of the people of God reserves the ultimate right to authenticate the
meaning of a text as interpreted by an individual. The problem of subjectivism and the fear of overlocalization of the meaning are countered by this
community aspect and by an awareness of the basic unity of the human
race, a unity guaranteed by the Holy Spirit through whom God makes all
things new.

Third, as God, the real author of the Bible, is the same today, yesterday,
and forever (Rev 1:4, 8; 4:1), it becomes possible to discern those interpretations that are in accordance with the one will and intention of God,
which is to give and promote life in all its fullness (John 10:10), as this has
been manifested in the course of biblical history. Any interpretation that
fails to do this in spirit and in truth becomes suspect and should be regarded as inauthentic. This is the one aspect of the Bible that has justified
the hermeneutics of the poor and the oppressed as well as feminist hermeneutics or interpreting the Bible from women's perspective.[12] Even if in
some cases the meaning of the Bible purportedly discovered is for its own
time only (Hab 2:3), such a meaning must be in tune with this universal
intention of God to liberate, save, give, and sustain life.

Finally, social location need not be confined to the small world of the
reader. If this location includes such issues as race, sex, and class, then its
scope must be widened to embrace the global dimensions in which these
realities occur. Sexism is a universal phenomenon, even as it is a particular
one. The same applies to racism and classism. This means that interpreting
the Bible from different social locations or reading from this place needs
not exclude the possibility of reading it from a global perspective. Rather,
those readings that deal with these universal issues deserve special attention

---

11. T. Okure, *The Johannine Approach to Mission: A Contextual Study of John 4:1-42*
(Tübingen: Mohr, 1988) 293, 311.

12. See E. Tamez, *The Gospel of the Oppressed* (Maryknoll, N.Y.: Orbis Books, 1982);
T. Okure, "Women in the Bible," *With Passion and Compassion: Third World Women
Doing Theology* (ed. V. Fabella and M. A. Oduyoye; Maryknoll, N.Y.: Orbis Books, 1988)
47-59.

and become privileged standpoints for examining the interaction between the social location of the interpreter and the text. In what follows, I wish to illustrate how the current concern to read the Bible from women's perspective has enhanced my interpretation of the New Testament divorce texts seen in a global perspective.

An Example: Reading the New Testament Divorce Texts Globally

The Method

There is no doubt that of all the current social locations for reading the Bible that of women is the most explosive and universal. Women constitute half of humanity viewed ontologically, and more than half viewed numerically. They are there in class, race, and all other social locations. Yet for centuries they as a sex have been treated as subhuman, or "misbegotten males," and denied full participation in the life of the church and society.

The Bible has played a decisive role in shaping this human attitude toward women, especially in the Judeo-Christian tradition. Since the Bible is regarded as the word of God, a privileged place for discovering the will of God for humanity, its statements about women, though in most cases culturally conditioned, have been taken as gospel truths that must not be contravened.[13] This applies particularly to those statements about the ontological inferiority of women to men and their subjection in church and society (1 Cor 11:3-10; 14:34-36; 2 Cor 11:3; 1 Tim 2:11-15).

In the last three decades, women and some men theologians have contested this patriarchal reading of the Bible that seeks to sustain the status quo in church and society. It has been noted that the Bible itself is the product of a patriarchal culture and that this patriarchy is a sin against God and humanity. This awareness has given rise to a reading of the Bible from women's perspective, or feminist hermeneutics, an aspect of feminism that Mercy Oduyoye describes as "shorthand for the proclamation that women's experience should be an integral part of what goes into the definition of being human.... It emphasizes the wholeness of the community as made up of male and female beings."[14] Feminist hermeneutics seeks to do this through a holistic reading of the Bible that recognizes the equal rights and dignity of men and women as intended by God in creation and redemption, the whole of the paschal mystery, and by highlighting those patriarchal aspects of the biblical cultures that are responsible for

---

13. The most significant documents of the Catholic Church on this issue are *Inter insigniores* ("On the Ordination of Women," 1977) and *Mulieris dignitatem* ("On the Dignity of Woman," 1989), both by John Paul II.

14. M. A. Oduyoye, *Hearing and Knowing: Theological Reflections on Christianity in Africa* (Maryknoll, N.Y.: Orbis Books, 1986) 121.

either the exclusion of women's contributions from the biblical story or the downplaying of their significant contributions as recorded in the story.[15]

Elsewhere I have articulated my own understanding of feminist hermeneutics, which I prefer to call reading the Bible from women's perspective.[16] Here I will mention one key feature of this approach that I wish to apply in reading the New Testament divorce texts. No one would dispute the statement that women are different from men, and vice versa. But many would still dispute the consequent statement—that women have a distinctive way of viewing reality that is different from men's and unique to them—and the practical ramifications of that statement. But thanks to psychology and the social sciences, it is now generally recognized that sexuality is not simply a matter of biological makeup but "is a gift that touches human persons on all levels of their existence."[17]

One of the distinctive features of women is that they are by nature intuitive, creative, and innovative, and African women particularly so. As people uniquely covenanted with life, they have a concern not only for their sex but for all humanity. Indeed, feminism properly understood is a human revolution that surpasses all other major revolutions in history, such as the industrial and the scientific revolutions. This is because, unlike these other revolutions, it deals with humanity itself and works for the restoration of the equal rights and dignity of men and women as originally intended by God (Gen 1:26-28). It is this creative and comprehensive approach that I wish to apply in interpreting the New Testament divorce texts in a global perspective in order to highlight their implications for the man-woman relationship outside the context of marriage.

Conjointly created as male and female in the image and likeness of God, men and women find the peak of their relationship in the context of marriage where the two become one flesh (Gen 2:24).[18] But in the sinful human location (Genesis 3), the woman as wife and mother both finds and loses her identity as a human being. As mother, her salvation lies in childbearing (1 Tim 2:15); as wife, she becomes the property of the husband who owns even her very sexuality (Deut 22:13-27).

The same plight of woman obtains in most traditional African cultures. The woman as wife is viewed as the "eater of the husbands' property" (in Ibibio, *adia mkpo ebe*); she is married with the husband's money and is to bear *his* children, look after *his* needs, and provide for *his* comfort. This

---

15. A classic treatment of the problem is E. Schüssler Fiorenza's *In Memory of Her: A Feminist Reconstruction of Christian Origins* (New York: Crossroad, 1984).

16. T. Okure, "Feminist Interpretations in Africa," *Searching the Scriptures,* vol. 1, *A Feminist Introduction* (ed. E. Schüssler Fiorenza; New York: Crossroad, 1993) 245–54.

17. H. Peschlke, *Christian Ethics: A Presentation of Special Moral Theology in the Light of Vatican II* (Dublin: C. Goodlife Neale, 1987) 375. See also, from Vatican II, *Gaudium et spes* ("The Church in the Modern World") nos. 47–52.

18. See T. Okure, "Biblical Perspectives on Women: 'Eve, the Mother of All the Living' (Gen 3:20)," *Voices from the Third World* (Philippine edition), 8/2 (1985) 17–24.

predicament of the woman as a being who exists only for the man is best summed up in the reply of a young girl in Sierra Leone in the course of a catechism class. To the question "Who made you?" she replied, "God made me for man." She learned this answer by way of intuition or through observing the place of women in her sociocultural location, not from any written code.

Jewish biblical law recognized divorce, but only a certain kind: a husband could divorce his wife (she was his property and so could be let go at will), but a wife could not divorce her husband. In traditional African societies, divorce was not very common. Even if the woman was barren, the practice of polygamy could allow her to remain in the husband's house while second or third wives bore the much-cherished children. The Gospels, on the contrary, record statements of Jesus prohibiting divorce (Matt 19:1-12; Mark 10:1-12; Luke 16:18) on the basis of the created order willed by God (Gen 1:26-27; 2:21-24). Outside the Gospels, the statements in 1 Cor 6:16; 11:2-12 (esp. vv. 7-9); and Ephesians 24–32 on the relationship of woman to man in the context of marriage shed light on our search for a fuller meaning of the Gospel passages.

I will first interpret these texts in their literary and historical locations; then, using the creative and comprehensive approach, I will draw out their implications for man-woman relationships outside the context of marriage. The rationale for this proposed method of reading is, first, that marriage and divorce constitute the closest union and separation, respectively, in man-woman relationship. This applies irrespective of sociocultural and geographical locations. Second, the inner logic of the texts themselves justifies reading them anew in a global context.

Analysis of Texts

The Synoptic passages listed above deal with the issue of the permissibility of divorce. Divorce signifies the dissolution of a validly contracted marriage. It frees the partners to remarry if they so choose. In Judaism, as mentioned above, only the husband could divorce the wife, with or without the "writ of separation" (the *get*). This was a legal document by which the man testified that the woman was no longer his wife. Without this document, the woman was not free to remarry, even though the husband was.[19] In the Roman world, on the contrary, a woman could divorce her husband. That she could possess property meant that she could easily become independent of her husband.[20] Indeed, scholars believe that Mark's version of

---

19. See, for instance, A. Cohen, *Everyman's Talmud* (New York: Schocken Books, 1975) 64–168.
20. Schüssler Fiorenza, *In Memory of Her,* 314.

the story is aimed at Herodias, who divorced her husband, Philip, to marry his brother Herod Antipas (Mark 6:17-29).

In Matthew and Mark, the episode is placed immediately before the incident where parents bring children for Jesus to bless but are turned away by the disciples to the displeasure of Jesus. This may draw attention to another type of divorce, namely, that of children from the world of adults (Matt 14:21).

In Matthew, the episode constitutes a leading event in the section that is commonly described as "the approaching kingdom" (Matthew 19–26). This linking of the question about divorce and the "approaching kingdom of heaven" is perhaps not accidental. The link is found in Matt 19:4-5 and Mark 10:6-8, namely, the reference to what was from the beginning. In this context, the kingdom of heaven means the restoration of God's reign or will for humanity as intended "from the beginning." This happens in a new way in Christ. Hence the episode opens that phase of Jesus' ministry in which he goes to complete his mission in Jerusalem and thus usher in definitively this reign or kingdom of God. This eschatological context (the definitive completion of Jesus' mission) reinforces the protological one (what was from the beginning [Gen 1:26-27; 2:24]) and calls one to look for a meaning of the passages that addresses the issue of the indispensability of the man-woman relationship in all spheres of life.

Traditional interpretations of these passages focused on the differences between the Matthean and Markan accounts—in terms of their literary form (a controversy apothegm in Matthew and a scholastic one in Mark) and their structural sequence of thought—and on the meaning of the exception clause in Matthew. It is said that, unlike Mark, Matthew presupposes divorce and is concerned only with the grounds for it and remarriage after it (19:9).

While these and other contemporary debates on these passages continue unresolved, the following affirmations emerge from them. First, Jesus' dialogue partners, the Pharisees and experts of the Torah, accept divorce as a given of the law of Moses (Deut 24:1-4). But Jesus rejects it on the grounds that the stipulation in the Mosaic law was only a concession due to the people's unwillingness to be taught (Matt 19:10). This concession went against the created order established by God. This order is that "from the beginning" God created humanity as male and female and as destined to become husband and wife (Matt 19:5; Mark 10:7). The marriage of a man and a woman makes concrete this unity of the human race, male and female (Gen 2:24). The Yahwistic account graphically illustrates this unity by the creation of the woman out of the man's rib as bone of his bone and flesh of his flesh (Gen 2:21-23).

Jesus cites this oneness of flesh (or body, according to some translations, for example, the New Jerusalem Bible) as the solid grounds against divorce. Through marriage, the two become again one flesh as it was "from the beginning." He concludes that given this divine provision, whereby the husband and wife belong to each other as do parts of a person's body, no human being under pretext of a human law has the power or right to separate the two. Human law cannot invalidate God's action. Paul makes a similar case when he argues in Gal 3:17 that the law on circumcision, coming centuries later and being exclusive to Jews, cannot invalidate God's promise to Abraham, a promise that was a free gift whose scope was universal: "In you all the tribes of the earth will bless themselves" (Gen 12:3).

Second, the inner logic of the Matthean passage argues against the belief of some scholars that Jesus here takes divorce for granted and is interested only in the grounds for it and remarriage after it. This interpretation is based on Matthew's allegedly Jewish origin. But it was not only the Jews who accepted divorce. As mentioned above, the Hellenistic-Roman world also did. If the question were merely the grounds for divorce or separation without remarriage, the disciples' "extreme" reaction to the effect that if such is the case between husband and wife it is better not to marry at all (Matt 19:10) would make little sense. Jesus' reiteration of God's intent applies universally to both Jews and Gentiles who legally practiced divorce. Even in the Jewish tradition itself, postexilic Malachi (1:13-16) expressly decries divorcing one's wife.

Jesus' reply to the Pharisees contains two points that are often overlooked in traditional interpretations but that deserve mention. The first is that contrary to Jewish practice of the time, and that of most human societies of all times, Jesus holds the husband guilty of adultery (Matt 19:12) *against the wife* (Mark 10:11) if he divorces her and marries another. Luke (16:18) imputes the adultery to both the man who divorces the wife and the one who marries her, not to the woman. This indeed was something new.

In Jewish as in most other societies, the adultery of the husband against the wife was not an issue (Num 5:11-31). Adultery signified only the marital unfaithfulness of the wife to the husband. This is because the sexuality of the wife was said to belong to the husband who, besides, could marry more than one wife (see Deut 22:13-27; *Yebam.* 44, 65a; and the answer of the Sierra Leonian girl mentioned earlier). Biblical passages are replete with the comparison of Israel to an adulterous wife. Hosea 2 and Ezekiel 16 are classic examples. Jewish law forbade coveting another man's wife (Exod 20:17; Deut 22:22), his property. In short, the husband of the abused woman was the person offended, not the wife of the adulterous husband. She had no rights over his body.

By declaring the husband to be guilty of adultery as much as the wife, and against the wife, Jesus corrects this traditional practice. The man is guilty because once married his sexuality belongs as much to the wife as hers belongs to him (1 Cor 7:3-5). The two have become one flesh. By saying this, Jesus equalizes the status and rights of the man and woman in marriage and holds both accountable for its indissolubility. In my view, this innovation is much more fundamental than the one often noted by scholars, that Jesus conceded to the woman the right to divorce her husband, something that the Jewish law ruled out. Jesus further grounds this equality in status and dignity of the husband and wife on the fact that "in the beginning" God created them male and female (in the divine image and likeness [Gen 1:26-27]). This reinforces the fact that they have now become one flesh or body. We may press this concept of the body further. Parts of a person's body belong to the body on equal terms. Each is unique and necessary for the body to function perfectly (1 Cor 12:4-30). So it is in the marital relationship between husband and wife. Ephesians (5:28-33a) brings this argument to a climax by viewing the marital union as a symbol of the union between Christ and the members of his body, the church (v. 32).

The second important point in Jesus' reply to his interlocutors concerns the references to Gen 1:26-27 and 2:24 as the protological reasons against divorce. The reference to 2:24 requires little explanation. I see this verse as playing the same role in the Yahwistic narrative (Gen 2:1-24) as do dominical sayings in various Synoptic passages. The whole narrative is woven around it, derives from it, and leads to it.[21] It is in the context of marriage that man and woman best live out their unity and oneness as a human species, as Mal 1:15 also testifies. But the case for Gen 1:26-27 is not so evident because it is not concerned with the marital union of the male and female. Why then did the Synoptic Jesus cite it as a reason against divorce? One reason is that in its own literary contexts Gen 1:26-27 is related to marriage only through verse 28a: "Increase, multiply, and fill the earth." In Jewish as in African thought, the goal of marriage is the begetting of children (Mal 1:15); in this way the Jew fulfilled God's injunction in Gen 1:28a. Contrary to the statements of some of the rabbis, the task of peopling the earth is given to humanity made up as male and female. In that task there is no superiority or inferiority, but only mutual cooperation. But procreation or peopling the earth was not the only task that God assigned to humanity created as male and female "from the beginning." God also assigned to them, as equal partners, the task of ruling over and tending creation (Gen 1:28b). Therefore, partnership between the male and female applies in the whole of life, not only in marriage. It underlines the co-responsibility of the man and woman in and for creation. This is not something confined to one sex. Herein lies the core and basis of the reinterpretation of the New Testament divorce texts that I wish to underline in this essay.

I had earlier defined divorce as the dissolution of a validly contracted marriage. But marriage implies more than begetting children, or the right to sexual relationship between partners. It establishes a whole new way of belonging between a couple, one that affects every facet of their life to-

---

21. See Okure, "Biblical Perspectives on Women."

gether but that is severed by divorce. Since sexuality is "a gift that touches human persons on all levels of their existence,"[22] it affects and should be made to affect all societal needs and structures. This means that for the proper ordering of society, the contributions of the male and female as man and woman are required.

As divorce in a family disrupts the life of that microcosmic society, so does it disrupt human life in the macrocosmic society. The same divine law that prohibits divorce in the small unit of the family prohibits divorce in the larger unit of the human family. Yet over the centuries, this latter divorce has occurred in all walks of life: political, social, economic, and religious; it is comprehensively termed patriarchy. Over the centuries it has been practiced in both church and society. Women have been marginalized and excluded from leadership positions in church and society. Worse still, this sinful order of things has been attributed to God's will said to be revealed in the Scriptures and by Christ.

Man's divorce of woman therefore exists not only in marriage but in all spheres of human undertaking. Existing societal and church structures have been built over the centuries with only contributions from the male sex. Such systems have been warped because they are not fully human. The result has been the gradual disintegration of human society itself through such forces as militarism, wars, nationalism, the exploitation of women and the poor, corruption, greed, the despoiling of the earth, and so forth. In my view, the most striking of the cumulative results of man's divorce of woman is the current universal dissolution of the institution of marriage itself. In other words, the divorce of the woman from the man in the wider, macrocosmic human family has finally infiltrated and corroded the microcosmic unit, the family. Hence, feminism, which seeks to redress this situation, is not simply a women's issue but a human issue. For to the extent that women, the ontological half of humanity, are treated as inferior to men, to that extent is the whole of humanity deprived, degraded, and prevented from realizing its full potential as God had intended for it from the beginning. As the Reverend Jesse Jackson once said, one person cannot keep another permanently in a ditch without staying in the ditch with the other.[23]

Throughout its history, the church has rejected divorce in the small unit of the man-woman relationship—that is, as husband and wife—out of fidelity to the divine will expressed in the New Testament passages that we have been considering, passages set against an Old Testament background (Gen 1:26-28, 28a). Today, we hear Jesus say in the New Testament passages under consideration that "from the beginning it was not so." Fidelity to the same God based on the same Scripture evidence should lead

---

22. See Peschlke, *Christian Ethics,* 375.
23. A statement made during his campaign as a U.S. presidential candidate in 1984.

the church to reject its own discriminatory policies toward women, which for centuries have barred women from participating fully in the life of the church.

The current desire to build a new world order and bring about a renewed face of the church and of humanity demands that substantial room be made for the full participation of women, with equal rights and opportunities in all spheres of church and societal life.[24] In other words, if humanity is ever to attain to its full dignity as destined by God (Gen 1:26-28), both men and women will have to recognize and uphold in practice the dignity of women as being in every respect equal to that of men. This too is an integral aspect of the obedience to Jesus' injunction that what God has united and continues to unite (the tense of the Greek here is the perfect), no human being should separate.

Conclusion

First, this study has endeavored to show that as social location influenced the lives of the people recorded in the Bible, so it did the lives of the authors of the Bible. Consequently, it cannot but influence the life of the interpreter/ reader of the Bible. A variety of interpretations of the same text is natural and inevitable.

Second, since the Bible is the inspired word of God, it becomes necessary to establish the meaning of this word in its own context before claiming its meaning for one's own context. The inner truth of the text should not be sacrificed for personal views of the interpreter because that breaks the dialogic give-and-take between the text and the reader. Reading the text within its own sociocultural context in faith and listening to what the Spirit is saying to the community of believers in any given location helps to guarantee fidelity to the inner truth of the passage in any social location.

Third, those interpretations that have a universal scope even as they are particular and that seek to promote the truth of the gospel that Jesus came to give life in all its fullness are to be specially encouraged. To illustrate this, this study ended by showing that the current hermeneutical issue of women's place in church and society can affect our understanding of the New Testament divorce texts in a new way.

Finally, concern with the influence of social location on the activity of the interpreter implies that the reader/interpreter is willing to gain a better understanding of the word of God and so allow this word to influence his or her personal life as well as that of his or her readers. It is this faith and life concern that gives meaning to this whole exercise. In the last analysis, reading from this place, or the issue of the interaction between the text and

---

24. See John XXIII's encyclical *Pacem in terris* ("Peace on Earth"), 39–41.

the social location of the interpreter, rests on the belief that the God who speaks through the living Bible also wishes to speak to successive generations of peoples in their different social locations through this same Bible. Authentic reading enables the reader to hear and respond to this divine message of life.

Part Two —————————————————————

Readings from Asia

4

Pentecost and the Intifada

Naim Ateek

Palestinian Christians trace their Christian faith to apostolic times. They point to the fact that from the very beginning the early church was composed of Jews and Gentiles. It was a melting pot of several ethnic groups—Jews, Romans, Greeks, Nabatean Arabs, and others who were living in the area. By the fifth century, Palestine had become predominantly Christian with hundreds of churches and monasteries built all over the region.[1] Gradually, after the seventh century and the coming of Islam, the Arabic language replaced Aramaic and Greek. The Christian community, however, remained in its homeland, Palestine, and continued its life and witness for Christ.

From early times, Palestinian Christians felt privileged to be living in the land that has been hallowed by the coming of Christ. Their proximity to the holy places gave them an unsophisticated spirituality coupled with a simple and down-to-earth understanding of the text of Scripture, both the Old and New Testaments. They saw themselves as heirs of the heritage and legacy of the early Christian community, a community that had opened its doors to all those who by faith were willing to come in. Membership was no longer seen as confined to one ethnic group of people, but rather in terms of a renewed covenant that included people of all races and ethnic backgrounds. They believed that Christ had given them a radical new definition of God as well as a new definition of the people of God.[2]

As the church moved into Christendom with Constantine, associating itself with power and becoming itself powerful, Palestinian Christians as well as most Eastern Christians did not enjoy that status for very long. To begin with, most of the Eastern Christians found themselves cut off from the rest of Christendom as a result of the christological controversies. Many of them were discriminated against by fellow Christians because of their theology and politics. Moreover, after the Muslims' takeover of most of the Middle East and North Africa in the seventh century, Eastern Christians

---

1. R. L. Wilken, *The Land Called Holy: Palestine in Christian History and Thought* (New Haven: Yale Univ. Press, 1992).

2. See N. T. Wright, *The Climax of the Covenant* (Edinburgh: T. & T. Clark, 1992) 231–57.

continued their life under Islam without the privileges of Christendom. Living in power and with power has colored and conditioned the life of the church in the West. In the East, however, the church sustained a pre-Constantinian context of life. In other words, the church remained without state or secular power or privilege—a church that was beset by antagonists from all sides who could turn hostile depending on the whim of the ruler; a life that could be easily characterized by vulnerability.

In spite of the many limitations on the life of the church in the East, this type of existence had some important advantages. For one, it kept the church much closer to the original setting and milieu of the New Testament. The church of New Testament times did not enjoy secular power. It had no privileges with the civil authorities. It was vulnerable. It was in the world but not of the world. It had to live with total dependence and on trust in God rather than the protection and support of the state.

To be close to the original milieu of Scripture is to be able to receive certain insights from the geography of the place as well as the text that might not be easily accessible to others. One can relate to the text without undue contextual analysis. There is an almost natural bridge between the reader and the text, namely, the pre-Constantinian context of life.[3]

Although many Christians in the world today live in such a context and feel close to the original setting of the New Testament, this situation is especially applicable to Palestinian Christians. They live in the very country where Jesus lived. Their country today is under occupation, precisely as it was when Jesus lived. They agonize daily over issues of injustice and oppression.

Several years ago, when I was preparing a sermon for the Sunday after Easter and looking at the appointed Gospel reading from John 20:19-23, I was struck by its unclouded relevance to my fellow Palestinian parishioners. The text read in part, "When...the doors of the house where the disciples had met were locked for fear of the Jews, Jesus came and stood among them and said, 'Peace be with you.' After he said this, he showed them his hands and his side." The connection between the text and the situation of those Palestinian Christians was clear. Where else in the world today except in Palestine do we find people who go behind shut doors "for fear of the Jews"? In other Third World countries, the preacher or expositor of this text might apply it to the presence of death squads or vigilantes, but in Palestine this text has a special ring of reality. For most Palestinian Christians, Christ's salutation, "Shalom," is far different from the cheap shalom that the Israeli army can give them. Moreover, the signs of Christ's suffering shown in his hands and side carry great meaning for the solidarity of

---

3. It is important to point out that today many Christians throughout the world live in a post-Constantinian or postcolonial context rather than a pre-Constantinian context. Yet the context of Eastern Christians can still be best described as pre-Constantinian.

Christ with Palestinian Christians. Christ who suffered but was now victorious was standing "in the midst" of the disciples who were afraid. He was not leaving them alone; he was there giving them his peace. He was also commissioning them to go and be his witnesses. The comfort and encouragement of such passages cannot be overexaggerated. The text has great relevance and urgency for Palestinian Christians. It is only by keeping this background in mind that we can now turn to the experience of Palestinian Christians and their understanding of Pentecost and the intifada.

The Situation in Life

There are two basic methods in biblical interpretive preaching. The first begins with the text, studies it, exegetes it, and then attempts to apply it to people in their present daily life. The second does the very opposite. It begins with the situation in life of the people, studies it, analyzes it, understands its implication for daily life, and then goes to the biblical text to find illumination and illustration. In the first method, the biblical text acts as a guide to its application in people's lives. In the second, it acts as a way of either confirming or judging the event. The former is the more traditional way of biblical study; the latter is more often used by liberation theologies. Both are valid and proceed from contexts that shape the reading of the text.[4]

Some people prefer to begin with the relevance of their situation in life. They understand it well and experience their vivid reality daily. They are captured by the negative or positive impact of that reality. They would need, therefore, to test their reaction or response to it in light of the word of God—the Bible. The topic before us suggests the use of the second method. Through their experience of the intifada, Palestinian Christians have been able to understand the meaning of Pentecost in a new and fresh way. In order to grasp what happened, it is important to state briefly the political background to the Israel/Palestine conflict.

The seeds of the conflict go back almost a hundred years when some Jewish leaders in Europe were beginning to evaluate the brunt of living among Western Christians and the toll it had exacted on Jewish life. The Jewish community of Europe, which had suffered considerably from anti-Semitism, was subjected to oppression and pogroms. Indeed, the rise of Zionism as a nationalist movement, whose objective was the creation of a political state for Jews, was viewed by some Jews as the right reaction

---

4. D. Rensberger (*Johannine Faith and Liberating Community* [Philadelphia: Westminster, 1988] 109) argues that "to refuse to consider the bearing of the biblical text on the issues posed by liberation theology merely legitimates some other 'forced' political interpretation of the text, namely, that of traditional Christian theologies. For no theology by which any individual or church lives or has ever lived is without a social and political component."

to such a state of affairs. The aim of the Zionist movement was to provide Jews with a home where they could be free from anti-Semitism and assimilation.

Zionism was nourished by the spirit of colonialism at the time. Palestine was to be colonized.[5] No consideration was given to the people of Palestine who had lived there for thousands of years. In fact, one of the potent mottos used by the Zionists was "a land without a people for a people without a land."[6] Many of them thought or deluded themselves into thinking or used it as a ploy that the land of Palestine was empty and that they could simply go back and claim it. Palestine had over half a million Palestinian inhabitants at the time.[7] Most of them were Muslims, but there were also a sizable number of Christians as well as a small Jewish community.

Zionism as a nationalist movement had to clash eventually with Palestinian nationalism. The former aimed at making Palestine as Jewish as England was English. The latter was committed to the independence of Palestine for all Palestinians, whether adherents of Islam, Christianity, or Judaism. Palestinian nationalism aimed to prevent the Zionist dream of turning Palestine into a Jewish state.[8]

Palestine came under the British mandate after World War I. Before too long, the British found themselves caught between the aspirations of the Palestinians and the Zionists. Some of the Zionist Jews were already living in the country. Many others were agitating and clamoring to come in. On the one hand, the Zionist Jews were insisting that Britain should honor its Balfour Declaration of 1917, which promised the creation of a homeland for Jews in Palestine.[9] They wanted the translation of this declaration into clearer policies, especially in terms of facilitating Jewish immigration into the country. On the other hand, the Palestinians were demanding the independence of Palestine as a right of self-determination for its inhabitants and the curtailing of Jewish immigration, which was upsetting the demography of their country. Moreover, they were constantly reminding the British of

---

5. E. Said, *The Question of Palestine* (New York: Vintage Books, 1980) 68–82.

6. This often-used slogan of the Zionists was originally based on the words of the Earl of Shaftesbury, one of the strongest advocates of Jewish restoration in Palestine in the nineteenth century, long before the rise of Zionism. The original words that he wrote in his diary on May 17, 1854, referring to Palestine and the Jewish people, were: "There is a country without a nation and a nation without a country." The earl was a deeply religious man, who read the Bible and looked forward to the fulfillment of its prophesies. He never doubted that the Jews were to return to "their own land." See the Earl of Shaftesbury, *The Jerusalem Bishopric and Its Connection with the London Society for Promoting Christianity amongst the Jews* (London: London Society House, 1887) 14–15.

7. J. L. Abu Lughod, "The Demographic Transformation of Palestine," *Transformation of Palestine* (2d ed.; ed. I. Abu Lughod; Evanston, Ill.: Northwestern Univ. Press, 1987) 140.

8. For a more detailed understanding of Palestinian nationalism, see R. Radford Ruether and H. J. Ruether, *The Wrath of Jonah* (San Francisco: Harper and Row, 1989) 92–130.

9. For a brief but sharp study of the Balfour Declaration and its background, see A. M. Lilienthal, *The Zionist Connection: What Price Peace?* (New York: Dodd, Mead, 1978) 12–28.

their promises to the Arabs during World War I regarding the independence of the Arab countries after the war.[10]

The tensions between the two groups grew increasingly worse, leading to greater violence and bloodshed. The Zionists were successful in managing the entrance of tens of thousands of legal as well as illegal immigrants into Palestine. It was, however, the accession of Hitler to power and ultimately World War II and the tragedy of the holocaust that began to turn the tide in favor of a solution to the Jewish problem on the land of Palestine. Between 1933 and 1945 over two hundred and fifty thousand Jews came into the country. The Jewish population of Palestine had grown from approximately 11 percent in 1914 to over 31 percent in the late 1940s.[11] The Zionist demand for a legal right in the country had by then achieved much international sympathy and backing.

Undoubtedly, the holocaust played a significant role in having world sympathy side with Jews and Zionism. Indeed, due to the holocaust, many Jews, including religious Jews who used to consider Zionism as an aberration because of its secular and antireligious position, were won over to its camp. In those days most people in the world were not even aware of the blatant injustice that was being perpetrated on the Palestinians. What mattered to many Westerners was the need for Jews to find a safe haven away from the evil of anti-Semitism.[12] One should also not underestimate the power and support of many Christians in Europe as well as North America who were, out of biblical conviction, promoting the return of Jews to "the promised land."[13]

Over fifteen international commissions were sent to Palestine during the British mandate to assess the deteriorating situation and propose remedies. It was clear in many of the reports that the heart of the issue was the imposition of a Jewish dream on a Palestinian majority. During this period, the Zionists worked through both Jews and Christians in the West and were able to promote their cause among Western leaders much more successfully and forcefully than the Palestinians. Their aim was to get a legal footing in Palestine. This was achieved in 1947, through the help of the United

---

10. See ibid., 12–28.

11. C. Chapman, *Whose Promised Land?* (Oxford: Lion, 1992) 20–21.

12. Anti-Semitism and the holocaust have continued to be used as a potent weapon to silence any criticism of Israel long after its establishment as a state. The Jewish people have been caught between the tragedy of the holocaust and their empowerment in the creation of the state of Israel. For an analysis of this phenomenon and its consequences for Jews, see the writings of M. Ellis, *Toward a Jewish Theology of Liberation* (Maryknoll, N.Y.: Orbis Books, 1987), and *Beyond Innocence and Redemption: Confronting the Holocaust and Israeli Power* (San Francisco: Harper and Row, 1990).

13. For a fascinating account of some of the early Christian Zionists, see Y. Ariel, *On Behalf of Israel* (New York: Carlson, 1991). On the support of Israel by some evangelical Christians after 1967, see G. Halsell, *Prophecy and Politics: The Secret Alliance between Israel and the U.S. Christian Right* (Westport, Conn.: Lawrence Hill, 1986), and D. Wagner, "Beyond Armageddon," *The Link* 25/4 (October/November 1992).

States and other countries that were able to pass a resolution through the United Nations for the partitioning of Palestine into two states, one Jewish on 52 percent of the land and the other Palestinian on 48 percent.[14] In that year Palestinians comprised "69 percent of the population of Palestine and owned or were settled in 94 percent of the land."[15]

The Palestinians refused the partitioning of their country, like the real mother who refused to permit the division of her son into two parts before King Solomon (1 Kgs 3:16-28). The Palestinians demanded that Palestine should remain one unit for all of its inhabitants, be they Muslims, Jews, or Christians. By then, however, the tension in Palestine had erupted into a full-scale armed conflict within the country. The Zionists proved too much for the Palestinians and instead of claiming the 52 percent allotted them by the United Nations, they were able to sweep through and occupy approximately 77 percent of Palestine. Consequently, about 750,000 Palestinians were displaced by the Zionists. Some of them were forced out; others fled in terror from the onslaught of the Zionists. They were never permitted to return to their homes in violation of UN resolutions. In order to prevent Palestinians from repatriation, Israel destroyed 394 Palestinian towns and villages.[16] The Zionists were able to consolidate their control over the 77 percent of Palestine that they had declared to be the state of Israel. Most of the Palestinians had become refugees living in makeshift camps throughout the neighboring countries. The United Nations tried but was unable to implement its resolutions on Palestine, including the one regarding the repatriation of Palestinians refugees, because of Israel's adamant position.

The years started passing with no just solution in sight. Neither the Palestinians nor the Arab countries accepted the legitimacy of the creation of the state of Israel in Palestine. Those Palestinians attempting to return to their homes were either killed or thrown back across the armistice boundaries. Clashes between Palestinians and Israeli Jews became very frequent all the way up to 1967, when the whole area was again on the brink of war. With a preemptive strike, Israel was successful in occupying the eastern part of Palestine (the West Bank of the River Jordan) as well as the Gaza Strip, that is, the remaining 23 percent of Palestine. The former had been under Jordanian rule since 1948; the latter, under Egyptian rule. In addition, Israel was able to sweep through and occupy the whole of Sinai from Egypt and the Golan Heights from Syria.

---

14. For insight into the pressures, bribes, and threats used by the U.S. government and American Zionists, see Lilienthal, *Zionist Connection*, 46–100.

15. Chapman, *Land*, 28.

16. For a documented account of these towns and villages, see the study prepared by F. Jaber of the Royal Committee for Jerusalem Affairs, Amman, Jordan, in *Lest the Civilized World Forget: The Colonization of Palestine* (New York: Americans for Middle East Understanding, 1992) 13–47. The group that published this study is located at 475 Riverside Drive, Room 241, New York, NY 10115.

As far as the Palestinian conflict was concerned, the whole of geographical Palestine had now fallen into the hands of Israel. The Palestinians in the newly occupied territories came under Israeli military rule. As the army consolidated its control over the West Bank and Gaza, Israel began to confiscate Palestinian land and build Jewish settlements on it. Israel started to enact oppressive military orders in order to further control the Palestinians. It started to do whatever it could to make the life of Palestinians difficult, thus encouraging them to emigrate. Through military conquest of the rest of Palestine, Israel was attempting in its own way to further implement the Zionist dream of expanding the territory of the Jewish state.[17]

During the following twenty years, between 1967 and 1987, Israel did its utmost to control the Palestinians of the West Bank and Gaza. Without paying attention to international law, including the Fourth Geneva Convention, Israel was working at an alarming speed to create irreversible trends, orders, and institutions. It built a ring of illegal suburbs around Jerusalem on confiscated Palestinian land, aimed at Judaizing the whole of the city. It enacted over fourteen hundred military orders to control the Palestinians. It extracted much taxation from the Palestinians, contravening international law. It confiscated more Palestinian land and built over 170 settlements throughout the West Bank and Gaza and moved over two hundred thousand of its citizens to live there.[18] Although Palestinians have been living for millennia in Palestine, they are regarded by Israel today as strangers and resident aliens on the land.

This powder keg had to explode, and it did in December 1987. After living under occupation and oppression for twenty years, the Palestinians began the intifada. It was a popular uprising of the whole Palestinian community of the West Bank and Gaza. The objective was to throw off the yoke of the oppressor. The Arabic word "intifada" means "to shake off." It is the same word used by Christ when he told his disciples to "shake off" the dust from their feet if any town did not receive them (Mark 6:11). The Palestinians were trying to shake off the occupation of their country. Two things happened simultaneously: the younger people, including men, women, and children, started throwing stones at the Israeli occupying army and people; and the older Palestinians started closing their shops and businesses in a series of massive general strikes that lasted for weeks and months. The Palestinians have been living in the experience of intifada since December 1987.[19]

---

17. The World Zionist Organization proposed in 1919 the area needed for the establishment of a Jewish state. Besides the whole of Palestine, it included parts of Lebanon, Syria, and Jordan. See F. Epp, *Whose Land Is Palestine?* (Grand Rapids: Eerdmans, 1970) 15.

18. In contravention of international law, Israel has built 150 settlements on the West Bank with an estimated 85,000 Israeli Jews living there; 9 settlements around Jerusalem with 140,000 inhabitants; and 16 settlements in Gaza with 5,000 inhabitants. See *Al-Quds* (Jerusalem daily newspaper), December 13, 1991.

19. For a better understanding of the intifada, its dynamics, and its impact on Palestini-

What Did the Intifada Do to the Palestinians?

Before the intifada started, the life of the Palestinian community under occupation was one of fear, hopelessness, despair, weakness, disorganization, and demoralization. No future was in sight. Everything around them looked gloomy. Then on December 9, 1987, at the funeral of four Gazans killed by Israelis, Palestinians started throwing stones at Israeli soldiers, who responded with live bullets. The intifada had started. It was a spontaneous reaction against an oppressive regime that was literally getting away with murder.

The intifada caught like fire. It spread quickly throughout the West Bank and Gaza. It could not be quelled or contained. It drew Palestinians together and attracted many others. It was totally unexpected. It was not planned or calculated by the Palestinians.

Palestinians as well as others have tried to analyze the causes and background of the intifada, but many admit they cannot completely fathom the depth of what happened. The intifada is greater than any analysis of it. No scientific analysis can do justice to the real event. In other words, the real event exceeded the expectation of the people. This historic event changed many peoples' lives. In those first few weeks and months of intifada, the Israeli occupying forces were very harsh in their reaction against the Palestinians, but the people were still exuberant. They had finally broken many chains that the Israelis had imposed upon them.

To begin with, fear was vanquished. The Israelis, through quick and brutal actions, had struck deep fears within the Palestinians, paralyzing them, but the intifada brought that to an end. Palestinian youth were fearlessly confronting the soldiers. Young and old, men and women were not succumbing to Israeli tactics aimed at perpetuating the myth of Israel's invincibility and inviolability. In the face of machine guns and tear gas, Palestinians were using slingshots and stones. Despair turned into hope, weakness into strength, fragmentation and disorganization into unity and solidarity. A new life had touched the whole of the community. It was contagious. People had become witnesses to a new and living experience that had left an indelible imprint on their lives. They were shouting it from the rooftops. People everywhere were relating their own experiences as well as the experiences of others. The experience of the intifada had preceded any belief in a doctrine of intifada. The historical event came before any theologizing about it.

The intifada has not touched the Palestinians alone. It has called the attention of many people to their plight and in turn converted them to their

ans, Jews, and expatriates, see Z. Lockman and J. Beinin, eds., *Intifada: The Palestinian Uprising against Israeli Occupation* (Boston: South End, 1989). See also J. R. Nassar and R. Heacock, eds., *Intifada: Palestine at the Crossroads* (New York: Praeger, 1990).

cause. It has changed the attitude of many people to the Israel/Palestine conflict. Indeed, because of the intifada, a new life has entered the dry bones of the Palestinians, and a new spirit has come upon them, bringing about a radical change in them.

Pentecost and the Intifada

The intifada caused many Palestinian Christians to better understand what happened at Pentecost and to comprehend its meaning for them today. Pentecost can best be described as an intifada. Jesus had told his disciples, "You shall receive power when the Holy Spirit has come upon you, and you shall be my witnesses in Jerusalem, and in all Judea, and Samaria, and to the end of the earth" (Acts 1:8). They did not fully comprehend what he meant by those words. Indeed, they were still afraid. When they met, they met behind closed doors. It was apparent that they were frustrated and in despair. "We had hoped that he [Jesus] was the one to redeem Israel" (Luke 4:21). They were weak and disorganized. Some of them decided to return to their original professions (John 21:3). But when the unexpected happened and the Holy Spirit was poured out, the change was incredible. It was an intifada caused by the Spirit of the living God being poured into the lives of the early disciples. It was an empowerment by the Spirit that the followers of Jesus received and that could not be hidden or contained. A new dynamic reality was visible in their lives. This was precisely the experience of the Palestinians. From fear and weakness, they emerged empowered as a result of the intifada.

The same people who were weak before Pentecost had become strong. They were not replaced by a stronger group of people. The weak had been transformed, renewed, and remade by God. The Holy Spirit had given them a new vitality. They were able to go public and were no longer afraid of being intimidated by the civil or religious authorities. They saw themselves empowered by God to carry out a new responsibility by openly witnessing to what God in Christ had done to them. Their intifada gave them the willingness to bear the responsibility of witness and gladly suffer the consequences. Indeed, they were no longer afraid to suffer for the truth of the gospel. Their new courage was exhibited by going out and fearlessly confronting the hostile religious leaders. Their witness for Christ immediately started to bear numerical results (Acts 2:41). Many people were attracted to them because of their witness to the truth and the sincerity of their cause (Acts 2:47). They lived daily in expectancy and hope of the coming of God's kingdom. Almost everyone of these statements genuinely reflect the Palestinian experience of intifada and the total change that had drastically taken place.

Pentecost marked the beginning of the "shaking off" of many shackles that had bound the disciples' lives and thinking. It opened new vistas for them in understanding God's will for the world as revealed anew in Jesus Christ. In other words, their view of themselves as well as their view of God and the world had undergone a dramatic change. Pentecost was a religious and spiritual intifada of great magnitude. It was eventually able to shatter the bigotry and prejudice of the disciples against non-Jews and make them recognize that the church was open to all people irrespective of their ethnic backgrounds. It accentuated the fact that God had no favorites.

Moreover, Pentecost was an intifada that could not be extinguished by the religious leaders of the time. Similarly, in spite of its great military strength, the Israeli army could not crush the Palestinian intifada. No degree of ever-harsher policies and actions against them could break the new spirit that had engulfed the whole community.

The intifada of Pentecost created a new spirit within the early Christian community that drew the members closer together in unity. There was a high degree of empathy and care for one another. This in turn issued in better organization in order to meet the needs of the new emerging community of believers (Acts 6:1-7). Again, Palestinian Christians were able to identify immediately with the new organization within the early apostolic community of believers because of their experience in the intifada. Neighborhood committees began to spring up in the various towns and villages of the West Bank and Gaza. Through the general strikes the Palestinians were sending strong signals to the government of Israel that the occupation of their country must cease, but those strikes were also exacting a toll on many Palestinian families. Many people, therefore, were collecting food for needy families. Some bakeries were giving bread for free to help. Grocery shops were also doing their share by selling goods at greatly reduced prices to the poor. One could feel the general solidarity within the whole of the community. In spite of the increasing external pressures, there was a new inner spirit that was holding the community together. This was very similar to the events in the early church.

The intifada of Pentecost caused two immediate reactions. While it gave the followers of Jesus hope and empowerment, it provoked a storm of anger and confusion among the religious and civil authorities. Again, this matches the experience of Palestinians in their own intifada. As the Palestinian people themselves were empowered, the Israeli army was showing signs of confusion and was frantically trying to find ways to suppress and crush their spirits.

Finally, no scientific, theological, or philosophical analysis could do justice to what really happened at Pentecost. Luke was trying to express the inexpressible and to describe the indescribable. Therefore, the truth of that great event is presented in the form of a narrative. No other method could have done it justice. It is a story that tries to reflect the birth of a new consciousness within a group of believers. It is an account that tries to give some reasons for the emergence of a new dynamic community. The actual experience of intifada had exceeded all of their expectations. Likewise, the truth of intifada is best expressed by the stories of men and women who relate them in order to convey the new consciousness that has gripped their community.

The Signs of the Spiritual Intifada

As I mentioned earlier, at the height of the Palestinian intifada, I preached a sermon using the analogy of intifada to talk about Pentecost. After the service a group of Palestinian Christians met together to reflect on that experience. The result was extraordinary. Many of them started for the first time to really apprehend what had happened in the early church by simply talking about their experience in the Palestinian intifada. At the end of the session, I asked them whether they could identify and name the signs of the spiritual intifada that is so much needed in the church today. Again, by being in touch with their experience within their own Palestinian community, they were able to identify four important points.

1. Once the intifada takes place, a new power is felt in the life of the person and the community—a power that is revolutionary and causes total change; a new spirit that grips both the individual and the community and sets them in a new direction.

2. Once the spiritual intifada happens, those who are involved cannot go back to a preintifada existence. Many battles still remain to be fought against the obstinacy of the present unjust structures and the pervasiveness of evil in the world, but there is no turning back. The chains have been broken. The taste of freedom has been experienced. The war against evil and injustice has been won through the death and resurrection of Christ. The new life in Christ that they have received will continue.

3. The spiritual intifada must impact other people. It cannot be contained or hidden. Those who have been touched and transformed by it must bear witness. The intifada has to reach out to others, attract them, and bring them into its fold. Indeed, it will encounter great resistance. Its adversaries are many. There are forces that will try to crush it, but it will be victorious at the end since it is founded on truth.

4. This intifada has the potential of changing the world. It is capable of creating a world where justice, peace, and reconciliation are open to all. And the first intifada on Pentecost did take place and did change the lives of many people. Palestinian Christians believe that they are the offspring of those who were first impacted by it. It vindicated the justice and love of God in the death and resurrection of Christ. It gave people a new life. It gave them freedom from evil and a new peace that the world could not give.

Today, that same original intifada of Pentecost calls Palestinian Christians to work against injustice and oppression in their country. It challenges them to strive for justice in ending the occupation of the West Bank and Gaza and establishing their state alongside the state of Israel. Furthermore, it calls them to work for peace and reconciliation among all the people of the land; to restore humanity to all those who, in the process of the conflict, have been dehumanized—the Palestinians as the oppressed and Israeli Jews as oppressors; to lift the banner of freedom and democracy to all who hunger and thirst for it. This same spiritual intifada continues to call Palestinian Christians to a renewed commitment to Christ, to keep its fire burning within them, and to strengthen their witness for him.

It has become undoubtedly clear that many Palestinian Christians have been able to rediscover afresh the meaning and relevance of the first-century event for their lives today. By beginning with their own context in life, namely, the experience of the Palestinian intifada, they have been able to grasp and be renewed by the profound significance of the Pentecost intifada for their faith commitment today.

Postscript

The Palestinian intifada has been unable to sustain its initial momentum. Some Palestinians would insist that it has only changed course. Others would hold that many pressures from inside as well as outside the Palestinian community have weakened it and have created tensions and divisions within the ranks of the Palestinians. At the same time, the injustice and oppression by the occupation forces have continued unabated. Again, one finds great similarities with what happened in the life of the church as it journeyed in history.

Yet, even as the Palestinian intifada wanes, it remains for Palestinians a beacon of light. It is that event par excellence from which they will continue to draw both inspiration and strength. The intifada is held up as that event that set the right standard by which many events should be judged. It reflected the best that the Palestinian community was able to show in courage, sacrifice, and determination. It will continue, therefore, to judge any halfheartedness or mediocrity within the Palestinian community. It can always shed light on genuine motives, authentic action, and true integrity.

The intifada judges equally the United Nations, the United States, and the Arab countries. It finds many of them wanting in their double-standard morality and in their inability to redress the grave injustice done to the Palestinians. It should awaken and disturb people's consciences, especially those who have become numb and apathetic to the cry of the oppressed—those who have become "at ease in Zion" (Amos 6:1); those who "abhor justice and pervert all equity, who build Zion with blood and Jerusalem with wrong!" (Mic 3:9-10). Similarly, the intifada of Pentecost continues to judge the church and to find it wanting. It will continue to stand as that great event that serves as a model as well as a point of reference to the church and out of which Christians still receive inspiration and strength.

5

On John 7:53–8:11:
A Well-Cherished but Much-Clouded Story

Hisako Kinukawa

Readings of the Story

This essay focuses on the social and historical context of "the woman caught in adultery" (John 7:53-8:11) and reconstructs who she actually was and the cause of her suffering. My Japanese feminist perspective helps me see her as a victim of sexual violence wielded by men. This perspective helps correct inaccuracies in the way she has been remembered. My conclusion will be that the story has been so clouded by androcentric ideology on sexuality at different stages of the tradition and church history that it has become difficult to read Jesus' revolutionary message in it.

Because of the complicated textual evidence, not many commentators have dealt with the story's context.[1] Some have treated the story in an appendix.[2] Despite this scholarly neglect, the story has quite often been told in churches, and it has become one of the most popular stories in the Bible. It has served in some cases as an excellent model of the faith of sinners; in other cases, repentance is emphasized. It has also been said that the story describes Jesus' personality and behavior both typically and vividly. The story, then, has been well-cherished in the history of the churches and used to give a lesson on the essence of the gospel.

But in what sense? The usual titles of the story, such as "A Story of the Adulteress" and "The Woman Caught in Adultery," seem already to suggest that the woman has one-sidedly been connected with sinfulness. This misunderstanding of the story involves "a decisive reshaping of the text."[3]

---

1. The following three exceptions have comments on the story in its context: G. R. O'Day, "John," *The Women's Bible Commentary* (ed. C. A. Newsom and S. H. Ringe; Louisville: Westminster/John Knox, 1992); S. Schulz, *Das Evangelium nach Johannes* (Japanese ed.; Tokyo: NTD, 1975); S. Takahashi, *Yohaneden Kogi* (The Gospel according to John) (Tokyo: Taisindo, 1967), vol. 3.

2. C. K. Barrett, *The Gospel according to John* (London: SPCK, 1955); R. H. Lightfoot, *St. John's Gospel: A Commentary* (London: Oxford Univ. Press, 1957).

3. G. R. O'Day, "John 7:53—8:11: A Study in Misreading," *Journal of Biblical Literature* 111 (1992) 631.

82

An example of a typical reading of the story is found in Augustine, who describes the relationship between Jesus and the woman in these terms: "The doctor with the sick woman. Pity with the pitiable." He continues:

> Sinners, it is true, had not dared to condemn her, had not dared to stone a sinner when they looked into their hearts and found themselves to be the same. But the woman was still in peril of her life because one who was without sin had stayed behind to judge her.[4]

Augustine conflates the scribes and the Pharisees with the woman—all are sinners—and makes the confrontation of the sinful woman with the sinless Jesus the pivot of the story. Thus, Jesus' forgiveness of sin is presented as the grand grace granted to the "sinful" believers.

Another example of an early interpretation of the story involves seeing Jesus' forgiveness of the woman's sin as having the precondition of her repentance. In reference to this interpretation, some scholars cite the *Apostolic Constitutions* (2.24), which date to some time between the end of the second century and the beginning of the third century. These scholars also point to early knowledge and use of this story in the Christian communities.[5] They suggest that the literal meaning of Jesus' forgiving the capital crime of adultery was too radical for the early Christian churches to accept—especially churches in the eastern part of the Roman Empire, which needed to insist on their moral austerity against Roman pagans.[6] All of this, some interpreters say, may suggest that the emphasis on repentance was not in the original text and was a creation of the church.

The story could be threatening if one feels "a fear and a resistance to Jesus' perceived antinomianism," as Calvin did.[7] "Nomianists" could not accept that grace was given by Jesus to the "sinful" woman without repentance. Yet according to the law, it is not she but her accomplice who should be caught as the principal offender. Thus, in interpreting this story, proper "nomianists" take it for granted that only women are accused as far as sexuality is concerned. An ambivalent attitude toward laws and sexuality may be detected in this interpretation, but I see here the reflection of an androcentrically biased hermeneutics that pushes the responsibility of the sexual relationship onto the woman only. Gail O'Day points out that the text would evoke men's fear that wives might be adulterous with im-

---

4. Augustine, "Sermons," *The Works of Saint Augustine: A Translation for the 21st Century* (trans. E. Hill, O.P.; New York: New City Press, 1990) 1:311.

5. See, for example, Lightfoot (*Gospel*, 346–47): "It is there cited as a lesson to bishops who were thought to be too severe in dealing with penitents."

6. S. Arai, *Sinyaku Seisho no Joseikan* (Women in the New Testament) (Tokyo: Iwanami, 1988) 342; B. Witherington III, *Women in the Ministry of Jesus: A Study of Jesus' Attitudes to Women and Their Roles as Reflected in His Early Life* (London: Cambridge Univ. Press, 1984) 144 n. 90.

7. O'Day, "John 7:53—8:11," 634–35.

punity.[8] O'Day raises a question about the strong polarity between Jesus and the woman.[9] She wonders whether the final exchange between Jesus and the woman is the focal matter of the story. She says: "By highlighting the woman's sin, and hence her unworthiness as a candidate for grace, the rest of the text is reduced to prolegomena."[10] She draws attention to the "larger social questions of Jesus' relationships to the religious establishment and the challenge he presented to the status quo."[11] O'Day thus expands our perspective by socializing the issue of the story.

Churches in my country, Japan, have also traditionally emphasized the unilateral grace Jesus granted the sinful. This, I argue, has blurred the focus on the issue embedded in this story. Before getting to my reading of the story from a Japanese feminist perspective—which is different from O'Day's feminist view—I want to shed some light on what seems to have been hidden behind the text.

Hermeneutics of the Story

Commentators are unanimous in saying that John 7:53—8:2 is a later addition to the original story.[12] O'Day divides the whole story into two parts: introduction (7:53—8:2) and central conflict (8:3-11). The introduction sets the context for the encounter. If the woman was brought to Jesus while he was teaching in the temple, as the story says, Jesus must have been in the women's court, where only women were allowed. The temple symbolizes the center of religious authority and orthodoxy, but the women's court may symbolize the kind of people with whom Jesus identified himself. We may very well see the redactor's sensitivity at work at this point.

In the following section the scribes and the Pharisees pose a question to Jesus, who makes a double response (8:6-7, 8-11). O'Day notes the parallels to be observed in these two responses of Jesus.[13]

Why Is Only the Woman Caught?

"The scribes and the Pharisees brought a woman who had been caught in adultery; and making her stand before all of them... " (8:3). The woman, then, was caught *in flagrante delicto,* and we can hardly go through the verse without wondering where the other party in this adultery has gone.

---

8. Ibid., 639.
9. Ibid., 634.
10. Ibid.
11. Ibid.
12. See, for example, Schulz, *Das Evangelium*; Arai, *Sinyaku Seisho no Joseikan*; Witherington, *Women*; O'Day, "John 7:53—8:11."
13. O'Day, "John 7:53—8:11," 631.

We need to explore the purpose of this omission, seeking to grasp why the story is apparently interested only in the woman. Before I deal with this issue, I would like to see what constituted adultery in Jesus' time as well as examine a parallel situation that Japanese women experienced not so long ago, so that we may have a proper background to deal with this issue.

Adultery in Jesus' Time

The biblical writers set up detailed laws on adultery but little restriction on prostitution. This inconsistent situation is legitimized by the double standard applied to men's and women's sexual behavior.

The Old Testament gives strict rules regarding adultery. For instance, Lev 20:10 and Deut 22:22-29 explain in detail the commandment, "You shall not commit adultery" (Exod 20:14). In Israelite society, adultery was defined as a man having sexual relations with either (1) a married woman, (2) an engaged virgin, or (3) a nonengaged virgin. If a man committed adultery, he was to be killed, except in the case of adultery with a nonengaged virgin. In this case, he was obliged to marry her himself and was never allowed to divorce her.

A man convicted of adultery was punished on the basis that he had infringed on the owner's rights over the woman. He was punished because he had affected the honor and property of the other male party, not the rights of the woman. If the woman involved in the sexual relationship was married or engaged, she was killed; if not engaged, she was obliged to marry the man because she had insulted her owner. Adultery was an insult of honor and an attack on another man's possession. It was an infringement on the marital relationship of one man by means of sexual relationships between his woman and another man, or an insult to a father's honor and an attack on his possession by causing his daughter to lose her virginity. It was essential for a father to keep his daughter a virgin so that he could transfer her from his household to that of her husband.

At a glance, the teaching on adultery seems to call for inviolability and purity in marital relationships. However, the teaching was altogether one-sided and given only from a male viewpoint. Women's dignity or human rights were hardly taken into consideration. If the tokens of virginity were not found at her marriage, a woman would be stoned to death (Deut. 22:13-21), while a man would never be questioned about his virginity. If a husband became suspicious that his wife might have defiled herself, he could take her to the priest, who would then administer a number of severe tests to find out the truth (Num 5:11-31). A woman, however, had no recourse against her husband if he had defiled himself. Women simply were not taken to be human beings with rights equal to those of husbands or fathers. Women were thus humiliated as a part of men's property. They were fully objectified.

The Parallel Situation Experienced in Japan

In Japan matters concerning sexuality have traditionally been considered as improper for public discussion. Actually, the Japanese have a hard time finding appropriate words for English words such as "sex," "gender," and "sexuality." Nevertheless, much sexual abuse or violence has been repeatedly committed both openly and in secret by men.

From 1899 to 1947, adulterers in Japan were sentenced according to the provisions of a civil law that gave all the power in the family to the heads of households for the purpose of supporting the "*Ie*-system" (*Ie* = household) and preserving male genealogy. No marriage could be permitted without the permission of the heads of both families. Once a woman was married, she was considered incompetent, unable to enter into any contract without her husband's supervision and to take care of her own property. Her only value was in giving birth to a boy who would carry on her husband's lineage. Her experience had thus much in common with the experience of women in the biblical world.

Adultery was seen as a violation of a man's property in Japan as well as in Israel. In Japan, if a wife had sexual relationships with another man, the man was guilty of violating her husband and had to compensate him. A man, even if he had a wife, was free to have sexual relationships with any unmarried women. Even if he had sexual relationships with someone's wife, he was not guilty unless he was sued for damages by her husband. And it was often the case that the husband would not sue the man who had a sexual relationship with his wife because he was more afraid that his wife's misdeed would become known. When a wife committed adultery, she could be divorced with no appeal. A wife could be sued for adultery and sentenced to two year's imprisonment. But a wife had no right to sue her husband for adultery. The law was absolutely one-sided.

Both in Israel and in Japan, adulterous women were hardly even "accomplices" of the adulterous men. Women, as nonpersons, became only defective property and were to be thrown away or sentenced to punishment. It was unthinkable for wives to run away from their homes.

Even though the civil law regarding adultery was completely abolished in Japan, the mentality that nourished it has not disappeared. There has been a tacit understanding that women are objects when they play the role of men's sexual partners. This applies even to those women who are legally and happily married. And if an adulterous relationship is disclosed, there is still a tendency for the shame and sin to be one-sidedly put on the woman. Therefore, the women try to internalize the shame so that they may not bring disgrace on their families or the social communities to which they belong. Even in cases of rape or sexual harassment, women are often blamed for having caused men to commit those acts. To avoid alienation from their social circles, women prefer to hide their victimized experiences. Once a woman speaks up about such an experience, she may be considered a slut rather than a victim. The underlying idea is that women are seductive, physical, shameful, and sinful.

Social Context of the "Woman Accused of Adultery": Dishonor

We need now to put our biblical story back into such a social context and meet the woman in these humiliating circumstances. In this way we can reconstruct the primitive encounter that might have occurred between the woman, Jesus, and the scribes and the Pharisees. O'Day says that the woman "is an object on display, given no name, no voice, no identity apart from that for which she stands accused."[14]

Thus the woman must have felt utterly humiliated and ashamed as she was forced before the curious eyes of the public. There was no worse dishonor for her and her family than to be blamed for a sexual crime. The story—which, again, makes no reference to the adulterous male— apparently reflects a male-centered bias that leads men to ill-treat women for the sake of men's honor.

A Case: Comfort Women

Given such an androcentric viewpoint about sexuality, it is not surprising that, during World War II, the Japanese military government installed numerous "comfort houses," or brothels, for soldiers. Imperialism and colonialism justified such a one-sided ideology on sexuality and drove the government to hunt for young, inexperienced girls from Asian countries as "comfort women."

In 1938, after the massive "rape of Nanjing" provoked strong anti-Japanese feeling among the Chinese people, the Japanese imperial government organized the comfort houses to arouse the fighting spirit of the soldiers, to keep a high military morale, and to suppress the soldiers' hostility toward senior officers, a feeling bred in the severely disciplined military life. To control the spread of venereal disease, it was deemed necessary to put comfort houses under military control. As the troops moved, the comfort women were also taken to the new battlefronts. Soldiers received military-issued coupons and made use of women to satisfy their sexual desire.

The first comfort house was started in Shanghai. It consisted of one hundred women: twenty Japanese women of about thirty-five years of age and eighty Korean women under twenty years of age. In the end, innumerable young women were forced to serve as comfort women. It is said that more than two hundred thousand women from Korea, China, Taiwan, and

---

14. Ibid., 632.

other parts of Asia were tricked under false pretenses and made to "serve." Young, virgin girls were intensively sought. They were to "console" ten to sixty soldiers every day. Their living conditions were desperate. The painful experience of forced sexual relationships caused great harm, both physically and mentally, to their health. Many died of atrocious sexual harassment. The system was nationally organized and justified under the name of the emperor, a living god. Japan cannot deny that it committed a national crime against the Asian countries it colonized.[15]

Such a system can easily be established if women are objectified and not regarded as humans, as I have already pointed out. These women were actually considered part of the baggage. According to eyewitness accounts, they were transported as if they were horses or weapons. This is one of the reasons it is difficult to get information about comfort women.

The comfort women should be seen as sexual slaves raped by a nationally institutionalized system. We can fully understand this only if we see the crime from the perspective of sexual violence. Only then can we detect a multilayered discriminatory structure.[16] Racial and sexual discrimination were integrated and made use of by the militaristic ideology, and the women were forced into sexual enslavement based on a patriarchal ideology, in other words, a double standard on sexuality. Soldiers separated sexual pleasure from procreation. For procreation they had wives in their homes; for sexual pleasure they had the comfort women. They asked their wives to be faithful to them while they demanded that other women victimize themselves for them. In addition, since they did not want to get infected by venereal diseases, they molested only young, strictly monitored girls captured outside Japan.[17]

Now we need to inquire into another serious issue: the reason those comfort women had to keep silent for the past fifty years. The first voice of the comfort women was heard only a few years ago. Even though they were all drafted under the name of the emperor, they were simply thrown away like trash at the end of the war. Though all the foreign victims were almost completely neglected by the Japanese government, men drafted from Asian countries could still go back home with their heads held high. The defeat of Japan in the war should have been the liberation for all the foreign victims. However, most of the comfort women could not help but interpret their experience as shameful, and many killed themselves. They could not even

---

15. A. Carter, "Comfort Women: Contesting History," *Japan Christian Activity News* 702 (1992) 5; M. Fukushima, "Comfort Women: Legal Action," *Japan Christian Activity News* 701 (1992) 8.

16. Carter, "Comfort Women," 5.

17. K. Hwangbou, "The Issue of Forced Military Prostitution from the Perspective of Korean Women Residents in Japan: Caught between Racial Discrimination and Sexual Discrimination," *Joseigaku Nempo* (Annual Report of Women's Studies Society) 13 (1992) 43–44.

think of going home because they were bound by a Confucian morality that had taught them virginity was the most important virtue. Their bodies were defiled, and they had brought disgrace on their families. So those who dared to go back to their home countries have not returned to their homes but have lived in seclusion. It has been impossible for women who were brought up under the Confucian patriarchal traditions to talk about being sexually victimized. As a result, the horrifying memories of violence have been hidden deep inside them, and they have never been healed of the physical and mental wounds they got from their painful slavery.[18]

Here is the dynamic of sexual crime that silences female victims by blaming them for losing their chastity and being a dishonor to their families and their societies. It is expected that women victims must feel ashamed of themselves and not claim that they suffered from sexual violence or rape. The culture and society that force them to keep such crimes hidden must be accused of collusion in committing inexcusable sexual violence. History has clearly taught us that the ideology that supports and sustains sexism must be surfaced and undermined.[19]

Why Stone the Woman Only?

In the biblical story the larger social or political context will help us see what has remained untold and what the real issue is. The woman in adultery asks us to stand on her side, but most commentators simply take her as symbolizing sin and hardly extend their imagination to her social situation or background.

"They said to him, 'Teacher, this woman was caught in the very act of committing adultery. Now in the law Moses commanded us to stone such women'" (8:4-5). If the main issue raised here by the scribes and the

18. Fukushima, "Comfort Women," 8; Carter, "Comfort Women," 5. Hwangbou ("Forced Prostitution,"40, 43) cites Confucian teachings that support the idea that men are superior to women and shows they are still prevalent in Korea, from where most comfort women were drafted. Examples of these are the following: the teaching of the "three obediences" (as a daughter, she should obey her father; as a wife, her husband; and as a widow, her son); the teaching of gender role difference (while men are to work outside, women are to stay in their homes); the teaching of one-minded devotion (a woman should be obedient only to her husband); and the teaching of the seven vices that result in divorce (lack obedience to her parents-in-law; inability to produce a male heir; talkativeness; propensity to theft; disease; jealousy; and lechery). There is also an incredible teaching that wives are to be beaten every three days so that they may be kept subservient. The teaching justifies husbands' ordinary violence against their wives.

19. Y. Ebara, "On Comfort Women," *Sisou no Kagaku* (1992) 32. For the last few years, the issue has been dealt with from the perspective of the violation of human rights. Responding to the circumstances, more comfort women have spoken out and filed suits in courts in Japan and also in the United Nations. Various civilian groups have worked to press the Japanese government to make public historical resources, to confess the sins committed, to express repentance, and to ask forgiveness. In 1992 several international investigating committees, both private and under the United Nations, started working to find a breakthrough for changing the obstinacy of the Japanese government in this regard.

Pharisees is the definition of the legal measures of adultery, the principal offender in this case should surely be the man who committed adultery: he, after all, is the one who has infringed on another man's property and honor. It would seem that the woman should be questioned only after the man is charged. However, the way the scribes and the Pharisees describe the law (commanding them "to stone such women") presupposes that women are generally the ones to whom the death penalty is applied. Here again we detect the androcentrically biased consciousness regarding sexual morality. Men are excused from the beginning and never surface. On the other hand, the woman, objectified, treated as though she is a bitch and made use of by the religious authorities who claimed to be guardians of the law, is forced into agony because she has dared to treat her own body as she wished.

The scribes and the Pharisees address Jesus as "teacher"—pretending to pay tribute before they confront Jesus with a trick, through which they try to control what happens in the temple and entrap Jesus in order to ruin his popularity. They flare up at Jesus for displaying an undisguised sense of authority. To disguise their hostility toward Jesus, they make use of the victimized woman. I wonder if they would have behaved in the same way if the male party had been caught and brought before the public. But then if that had been the case, the tradition would probably not have transmitted the story, and the story would not be in the Gospel.

A Perfect Chance for Entrapping Jesus

The scribes and the Pharisees inquire of Jesus with much emphasis on the "you": "Now what do you say?" They say this to test him so that they might have some charge to bring against him. They mean to test Jesus' setting himself against Moses or against the Roman law.

The woman's case affords them a perfect chance for entrapping Jesus with malicious forethought. According to John 18:31, the Jews had no power to sentence someone to capital punishment. If that is the case and Jesus responds that the woman should be put to death, he can be accused of usurping Roman power. But if Jesus takes the opposite view, he is in conflict with the law of Moses. He can thus be cornered into an impasse. This is why the scribes and the Pharisees focus on genuinely legal discourse. The woman and Jesus are turned into objects for this technical legal discourse. The woman becomes a point of law, and Jesus is to give the final judgment. No concern is paid to the social or religious circumstances that have brought about such consequences for this woman. And the woman has no right or power to defend herself except to keep silent.[20]

"Jesus bent down and wrote with his finger on the ground" (John 8:6b). He does not reply to the question directly nor give any direction regard-

---

20. Lightfoot, *Gospel,* 347; O'Day, "John 7:53—8:11," 638; Takahashi, *Kogi,* 40.

ing what should be done to the woman. Most commentators interpret his action as indicating his refusal to be entrapped by the conspiracy. R. H. Lightfoot refers to T. W. Manson's interpretation of Jesus' action as "a well-known practice in Roman criminal law, in accordance with which the presiding judge first wrote down the sentence and then read it aloud from the written record."[21] His action surely does not show his lack of resolution, but rather symbolically shows him smashing his opponents' self-righteous arrogance and frustrating their cocksure scheme. He could also be refusing to treat the woman as a sinner. Nevertheless, the aim of the scribes and the Pharisees is to cross-examine him until they successfully make him speak. So "they kept on questioning" (v. 7).

Then, "he straightened up and said to them, 'Let anyone among you who is without sin be the first to throw a stone at her' " (v. 7). To reply to a legal question, Jesus in effect resorts to an answer that might be considered appropriate in the light of their laws.

Why Is the Woman a "Sinner"?

The story seems to presuppose that the accused woman has been arraigned for sin, and almost all interpreters take the story as it is and comment on that presupposition.

"And once again he bent down and wrote on the ground. When they heard it, they went away, one by one, beginning with the elders; and Jesus was left alone with the woman standing before him" (vv. 8-9).

Ben Witherington comments as follows:

> By implication Jesus pronounces this woman guilty by saying, "If..."
> He applies the principle, "He who reproves others, must himself be
> above reproach in the case at issue." It is the motives of the witnesses
> and their own culpability, not the woman's lack of sin, which decides
> the matter here.[22]

Saburo Takahashi, making reference to Jesus' answer regarding the sinfulness of all the people, says that all present could not help but withdraw in silence, overwhelmed by Jesus' spiritual severity and pierced by the consciousness of their own sinfulness in the depths of their hearts.[23] Sasagu Arai interprets Jesus' answer as pointing to the fact that everyone is capable of committing adultery. Thus, Jesus' words reinforce the fact that no one has the right to accuse the adulterous woman: Who can stone her to death only on a charge of adultery? Looking at the reality of human weakness, Arai puts the scribes and the Pharisees on the same level as the

---

21. Lightfoot, *Gospel,* 347.
22. Witherington, *Women,* 22.
23. Takahashi, *Kogi,* 44.

woman. Although Arai also refers to Jesus' words in the Gospel of Matthew (5:27-28: "You have heard that it was said, 'You shall not commit adultery.' But I say to you everyone who looks at a woman with lust has already committed adultery with her in his heart"), he does not seem to be concerned about the dehumanizing situation in which the women of the time were enslaved.[24]

By identifying the scribes and the Pharisees as sinners along with the woman, Jesus succeeds in saving her from punishment, but at the same time Jesus fails to let them see how much she has been objectified, ill-treated, and victimized. What would help her are words that pull her out of her dehumanized position and place her on the same level as the men.

O'Day takes Jesus' words as "an invitation to discern the answer themselves." Her interpretation is similar to Arai's except for her argument that "Jesus nullifies the presumed control of the scribes and Pharisees and places them on the same level as the woman."[25] According to this interpretation, Jesus succeeds in humiliating the scribes and the Pharisees by bringing them down to the level of the "sinful" woman and making the passing of any judgment impossible. But by not taking any notice of the circumstances particular to the woman, Jesus—as he is presented in the Gospel—fails to reach the core of the issue: the question of why only the woman was dragged out, exposed before the public in shame, and accused of guilt worthy of death. It seems to me that if little attention is paid to this question, we lose the point of the story.

"Jesus straightened up and said to her, 'Woman, where are they? Has no one condemned you?' She said, 'No one, sir.' And Jesus said, 'Neither do I condemn you. Go your way, and from now on do not sin again'" (vv. 10-11). Jesus' words seem to evoke from the men an internalized or spiritualized understanding of sin and have the actual power to move people away from the place. I doubt if these words were original to Jesus, and I cannot deny my suspicion that the whole story has been much influenced by an early church that individualized the concept of sin. When I think of the confident insistence of the scribes and the Pharisees on their own purity, a result of their adherence to every point of the law, at most I can see Jesus' irony wasted on a self-satisfied and self-righteous people.

How Can Both Parties Be Equal?

O'Day draws our attention to the structural parallels between verses 6b-7 and verses 8-11. She finds the thrust of the text revealed in the verbal similarities and scenic parallels of the two sections. What she reads from the parallel is the equal treatment given by Jesus to the scribes and the Pharisees

---

24. Arai, "Seisho," 342.
25. O'Day, "John 7:53—8:11," 632, 636.

and the woman. She reinforces this reading by pointing to how Jesus addresses each party in order to establish them as social and human equals.[26] Further, she points out a chiasmus found in verse 7b and verse 11b. From that she concludes, "Both the scribes and Pharisees and the woman are invited to give up old ways and enter a new way of life." Similarly, "The scribes and Pharisees are invited to give up the categories by which they had defined and attempted to control life." The woman is challenged "to participate in a new future for herself that will allow her to live not as a condemned woman but as a freed woman."[27] O'Day does not investigate further and does not ask how it is possible for such a woman to live in such a way. To conclude this way, I am afraid, will lead us to overlook the long history of miserable women who have been objectified, dehumanized, and abandoned by the arbitrariness of men. To become equal with men is not that simple for such women. If we stop our inquiry at this level, we only see Jesus humiliating the scribes and the Pharisees but not standing with the woman who suffered most. This Jesus is not revolutionary at all.

It is interesting that Witherington regards the woman as treated like a "scapegoat responsible for social ills." Although this may point to social discrimination against women in the society, he seems to put more emphasis on Jesus' criticism of the scribes and the Pharisees as those "who fail to live up to their responsibility of being examples of virtue for the community."[28] Maybe that is why he cannot go beyond saying that Jesus does not pronounce the woman's sin forgiven. Though rejecting the legalism that the scribes and the Pharisees cling to as discriminatory against women and referring to the fact that a man's lust is not taken as seriously as a woman's seduction, Witherington considers that repentance is necessary for her salvation. Thus he locates himself close to Calvin's nomianism.[29] Just like Witherington, Lightfoot takes Jesus' final words to be "neither of condemnation nor of forgiveness, but a charge to forsake her former way of life."[30] Thus he also implies that what is lacking here is her repentance. Takahashi suggests that Jesus' words, full of sympathy and pity, may empower her to repent and forsake her sin.[31] They all agree in suggesting that it is the woman's repentance that is at issue.

The only exception may be found in Arai's comments that Jesus' words in verse 11b ("and from now on do not sin again") are not original but were added later by the church and that therefore Jesus accepted the "sinful" woman as she was with no condition. If this is the case, Arai explains, the image of Jesus in this story belongs to the oldest layer of Jesus tra-

---

26. Ibid., 636, 637.
27. Ibid., 637.
28. Witherington, *Women*, 23.
29. Ibid.
30. Lightfoot, *Gospel*, 348.
31. Takahashi, *Kogi*, 44.

ditions.[32] Furthermore, he assumes that the story reflects the problem of apostasy confronted by the church of the fourth century. The content of the story was thus transformed with the additional phrase that made it possible for the church to interpret it in the sense that even those who commit adultery in a moral or religious sense could be reaccepted by the church only if they repented. Considering the complicated textual history, this seems to me to be the most probable explanation.[33]

My Reading of the Story

Standing on the Side of the Woman

Based on the preceding analysis, I would like now to reread the story by standing on the side of the woman. First, she would have been aware that if she committed adultery and were caught, she would be put to death according to the law. The scribes and the Pharisees also understand that point and put the case to Jesus. Second, as I have already pointed out, we do not see here the principal offender, that is, the man who infringed on the property and honor of another man. The scribes and the Pharisees, all men, are accusing the woman only. How could they let him escape from the scene of the crime? There is no excuse not to see him there. Most likely, it is simply another example in which only a woman is found guilty when a crime is committed by both a man and a woman. This has been repeatedly experienced by women, especially in sexual relationships. Third, are these men themselves responsible for such sexual conduct?

If she dared to have a sexual relationship with another man while being fully aware of the death sentence, and if we take into consideration the humiliating circumstances that hedged her in as her husband's property, there are only two possible interpretations for her action. One is that she was forced by a man and fell prey to his lust. While she was upset, he fled away. The other more plausible interpretation is that she took the action on her own initiative. Then her action could be called, in some respects, revolutionary. For a woman under such restrictions, adultery could have been her only form of protest or revolt. She might have spent years of tears enduring her husband's sexual violence and finally passed the bearable limit. Adultery might have been the only means through which she could offer resistance to her husband. I can find no evidence for this in the text, but I cannot help but interpret the text in this way. This I have learned from the history of the suffering of women on account of the arbitrary violence of men—a history played out in ancient Israel and also in Japan and other Asian countries. The story calls to us due to the tragic circumstances into

---

32. Arai, "Comfort Women," 368.
33. Ibid., 349.

which women have been cornered. We cannot say that this is a beautiful pericope.

How Can Jesus Be on the Side of the Woman?

Finally, I would like to examine Jesus' words to the woman to see if these words have brought liberation to her. If Jesus deals with the woman in such an inhuman situation by using the words of the text, I cannot say he is on her side. When he says, "Neither do I condemn you," he of course does not mean that he is also guilty. Instead, the statement means that he does not pronounce judgment on what has happened. Thus, the statement may presuppose that Jesus thinks adultery is a crime to be personally charged according to the law. But Jesus is the very person who has undermined his opponents' ideology of dependence on the law and neglect of the real issue. There would seem, then, to be a contradiction here, and it is very hard to accept the statement as having originated with Jesus.

At the end he instructs her, "Go your way, and from now on do not sin again." This is a very harsh sentence if we consider her circumstances, circumstances that do not allow her to have recourse to any other means except "sinning." There are two things to be pointed out. First, as mentioned above, this "sinning" was possibly the only way she could manage to escape from her predicament. It might have been that she could gain her "liberation" only through committing the "sin." We cannot see in Jesus' words a perspective that is in solidarity with her desperate situation, nor do we find any help to get her out of her oppressed life. It is absolutely unlike Jesus not to overturn the very roots of the injustice. Second, a question remains unanswered if Jesus, by his phrase "Go your way," is telling her to go back to her husband and continue her married life. She has not been liberated by these words if she is again bound by her husband, from whom she may have been trying to be freed. Her "sinning" has involved a grave risk on her part. She needs the deepest empathy at this point. And the empathy to see her as a victim of male sexual violence should be the key to take us closer to the core of the issue and see what is to be the good news to such a woman. To expect her to escape from male sexual violence if the only way she can do so is to commit another sexual crime is an illegitimate and suffocating way to deal with her.

Thus I must conclude that Jesus' words are not on the side of this woman, who finds no way out no matter which way she turns, without the right to divorce or to act on her own decision. And so these words, I submit again, did not originate from the mouth of Jesus. And this conclusion agrees with what Arai says, though the reasons are much different.

Around the fifth century, when this story found a place in the Gospel, sin was already viewed as largely an internal and individualized matter. For that situation, the story was meaningful, and we can see why the original story was doubly clouded by Christian individualization of sin and emphasis on repentance. These two characteristics are reflected in the story and have influenced the whole history of the church.

The story is further evidence that a biased worldview and a biased social structure reciprocally affect and justify each other. So we must be conscious of the danger of dealing with the two separately. In the case of this story, the tradition justified by the church permeated the story until it changed the primitive tradition and took control of the rest of church history.

Consequently, I cannot be persuaded by what O'Day says about the many relationships formed between Jesus, the woman, and the scribes and the Pharisees. If the issue is settled as she proposes—that is, by Jesus putting the two parties on the same level and inviting them to renew their way of living—they emerge as hypothetically equal but not truly equal because of the patriarchal imbalance of power.

I have tried to show in this essay that in order to get hold of the true story of this woman, we need to go through certain steps of critical social and interpretive analysis. First, we must distinguish historical layers of interpretation added to the story by the experience of church history and the perspective of patriarchy. That also helps us to see how sexuality has been viewed in different social and historical contexts, including the biblical world. Second, we must take the vantage point that sexuality as a whole has been biased and warped for male convenience. This fact has resulted in a dualistic understanding of women as being sinful and a disregard for the basic human rights of women. Third, the male-centered offense committed against women's sexuality and personhood must be surfaced to equalize the relationship between women and men. Fourth, and most importantly, a feminist reading of this text should recognize the sinfulness of patriarchal social structures and refrain from convicting the woman, the most subjugated and powerless character in the story, as sinful in order to make her a model for the way to repentance.

__ 6

Exile and Return in the Perspective of 1997

_____ Archie C. C. Lee __

On July 1, 1997, the sovereignty and jurisdiction of the present British crown colony of Hong Kong will revert to the Chinese government. The Hong Kong of 1841, "a barren island with hardly a house upon it,"[1] has been transformed into a flourishing city of the Orient since becoming a British colony in 1842. When defeated in the infamous Opium War with the British, China was forced to cede the island of Hong Kong to Britain under the Treaty of Nanking. Another unequal treaty, the Convention of Peking, was signed in 1860; it allowed the British to take the southern part of the Kowloon Peninsula, together with Stonecutters Island. Subsequently, by the Second Convention of Peking, in 1898, the British leased from the Chinese government for ninety-nine years New Kowloon, the New Territories, and 250 outlying islands, which together constitute 92 percent of the land area of the present Hong Kong.

This lease period of ninety-nine years will come to an end in 1997. The two sovereign states, Britain and China, held a series of talks in the early 1980s on the future of Hong Kong, which concluded with the signing of the Sino-British Joint Declaration of 1984. According to the declaration, Hong Kong will cease to be a British colony and become a special administrative region (SAR) of the People's Republic of China under the guiding principles of "One country, two systems" and "Hong Kong people ruling Hong Kong." Both countries will also work to ensure the present stability and prosperity of Hong Kong, while China promises to keep the existing capitalist system and lifestyle unchanged for fifty years, that is, until 2047.

Although China has repeatedly assured the people of Hong Kong, especially the business circles, that their way of life and the capitalist system will remain unchanged and that their interests will be taken into account, they know that 1997 constitutes a historical demarcation for Hong Kong and that, for better or for worse, Hong Kong will undergo fundamental changes

---

1. An impression of Lord Palmerston, the British foreign minister in 1841, quoted in G. B. Andacott (*A History of Hong Kong* [London: Oxford Univ. Press, 1958] 22). K. N. Wang, the general secretary of the Hong Kong Christian Institute, provides a brief review of Hong Kong's past and a description of the present dilemma in an unpublished article, "Hong Kong: A Modern City at Risk."

at that time. There is fear, anxiety, feelings of uncertainty, and a crisis of confidence among the people of Hong Kong. Many Hong Kong citizens are either exiles from China or the children of exiles and, as such, victims of political unrest and turmoil in China. The most recent large-scale influx of refugees into Hong Kong took place after the Communist takeover of the mainland in 1949 and the subsequent political crises and persecutions in China. Such people have longed for a return to a liberated and free homeland. The dream provides sustaining power for many. The irony is that the scheduled restoration in 1997 has not gladdened the hearts of the people but, on the contrary, has made them anxious and fearful.

Such a social context certainly shapes one's interpretation of the biblical texts. This concrete situation leads many Christians and biblical scholars in Hong Kong to a more profound understanding of the insights of the Bible, with the prophetic books becoming especially alive. The present experience and dilemma of those of us in Hong Kong help us to appreciate the struggles of the Israelite exilic communities and their reaction to the invitation to return to Jerusalem. I shall examine Jeremiah 29 from the perspective of 1997 to see how our social location contributes to our understanding of the idea of exile in the letter of Jeremiah and the theme of return in Jer 29:1-14.

Analysis of the Social Location

Very few will deny that, no matter how objective we claim our biblical interpretation to be, we are bound by our own background and that our context either sets limits to our understanding or enables us to gain insight that would otherwise be hidden from us.

The sociopolitical situation of Hong Kong is characterized by a series of deepening crises. The crisis of confidence had set in even before the signing of the Sino-British Joint Declaration (1984). It came rapidly to a climax after the Beijing Tiananmen Square massacre on June 4, 1989. Between 1984 and 1989, 150,000 Hong Kong citizens emigrated to other countries: in 1989 alone 54,000 left the city; in 1990, another 71,000 left. It is estimated that 600,000 people will choose voluntary exile in the lead-up to 1997, at the rate of more than 1,000 people a week. Almost all of these emigrants are highly trained professionals, investors, businessmen, and middle-management personnel. They leave the city with their expertise, skills, and capital. In the long run this massive brain-drain will badly affect the infrastructure of the community. A post-June 4 survey indicated that 85 percent of chartered surveyors, 80 percent of accountants, 60 percent of lawyers, and 58 percent of physicians intended to leave by 1997.[2]

---

2. "Home Away from Home," *Asia Magazine,* April 6–8, 1990, 18; S. Seibert et al., "Hong Kong Blues," *Newsweek,* April 16, 1990, 12–17.

Just from reading the titles of some of the numerous articles published in Hong Kong—for example, "An Unholy Alliance,"[3] "Hong Kong: Two Countries, One Victim," "Whither the Hong Kong Experiment?"[4]—one immediately gets a keen sense of the bitterness and disappointment of the Hong Kong people. China has tried to interfere in every sphere of life in Hong Kong through all sorts of means and with increasing audacity. There are pro-China groups that come out loud and clear on behalf of loyalty to China at the expense of the interest of Hong Kong. Indeed, "an unholy alliance" is a vivid phrase adopted by Emily Lau, a leading reporter who in 1991 won the first direct election of the legislative council ever conducted in the 150 years of the history of the colony, to portray the cooperation of the conservative leadership, the institutional church, and the business circles of Hong Kong.

The political conflict between the British and the Chinese governments over the electoral reform proposals for the 1995 election created strained relations between the two powers. The Hong Kong community has been split down the middle. Different political affiliations have been operative among social groups and political parties in Hong Kong. The Chinese leadership has been adamant on the political issue. Several key figures from among the Chinese leaders have strongly and personally attacked the Hong Kong governor, Chris Patten, who initiated democratic reforms with strong support from the British administration in London. They have constantly insisted on holding Governor Patten responsible for the consequences resulting from their retaliatory actions. They have refused to cooperate with the British even on matters that are beneficial to the welfare and livelihood of the Hong Kong people. Political disputes have spilt over to nonpolitical issues.

At a time of tense relations with Britain, the Chinese announced the appointment of the second batch of Hong Kong affairs advisers, all of whom are from the pro-China social and political groups and business community. Grassroots and prodemocratic elected members of the legislative council are not represented. There are signs that China has started its own plan to set up "a new kitchen" to prepare for the takeover without negotiation and cooperation with the British. The Basic Law of the Hong Kong Special Administrative Region stipulates that the members directly elected to the legislative council in 1995 will continue their term of service beyond 1997 in order to maintain continuity and stability, but there are fears that this idea of a "through train" will be totally discarded.

It is easy to see that the Chinese tactics are to identify and reward people who go along with Chinese policy and who are in sympathy with the Chinese way of dealing with Hong Kong. Those who hold contrary views feel

---

3. E. Lau, "An Unholy Alliance," *Far East Economic Review,* October 24, 1987.
4. K. N. Wang, *Hong Kong 1997: A Christian Perspective* (1991) 21–30, 68–79.

the pressure of intimidation and isolation. Public opinion in the territory is being polarized, and many people simply feel it is safer to keep silent.

Ninety-eight percent of the people of Hong Kong are Chinese and acknowledge Chinese sovereignty over the land of Hong Kong. But they are caught in a dilemma because many of them left China during the various periods of political disturbances and have witnessed oppression and human rights abuses by the Chinese Communist party. Furthermore, there is a great gulf between the two places in terms of political ideologies, standards of living, lifestyles, and basic social and human perceptions. Although the Joint Declaration and the Basic Law are important political documents, there are conflicting interpretations on significant points. Many Hong Kong residents are very much afraid of the uncertainty that the future holds. Returning to a strange motherland is not the hope of many of those who were born in Hong Kong.

In the case of the people who intend to stay in Hong Kong, the "return," of course, will not involve taking a journey back to the homeland, as the exilic community in Babylon had to do. Whether one likes it or not, the land and its people are to be handed over to China. If one does not wish to be part of this, the only options available are to embark on a second exile to foreign countries or obtain a foreign passport as a way of securing an exit in case of emergency. This is what the wealthy capitalist and business community as well as the professional classes are trying to do. For 90 percent of the population of Hong Kong, however, their fate has been determined by the negotiation and agreement of the sovereign states without their participation. How to preserve the present living conditions and to guarantee the freedom that is so precious are questions that continue to occupy the mind of Hong Kong citizens who, like it or not, have to face up to the reality of the return in 1997.

Interpretation of Jeremiah's Letter (Jeremiah 29) from the Social Location

The letter of Jeremiah to the exiles in 597 BCE (Jer 29:4-7) has a special appeal to the Chinese refugees who were exiled from their homeland either by force or by choice and settled in the British colony of Hong Kong:

> Thus says the LORD of hosts, the God of Israel, to all the exiles whom I have sent into exile from Jerusalem to Babylon: Build houses and live in them; plant gardens and eat what they produce. Take wives and have sons and daughters; take wives for your sons, and give your daughters in marriage, that they may bear sons and daughters; multiply there, and do not decrease. But seek the welfare of the city where

I have sent you into exile, and pray to the Lord on its behalf, for in its welfare you will find your welfare.

The word of Jeremiah has been well heeded by the emigrants to Hong Kong. They abandoned their country and gave up the hope of immediate return; some even left behind the idea of returning altogether. The history of Hong Kong testifies to their acceptance of the situation under the rule of a foreign power. They have worked hard to make their settled life in an alien land a miracle. "Build houses and live in them; plant gardens and eat what they produce. Take wives and have sons and daughters." These they have done well, making Hong Kong a prosperous city. They have sought the welfare of the city with the understanding that in its welfare they would find their own welfare. The major difference between them and the Israelites is that the refugees and immigrants to Hong Kong did not have a sense of being punished by the divine as a collective whole, nor did they have any idea of being sent by the divine to a foreign city on purpose.[5] However, the reality of being exiled to an alien land under foreign rule and the conviction that the only hope for the future lay in their own positive attitude toward the new environment are basically the same.

Both the Jewish exilic community and the Chinese community in Hong Kong enjoyed a certain degree of freedom. Like us, "They were allowed to live according to the customs of their fathers and were allowed to buy property (cf. Jer 29:5) and even slaves (Ezra 2:65)."[6] In both cases there was a strong national and sentimental link between the exilic community and the motherland. Many of the Chinese in Hong Kong have relatives in the mainland for whom they provide. It is not surprising, then, to learn that "the exilic Jews sent expensive presents to Jerusalem."[7] Quite a number of Chinese have participated in the administration of the political as well as civil structure of the colonial government. Likewise, some Jews "served in the imperial administration of Assyria and Babylon."[8]

There is consensus among commentators that the letter in Jer 29:5-7 is authentic. Disagreement arises with regard to the extent of it, specifically whether verses 8-9 and 10-14 belong to the letter proper or not.[9] Daniel Smith speculates from the "response" to the letter in verse 28, which

---

5. For the exile as a divine judgment and restoration as an act of mercy, see P. R. Ackroyd, *Exile and Restoration: A Study of Hebrew Thought of the Sixth Century BC* (London: SCM, 1968) 239.

6. B. Oded, "Judah and the Exile," *Israelite and Judean History* (ed. J. H. Hayes and J. M. Miller; London: SCM, 1977) 483.

7. Ibid.

8. A. Malamat, "Exile, Assyria," *Encyclopaedia Judaica* 6:1035.

9. It is not difficult to take vv. 16-20, having Deuteronomic influence, as not integral to the message to the exiles. These verses are not included in the LXX; see D. L. Smith, "Jeremiah as Prophet of Nonviolent Resistance," *Journal for the Study of the Old Testament* 43 (1989) 96–97, 105 n. 7.

mentions only the permanent stay in Babylon without any mention of the return, that the original letter contained only verses 5-7.[10]

Set in the context of chapters 27–29, the letter has always been seen as related to the issue of prophetic conflict.[11] Smith, however, observes that the letter has a special meaning of its own when taken as an important political document to the exiles, advising them to abandon violent action or revolt against the Babylonians. His analysis of the words "build," "plant," and "marry" in connection with Deuteronomy 20 and 28 and Isaiah 65 enables him to arrive at the conclusion that "Jeremiah is not simply advising a settled existence, but using the Deuteronomic exemptions from warfare to declare an 'armistice' on the earlier community."[12]

Obviously, the peace and stability of Babylon provided the right ingredients for the exilic Jews to develop. Therefore, "the spiritual centre of Jerusalem and Judah was transferred to Babylon, and there it remained for some decades, until the first of the exiles returned home."[13] Jeremiah's letter is actually in favor of the policy of accommodation to and cooperative political activities in the new situation. The Jews did assimilate to Babylonian life and culture. Both Sheshbazzar, the Jewish prince to be made governor in Judah, and Zerubbabel, leader among the returning exiles and son of Shealtiel, son of Jehoiachin, have Babylonian names, which is an indication of a "certain degree of assimilation to Babylonian conditions."[14]

Further, since Cyrus did not force the Jews to return to Palestine, many of them remained in the diaspora, not wanting to make that long and hard journey back to Jerusalem. Considering the time gap between the first exile in 597 and the defeat of Babylon in 539 BCE and the edict of King Cyrus of Persia (Ezra 1:1-4), one is not surprised to see the lack of enthusiastic response to the call to return. Although the return was regarded by the exilic community as a sign of hope and of God's grace and some did return to participate in the restoration and rebuilding of Jerusalem and its temple, many struggled with the idea of going back. We in Hong Kong can appreciate the kind of struggles the Jews in Babylon faced when they were allowed to return.

There were obviously very few deportees who returned from exile. Robert Carroll underlines the point that

---

10. Ibid.

11. See J. Crenshaw, *Prophetic Conflict: Its Effect upon Israelite Religion* (Berlin: de Gruyter, 1971).

12. Smith, "Jeremiah," 102.

13. J. A. Soggin, *A History of Ancient Israel* (Philadelphia: Westminster, 1985) 256.

14. G. Widengren, "The Persian Period," *Israelite and Judaean History,* 520; see P. Dutcher-Walls, "The Social Location of Deuteronomists: A Sociological Study of Factional Politics in Late Pre-exilic Judah," *Journal for the Study of the Old Testament* 52 (1991) 87–88.

those who went into exile in 597 were not those who returned in the century following the fall of Babylon in 539. Few, if any, of the original exiles lived so long that they could even contemplate returning to a land which they had left in their youth. The bulk of those who "returned" had never known life in Palestine—it was a new and risky venture for them.[15]

Carroll further comments that "most of the generation of those departed in 597 and 587/6 will no longer have been alive; many of the younger people may not have felt an urge to go to unknown Palestine, even if it was presented as the land of their fathers."[16] Siegfried Herrmann also acknowledges "the possibility that the return did not take place at once."[17] He doubts that after such a long period of exile anyone would be ready to return.

It would be helpful for our understanding of the exilic community if we had more information concerning their anxiety, uncertainty, and fear in their struggle to return to Palestine. Herrmann recognizes that "there has been no sources from Syria and Palestine to give us more details about the transition from Babylonian to Persian rule."[18] The Cyrus edict does not mention the return of the exiles from Babylon. Due to the Persian interest in fostering local cultic traditions, Cyrus might have been more concerned with the building of the temple than with the return of the deportees.[19]

Interpretation of the Return (Jer 29:10-14) from the Context of Hong Kong

Reading the letter of Jeremiah within the context of Hong Kong, one naturally tends to focus upon the notion of restoration. Given that, I will look beyond the letter proper (29:4-7) to the proclamation of salvation with regard to the return (29:10-14). The redactors of this text interpreted and presented the prophecy of Jeremiah from their own social location within the exilic community. Robert Carroll makes the following observation regarding Jeremiah:

---

15. R. P. Carroll, *Jeremiah* (Old Testament Library; London: SCM, 1986) 558.

16. Ibid. In reflecting upon Jeremiah's letter to the exilic community in Babylon, L. Trepp (*A History of the Jewish Experience* [New York: Behrman House, 1973]) sees basic Jewish thinking in the letter to the effect that dispersion is God's will with a divine purpose. The Jewish community in Babylon did not end with the return. Diaspora has from then on been recognized as "a permanent possibility" (32).

17. S. Herrmann, *A History of Israel in Old Testament Times* (London: SCM, 1975) 301.

18. Ibid., 298; Carroll, *Jeremiah*, 75.

19. The fact that the rebuilding of the temple did not actually begin until the reign of King Darius may prompt us to conclude that most of the returnees went back only after 521; see Herrmann, *History of Israel*, 301.

The life of Jeremiah presented in the tradition is neither a historical nor biographical feature, but part of the interpretation and presentation of the redactors; throughout the tradition there is a good deal of evidence for a complex use of prophecy which provides many insights into community struggles of the sixth century.[20]

In his commentary on Jeremiah, Carroll goes further by arguing that a fifth-century dating should not be excluded for some of the passages of Jeremiah, with 24:1-10 and 29:10-19 cited as examples.[21] I shall return to this in the following paragraphs. Here I wish only to argue that when the text of Jeremiah was being shaped in the hands of the redactor of verses 10-14, the major issue was probably simply that the time for the stay was up. The exiles had been in Babylon for decades: "For thus says the Lord: Only when Babylon's seventy years are completed will I visit you, and I will fulfill to you my promise and bring you back to this place" (Jer 29:10). This verse may very well reflect the present location of the community, the time when the seventy-year[22] stay was about to be completed.

It is very likely that various groups representing different interests, orientations, and interpretations of the event made their conflicting voices heard, though no set of criteria can with certainty distinguish the conflicting views of the opponents. We in Hong Kong too are bombarded every day by opposing views and conflicting interpretations of the political events relating to the relations between Hong Kong, China, and Britain. These views and interpretations represent the political loyalties and interests of the groups or circles concerned. Daniel Smith interprets the prophetic conflict theme of Jeremiah 27–29 in terms of a crisis of leadership: "The split is between those who advocate a limited cooperation and those who advocate open, and frequently violent, rebellion."[23] Jeremiah 27–29 thus presents different attitudes to and evaluations of the exile and the return as political events.

Many commentaries assert with regard to Jeremiah 29 that verses 10-14 are secondary, with "heavy deuteronomistic editing."[24] For instance, J. Philip Hyatt sees ideas and phraseology of the Deuteronomist in chap-

---

20. R. P. Carroll, *From Chaos to Covenant: Prophecy in the Book of Jeremiah* (New York: Crossroad, 1981) 267.

21. See Carroll (*Jeremiah*, 63–82) on the function, setting, and date of Jeremiah.

22. On the theme of "seventy years," see ibid., 495; idem, *From Chaos to Covenant*, 203–4; M. Weinfield, *Deuteronomy and the Deuteronomic School* (Oxford: Clarendon, 1972) 143–46; and Ackroyd, *Exile and Restoration*, 240–44.

23. D. L. Smith, *The Religion of the Landless: The Social Context of the Babylonian Exile* (Bloomington, Ind.: Meyer, Stone and Co., 1989) 135.

24. See, for example, Carroll, *From Chaos to Covenant*, 189; idem, *Jeremiah*, 67. E. W. Nicholson tabulates the positions of scholars on the original letter of Jeremiah in *Preaching to the Exiles: A Study of the Prose Tradition in the Book of Jeremiah* (Oxford: Basil Blackwell, 1970) 98. Critics hold that Deuteronomistic editors had a determinative influence in shaping Jeremiah 27–29; see B. O. Long, "Social Dimensions of Prophetic Conflict," *Semeia* 21 (1982) 40.

ter 29, especially in verses 10-20. Some of the prophet's own teaching may be in verses 10-14, but Hyatt admits that the passage has been "revised to such an extent that we cannot recover his words with precision."[25] One can go a step beyond this to assume with Robert Carroll that the texts of Jeremiah represent certain religiopolitical factors at work and a diversity of influences of factional politics that shaped the editing of the book: "The different cycles of material in the book reflect distinctive interests, and these may be identified with various social circles active after the fall of Jerusalem and during the Persian period."[26] As a matter of fact, the book of Jeremiah contains allusions and references to the return of exiles (16:14-15; 20:18-21; 31:7-9, 12-14) and the end of the Babylonian period of power after seventy years (25:11-12; 29:10) or three generations (27:7).[27]

Carroll takes Jer 29:10-14 as part of the collections of salvation material (Jer 12:14-17; 16:14-15; 23:7-8; 30; 32–33). Reading the passage in connection with the denigration of the Judaean communities in favor of the returning exiles in 24:4-10, he interprets the conflict and polemic in relation to the power struggle and fight for legitimacy of power between Judaeans and the returning exiles in the time of Ezra and Nehemiah.[28] If this tentative analysis of the influences of the returning exiles is correct, a fifth-century dating for the redaction of the book of Jeremiah may well be contemplated. Jeremiah 24—a product of the propaganda of the exiles of the 597 deportation, who claimed priority over those of the second deportation in 586 and superiority over the Judaean group that had remained in Jerusalem—exhibits some elements of lateness, especially the adoption of the motifs of verse 6 (cf. 1:10).[29]

There are close links between Jeremiah 24 and Jeremiah 29. Both chapters make the claim that the events they describe took place after the first deportation (24:1; 29:2). Both texts uphold the promise of return to the land (24:6; 29:10, 14) and assure the returning exiles of Yahweh's favor for them. A plan of peace and prosperity oriented toward a hopeful future is proclaimed in the form of a divine oracle (29:11). In contrast with the fate of those who were left behind in the land, Jer 24:6-7 reports Yahweh's comforting words:

I will set my eyes upon them for good, and I will bring them back to this land. I will build them up, and not tear them down; I will plant them, and not pluck them up. I will give them a heart to know that

25. J. P. Hyatt, "The Deuteronomic Edition of Jeremiah," *A Prophet to the Nations: Essays in Jeremiah Studies* (ed. L. G. Perdue and B. W. Kovacs; Winona Lake, Ind.: Eisenbrauns, 1984) 260.
26. Carroll, *Jeremiah*, 70.
27. Ibid., 68.
28. Ibid., 70–71.
29. Cf. Carroll's interpretation of Jer 24:1-10 (ibid., 482–88).

I am the LORD; and they shall be my people and I will be their God, for they shall return to me with their whole heart.

While Jeremiah was told in other passages not to pray for the people (7:16; 11:14; 14:11), Jeremiah 29 twice stresses the importance of prayer by the people (v. 7 and v. 12). In the letter proper the people are urged to pray for the foreign power, the Babylonians. On the return, they are invited to pray for their own welfare and are promised that their prayers will be heard. As in 24:7, so here in 29:13 the "heart" of the people plays a part in reestablishing the relationship with Yahweh in their restoration of the land. In both passages, therefore, the future of the returning exiles depends on the divine initiative, but the positive response of the people is equally significant. Restoration is not simply promised in 29:10-11—its fulfillment relies on certain conditions (29:12-14). William Holladay points out the difference between 29:4-7 and 29:10-14 in terms of the welfare theme; in the letter the welfare of the exilic community is tied up with that of Babylon (v. 7), but in 29:10-14 the welfare of the returning exiles is assured and proclaimed in the plan of Yahweh, who wills welfare and not evil (v. 11).[30]

Besides the differences in the approaches to welfare among the letter (29:4-7), the addition to it (29:8-14), and the elements of Deuteronomistic editing in the oracle on the return, one may observe that 29:8-14 undercuts the impact of Jeremiah's teaching of a long-term exile with normal social life. "Building houses," "planting gardens," as well as "marrying and giving in marriage" are "all long-term projects which produce a firmly established society with an open-ended future."[31] The ideas in the letter are very revolutionary, to the extent that a permanent settlement is advised and intermarriage is not excluded. The seventy-year theme, however, seems to undermine and change the intention of the letter, which advises a permanent stay in the diaspora.

If 29:10-14 is not taken as coming from the historical setting of the exile but rather from the setting of the returning community, as "a post-exilic creation" and "an after the event proclamation,"[32] then its function is not that of a warning against the brevity of Babylonian domination but rather that of an invitation to join in with the return movement with assurance of a hopeful future. It is also propaganda on the part of the returning exiles on behalf of their superiority and legitimacy of power.

Evaluated from this perspective, the oracle in verses 8-9 may also assume a different setting and function. It is now placed right after the letter and before the oracular statement on the return in verses 10-14. It denounces the prophets, diviners, and interpreters of dreams whose activities became

---

30. W. Holladay, *Jeremiah* (Hermeneia; 2 vols.; Philadelphia: Fortress, 1986) 2:141.
31. Carroll, *Jeremiah*, 556.
32. Ibid., 557–58.

popular and in greater demand as the people became increasingly preoccupied with the uncertainty of the future.[33] This is evident as well in this difficult time for Hong Kong, when we are facing the issue of a future that is totally beyond our control. We too witness a growing need to call upon fortune-tellers, palm readers, diviners, and feng-shui experts who are believed to have the capability of telling us our fate and foretelling our future. The people look for all sorts of means through which they can understand the divine will and gain some knowledge of the unknown.

Robert Carroll takes verses 8-9 in the context of chapters 27–29 and interprets them in the context of prophetic conflict. He views Jeremiah's letter as providing an explanation for the permanence of the new life in a foreign country in contrast to the oracles of the prophets, diviners, and dreamers, who claimed that the exile would be short. Carroll sees some difficulties in such an interpretation: "The point could have been made much more clearly in the text, if that is indeed what vv 8-9 purport to be."[34] The experience of those of us in Hong Kong allows us to read the oracle in verses 8-9 more clearly: it is a warning against seeking advice, guidance, and assurance from sources other than Yahweh in times of uncertainty. The words of Yahweh in verses 10-14 revealed Yahweh's plan for the people's welfare and a hopeful future. In such a context, verses 8-9 may presuppose an exilic community struggling with the issue of return. The prophets, diviners, and dreamers are those among the exiled in Babylon to whom the exilic community turned. The text warns against seeking guidance from those not sent by Yahweh. Instead, they shall seek Yahweh with all their heart, and a word of assurance is then given that they shall indeed find Yahweh (29:12-14).

Conclusion

Robert Carroll has stated succinctly that what constitutes a prophetic book may include the original utterance and the subsequent literary elaboration; he states also, in reference to Jeremiah, that "the social location of the elaborated text is unknown and yet scholars developing theories about the production of the book of Jeremiah need to give some thought to this important issue."[35] It is not difficult to grasp the ideological position of groups competing for political power. Reading the elaborated written text, one is struck by the conflict of different interests on the eve of the return and upon the exiles' arrival in Jerusalem. The book of Jeremiah contains basic

---

33. Ibid., 556; Holladay, *Jeremiah,* 2:141.
34. Carroll, *Jeremiah,* 557.
35. R. P. Carroll, "Arguing about Jeremiah: Recent Studies and the Nature of a Prophetic Book," *Congress Volume* (ed. J. A. Emerton; Leiden: Brill, 1991) 232.

elements of Jeremiah's word that have been reshaped, recast, and reinterpreted in the later context of the exilic community and the returning exiles, who were caught up with the issue of return and restoration. The word of Jeremiah was seen as serving the religious needs of the community in exile. My interpretation of Jer 29:1-14 from the social location of Hong Kong has revealed the same basic struggle over the issue of return within the exilic community. It is hoped that approaching the biblical texts from the social context of the interpreter may in some small ways contribute to solving the difficulty of "intense criticism" but "thin interpretation" not only in Jeremiah studies but also in critical scholarship as a whole.[36]

---

36. W. Brueggemann, "Jeremiah: Intense Criticism/Thin Interpretation," *Interpretation* 42 (1988) 268–80.

__7__

Laughing at Idols:
The Dark Side of Biblical Monotheism
(an Indian Reading of Isaiah 44:9-20)

George M. Soares-Prabhu

Biblical interpretation, which in mid-twentieth century moved from an author-oriented historical criticism (until then the only method accepted as legitimate in the academy) to a text-based literary criticism, is now moving from literary criticism to reader-response criticism and intertextuality. Because of this the focus of its hermeneutical interest has shifted from the author to the text and from the text to the reader. This double shift is the result of two related postmodern movements: the collapse of positivism, which put an end to the "fantasy" that historical exegesis is "a straightforward disinterested philological exercise" that is "neither theoretical nor ideological,"[1] and a growing awareness in biblical hermeneutics that the meaning of a text is not some fixed "author meaning" (what the author intended to say) embedded in the codes of the text but the trajectory of the meanings that emerge when the text, as a polysemic linguistic structure, interacts with a succession of readers, each of whom reads it from his or her own place.[2] The interpretation of a text, then, is best imaged as a fruitful "conversation" between text and reader,[3] in which the reader (not the implied reader of the literary critic, but the real reader who reads the text from a concrete historical setting) plays a decisive role.[4] "One's social location or

---

1. G. Phillips, "Exegesis as Critical Praxis: Reclaiming History and Text from a Postmodern Perspective," *Semeia* 51 (1990) 12; see also G. M. Soares-Prabhu, "The Historical Critical Method: Reflections on Its Relevance for the Study of the Gospels in India Today," *Theologizing in India* (ed. M. Amaladoss, G. G. Sauch, and T. K. John; Bangalore: Theological Publications in India, 1981) 314–23; D. Tracy, *Plurality and Ambiguity: Hermeneutics, Religion, Hope* (San Francisco: Harper and Row, 1987) 47.
2. J. Severino Croatto, *Biblical Hermeneutics: Toward a Theory of Reading as a Production of Meaning* (Maryknoll, N.Y.: Orbis Books, 1987) 13–24; P. Ricoeur, *Interpretation Theory: Discourse and the Surplus of Meaning* (Fort Worth: Texas Christian Univ. Press, 1976) 25–37.
3. H.-G. Gadamer, *Truth and Method* (London: Sheed & Ward, 1975) 321–24.
4. G. M. Soares-Prabhu, "Two Mission Commands: An Interpretation of Matthew 28:16-20 in the Light of a Buddhist Text," *Biblical Interpretation* (forthcoming); J. Voelz,

rhetorical context," as Elisabeth Schüssler Fiorenza has written, "is decisive of how one sees the world, constructs reality, or interprets biblical texts."[5]

What Is an Indian Reading of the Bible?

This essay proposes a self-conscious reading of a biblical text from one such social location—the confused, agitated, plural world of India today. Because of its complexity and "otherness," India is an unusually interesting place from which to read the Bible. Its "outside," that is, its social situation, is defined (as I have suggested elsewhere) by its three dialectically interrelated factors of a *poverty* so stark and widespread that words cannot convey what it is; a *religiosity* so pervasive and pluriform that it has (at least until now) allowed the major "word religions" to live together in tolerable harmony, alongside the cosmic religions of India's aboriginal peoples and the exiled religions of refugee groups like the Zoroastrians of Persia or the Lamaists of Tibet; and a social system (*caste*) so brutal that it is quite certainly the most oppressive system existing in the world today, outdoing apartheid for the damage inflicted on human beings.[6] India's "inside," or its cultural world of shared perceptions and values, has been shaped (as I shall suggest below) by a specifically "Indian mind," which reaches back three millennia into history and includes a long, sophisticated, and self-conscious tradition of scriptural interpretation.[7]

Reading the Bible from a place as complex as this can mean many things. It may mean, for instance, using traditional Indian methods of interpretation to interpret the Bible, reading the Bible in the light of specifically Indian social concerns, or reacting to the Bible with an Indian mind, that is, with the sensibilities proper to an Indian culture.[8]

These three ways of reading the Bible are obviously not mutually exclusive. They may and indeed should overlap. Ideally, one ought to read the

"Multiple Signs and Double Texts: Elements of Intertextuality," *Intertextuality in Biblical Writings: Essays in Honour of Bas van Iersel* (ed. S. Draisma; Kampen: Kok, 1989) 27.

5. E. Schüssler Fiorenza, "The Ethics of Biblical Interpretation: Decentering Biblical Scholarship," *Journal of Biblical Literature* 107 (1988) 5.

6. G. M. Soares-Prabhu, "From Alienation to Inculturation: Some Reflections on Doing Theology in India Today," *Bread and Breath: Essays in Honour of Samuel Rayan* (ed. T. K. John; Anand: Gujerat Sahitya Prakash, 1991) 62–71.

7. See M. Biardeau, *Théorie de la connaisance et philosophie de la parole dans le brahmanisme classique* (Paris: Mouton, 1964); K. K. Raja, *Indian Theories of Meaning* (Adyar Library Series 93; Madras: Adyar Library, 1963).

8. I have suggested elsewhere ("Two Mission Commands") that we can study the Bible in the light of Asia's social concerns and Asia's pluriform religious traditions by matrixing biblical texts with stories of Asia's broken humanity and texts from Asia's religious scriptures. I have tried to do the latter by comparing the mission command of Jesus in Matt 28:16-20 with that of the Buddha in Mahavagga 11.1 of the Vinaya Texts. This is analogous to reading a text with an "Indian mind," except that that "mind" here is focused through a religious text.

Bible in India in the light of Indian concerns, with a sensibility that is Indian, using where helpful traditional Indian methods of interpretation. This in fact is what exegetes in India would naturally do, except that the colonized consciousness imposed on them by a colonial Christianity and their affiliation with a guild of biblical scholars that, though multinational in its membership, still remains adamantly monocultural in its outlook serve to alienate them from their traditional culture and prevent any local reading of the text.[9] In India, a reading of the Bible from "this place" instead of being a natural process (as a reading of the Vedas or of the Pali Canon would be) becomes a reading against the grain, which needs to be undertaken with considerable self-conscious effort.

It is just such a self-conscious Indian reading of a biblical text that I attempt here, focusing on the third approach described above. I shall try to read Isa 44:9-20 (a biblical text that is particularly responsive to a critical Indian reading) with an Indian mind. But this inevitably brings up questions as to whether there is in fact an Indian mind, what this Indian mind is, and how it can be used for a fruitful reading of the Bible. I shall try to answer these questions before attempting an Indian reading of Isa 44:9-20.

The Indian Mind

India is a "place" inhabited by more than eight hundred million people, who speak some 1650 different languages and dialects and live at levels of technical sophistication ranging from the near Stone Age to the post-atomic era.[10] The bewildering diversity of India has to be experienced to be believed. Cultural anthropologists are therefore wary of holistic explanations of Indian culture that latch on to the overarching unities of the "great tradition" of Sanskritic Hinduism while glossing over the many regional diversities of the "little traditions" of popular religion.[11] Such caution is justified. But one can, I believe, still speak legitimately of an Indian way of experiencing reality. Hinduism, which is as much a culture like Hellenism as it is a religion like Judaism,[12] has permeated the whole of the subcontinent, giving it "a deep underlying fundamental unity far more profound than that produced by either geographical isolation or political superiority,... a unity which transcends innumerable diversities of blood, color, language, dress manners and sect."[13] Nothing (not even the other so-called minority religions) quite escapes the pervasive influence of this subtly unifying yet intrinsically pluralist culture. Even if it does not include the whole of the In-

---

9. Soares-Prabhu, "From Alienation to Inculturation," 71–78.
10. Ibid., 59–60.
11. J. Leavitt, "Cultural Holism in the Anthropology of South Asia: The Challenge of Regional Traditions," *Contributions to Indian Sociology* 26 (1992) 12–20.
12. R. C. Zaehner, *Hinduism* (London: Oxford Univ. Press, 1962) 1–2.
13. V. Smith, *The Oxford History of India* (Oxford: Oxford Univ. Press, 1919) x.

dian cultural reality, an "Indian mind" certainly reflects the most significant area in it.

What then is this Indian mind? In a seminal article of stunning insight, the poet A. K. Ramanujan has suggested that Indian thinking has as its archetypal model the grammar of Panini rather than (like Western thinking) the mathematics of Euclid and so tends to be context-sensitive rather than context-free.[14] Indian thinking is therefore always contextual. It tends to avoid abstract, universally valid judgments about things in general, preferring instead to evaluate persons, events, and things in terms of the specific contexts in which they occur.

Because of this sensitivity to context and therefore to the concentric series of contexts in which persons, events, and things appear, Indian thinking experiences *all* reality as an interconnected, interrelated, and interdependent whole. It is, therefore, cosmocentric and not (like Western thinking) anthropocentric in its orientation. The cosmos (not just humankind) is always the horizon of the Indian experience. This makes Indian thinking holistic and inclusive. It always tries to grasp the whole because things have meaning only as parts of this whole. Because of this passion for wholeness, the Indian mind is prepared, as Troy Organ has said, to risk the chance of error rather than the loss of any part of truth.[15] Its thinking is therefore inclusive not exclusive. Truth is defined not by exclusion (A is A because it is not B) but by identity (A is A whether or not it is also B), so that to affirm something is not necessarily to deny its opposite.[16] Indian thinking is therefore tolerant of ambiguity and is able to hold together seemingly contradictory aspects of reality as complementary parts of a never fully to be apprehended whole.[17]

Perhaps the most striking manifestation of this tolerance of ambiguity is the way in which Indian thinking holds together the undivided oneness of the Absolute Brahman ("the one without a second") with the infinite variety of forms in which the Absolute is expressed. The radical monism of India has its obverse in its radical polytheism. No religious tradition has insisted so resolutely on the oneness of the Absolute as Hinduism has done; none has generated so vast a variety of marvelous images in which the Absolute is to be encountered. The cosmocentric and visual mind of India, which is more interested in "seeing the divine image" than in hearing the divine word, has developed a radically polytheistic consciousness that offers a complementary alternative to the biblical myth of aniconic monotheism

---

14. A. K. Ramanujan, "Is There an Indian Way of Thinking? An Informal Essay," *Contributions to Indian Sociology* 23 (1989) 47–55.

15. T. Organ, *The Hindu Quest for the Perfection of Man* (Athens: Ohio Univ. Press, 1970) 54.

16. R. Panikkar, *Kultmysterium in Hinduismus und Christentum: Ein Beitrag zur vergleichende Religionstheologie* (Freiburg: Karl Alber, 1964) 39–41.

17. G. M. Soares-Prabhu, "Interpreting the Bible in India Today," *The Way Supplement* 72 (1991) 76–77.

that has so largely determined habits of thinking in the West.[18] In many ways, then, the intensely visual, pluriform, inclusive, cosmocentric Indian mind is the polar opposite of the word-oriented, exclusivist, anthropocentric mind-set of the Bible. Reading a biblical text with an Indian mind can therefore be a disconcerting experience.

An Indian Reading

The experience is especially disconcerting when the text chosen is one as offensive to Indian sensibilities as Isa 44:9-20. This is a satirical taunt song that contains the most elaborate and forceful critique of idolatry to be found anywhere in the Bible. In India, where "idol worship" is a normal and edifying religious practice (as effective, it would seem, in promoting spiritual growth as the Muslim *namaz* or the Christian mass) and where the "idols" worshiped are recognized as visual theologies of great depth and power,[19] such a text will provoke reactions very different from the approval[20] or mild apology[21] it arouses in the West.[22] The Indian reader is scandalized by a text from Scripture that offers what seems to be a dishonest caricature of a meaningful religious practice and that does this in a literary form (satire) that one does not expect to find in a religious book. A religious text may, indeed must, condemn the evil that people do, but it ought not to poke fun at the people themselves! Satire, which does this, lacks compassion. And since compassion is a mandatory dimension of any religious text, it is difficult to see how satire can figure in a religious book. I certainly do not recall any text from the Hindu or the Buddhist Scriptures that toys with satire. For all its literary finish,[23] then, the satire in Isa 44:9-20 poses from the start problems for an Indian reader.

---

18. D. L. Eck, *Darsan: Seeing the Divine Image in India* (2d rev. ed.; Chambersburg, Pa.: Anima Books, 1985) 22.

19. Ibid., 17; H. Zimmer, *Myths and Symbols in Indian Art and Civilization* (ed. J. Campbell; Bollingen Series 6; Princeton, N.J.: Princeton Univ. Press, 1972) 130–36, 148–56.

20. G. A. F. Knight, *Servant Theology: A Commentary on the Book of Isaiah 40–55* (International Theological Commentary; Grand Rapids: Eerdmans, 1984) 79–81; J. D. Watts, *Isaiah* (Waco, Tex.: Word Books, 1985–87) 2:146.

21. K. Elliger, *Deuterojesaja*, vol. 1, *Jesaja 40.1-45,7* (Neukirchen-Vluyn: Neukirchener Verlag, 1978) 440–41; J. L. McKenzie, *The Second Isaiah* (Garden City, N.Y.: Doubleday, 1968) 68–69; P. Volz, *Jesaia II* (Leipzig: Deicherische Verlag, 1932) 52; C. Westermann, *Isaiah 40–60* (London: SCM, 1969) 151.

22. Significantly, E. John Hamlin, in a commentary written for the Third World (*A Guide to Isaiah 40–66* [Delhi: ISPCK, 1989] 67), is the only commentator I know who shows awareness of the problem that such an anti-idol tirade might pose to readers living outside the Christian world. He is at pains to point out that Second Isaiah is not referring to the religious institutions of non-Christians today—though of course, equally, he is!

23. Knight, *Servant Theology*, 79; Westermann, *Isaiah*, 150.

But the unease that it generates in an Indian reader must not prevent the reader from listening to the text. There is always the danger that reading such an idol-baiting text from this polytheistic place might be as unjust to the text as the text has been to the idol worshipers it so offensively satirizes. This danger is doubly real in India. For India is not only a place in which a context-sensitive culture biases readings in favor of the reader who brings a new context to the text;[24] it is also a place that has not yet undergone its "Enlightenment." Readings of texts from such a place tend to be precritical, subjective readings, in which the reader, whether it is Mahatma Gandhi reading the Bhagavad Gita[25] or Osho Rajneesh reading the Gospels,[26] is unable to distance himself or herself sufficiently from the text to hear what it has to say. Not surprisingly what the reader hears in the text is only the echo of his or her own voice. A responsible Indian reading, which wants to respect both the utterance of the text and the preunderstanding of the reader, must include, then, a critical moment, without which the reading will dissolve into mere subjective reaction.

The reading of Isa 44:9-20 that I attempt here will therefore begin with a critical reading of the text. This reading will not be a historical reading concerned with a detailed reconstruction of the history of the text nor a literary reading attempting to spell out its literary structure or rhetorical strategy. It will be what might be called a theological reading that tries to find out the overall meaning of the text as it now stands in the Bible and then reacts to what the text is saying from an Indian point of view.

An Indian Reading of Isaiah 44:9-20

To do this, the Indian reading of Isa 44:9-20 that I propose will proceed in three steps. It will (1) situate the text in its literary and sociological *context;* (2) spell out the *structure* of the text as accurately as possible; and (3) reflect on the *significance* of what the text has to say to a reader in India today.

---

24. See Ramanujan, "Indian Way of Thinking," 53. There is a splendid illustration of this in the Brhadāranyaka Upanishad 5.2.1-3, where "what the thunder said" ("da, da, da") is interpreted differently by gods, humans, and demons. For the gods who are given to pleasure, "da" means "control yourselves" (*dāmyata*); to humans given to greed, it means "give" (*datta*); to demons given to cruelty, it means "be compassionate" (*dayadhvam*).

25. M. Gandhi, *The Gospel of Selfless Action; or, The Gita according to Gandhi* (trans. and ed. M. Desai; Ahmedabad: Navajivan, 1946).

26. Bhagwan Shree Rajneesh, *The Mustard Seed: Discourses on the Sayings of Jesus Taken from the Gospel according to Thomas* (2 vols.; Pune: Rajneesh Foundation, 1975); idem, *Come Follow Me: Talks on the Sayings of Jesus* (4 vols.; Pune: Rajneesh Foundation, 1976–77); idem, *I Say unto You: Talks on the Sayings of Jesus* (2 vols.; Pune: Rajneesh Foundation, 1980).

The Context of Isaiah 44:9-20

Isaiah 44:9-20 is part of Second Isaiah, a work composed during the exile, the gravest crisis in Israel's history.[27] Crises are often moments of creativity, and it is precisely during the exile that Israel's "breakthrough to monotheism" took place.[28] The breakthrough was prepared for by prophetic movements in preexilic Israel and Judah that attempted to assert, though with only limited success, the exclusive worship of Yahweh. But it was only with the exile that what Bernhard Lang has called "the Yahweh alone movement" triumphed. It succeeded so well that not just monolatry but genuine monotheism—a monotheism possibly catalyzed by the Zoroastrianism of the emerging Persian Empire[29] and certainly colored by the harsh conditions of its origins—became consciously and even aggressively the faith of the people as a whole. Now indeed "polytheistic Israel is dead, and out of its ashes arises [monotheistic] Judaism."[30]

Composed toward the end of the exile, Second Isaiah offers some of the earliest and most forthright expressions of this monotheism. Second Isaiah's insistent monotheism is soteriological: it provides the basis for his proclamation of the certain and imminent return of his exiled people. Second Isaiah is preeminently the prophet of the return,[31] and his certainty about the coming return of his people is based not just on his reading of the political situation, in which the growing power of Cyrus presages the fall of Babylon, but on his faith in Yahweh as well. He is convinced that Yahweh, Israel's God, is the only "true" God. Yahweh has created the universe and controls the events of history. He[32] is therefore able to save his people, and, as his past interventions in their history (especially the exodus from Egypt and the conquest of Canaan) as well as his present activity in the events they are witnessing (especially the victories of Cyrus) show, he

---

27. The "oracles" in the book were mostly delivered in Babylon during the latter part of the exile, probably after 550 BCE, the year in which Cyrus began his victorious campaign. But they were put together later, possibly after the return from exile, by the disciples of the prophet, among whom we must reckon Third Isaiah, the author of Isaiah 56–66. See P.-E. Bonnard, *Le Second Isaïe: Son disciple et leurs éditeurs, Isaïe 40-66* (Paris: Gabalda, 1972) 315–19; McKenzie, *Second Isaiah*, xvii–xxiii; Carroll Stuhlmueller, "Deutero-Isaiah: Major Transitions in the Prophet's Theology and in Contemporary Scholarship," *Catholic Biblical Quarterly* 42 (1980) 4–5; Westermann, *Isaiah*, 3–8, 27–30.

28. Bernhard Lang, *Monotheism and the Prophetic Minority: An Essay in Biblical History and Sociology* (Sheffield: Almond Press, 1983) 41.

29. Ibid., 46–47.

30. Ibid., 41.

31. N. H. Snaith, "A Study of the Teachings of the Second Isaiah and Its Consequences," *Studies on the Second Part of the Book of Isaiah* (ed. H. M. Orlinsky and N. H. Snaith; Leiden: Brill, 1977) 147–49; A. S. Kapelrud, "The Main Concern of Second Isaiah," *Vetus Testamentum* 32 (1982) 52–56; Lang, *Monotheism*, 44.

32. I try to avoid sexist language in speaking of God but use the masculine pronoun for Yahweh. Yahweh is not simply to be identified with "God," but is rather a specific (male) image of the divine.

also intends to do so.[33] "The unique power and might of the ONE GOD," as Norman Snaith sums it up, "is the guarantee of the return."[34]

This saving message of the prophet has been spelled out, rhetorical criticism suggests, in extended poems or persuasive "speeches."[35] These, however, are not of one piece but have been compiled by the prophet or a disciple of his out of the smaller formal units detected by the form-critical study of the text.[36] There is, as might be expected, no consensus about the number, origin, or extension of either the larger "poems" defined by rhetorical critics or the smaller forms that the form critics have identified.[37] Many scholars do, however, agree that Isa 44:9-20 is part of a larger section extending from 44:6 to 44:23.[38] Some believe that it has been inserted into an originally unified poem, 44:6-8 + 21-22, in which "a complete trial speech and a complete assurance of salvation combined to form a single oracle."[39] But form-critical criteria suggest that verses 21-22 are a separate unit in the form of a _Mahnrede,_ that is, an exhortation to conversion.[40] It seems best, then, to take 44:6-23 as a composition of four distinct units, each with its own particular form. A trial speech affirming the uniqueness of Yahweh (vv. 6-8) is followed by a satirical taunt song denying any reality to idols (vv. 9-20), then by an exhortation calling on Israel to turn to Yahweh (vv. 21-22), and finally by a jubilant hymn, characteristic of Second Isaiah, which rejoices at the redemption that is certain to be soon accomplished (v. 23).

If, as Frank Matheus surmises,[41] the hymn in verse 23 is the culminating point of the section and brings to a focus the themes that have been touched

33. R. J. Clifford, _Fair Spoken and Persuading: An Interpretation of Second Isaiah_ (New York: Paulist, 1984) 14.

34. Snaith, "Teachings," 149.

35. J. M. Muilenburg, "The Book of Isaiah: Chapters 40–66," _The Interpreter's Bible_ (Nashville: Abingdon, 1956) 5:384–86; Clifford, _Fair Spoken,_ 4.

36. J. Begrich, _Studien zur Deuterojesaja_ (Munich: Kaiser, 1969) 13–67; Bonnard, _Second Isaïe,_ 32–33; R. F. Melugin, _The Formation of Isaiah 40–55_ (Berlin: de Gruyter, 1976) 175; Westermann, _Isaiah,_ 11–21.

37. Stuhlmueller, "Deutero-Isaiah," 1.

38. Bonnard, _Second Isaïe,_ 154; E. J. Kissane, _The Book of Isaiah_ (2 vols.; Dublin: Browne and Nolan, 1943) 2:61; K. Marti, _Das Buch Jesaja_ (Tübingen: Mohr, 1900) 301; Muilenburg, "Isaiah," 505. This is true whether Isa 44:9-20 is taken to be a composition of Second Isaiah (Clifford, _Fair Spoken,_ 110; F. Matheus, _Singt dem Herrn ein neues Lied: Die Hymnen Deuterojesajas_ [Stuttgart: KBW, 1990] 70–71; Muilenburg, "Isaiah," 505; Volz, _Jesaia,_ 51–52) or, as seems more likely, not (Elliger, _Deuterojesaja,_ 416; McKenzie, _Second Isaiah,_ 67; Westermann, _Isaiah,_ 147); and whether it is to be read as prose (Knight, _Servant Theology,_ 79; McKenzie, _Second Isaiah,_ 67; Volz, _Jesaia,_ 51), poetry (Muilenburg, "Isaiah," 510; Westermann, _Isaiah,_ 148), the rhythmic prose of rhetorical speech (Elliger, _Deuterojesaja,_ 416–17), or, possibly, as poetry overlaid with prose glosses.

39. Westermann, _Isaiah,_ 139, following B. Duhm (_Das Buch Jesaia_ [5th ed.; Göttingen: Vandenhoeck & Ruprecht, 1968] 331); Marti, _Jesaja,_ 301; Muilenburg, "Isaiah," 505.

40. K. Arvid Tängberg, _Die prophetische Mahnrede_ (Göttingen: Vandenhoeck & Ruprecht, 1987) 111–13; Elliger, _Deuterojesaja,_ 442–45.

41. Matheus, _Singt dem Herrn,_ 72–73.

on in all the preceding parts, the base of the section is made up of the trial speech in verses 6-8 and the satire on idols in verses 9-20. As the positive and negative ways of affirming the uniqueness of Yahweh, these two texts ground the assurance of redemption that the hymn celebrates. The exhortation in verses 21-22 functions as a link that joins the mutually reinforcing affirmations of Yahweh's uniqueness in verses 6-8 (Yahweh is the only God) and verses 9-20 (the idols are no gods at all) to the celebration of redemption in the hymn of verse 23. It defines Israel's response to Yahweh's self-affirmation. Israel is exhorted to return to the only God who has redeemed it (44:21). Such a return will lead to the redemption of Israel, that is, to its return from exile. The hymn in verse 23 is a cry of exultation at this certain and imminent return. The passage, therefore, forms a coherent unit whose structure may be diagrammed as shown in the following figure.

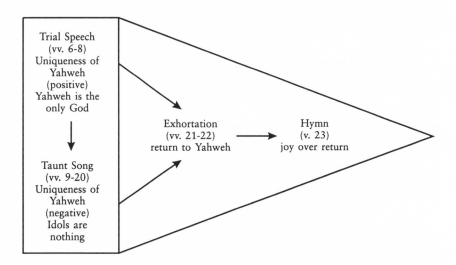

The whole passage is held together by the theme of redemption. In the trial speech (vv. 6-8) Yahweh declares himself to be Israel's king and redeemer (*melek yiśrā'ēl wᵉgō'ălô*). In the exhortation (vv. 21-22) Israel is invited to turn to Yahweh because it has been redeemed by him (*šûbâh 'ēlay kî gᵉ'altîkā*). The concluding hymn (v. 23) is a triumphant cry of joy at the redemption accomplished by Yahweh (*rānnû šāmayim ... kî gā'al yhwh ya'ăqōb ûbᵉyiśrā'ēl yitpā'ār*). Isaiah 44:3-23 is thus a sort of gospel within a gospel, a compact summary of the "good news" of imminent salvation proclaimed by Second Isaiah. It offers the assurance of "redemption," based on the conviction that Yahweh, the LORD of hosts, the first and the last, is the only God (44:6-8), and so the ultimate controller of nature and of history. The satire on idols (vv. 9-20), though it lacks the catchword "redeem" (*g'l*), and in other ways too differs so considerably from the rest of Second Isaiah that it can scarcely be his work,[42] fits into the passage because it latches on to the affirmation of Yahweh's uniqueness. If Yahweh is the only God, then the idols of the nations must "profit nothing" (*bal-yôʿîlû*). The satire on idols (vv. 9-20) and the trial speech in which Yahweh presents himself as the only God (vv. 6-8) thus form a tight unit recognized as such by the punctuation of the Masoretes and the spacing of the text in 1QIs*ᵃ*.[43] The two contiguous texts are the two mutually reinforcing sides of a single affirmation about the uniqueness of Yahweh, and this is the theological basis of Second Isaiah's exhortation to repentance (vv. 21-22) and his celebration of imminent redemption (v. 23). Whatever may have been the original function of the satire (possibly an argument to prevent the defection of the exiles to the gods of Babylon, which, as the gods of the conquering people, must have exerted a strong fascination on them), it now serves to bring out the uniqueness of Yahweh as the only true God.

This uniqueness is affirmed in a formula that is found in variant forms elsewhere in Second Isaiah (Isa 43:11; 45:5, 14, 18, 21) as well as in Deuteronomy (4:35, 39) and the Deuteronomic Historian (1 Kgs 8:60; 2 Kgs 19:19). In its basic form this formula reads: "Yahweh is God, besides him there is no other" (*yhwh hûʾ haʾĕlōhîm milᵉbaddô/mibbalʿadô ʾên ʿôd*). This implies, to use Hans Wildberger's convenient distinction, not just the *Einzigartigkeit* (uniqueness) of Yahweh but his *Einigkeit* (singularity) as well.[44] Yahweh is unique not just qualitatively but also numerically. He is not just incomparably the greatest ("Who is like me?"), he is the only one ("there is no other"). This leap into monotheism shapes the polemic against idols that we find here (and elsewhere) in Second Isaiah. But it is also, as I shall suggest, shaped by it.

The Structure of Isaiah 44:9-20

What, then, does this anti-idol polemic say? Although its overall meaning is plain, its details are often obscure. For unlike the beautifully balanced satire of 46:1-4 (probably the work of Second Isaiah himself), Isa 44:9-20 (which is almost certainly not by him) reads awkwardly. It is an overlong piece, so irregularly written that it is disputed (as we have seen) whether it is poetry, prose, or the sort of rhythmic prose that is common in rhetorical discourse. The passage is full of obscurities due to faulty textual transmission[45] and

---

42. Westermann, *Isaiah*, 146.

43. Elliger, *Deuterojesaja*, 414–15.

44. H. Wildberger, "Der Monotheismus Deuterojesajas," *Beiträge zur alttestamentlichen Theologie: Festschrift für Walter Zimmerli* (ed. H. Donner, R. Hanhart, and R. Smend; Göttingen: Vandenhoeck & Ruprecht, 1977) 507.

45. See Elliger, *Deuterojesaja*, 408–14. Two are specially troublesome: (1) In v. 12 *ḥārāš barzel maʿăṣād* (the worker in iron, axe) makes no sense at all. In the translation I give below I have rendered *maʿăṣād*, found elsewhere only in Jer 10:3 and whose meaning (axe) is therefore by no means certain, as "tool"; following the LXX, I have also, with Westermann

abounds in repetitions that interrupt and confuse the flow of the text. These repetitions are clearly secondary expansions added to the text in the course of a long and complex history of tradition.[46] This history is of course not relevant to our Indian theological reading, which takes off from the text in its final form. I give, therefore, a near literal translation of the text as it now appears in the Bible. The translation has been arranged so as to show the parallelisms (v. 12 ‖ v. 13) and duplications (v. 15 = vv. 16-17; v. 18 = v. 19) that appear in it, as the fruit of its long tradition history, and to indicate (by the numbers with points: 1.0, 2.1, and so on) the structure that I find in the text and will explain below.

Isaiah 44:9-20

1.0 ⁹All those who make idols are nothing,
and the things they treasure do not profit;
Their witnesses neither see nor know, and so they will be put
    to shame.

2.1 ¹⁰Who would fashion a god or cast an image that brings no profit?
¹¹Look, all his fellows (*habērin*) will be put to shame;
for the artisans (*hārāšîm*) themselves are merely human.
Let them gather together; let them stand up.
They will be terrified (*phd*) and put to shame (*bws*) together.

2.2
¹²The artisan in iron (*hārāš barzel*) [sharpens] a tool and fashions (*p'l*) [an idol] over coals. With hammers he makes it (*ysr*) and fashions it (*p'l*) with the strength of his arm. He gets hungry and loses strength; He drinks no water and grows faint.

¹³The artisan in wood (*hārāš ʿēṣîm*) stretches out a line. He marks out [an idol] with a marker. He shapes it (*ʿśh*) with chisels; and with a compass he marks it out. He shapes it (*ʿśh*) in human form, with human beauty, that it may dwell in a shrine.

2.3 ¹⁴[He goes out] to cut down cedars, or takes a cypress or an oak and makes it grow strong among the trees of the forest. He plants a pine and the rain makes it grow.

(*Isaiah*, 145), inserted *yēhēd* (from *hdd* = to sharpen) after it. (2) Verse 14 begins with a construct infinitive *likrot-lô ʾărāzim* (to cut for himself cedars), which obviously requires a principal verb. Following Marti (*Jesaja*, 303), I have added *hālak* (he goes) to the beginning of the verse.
46. Elliger, *Deuterojesaja*, 414–22.

¹⁵And then it is people's [fuel] for burning (*b'r*); and he takes some of it and warms himself. He also kindles (*šlq*) a fire and bakes bread.

¹⁶Half of it he burns (*śrp*) in the fire; over this half he [cooks] flesh and eats it; he roasts a roast and is satisfied.
He also warms himself and says "Aha! I am warm; I feel (*'h*) the fire."

Then he fashions (*p'l*) a god (*'ēl*) and worships it (*šhh*); he shapes (*'śh*) an idol (*pesel*) and bows down before it (*sgd*).

¹⁷The rest he shapes (*'śh*) into a god (*'ēl*), into his idol (*pesel*); he bows down before it (*sgd*).

2.4

¹⁸They do not know (*yd'*) and they do not understand (*byn*), for their eyes are blocked (*thh*) from seeing and their hearts from understanding.

¹⁹They do not reflect (*swb*) in their hearts, they do not know (*yd'*), they do not understand (*byn*) [enough] to say:
"Half of it I burned (*śrp*) in the fire,
and I also baked bread on its coals.
I roasted meat and have eaten.
Shall I make a detestable thing?
Shall I bow down to a block of wood?"

3.0 ²⁰He herds ashes. A deceived heart leads him astray (*nth*). He cannot save himself nor say, "Is there not a lie (*šeqer*) in my right hand?"

In spite of its apparent lack of form, the anti-idol satire of Isa 44:9-20 has been, I suggest, carefully structured. An introduction (1.0) and a conclusion (3.0) frame the main body of the satire, which can be subdivided into four parts (2.1-4). Looking at each of the three main sections of the structure we find the following.

1. The satire begins with an introductory verse (v. 9) that spells out the content of its polemic in terms of three explicitly stated themes. It speaks about the *makers* of idols who are (it says) engaged in useless labor (v. 9a); about the *idols* they make and treasure, which profit for nothing (v. 9b); and about the *worshipers* of the idols (called "witnesses" probably to integrate the polemic into the trial speech that precedes it)⁴⁷ who "neither

---

47. Assuming that 44:9-20 is not by Second Isaiah but an oracle introduced by a later editor into his text, vv. 9-11 might be the redactional link fashioned by the editor to join

see nor know" (v. 9c). All three themes are developed in the polemic that follows, not successively, in different strophes, as E. J. Kissane suggests,[48] but more or less together and always under the rubric of the "makers of idols." For the whole satire is ostensibly about these idol makers. They are the subject of every sentence in the text. But the makers of idols are also their worshipers (vv. 15b, 17), and in making their idols they tell us what these idols are (vv. 12-13).

2. The reflection on the makers of idols proceeds in four steps. It begins (2.1) with the observation that the makers of idols are merely human and are therefore unable to meet the challenge of the God of Israel, who claims to be the only God (vv. 10-11). Then (2.2) follows a description of their work in two parallel verses, which describe how an idol is made by a worker in iron and a worker in wood (vv. 12-13). The descriptions are objective, neutral, with no explicitly hostile note. Polemic begins at the next stage (2.3). Here the makers of wooden idols are shown planting trees to get wood (v. 14). They use part of the wood as fuel to warm themselves and cook their food and shape the rest into an idol that they worship. A terse description of this in verse 15 is repeated with more detail and color in verses 16-17. The polemic ends (2.4) with a comment on the blindness of those who make and worship idols. Once again, a first bare statement in verse 18 is repeated more forcefully in verse 19.

3. A concluding verse (v. 20) rounds off the satire, taking us back to its beginning. Its opening words, "He herds ashes" (rō'eh 'ēper), which, as B. Duhm suggests, describe a thoroughly futile activity,[49] remind us of the opening verse of the satire (v. 9a) in which the makers of idols are said to be in a state of emptiness and confusion (tōhû). The inability of the idol maker/worshiper to "save himself" affirmed in verse 20b gives specific and ominous form to the prediction in verse 9c that worshipers of idols will "be put to shame." And the last words of the satire ("He cannot . . . say, 'Is there not a lie [šeqer] in my right hand?'" [v. 20c]) are an extraordinarily precise and vivid illustration of the general indictment in verse 9 that the makers/worshipers of idols "neither see nor know."

The anti-idol satire of Isa 44:9-20 is therefore a tightly woven unit. An introduction and a conclusion thematically related to one another frame a description of idol making and its implications, set out in the four steps

---

the oracle (which would have begun at v. 12) to the trial speech (vv. 6-8) that immediately precedes. Not only are the makers of idols now spoken of as "witnesses" (v. 9b); they are also questioned about their activity (v. 10), invited to come together and stand up to testify, terrified because they have nothing to say in their defense, and covered with shame (v. 11b). The verses have been written up in juridical language not found elsewhere in the satire but appropriate to the trial scene that precedes. There is no need, then, for the emendation of 'ēdêhem into 'abdêhem, as proposed (with no textual support) by McKenzie (Second Isaiah, 66) and Volz (Jesaia, 51).

48. Kissane, Isaiah, 2:67.

49. Duhm, Jesaia, 336; Westermann, Isaiah, 151–52.

noted above. These steps mark an onward movement in the progress of the satire. From the general and dispassionate charges leveled against idol makers with which the satire opens (v. 9), we are led through a close description of how idols are made (vv. 12-13) and what the making of idols implies (vv. 14-19a), to the concrete, emotionally charged polemical questions with which the satire ends (vv. 19b-20).

The Significance of Isaiah 44:9-20

The satire of Isa 44:9-20 is one of several anti-idol texts in Second Isaiah (Isa 40:18-20; 41:5-7; 42:17; 45:16-17; 46:1-4, 5-7). In every one of these, the idols of the "nations" are contrasted with Yahweh, who is presented (or presents himself) as incomparable, not to be likened to any image (40:18; 46:5); as the "first and the last" (41:4; 44:6), that is, as a "lasting and creative presence in history"[50] or as the unique God who tolerates no other (44:8; 45:14). All the anti-idol texts thus serve a common purpose. They highlight the absolute uniqueness of Yahweh and ultimately the efficacy of Yahweh's saving power. This stands out in stark contrast to the "nothingness" and powerlessness of idols and of the gods they represent.[51]

But the anti-idol texts do this in different ways. Three of them (40:18-20; 41:5-7; 46:5-7) do so by merely describing, quite dispassionately, the *making of idols*. Made by skilled craftsman and set up so that they will not topple (*lō' yimmôt*), the idols are powerless, inanimate works of human hands. In other texts attention shifts to the *makers of idols* (Isa 45:16). In contrast to Israel, who will be saved by the Lord, these idol makers will be "shamed" (*bôšû*). Finally, in Isa 46:1-2 it is the *idols themselves* that are mocked. The text describes the (wrongly) anticipated flight of the great gods of Babylon, before the conquering advance of Cyrus.[52] Bel and Nebo are unable to save themselves and are carried off into captivity on pack animals, in striking contrast to Yahweh, who carries his people out of captivity: "I have made and I will bear; I will carry and I will save" (Isa 46:4).

The violence of the anti-idolatry polemic grows in intensity as we pass from the first set of texts to the second and the third and is carried a step further in our text (Isa 44:9-20). This text is the most comprehen-

---

50. A. Schoors in Stuhlmueller, "Deutero-Isaiah," 11.

51. R. J. Clifford, "The Function of Idol Passages in Second Isaiah," *Catholic Biblical Quarterly* 42 (1980) 464.

52. In any event, the anticipation of the prophet is not fulfilled. Cyrus does not chase out the gods of Babylon but treats them with respect, indeed claims legitimation from them. "I am Cyrus, king of the world, great king, legitimate king,...whose rule Bel and Nebo love, whom they want as king to please their hearts," intones the Cyrus cylinder (*Ancient Near Eastern Texts* 316). The tolerant, respectful attitude of Cyrus toward Bel and Nebo, however much it may have been a matter of imperial policy, stands in sharp contrast to the intolerance of the prophet who so loudly extols him as Yahweh's servant!

sive and ferocious attack on idols that we can find in Second Isaiah, or indeed anywhere in the Bible. Elements from the other anti-idol texts—the wholly human origin of the idols (44:12-13), their powerlessness and passivity (44:14-17), the shaming of the idol makers (44:11)—are all taken up here and intensified. And to these is added something new: a contemptuous ridiculing of people who worship idols. "Not the idol," notes John D. Watts, offering with obvious relish a neat summary of the prophet's attack, "but the worshipers are the object of laughter. They are *emptiness,* who *see nothing and know nothing.* They are *shamed, less than human* (v. 11), *a mind deceived.*"[53] Idol worshipers according to the satire of Second Isaiah are people so foolish that they can worship a block of wood, part of which they have used as fuel for their cooking fires (44:18-20):

> They do not reflect in their hearts,
>   they do not know,
>   they do not understand [enough] to say:
> "Half of it I burned in the fire
>   and I also baked bread on its coals.
> I roasted meat and have eaten.
> Shall I make a detestable thing?
> Shall I bow down to a block of wood?"

A Mistaken Understanding of Idolatry

Here lies the sting of the satire and its problem. The satire supposes that the idolater is foolish enough to bow down to a block of wood, part of which he has just used as fuel for his fire. But no idol worshiper in India or elsewhere ever does this. Even the "simplest" of them do not worship a block of wood. They are quite aware that their idol is and remains wood and stone. What they believe is that when an idol is "consecrated," the "god" (whether Bel or Marduk, or Shiva or Devi) comes to "dwell" in it. The idol then mediates the "real presence" of the divine—in somewhat the same way, it seems to me, that the "consecrated" bread and wine in the Christian Eucharist mediate the "real presence" of Jesus.[54] The satire's implied charge that idolaters are "bowing down to a block of wood" is then completely untrue. They are bowing not to the idol but to the god made

---

53. Watts, *Isaiah,* 2:145.
54. If anything, the traditional Roman Catholic understanding of the Eucharist in terms of transubstantiation seems to me more "idolatrous" (I use the word in a positive not pejorative sense) than anything in Hinduism. No Hindu believes that the "substance" of the idol is transformed into the substance of the god. The idol remains a symbolic focal point in which the divinity, or rather the power of the divinity, is manifested. Reflection on the Hindu understanding of the "divine image" might provide a good starting point for a new theology of the Eucharistic "real presence" that might be more satisfactory than the mechanisms so far proposed in Christian theology.

present in the idol—whether this god is conceptualized as a suprahuman member of an otherworldly pantheon (like the Vedic gods or the gods of Babylon) or (like the gods and goddesses of Hinduism today) as one of the "manifestations of the distinct powers springing from an unknowable 'Immensity.' "[55] Those who worship idols are not "transferring to a creature the adoration due to God alone" but are "adoring some object upon which has descended the glory of God, so that this object can become a point of departure for a slow and arduous ascent toward God."[56] The sin of idolatry, in the sense of "a mere bowing down to 'sticks and stones,' " lies, then, as Diana Eck (quoting Theodore Roszak) has pointedly asserted, wholly in the eye of the beholder.[57]

Commentators with rare exceptions have recognized this. But none seems to have faced up to the problem that this kind of anti-idol polemic poses. It is not enough to dismiss Isa 44:9-20 as a "rampageous satire,"[58] deplore its overenthusiastic polemic,[59] or justify it by simplistic (unbelievably simplistic!) condemnations of idolatry.[60] It must be recognized for what it is: a damaging and therefore sinful misrepresentation of a people's religion and culture. Such a misrepresentation must be judged either as polemically inspired libel or (what is surely more likely) as a remarkable display of prejudiced ignorance. It might be difficult to believe that someone who presumably lived among the Babylonians, shared their life, saw them at worship, watched them make their idols, perhaps even joined in their festivals, could be so crassly ignorant of what they really believed. But to the Indian reader such prejudiced ignorance is not unfamiliar. In a celebrated passage of his autobiography, Mahatma Gandhi recalls how during his school days "Christian missionaries used to stand in a corner near the high school and hold forth, pouring abuse on Hindus and their gods."[61] Like the satirist in Second Isaiah, generations of Christian mis-

---

55. A. Daniélou, *Hindu Polytheism* (Bollingen Series 73; New York: Pantheon, 1964) 9.

56. R. Panikkar, *The Trinity and the Religious Experience of Man* (Maryknoll, N.Y.: Orbis Books, 1973) 16.

57. Eck, *Darsan*, 21.

58. Westermann, *Isaiah*, 151.

59. McKenzie, *Second Isaiah*, 68.

60. C. R. North, "The Essence of Idolatry," *Von Ugarit nach Qumran: Beiträge zur alttestamentlichen und altorientalischen Forschung* (ed. J. Hempel and L. Rost; Berlin: Töpelmann, 1961) 158–60.

61. M. K. Gandhi, *An Autobiography; or, The Story of My Experiments with Truth* (trans. M. Desai; Ahmedabad: Navajivan, 1940) 24. The accuracy of Gandhi's observation was questioned by a Protestant missionary, H. R. Scott, who claimed to have been the only missionary in Rajkot at the time of which Gandhi wrote and denied ever having preached at the corner of the high school or having ever poured abuse on Hindus and their gods. Gandhi with scrupulous honesty published Scott's letter to him in the weekly journal *Young India* he was then editing (March 3, 1926) but went on to add: "Though the preaching took place over forty years ago the painful memory of it is still vivid before me. What I have heard and read since has but confirmed that first impression" (*Christian Missions: Their Place in India* [ed. B. Kumarappa; Ahmedabad: Navajivan, 1941] 6). Whether Gandhi

sionaries brought up on the anti-idol polemic of the Bible have gone on repeating the same distorted charges of idolatry against Hinduism, even though a lifetime spent in India ought to have taught them better. But layers of prejudice against "idolaters" effectively insulated them from the deeply religious world in which they lived and made them insensitive to the damage their missionary propaganda was doing by creating and perpetuating the "benighted heathen" image, which persists as "scratches" in Western thinking about India even today.[62]

For the Indian reader, what lends a touch of irony to this anti-idol polemic of the Bible is the perception that what makes the biblical authors so prone to see and condemn idolatry in others is the element of idolatry in their own religion. We see ourselves, it has been said, in the mirror of our own destructive criticisms. The religion of Second Isaiah, as seen from India, is in a sense as "idolatrous" as that of the people he mocks. True, his God has (at least since the monarchical period of Israel's history) no material image. In this Yahweh may have been unique.[63] But an image does not have to be material. Mental images are one of the eight kinds of "materializations" or images of the divine (*mūrti*) that Indian theology recognizes (Bhagvāta Purāna 11.28.12),[64] and Yahweh who cannot be represented by a material image is in fact thought of in a mental image, cast in the likeness of a human male. "The spirituality of Israel," as Raimundo Panikkar points out, is "based on the conception of a God who speaks, punishes, pardons, is jealous, ordains laws, can be offended and also appeased, who commands, promises, and concludes pacts with men"[65]—and, one might add, who leads his people in war, destroys their enemies, and demands strict "ethnic cleansing" to guard against their possible religious apostasy (Deut 7:1-5). Such a spirituality "belongs phenomenologically to the category of iconolatry [Panikkar's euphemism for idolatry]," for iconolatry consists in a "projection of God under some form . . . which may be mental or material, visible or invisible, but always related to our human representation."[66] Anthropocentric biblical thinking leads to a "jealous" anthropomorphic God, just as cosmocentric thinking leads to proliferation of a multitude of less dangerous because less seductive idols, as pluriform as the cosmos itself.

There is of course a radical difference between the worship of Yahweh,

---

was mistaken or (as seems more likely) Scott was overpresumptuous in imagining that he was the only missionary in Rajkot at the time does not really matter. Abuse of the kind Gandhi speaks about was common in missionary discourse and in missionary writings of the colonial era, and I have heard it often enough in my own days in school.

62. M. Singer, *When a Great Tradition Modernizes: An Anthropological Approach to Indian Civilization* (Delhi: Vikas, 1972) 11–21.

63. Lang, *Monotheism,* 23.

64. See Daniélou, *Polytheism,* 363.

65. Panikkar, *Trinity,* 14–15.

66. Ibid., 15.

the icon of the God of Israel, and the worship of an idol of Baal. The difference is not merely that the image of one is mental and that of the other material. In terms of the religious attitude (spirituality) implied, this difference may not amount to much. Both kinds of images lead to what Panikkar has called iconolatry, which he associates with *karma-marga,* the path of ritual or ethical action, which is the first of the three ways to salvation recognized by Hinduism.[67] Neither is the difference quite that suggested by Panikkar when he says: "The idol of Israel was certainly not an object made by hand or created by thought, an invention or discovery of man; it was Jahweh, the living and true God, the one who had revealed himself to Israel and made a pact with her, who was Israel's own special idol."[68] Could not the same be said of other idols that also are not merely human inventions but expressions of a religious experience and therefore of a revelation? Rather, the difference between Yahweh worship and Baal worship lies, I believe, in the two different horizons, monotheistic or polytheistic, in which these two analogous forms of iconolatry are situated. It is this monotheism of Second Isaiah that now needs to be examined.

A Nationalist Monotheism

The anti-idol texts of Second Isaiah are, we have seen, always associated with his assertion of the uniqueness of Yahweh and the absolute efficacy of his saving power. Idols are nothing because Yahweh is the only God, besides whom there is no other. Second Isaiah's anti-idol polemic is therefore the obverse side of his monotheism. But this obverse side is also its dark side. It reveals Second Isaiah's monotheism as an exclusivist and therefore inadequate understanding of God. For if Yahweh is truly God, the only God besides whom there is no other, then he must be the God not just of Israel but of all other peoples (of all idol worshipers!) as well.

God's concern cannot be monopolized by a single people but must reach out to all. God's all-pervasive presence cannot be restricted to any one temple or to any one "holy" land but must encompass the world. The gods that people worship cannot, then, be false gods or no gods. They may be (as Hinduism would say) inadequate representations of God, whose worship would be imperfect ways to reach God. But they cannot be "nothing." Every attempt to reach God must relate in some way to the only God that is. "The very notion of a false god," as Alain Daniélou puts it, "is an obvious fallacy. If there is an all-powerful, all-pervading divinity . . . how can we worship anything that is not Him?"[69] Krishna's reassurance in the Bhagavad Gita, "Even those who lovingly devote themselves to other gods and

---

67. Ibid., 11–19.
68. Ibid., 13.
69. Daniélou, *Polytheism,* 10.

sacrifice to them filled with faith, they really worship me, though the rite may differ from the norm" (9.23), makes more sense than the exclusive nationalistic monotheism of Second Isaiah, which speaks of Yahweh as the only God but makes him in fact the god of Jews only.

For, in Second Isaiah, Yahweh is "Jacob's King" (41:21); "the Holy One of Israel" (41:16, 20; 43:3; 49:2); "Israel's King and redeemer" (44:6); even Israel's "husband" (54:5). Israel is his people (43:1-3; 44:21), whom he has chosen (44:1), about whom he is deeply concerned (49:14-19; 51:1-3), for whom he is prepared to sacrifice other peoples (43:3-4, 14; 45:14; 49:22-23). Rarely has the closeness of Yahweh for his people been so clearly and forcefully expressed. But this is done at the expense of all the other peoples of the earth, for whom Yahweh, the only God, shows not concern, but hostility (47:1-15; 49:25-26), contempt (44:9-20), and large indifference. Except in a very few texts (to be discussed below) that may speak about Israel's role in the salvation of nations, Yahweh does not relate to other nations as their God. The nations are not invited to worship him; they are merely summoned to innumerable trial scenes (41:1-4, 21-24; 43:8-13; 44:6-8; 45:20-21) to attest to his incomparable supremacy. They are offered submission, not salvation. Even Cyrus, who is co-opted into Yahweh's service, is shown as a mere instrument in his hand. He is never treated as Yahweh's worshiper or made part of Yahweh's people. Second Isaiah's skewed monotheism leaves the nations (that is, all humankind except Israel) without any real God. Their own gods are nothing, but Yahweh refuses to be their God!

If this flaw in Second Isaiah's monotheism has not been perceived by most First Testament scholars, it is because, with a very few exceptions,[70] they take Second Isaiah to be a prophet of universalism.[71] Along with his breakthrough into monotheism, Second Isaiah, they believe, breaks out of Jewish particularism also to announce salvation to all nations. But the evidence for this is meager. The case for universalism rests on a handful of ambiguous texts. Indeed, if matters are pressed, it rests on a single pair of texts from the Servant Songs (42:1-4; 49:6) and their echoes in later strata of the tradition (42:6; 51:4).[72] "Within a fragmentary and unfinished piece of poetry [the Servant Songs]," as Carroll Stuhlmueller has put it, "Dt-Isa

---

70. Snaith, "Teachings," 155.

71. Wildberger, "Monotheismus," 529–30.

72. Isaiah 42:6 echoes 49:6. The Servant (?) will be made to be "a covenant for the people (*bᵉrît 'am*) and a light for the Gentiles (*'ôr gôyim*)." Isaiah 51:4 combines 41:1-4 with 49:6. Yahweh promises that his judgment (*mišpāṭ*) will become a light to the nations. The mission to be a "covenant for the people" refers to Israel, for Second Isaiah uses *'am* in the singular always for Israel, and only in the plural (except in 42:5 where the context requires a singular) for the Gentiles (Snaith, "Teachings," 157). "Light to the Gentiles" clearly indicates action on behalf of the Gentiles, but whether in their favor or against them (as 51:4 seems to suggest) is not clear. A third possibly relevant text, Isa 45:22, in which Yahweh urges all the ends of the earth (*kol 'apsê-'eres*) to turn to him and be saved, probably refers not to the Gentiles but to the worldwide salvation of dispersed Israel.

made the colossal leap from an exclusive concern for Israel's salvation and its concomitant antigentile attitude to world salvation."[73]

The leap from Second Isaiah's consistently antigentile attitude to a concern for world salvation would indeed have to be colossal—so colossal that one might well doubt if it was ever attempted at all. Whether the allegedly universalist texts really speak about the salvation of the Gentiles and not of a worldwide salvation of scattered Israel witnessed by Gentiles everywhere[74] is doubtful. And even if they do, they remain isolated texts, a few tiny sparks of lights that do little to illuminate the looming darkness. They offer at best hints and guesses of a genuine universalism, which do not change the strongly nationalist, antigentile thrust of Second Isaiah's work.

For an unbiased reader the impression left by Second Isaiah is certainly not one of concern for the Gentiles. The Book of Consolation, which abounds in hauntingly beautiful passages expressing Yahweh's patient, unforgetting love for his errant people, contains no word of appreciation or comfort for the Gentiles. Instead there are threats against those who oppose his people (41:11-12; 47:1-15), taunt songs addressed to their gods (Isa 44:9-20), and predictions of their eventual subordination to Israel (43:3-4; 45:14; 49:22-23; also 60:1-22). Here lies the core of Yahweh's attitude to the Gentiles in Second Isaiah. They are of interest to him only inasmuch as they can be of service to his people. Yahweh is prepared to give Egypt as Israel's ransom, Ethiopia and Sheba in exchange for it (43:3). He will make over to Israel the spoils of Egypt, Ethiopia, and the Sabeans, and hand over their people to Israel as its slaves (45:14). The rulers of the Gentiles are destined to be nursemaids (domestic slaves) for Israel's children. They will "bow down before you with their faces to the ground and lick the dust at your feet" (49:22-23). The world order envisaged here is unmistakable. Israel is to be the master race; the Gentiles are the "lesser breeds without the law." This should not surprise us, for a "chosen people," as I

---

73. Stuhlmueller, "Deutero Isaiah," 27. It is possible that these texts (particularly if the Servant Songs once had a life of their own) may originally have had a genuinely universalist sense. But as they now appear in the Book of Consolation they do not seem to go beyond the limits of Second Isaiah's nationalist monotheism, as this has been described above. Isa 42:1-4, which announces that the Servant will bring "justice" or more correctly "judgment" (*mišpāṭ*) to the nations, says no more than that he will bring to the nations the courtroom decision given at the many trial scenes described by the prophet, in which the claim of the other gods to divinity is rejected and Yahweh's claim to be the only god is upheld (Westermann, *Isaiah*, 95). Isaiah 49:6, which promises to make the Servant "a light to the nations" (*'ôr gôyim*) so that "my salvation might be to the end of the earth" (*lihyôt yᵉšû'ātî 'ad-qᵉsēh hā'āres*), may be saying no more than that the return from exile will be a sign to dazzle the whole gentile world (Snaith, "Teachings," 156). Neither text, particularly when read in their present context as part of the strongly nationalist proclamation of Second Isaiah, need suggest a genuine universalist vision in which Yahweh shows the same concern for the nations as he does for Israel.

74. Snaith, "Teachings," 155–57.

have suggested elsewhere, is only a step way from a *Herrenvolk*.[75] That so nationalist a prophet should be concerned about the salvation of the Gentiles is surely unlikely. The monotheism of the prophet remains adamantly exclusive.

Given the situation in which Second Isaiah lived, this is not surprising. The prophet wrote for a people who, because of the trauma of the exile, had reached a situation in which they had lost all confidence in their history. This, as in Nazi Germany or in Iran (and possibly in India today), is the seedbed of extremist nationalism and religious fundamentalism. "If a traumatic process obscures the creative appropriation of the past and blocks the transformation of what has been inherited into an open future, . . . fundamentalist reactions emerge," notes the psychologist Geiko Müller-Fahrenholz.[76] The nationalist monotheism of Second Isaiah is, I believe, such a fundamentalist reaction. Bernhard Lang alerted us long ago to the political factors at play in the emergence of Israel's monotheism:

> While Judah, as a political entity, is shattered by a superpower, the idea of the only god is born. Monotheism, then, is the answer to political emergency, in which no solution is to be expected from diplomatic manoeuvering or foreign military help. There is but one saviour: the only true God.[77]

This of course does not mean that the monotheism of Second Isaiah is simply the answer to a political emergency. Like any foundational religious insight (like the enlightenment of the Buddha or the proclamation of God as unconditional love by Jesus), it is the outcome of a religious experience: an insight into the ultimate significance of the world. Such a foundational experience cannot be explained in terms of sociopolitical factors only. Other peoples in bondage to Babylon did not make the breakthrough to monotheism; other itinerant charismatic preachers in Roman Palestine did not encounter God as "Abba." But sociopolitical factors may provide a favorable environment for an experience like this to establish itself as a successful religious movement, and they will certainly influence the form that this movement will take. The emergence of monotheism in Babylon, as we find it expressed in Second Isaiah, was colored by the "end of the world" situation of the people among whom it emerged. This gave it, I suggest, a nationalist and fundamentalist tone. It became an exclusivist monotheism in which the only God remained the God of the Jews only.

---

75. G. M. Soares-Prabhu, "The Unprejudiced Jesus and the Prejudiced Church," *The Way* 27 (1987) 13.

76. G. Müller-Fahrenholz, "What Is Fundamentalism Today? Perspectives in Social Psychology," *Fundamentalism as an Ecumenical Challenge* (ed. H. Küng and J. Moltmann; Concilium 1992/3; London: SCM Press, 1992) 14–21.

77. Lang, *Monotheism*, 54.

An Anti-gentile Bias

The result of this is that there is in Second Isaiah, indeed in the First Testament as a whole, a distinct anti-gentile bias that in some ways parallels the anti-Jewish bias that we find in some books of the Second Testament, like Matthew and John, that also emerged from a situation of a desperate struggle for self-definition and survival. Hostility or at best indifference toward the nations is characteristic of the Hebrew Bible. The texts collected by Werner Schmidt to demonstrate the "hope for the nations" proclaimed in the Bible[78] hardly make encouraging reading. A dozen stray texts speak not so much about the salvation of the nations as of their subordination to Israel and its God. If the nations are to be saved, it can only be by abandoning their history and accepting the history of Israel as theirs (Isa 2:2-4; 45:23; 55:3-5; 60:1-22; Jer 3:17; Zeph 2:11; Zech 14:16-19). This summons to alienation, only too familiar to the victims of the colonial Christian mission, is hardly a message of hope. Only the book of Jonah (a marvelous oddity in the Bible) and a very few texts, like the curious blessing of the nations in Isa 19:24 or the recognition in Mal 11:1 that acceptable worship can be offered by all peoples everywhere (not in Jerusalem only), make, I believe, a genuine breakthrough to universalism.

Less noticed than the anti-Judaism of the Second Testament, the anti-gentile bias of the First has been no less catastrophic in human history. For if the anti-Judaism of the Second Testament eventually provoked the horror of the holocaust, the anti-gentile attitude of the First, expressed in satires like those of Second Isaiah, resulted in the less-publicized but I suggest even more devastating destruction of the peoples and cultures in the "new" world and in colonized areas of the very old. The massive destruction of temples and of thousands of lovingly cherished religious texts in South America and in Asia (I think particularly of my own homeland of northern Goa where not a single Hindu temple was left standing) was the work not of the "barbarous" conquistadores lusting after gold and women but of the pious friars accompanying them, fired with zeal for the only god of the Bible and a paranoid hatred of "idolatry." The history of Christianity has been extraordinarily destructive of peoples and cultures, and this is surely at least partly because of the fanatical iconoclasm of the Bible, which is the dark side of its monotheism. For as Daniélou surmises:

> Monotheism is the projection of the human individuality into the cosmic sphere, the shaping of "god" to the image of man. Hence the monotheist commonly visualizes his "god" as an anthropomorphic entity who shares his habits, patronizes his customs, and acts according to his ideals. Religion becomes a means of glorifying his culture

---

78. W. H. Schmidt, *Alttestamentlicher Glaube in seiner Geschichte* (7th ed.; Neukirchen-Vluyn: Neukirchener Verlag, 1990) 319–24.

or his race, or of expanding his influence. He is one of the elect who follows the "Way of God" as if there could be a way that does not lead to "God." We can see all monotheistic religions fighting to impose their God and destroy other gods as if God were not one as they claim. Monotheism is basically the absolute exaltation of the worshiper's own deity over all other aspects of the divine, all other gods who must be considered false and dangerous.[79]

Whatever the theological validity of this analysis, it certainly seems to picture accurately the actual historical behavior of the monotheistic religions. They have been extraordinarily intolerant both toward other religions and toward dissident groups in their own.[80] Disclosing the hidden roots of this intolerance can be a function of "pluralist" Indian readings of the Bible, like the one attempted here. Such readings can then take their place beside the Jewish critique of the anti-Semitism of the Second Testament and the feminist critique of biblical patriarchy as one of the many ways in which a reading from another place can both defamiliarize and liberate the text.

79. Daniélou, Polytheism, 10.
80. G. M. Soares-Prabhu, "Religion and Communalism: The Christian Dilemma," Responding to Communalism: The Task of Religions and Theology (ed. S. Arokaisamy; Anand: Gujerat Sahitya Prakash, 1991) 142–43, 154–59.

8

A Voice from the Margin: Reading Matthew 15:21-28 in an Australian Feminist Key

Elaine M. Wainwright

> Feminism is unwrapping
> It's looking back over the past
> unwrapping our dusty sisters
> the ones neglected in his-story
> > the writers
> > the
> > thinkers
> > the lovers
> > the
> > challengers
> > the washerwomen
> Unveiling their splendour
> It's lining them up in our full view
> Seeing them wink at us
> > > Feeling
> > > less
> > > alone
> It's unwrapping ourselves and when we can
> being midwives in the unwrapping of each other
> It's shedding old skins seeing each other glisten
> It's getting bigger becoming whole
> It's discovering rooms we never guessed at
> in the house of ourselves rooms of power
> rooms of anger   rooms of pleasure   rooms of I[1]

---

1. P. Maitland, "Feminism Is," a poem published under the copyright of the author. The above is a small selection from a longer work by Maitland, an Australian woman whose words offer vision and hope while capturing the spirit of the task undertaken in this essay. The significance of the poem will be explored in the context of the essay that follows.

The ferment for this essay began in a recent experience that is perhaps paradigmatic of the specific reading site (location) from which the subsequent interpretive task could emerge. The scene was a gathering of students from three Christian denominations participating in a unit called "Women's Studies in Religion and Theology." The majority of the students were Australian-born and belonged to one of the three mainstream Christian denominations that constitute our college of theology. Others, however, were from different ethnic and cultural backgrounds. On the particular evening in question, we sought to hear the voices of indigenous Australian women and of those Australian women whose country of origin is not Australia and whose primary language is not English.

I listened first to Joan Hendricks telling us that we would not understand what she had to say about aboriginal culture until we had heard a little of her story of her own appropriation of her aboriginality after years of devaluation. This listening brought with it a deeper awareness of the multifaceted nature of women's experience, which we claim as the foundation for any of our feminist theological enterprises, and the limitation of gender studies that do not take account of the very polyvalence of women's experience. Lou Myles, an Australian woman of Filipino origin, very specifically challenged the hegemony of white, middle-class, Anglo-Australian feminism and its strong links in the religious arena with the Judeo-Christian tradition. Also, as each spoke of a woman's place within her culture of origin, it became clear once again that unilaterally defined patriarchy as a central analytical category would no longer suffice if we were to give voice to the experience of all women from different ethnic, cultural, socioeconomic, and religious backgrounds.

In this encounter, therefore, I was challenged to extend my own boundaries in a way that brought to consciousness a biblical story with which I was very familiar, namely, that of the Canaanite woman in the Matthean Gospel story (Matt 15:21-28).[2] While I had previously read the story from a feminist perspective,[3] that reading was undertaken within the context of completing a Ph.D. thesis in a culture other than my own. The present reading is grounded in six years of exploration of this and other biblical stories with and among Australian women and men on Australian soil. I envisioned the possibility of a new reading of the story and of that new reading being such as to be able to read me as reader,[4] extending my horizons and

---

2. Only subsequent to the decision to focus on this text did I discover that the parallel Markan story of the Syro-Phoenician woman provided the focus for E. Schüssler Fiorenza's *But She Said: Feminist Practices of Biblical Interpretation* (Boston: Beacon, 1992). Her text will provide a significant dialogue partner, given the commitment to critical, feminist biblical interpretation that we share. Our different social locations will, however, give rise to variously nuanced readings.

3. I have offered an extensive reading of this text in *Towards a Feminist Critical Reading of the Gospel according to Matthew* (Berlin: de Gruyter, 1991) 96–118, 217–51.

4. M. C. Parsons ("What's 'Literary' about Literary Aspects of the Gospels and Acts?"

particularly my feminist horizons still further. I was excited, therefore, at the prospect of rereading a very familiar story in the context of a project whose focus is that of social location and biblical interpretation.

In light of that focus, the movement of this essay will proceed from an initial explication in more specific detail of the particular social location and reading communities that provide the context for the text that follows. This will be brought into dialogue with the theoretical framework that gives shape to the reading, and the two will then provide the arena in which the dance of interpretation can take place. I use the metaphor of dance explicitly to describe the experience of interpretation that has captured me in the undertaking of this task and that I find most adequately articulated by Elisabeth Schüssler Fiorenza when she seeks to describe "the hermeneutical steps and rhetorical moves of a feminist critical hermeneutic and rhetoric of liberation":

> These steps are not simply linear and sequential, like the steps of a staircase, rather, like steps in a dance, they move backward and forward, encircle, repeat, and move ahead once more. The metaphor of movement and dance suggests that feminism is not defined by a core essence and substance but is embodied as a movement engendering change and transformation.[5]

Reading from This Site

Within the introduction, various aspects of my particular social location have emerged. Here, I shall seek to articulate simply and briefly those aspects of that location that I believe have consciously shaped my reading of the Canaanite woman's story. As an Australian woman of Anglo-Irish origin who is affiliated with one of the mainstream Christian traditions, I am, on the one hand, a participant in the dominant female culture of our nation. As female, however, I experience the exclusionary practices and ideologies that characterize both the society and the church to which I belong. Involvement in the women's movement in Australia during the past six years has brought an awareness of the many voices that speak of Australian women's oppression, liberation, feminism, religion, sexuality, and

---

SBL 1992 Seminar Papers [ed. E. H. Lovering; Atlanta: Scholars Press, 1992] 20) proposes that within what he calls a cultural-literary analysis "the critic must offer perceptive readings of the reader and his or her social location." This transformative aspect of the interpretive task is likewise addressed by S. M. Schneiders, albeit using different terminology (*The Revelatory Text: Interpreting the New Testament as Sacred Scripture* [San Francisco: Harper, 1991] 157–79).

5. Schüssler Fiorenza, *But She Said*, 9.

every aspect of their experience.[6] I cannot speak with all of these voices, and therefore my reading in the context of our varied lives makes no claim to universalism or feminism as a unilateral construct. I am concerned with how we as a human community hear the discourses that arise from our varied locations. The particular focus for this concern is our hearing these varied discourses within Australian feminism so as to expand our human horizons together as we seek to shape a new, transformed future for women in this land.

This reading is also informed by my participation in a variety of reading communities.[7] The first is that of feminist critical theorists, both national and global, and this intersects in some measure with the second, that of feminist biblical scholars. The third is the community of Christian women and men who have experienced both the biblical text and its interpretation within the context of their Christian churches as oppressive and who seek for ways in which that text may function, within communities of emancipatory praxis, as revelatory.[8]

From this location, I seek to undertake a twofold task. On the one hand, I will bring to light those ideologies of oppression—ideologies based not only on gender but also on gender linked to ethnicity, class, and religious affiliation—that are encoded in the Matthean text itself. These ideologies have functioned to shape value systems in the originating social locations of the text, and they have often been validated by its history of interpretation. They also serve to authenticate current ethical and cultural perspectives that are exclusive.[9] On the other hand, a reading against the grain of the text will seek to restore the centrality of the female character both to the particular story of the Canaanite woman and to the Matthean story as a whole. It will also go beyond the text to examine its rhetorical function within a feminist critical reconstruction of early Christianity.[10] This twofold pro-

---

6. Some of these voices are captured in *National Women's Conference 1990 Proceedings* (Canberra: Write People, 1990), the written record of the first conference of the National Foundation of Australian Women.

7. Here I use "reading community" to refer not just to that from which one reads a written text like the biblical text but also to the community from which one reads life as text.

8. This brief description is informed by a wealth of critical, feminist biblical scholarship that has informed this praxis; see, for example, Schüssler Fiorenza, *But She Said;* idem, *Bread Not Stone: The Challenge of Feminist Biblical Interpretation* (Boston: Beacon, 1984); and idem, *In Memory of Her: A Feminist Theological Reconstruction of Christian Origins* (New York: Crossroad, 1983); S. Schneiders, *Revelatory Text;* and idem, *Beyond Patching: Faith and Feminism in the Catholic Church* (New York: Paulist, 1991); R. Radford Ruether, *Women-Church: Theology and Practice* (San Francisco: Harper & Row, 1985); and many others too numerous to mention here but whose contributions have been significant.

9. This stage of analysis is given various names in scholarly literature. It is the "ideological analysis" referred to by Mary Ann Tolbert in her essay "A Response from a Literary Perspective," *The Fourth Gospel from a Literary Perspective* (ed. F. F. Segovia; *Semeia* 53; Atlanta: Scholars Press, 1991) 207–10; and the "hermeneutics of suspicion" that is now standard terminology in feminist critical theory and feminist biblical interpretation.

10. Schüssler Fiorenza discusses the complexity of such a reconstruction in *But She Said,*

cess is intimately linked to an examination of the rhetorical effect of the interpretation process on the reader, not just as individual but within the reading communities or social locations already articulated.[11]

Such a multifaceted task will entail a methodology that is likewise multifaceted. The new literary criticism with a focus on both narrative strategies and reader effects will provide a foundation, uncovering as it does the meaning of the text for the contemporary reader.[12] To this will be added an interface with the social and cultural worlds of the text within which its rhetorical function can be understood, thereby seeking the meaning-effect of the text in its originating context. Evelyn R. Thibeaux notes how these two approaches can work together under the rubrics of a rhetorical criticism that, she states, "encompasses the practices of both literary criticism and social science criticism and moves each in the direction of the other."[13] A feminist, critical, biblical and theological hermeneutics, which will inform all stages of the employment of this multifaceted method, will make it possible to take into account the ideological dimensions of textual meanings.

Reading Matthew 15:21-28

Text in Narrative Context—A Faint Whisper Is Heard

A significant aspect of the narrative approach to a text is its attention to the entire narrative as a unit and each pericope within that context. Initial attention will therefore be given to key characteristics of the unfolding narrative in order to situate the story of the Canaanite woman.

The reader of the Matthean narrative is invited from the outset into a symbolic universe that is androcentric, insofar as the males in Jesus' patrilineage are designated as key progenitors and the women in that lineage are rendered virtually invisible (Matt 1:1-17). The narrative focus on Jesus further underscores this perspective. Read in a different key, however, and against the grain of the androcentric register, the naming of the four women

---

80–101. At this stage too we unwrap our "dusty sisters," as Maitland's poem suggests, and line them up for our full view.

11. Schneiders (*Revelatory Text,* 196) calls this "the transforming effect on the reader of the interpretation process itself." This stage is likewise reflected in Maitland's poem. It is the "unwrapping" of ourselves as the text reads us enabling us to discover "rooms we never guessed at."

12. This is the formalist approach, which is text-centered and seeks the meaning inherent in the linguistic structures of the text. See M. A. Powell, *What Is Narrative Criticism?* (Guides to Biblical Scholarship; Minneapolis: Fortress, 1990).

13. E. R. Thibeaux, " 'Known to Be a Sinner': The Narrative Rhetoric of Luke 7:36-50" (paper presented to the Rhetoric and the New Testament Section at the 1992 SBL annual meeting) 3.

and Mary in the genealogy provides clues to the feminist reader regarding both the ethnic and the gender otherness surrounding the female in the symbolic universe that the narrative creates.[14] The significance of this otherness from the alternative perspective is its decentering of the androcentric perspective and patriarchal structures encoded in the text.[15]

Guided by these clues, the reader recognizes the significant absence of female characters and symbolism from the remainder of the prologue (1:1—4:17).[16] This reader is also aware of the androcentric perspective that characterizes the Sermon on the Mount (vv. 5-7), the beginning of Jesus' preaching of the *basileia*. As that preaching continues through the miracle narrative (vv. 8-9) and the missionary sermon (v. 10), the patriarchal structures encoded in the text and the androcentric perspective are further developed and emphasized, while the presence of three female characters, recipients of Jesus' healing ministry, continues the decentering function (8:14-15; 9:18-26). The appearance in the narrative of Peter's mother-in-law, the woman with the hemorrhage, and the ruler's daughter advances the subplot of female participation in the Jesus story and ministry, despite the fact that each is unnamed and two are introduced by way of their enmeshment in patriarchal family structures. From the naming and yet silencing of women in the prologue, the story moves to Jesus' calling of a woman to *basileia* ministry and her silent yet active response. She arose and she served, the verb used being *diakonein,* which in the early Christian communities designated ministry (8:14-15).[17] The woman with the hemorrhage of Matt 9:20-22 symbolizes the *basileia* when she crosses social boundaries, approaching Jesus from behind and initiating her own healing. The first explicitly female point of view is heard by the reader when this woman says to herself: "If I only touch his cloak, I will be made well" (9:21). It is this perspective that Jesus names "faith" (9:22).

As the reader moves into the narrative continuation of the Galilean ministry (11:1-16:20), the *basileia,* while linguistically male-centered, has been

---

14. Reference to Rahab, a Canaanite (1:5), and to Ruth, the Moabite (1:5), links ethnic to gender otherness in the genealogy. Scholars also discuss the ethnic origins of both Tamar (1:3) and Bathsheba (1:6), but there is less textual evidence in each case to support a claim of "foreigner."

15. I have treated this in detail in *Towards a Feminist Critical Reading,* 60–76, 155–76. See also J. Capel Anderson, "Mary's Difference: Gender and Patriarchy in the Birth Narratives," *Journal of Religion* 67 (1987) 183–202; J. P. Heil, "The Narrative Roles of the Women in Matthew's Genealogy," *Biblica* 72 (1991) 538–45; and J. Schaberg, *The Illegitimacy of Jesus: A Feminist Theological Interpretation of the Infancy Narratives* (San Francisco: Harper & Row, 1987) 20–77.

16. The presence of Mary in the birth narrative (1:18-25) and the mention of her with the child in the narrative that follows (2:11, 13, 14, 21) continue the decentering process, as does the female symbolism in 2:18. It is, however, but a faint whisper within the dominant key of patriarchy and androcentrism.

17. This aspect of the story has been developed in *Towards a Feminist Critical Reading,* 181–82. I have demonstrated there that the form of this story (8:14-15) parallels that of the call of Levi (Matt 9:9), which in turn is typical of the vocation/call story type.

developed narratively in confrontation with the established order, which was patriarchal and hierarchical.[18] The symbolic power of this confrontation continues within this section of the narrative in which the story of the Canaanite woman is located. Initially, the male Jesus is identified with Sophia/Wisdom, who is personified as female in the Hebrew Scriptures (11:1-19, especially v. 19). This identification may serve to decenter an androcentric reading that valorizes the masculinity of Jesus.[19] B. Rod Doyle in fact suggests that Matt 11:1—14:13a, as a narrative unit, is characterized by Wisdom and 14:13b—16:12 by the theme of bread.[20] Schüssler Fiorenza, on the other hand, links the imagery of Sophia with that of giving the bread of understanding and hence carries the imagery of Jesus-Sophia into the "bread section" in which the story of the Canaanite woman is found.[21]

The story, in fact, is placed narratively at the turning point of a chiastic structure that can be diagrammed thus:

A   The feeding of five thousand (14:13-21)
     + a disciple's little faith (14:28-33)

B   Jesus heals many (14:34-36)
     The tradition of the elders (15:1-20)

C   The Canaanite woman (15:21-28)

B'   Jesus heals many (15:29-31)

A'   The feeding of four thousand (15:32-39)
     + the disciples' little faith (16:5-12)

The theme of bread characterizes A, C, and A1, and it is linked to that of healing in B, B1, and C. The two come together in the story of the woman who pleads for healing for her daughter and who claims the crumbs of bread that fall from the patriarchal table. When the reader considers the inclusive call of Jesus-Sophia offered in 11:28—"Come to me, *all* you that are weary and are carrying heavy burdens, and I will give you rest"—together

---

18. S. Humphries-Brooks ("Indicators of Social Organization and Status in Matthew's Gospel," *SBL 1991 Seminar Papers* [ed. E. H. Lovering; Atlanta: Scholars Press, 1991] 45) claims that the narrative form is chosen because it is only through "emplotment" that this confrontation can be seen clearly. As a result, he claims that the text "ultimately constructs an audience aligned with the kingdom of heaven and thereby able to subject all characters in the story to evaluation by the ethics and politics of that kingdom." Schüssler Fiorenza (*But She Said,* 105–32) provides an excellent analysis of patriarchy both ancient and modern and its hierarchical nature.

19. While this interpretive possibility may be developed, it should also be noted that the symbolic link may function to masculinize the wisdom symbol, furthering the androcentric symbolic universe of the text.

20. B. R. Doyle, "Matthew's Intention as Discerned by His Structure," *Revue biblique 95* (1988) 42–45.

21. Schüssler Fiorenza, *But She Said,* 13.

with the feeding of men, women, and children with bread (14:21) and the healing of *all* that were sick in Gennesaret (14:34-35), the confrontation with the Canaanite woman set in the context of confrontation with the Pharisees and scribes likewise confronts the reader.

Text and Socio-Cultural Context: The Voice Bursts Forth as Shout

Read according to the androcentric perspective that characterizes the dominant Matthean narrative to this point, the story of the Canaanite woman is framed by references to Jesus. It opens with his withdrawal to the district of Tyre and Sidon (v. 21) and closes with his affirmation of the woman's faith (v. 28). Jesus is the master, or *kyrios,* with his disciples. As Schüssler Fiorenza claims: "Read in a *kyriocentric,* that is, master-centered, frame the story functions as one more variation of woman's story as outsider in the symbolic worlds and social constructions of male discourse."[22] The development of the text highlights even further the reasons why such a reading has dominated the history of interpretation of this text and continues to do so. When Jesus' withdrawal is interrupted by the heartrending cry of a Canaanite woman seeking healing for her daughter, Jesus fails to answer—"But he did not answer her at all" (v. 23). This response is totally uncharacteristic of Jesus' responses to similar requests, whether made by a Roman centurion seeking healing for his servant (Matt 8:6) or by the two Jewish blind men who cry out in the same way as the Canaanite woman (9:27).[23] The reader is given pause to think that whatever could give rise to such an extraordinary response must, in its own turn, be extraordinary. In the narrative to this point, the voice of a woman has not been heard, and yet here that voice is raised in public in the presence of males. Jesus is challenged to go beyond his offering of the fruits of the *basileia* to women as well as men (Matthew 8–9); he is challenged to remove gender boundaries so that women can participate in the public arena with men.

The intervention of the disciples, who in the androcentric world of the dominant narrative are characterized as male, further underlines the threat posed by the woman's appearance in a gender-structured world. They seek her dismissal because she is "shouting after us" (v. 23b). Their explanation may thus link the woman's shouting to women's ritual or cultic activity.[24] They draw forth a response to the woman's request from Jesus, but it is a particularist statement—"I was sent only to the lost sheep of the house of Israel" (v. 24; cf. 10:6)—that simply reiterates their desire to be rid of

---

22. Ibid., 12.
23. For a study of the rhetorical strategy of repetition that links the healing of the blind men with the Canaanite woman's story, see J. Capel Anderson, "Double and Triple Stories: The Implied Reader and Redundancy in Matthew," *Reader Response Approaches to Biblical and Secular Texts* (ed. R. Detweiler; *Semeia* 31; Atlanta: Scholars Press, 1985) 71–89.
24. This will receive further treatment below in relation to the woman.

the woman. Here, however, gender otherness has been extended to include ethnic otherness, doubly marginalizing the woman in a world whose center is characterized by maleness and Jewish ethnicity.

In a climactic rebuff following the woman's repeated call for help (v. 25), Jesus answers with the insulting parabolic saying, "It is not fair to take the children's food [those who belong in the household of the *kyrios* or male householder] and throw it to the dogs [those on the periphery, outside the house of the master]" (v. 26). In this response the twofold challenge offered to Jesus by the woman's cries is highlighted. The reference to "dogs" is not just a gentile slur but also a possible reference to those not learned in the Torah, women being particularly included in this group.[25] Marla J. Selvidge also draws attention to the fact that in some of the male-centered cults of the Greco-Roman world, especially that of Hercules, women and dogs were excluded.[26] Jesus' words, therefore, contain a further hint of the ritual or cultic dimensions in this story.

In the unfolding of this story, therefore, Jesus is treated as representative of the kyriocentric structures and discourse that characterize the Matthean narrative. He symbolizes that power that is vested in males and limited to the ethnic group that the most powerful males represent. It is a power that is divinely sanctioned within the androcentric narrative and that therefore leads to interpretations that seek to rescue Jesus from the ethnic and gender biases evident in the story. One such interpretation is that Jesus is testing the woman's faith.[27] This is the most commonly held interpretive perspective that I have heard among Christians, even those seeking communities of emancipatory interpretation and praxis, and it finds support within critical biblical scholarship.[28]

This androcentric register of the Canaanite woman's story, which renders her marginalized, underscores emphatically the power of male-centered discourse in general. This is a power that we experience in our Australian ethos in all the major arenas of public discourse—politics, science, the arts, sports, to name a few—so that even when a female voice is raised, as it is in this story, it is not heard or is marginalized by virtue of the power of the center to which it does not belong.[29] The effect of such discourse when it combines gender and race superiority is poignantly demonstrated in a short

---

25. For a discussion of the nuancing of this possible interpretation, see *Towards a Feminist Critical Reading*, 239–40.

26. M. J. Selvidge, *Woman, Cult, and Miracle Recital: A Redactional Critical Investigation of Mark 5:24-34* (Lewisburg, Pa.: Bucknell Univ. Press, 1990) 78.

27. Schüssler Fiorenza (*But She Said*, 161) provides further examples.

28. The most recent example of this interpretation is found in W. D. Davies and D. C. Allison, *A Critical and Exegetical Commentary on the Gospel according to Saint Matthew* (2 vols.; Edinburgh: T & T Clark, 1991) 2:549–50.

29. This was demonstrated most powerfully by students in a women's studies course as they shared the results of a week's media watch. It was also evident in recent Australian cabinet appointments in the newly elected federal government when only three women were given ministerial portfolios.

extract from the novel *My Place* by the Australian Aboriginal novelist and artist Sally Morgan. Toward the end of her story, when her grandmother Nan is dying, Sally describes a conversation between them in the context of her massaging Nan's aching back:

> "Ooh, that's good, Sally," she murmured after a while. As I continued to rub, she let out a deep sigh and then said slowly, "You know, Sal...all my life, I been treated rotten, real rotten. Nobody's cared if I've looked pretty. I been treated like a beast. Just like a beast of the field. And now, here I am...old. Just a dirty old blackfella."
>
> I don't know how long it was before I answered her. My heart felt cut in half. I could actually see a beast in a field. A work animal, nothing more.
>
> "You're not to talk about yourself like that," I finally replied in a controlled voice. "You're my grandmother and I won't have you talk like that. The whole family loves you. We'd do anything for you."
>
> There was no reply. How hollow my words sounded. How empty and limited. Would anything I said ever help?[30]

The virtual immutability of this male-centered discourse, evident in the grassroots interpretation of our Gospel text and in the history of its interpretation, demonstrates the effect of the power given to such discourse when sacralized or theologized. The reader's incorporation of the androcentric perspective of the text into a theology of Jesus fails to allow the ethic and the politics of the *basileia* to evaluate the character Jesus of the Matthean narrative.[31] Such a discovery alerts the attentive reader to the myriads of ways in which the male discourse of the biblical and theological traditions has likewise been prevented from a similar evaluation in light of the inclusive ethic and politics of the *basileia*. These traditions have therefore been continually drawn upon to support exclusive practices regarding ordination and liturgical participation of women, ministry and mission, decision making, and theologizing—to name just those that the story of the Canaanite woman challenges.

Amy-Jill Levine notes two characteristics of the narrative statement describing Jesus' introduction to this scene that may, however, point to a possible *basileia* story. Jesus withdraws or separates himself not just from the ethnic center of Galilee to the periphery depicted by Tyre and Sidon but also from the political agenda of the Pharisees and Herodians. Levine sees this not just as a movement from center to periphery but also as revealing an interest in mobility rather than the stasis that characterizes the members of the establishment, whom she says "remain in cities, palaces, and syna-

---

30. S. Morgan, *My Place* (Freemantle, Australia: Freemantle Arts Centre Press, 1987) 352.
31. See n. 18 above.

gogues."[32] It is there, on the periphery, that Jesus can receive the challenge of the *basileia*. This is further emphasized when the story is placed in context. In a confrontation with the "Pharisees and scribes" regarding tradition and traditional practices, Jesus offers the challenge: "For the sake of your tradition, you have made void the word of God,...teaching as doctrines human precepts" (15:6, 9b).

As our analysis has shown, however, Jesus' responses to the woman represent the center with its ethnic and gender boundaries, the human precepts. It is only the insistent and carefully crafted retort that the woman gives to Jesus' final rebuff that moves him to the periphery where he can, in fact, cut through those boundaries. It is here—in the woman's refusal to be silenced and her claim on the power of the *basileia*—that he recognizes a more expansive vision of that *basileia*. As Jesus is drawn into debate with the woman, who uses his discourse rather than her own but uses it finally (v. 27) against him, he is in fact changed. Jesus' point of view in this story as a whole is aligned neither with that of the *basileia* vision nor with that which the implied author has presented as the divine point of view in 12:18-21, but through the confrontation with this woman it moves into alignment with both. Human traditions of ethnic and gender specificity are overcome.

Such a reading of the Jesus story is in tension with the androcentric perspective, already acknowledged, that places Jesus always at the center. It also creates a similar tension for the reader, inviting her or him beyond the androcentric discourses and patriarchal structures that characterize society and Christian community, beyond the establishment of church and theological college, to hear the voice of those marginalized particularly because of gender, but to hear them in their ethnic specificity together with the religious and cultural differences that often characterize this specificity. The following words of Sennie Masian addressed to women at the 1990 National Women's Conference challenge us to hear the voices of Filipino women in Australia who now number approximately sixty-five thousand:

> It is a pity you never read, see or hear about them. It's twice a pity, and you are aware of this, that the majority of the people here in Australia are still ignorant of the existence of the career-oriented, skilful and professional Filipino women. They, as always, are collectively and sensationally labelled as the domesticated, low-status mail-order brides, often referred to with scorn and stigmatized;

---

32. A.-J. Levine, *The Social and Ethnic Dimensions of Matthean Salvation History* (Studies in the Bible and Early Christianity 14; Lewiston, N.J.: Edwin Mellen Press, 1988) 134–35. I wish to acknowledge my gratitude to Levine, who read an earlier draft of this essay and pointed out to me the anti-Semitism that appeared in my text. This too was a significant part of the process of this essay extending my feminist perspective as I seek to move beyond all forms of patriarchy.

categorized as poor, stereotyped as uneducated, parochial village people—and sometimes pigeonholed as prostitutes if unclassified in the above categories.[33]

Since it is on the margins that a new voice is heard, our attention shifts to the woman in the Matthean story. The introduction of the woman (v. 22) with the phrase "and behold," the Matthean focalizer, shifts the reader's attention from Jesus to her. She is to be the protagonist in the narrative, and indeed this is so if one recognizes that she initiates each movement in the story, each moment in the dialogue or debate that follows. Jesus, on the other hand, is characterized solely as respondent, as is indicated by the fourfold use of the verb "to answer" in relation to him (vv. 23, 24, 26, 28). It is, therefore, a story of the woman; it is her-story, a significant movement in the subplot of female characterization, and her voice needs to be heard above the noise of the dominant narrative.

She is not introduced into the narrative by her name, although later tradition will identify her as Justa,[34] but is identified as *Canaanite* and *woman*, two factors that, according to the patriarchal structures of early Christianity with their interlocking categories of discrimination encoded in the text, render her marginalized. Indeed, she is outsider or "other" because of her gender, her ethnicity, and her religious designation.[35] She is symbolic of and alerts the reader to the multilayered discrimination that women suffer in patriarchal and/or androcentric societies, whatever the particular manifestation of those characteristics in a given society or subsection of that society.[36]

She also "came out" (v. 22) from the region, locating both the story and the woman herself in the public arena, outside the confines of patriarchal domesticity. She is, therefore, symbolic of so many women today across the globe who refuse to be coerced by the politics of submission and who stand on the margins or in the new centers that women are creating in the public arena, engaged in transformative activity on behalf of women and on behalf of humanity.

It is from this position that woman's voice is heard as it is in the biblical story. The Canaanite woman's voice breaks into the male discourse just as her presence has broken into the male world of Jesus and the presumably

---

33. S. Masian, "The Profile of Filipino Woman—Not Read, Seen or Heard," *National Women's Conference 1990 Proceedings*, 183.

34. Later tradition, namely, the third- and fourth-century Pseudo-Clementine homilies, will identify as "Justa," as Schüssler Fiorenza notes (*But She Said*, 100).

35. The term "Canaanite" is indeed anachronistic, and its use would seem to be symbolic. G. R. O'Day ("Surprised by Faith: Jesus and the Canaanite Woman," *Listening* 24 [1989] 291) argues that this renders the woman Jesus' enemy, as her ancestors were Israel's enemies. This we can then nuance politically, ethnically, and religiously.

36. See R. Kelly, "Aboriginal Women's Role in Society," *Conference Proceedings*, 160–61.

male disciples.[37] The verb used to describe her, "to cry out," and the activity to which it points had strong ritual or cultic connotations, namely, the sacred cries of the female devotees of Dionysus, Cybele, or Isis.[38] In such cultic settings, women who were silenced and hidden by domesticity and the patriarchal family structure had a voice. Hers is, therefore, a public voice, and it is the first female voice heard in the narrative.

According to the cultural codes of the first-century Mediterranean world that are encoded in the text, this woman is "out of place." She is not, according to the narrative, accompanying male relatives and therefore is like a woman who is divorced or widowed. She is seen as sexually aggressive and hence dangerous.[39] She is not on the inside, the female space, but enters the story outside, in the public arena, the male space. The danger that her presence represents is perhaps lessened since the relationship implied by the story is that of supplicant to miracle worker. She comes seeking mercy. The ambiguity that our contemporary reading evokes is perhaps reminiscent of the ambiguity and tension that her presence in the story evoked for the first-century audience. For both reading communities, the opening of the story has certainly confronted gender codes as these operate religiously, culturally, and ethnically and prepared for the story of confrontation that is to follow. Jesus, the man of honor, withdraws from the center, the place where that honor would be less threatened, to the periphery, a place of tension and ambiguity, and there encounters a woman who is "out of place," a threat to that honor. The story is set for cultural ethnic and gender confrontation, a context according to the Gospel narrative in which a new understanding of God's dream for humanity is possible.

The extraordinary aspect of this story, for the reader, whether first-century or twentieth-century, is the words given to the woman: "Have mercy on me, Lord, Son of David; my daughter is tormented by a demon" (15:22). At a first level of reading, her plea—"Have mercy on me"— might be seen simply as the request of a supplicant seeking favor. When it is joined, however, to the confessional titles Kyrios (Lord) and Son of David, even those simple words of petition take on a different hue. If we look beyond this first plea to its repetition in verse 25, we find similar words: "Kyrios/Lord, help me." Even the final ironic twist that the woman

---

37. At this point in the narrative, only twelve males have been named disciples (10:1-4), although, as already indicated, the narrative contains a vocation story of a woman, Peter's mother-in-law (8:14-15), suggesting that the group following Jesus may be more inclusive than twelve men.

38. C. C. Kroeger, "A Classicist Looks at the Difficult Passages," *Perspectives on Feminist Hermeneutics* (Occasional Papers 10; ed. G. Gerber Koontz and W. Swartley; Elkhart, Ind.: Institute of Mennonite Studies, 1987) 14. This is developed further by R. and C. Kroeger, "An Inquiry into Evidence of Maenadism in the Corinthian Congregation," *SBL 1978 Seminar Papers* (ed. P. J. Achtemeier; Missoula, Mont.: Scholars Press, 1978) 331–38.

39. B. J. Malina, *The New Testament World: Insights from Cultural Anthropology* (London: SCM, 1981) 42–47.

gives to Jesus' parabolic statement is preceded by the reverential, "Yes, Lord" (v. 27). The voice given to this woman in the narrative is therefore significant.

A first-century reader would recognize the intertextuality operative here. Her cry for mercy and for help is characteristic of the Psalms, especially the psalms of lament, according to Gail O'Day's analysis.[40] It is the language of the religious insider. She also uses the confessional titles of the early Christian communities—Kyrios and Son of David. In seeking to understand the rhetorical effect of the woman's speech, I would agree with Schüssler Fiorenza that it cannot be historically contextualized in the life of Jesus[41] but must be located in early Christian controversy not only regarding cross-ethnic factors, as Levine describes this debate,[42] but also regarding gender.[43] The liturgical and theological language given to the woman (vv. 22 and 25), absent in the Markan account of the Syro-Phoenician (Mark 7:24-30), functioned within the house churches of the Matthean community, in their struggle surrounding the possible liturgical and theological leadership of women, to authenticate such words on the lips of a woman or to challenge a patriarchal or kyriocentric house church to such a possibility. If much of this shaping of the tradition took place during the oral traditioning process within the Matthean house churches, women may still have been significantly involved even if excluded from the final scribal role, as Antoinette Clark Wire argues.[44]

While, on the one hand, this story functioned rhetorically to challenge the community to or to authenticate an already existing *basileia* vision that was inclusive in terms of both ethnicity and gender, it had the effect, on the other hand, of underpinning a religious language system that was kyriocentric, an element in a power structure that was androcentric and hierarchical.[45] Schüssler Fiorenza demonstrates how this power oper-

---

40. For examples of the first plea in the Psalms, see Pss 6:3; 9:14; 26:7; 30:10; 40:5, 11; 55:2; 85:3; 122:3; for the second, Pss 43:27; 69:6; 78:9; 108:26; and 118:86. O'Day ("Surprised by Faith," 294–98) develops this intertextuality in relation to psalms of lament.

41. Schüssler Fiorenza, *But She Said,* 162; see also idem, *In Memory of Her,* 138.

42. Levine, *Social and Ethnic Dimensions,* 132 and elsewhere.

43. The significance of the gender question in the shaping of this story in the Matthean narrative is central to my analysis of it; see n. 3, above.

44. A. Clark Wire, "Gender Roles in a Scribal Community," *Social History of the Matthean Community: Cross-Disciplinary Approaches* (ed. D. L. Balch; Minneapolis: Fortress Press, 1991) 87–121. As the title of Wire's article indicates, she locates the compilation of the Matthean Gospel in a scribal community, but I would argue that she does not allow for sufficient oral traditioning within the Matthean communities, which enabled the traditions strongly influenced and shaped by women to significantly inform the final narrative. I would agree with her, however, that these traditions are finally refracted through the lenses of those performing the scribal task (see esp. 121).

45. Schüssler Fiorenza (*But She Said,* 12) introduces this term "kyriocentric," or master-centered, which describes well the axes of power that function within patriarchy. I find it particularly helpful in describing the religious language used by the early Christians to image Jesus and the rhetorical effect of that language.

ates "not only along the axis of gender but also along those of race, class, culture, and religion" or "interlocking systems of oppression."[46] It is a system of dominant power or power-over, and it is male-centered. As a result of the use of the language that characterized this system within early Christian traditioning, especially in relation to Jesus and divinity, the overarching religious and political system remained kyriocentric. Women's participation in certain emancipatory praxis was, therefore, always within a context that was patriarchal. The Gospel text that gave voice to the developing theological framework functioned to maintain this ideological structure.

As the text had a two-edged rhetorical function within early Christianity, it has a two-edged effect today, especially when the focus is on the woman's words in the dialogue. While feminist interpreters claim the initiative of the woman and her public voice, they struggle with the kyriocentric language and belief system that characterizes that voice. One of the most consistent struggles I have observed among those communities of feminist emancipatory praxis, or *ekklesia,* of women in which I have participated in recent years is with the imaging of Jesus, the risen one. The rejection of the Kyrios title is at the heart of this struggle.[47] It functions rhetorically for many women and some men as a powerful tool for maintaining the hierarchical and patriarchal structures and androcentric language and symbol systems operative within the Christian tradition. It functions, therefore, ideologically. Just as within the Matthean narrative alternative images, especially that of Jesus-Sophia, seek to decenter the dominant patriarchal and androcentric imagery, so too within our communities of faith, as they seek that emancipatory praxis that is supported by a *basileia* story with Jesus as its chief protagonist, images of liberation, especially female images, will need to be used and used abundantly.[48]

The Canaanite woman's request for the healing of her daughter who is severely demon-possessed—a request with which verse 22, the verse we have been considering, comes to an end—introduces another dimension into the symbolic universe of the narrative, namely, that of mother and daughter. It is, however, a relationship that in this story is shattered by the demonic, and it is from this that the mother seeks and obtains liberation.

---

46. Ibid., 123. See the entire chapter (103–32), in which Schüssler Fiorenza examines the structures of patriarchy under the name of the woman of our story, Justa. She titles the chapter "To Speak in Public: A Feminist Political Hermeneutics," inspired no doubt by the courageous woman of the Matthean story who dares to speak in public.

47. This is not a universal claim since the title may function in terms of emancipation within some cultural contexts. In this regard, see especially S. Thistlethwaite's account (*Sex, Race, and God: Christian Feminism in Black and White* [New York: Crossroad, 1989] 116) of the response of African American Christian women to the changing of that title in the translation project, *An Inclusive Language Lectionary.*

48. E. A. Johnson (*She Who Is: The Mystery of God in Feminist Theological Discourse* [New York: Crossroad, 1992] 56–57) advocates such a use of images in order to redress the imbalance in our imaging of God and Jesus. She also explores the alternative imaging of Jesus (150–69).

This aspect of the story has received little attention in the literature perhaps as a result of its secondary effect within the text.[49] It is this aspect of the story, however, that may have more significant rhetorical potential within different reading communities, two of which I will draw attention to below.

The first is that of feminist theorists who search for a symbolic system or a "female imaginary." Margaret Whitford, commenting on the work of Luce Irigaray, says of this transformation of the symbolic order with which Irigaray is concerned: "...The possibility of a female imaginary...would necessitate images or representations of women in which women could recognize themselves, or with which women could identify."[50] Later in the same article, Whitford translates Irigaray's own words, which make this even more explicit, especially in relation to our story: "To whomever is concerned today with social justice, I propose putting up in every public place images representing the (natural and spiritual) mother-daughter couple....Such representations are absent from public and religious sites."[51] She herself recognizes as do other feminist theorists that one of the problems that we face is that such images make very little difference in a society that accords so little subjectivity to the female. This is what we have seen happen as the image of the Canaanite mother and daughter vanishes behind the veil of an androcentric narrative. If, however, we bring them to light in a changing symbolic order, their story may indeed function to enhance the transformation process itself.

That this transformation process is indeed underway is demonstrated by the reflections of a woman who participated in a short course exploring a feminist reading of the Matthean Gospel. I share what she has written as illustration of the rhetorical function of this story within a different social location, that of the *ekklesia* of women seeking interpretations of biblical texts that function to liberate.

> I wrote this reflection having in mind the need for love and healing in mothers who have hurt their children. Particularly in mind were women who struggle daily to cope with the burden of caring for a child who is handicapped or who has a prolonged illness. As I sat with Matthew's account of the Canaanite women her first words to Jesus ("Have mercy on me....Lord, help me") stood apart from her statement about her daughter's condition in much the same way that nervous broken voices on my phone betray dark fears and shame as they go on to describe the medical condition of their

---

49. The woman's requests use the word "me," focusing attention on herself and her need. The request for the healing of her daughter occurs at the end of her opening request and receives no apparent attention in the unfolding narrative until the final narrative comment stating that her daughter has been healed (v. 28).

50. M. Whitford, "Irigaray's Body Symbolic," *Hypatia* 6/3 (1991) 97.

51. Ibid., 98.

babies. I longed to retrieve something of the power of that desperate Canaanite woman for the mothers sitting before images of serene Madonnas hearing the virtues of motherhood extolled and hating themselves more.

She could not stop the crying, terrible crying of the baby. Day after day, night after night it went on. Nothing comforted her for long... not feeding, not cuddling, not rocking, not singing—none of these motherly things comforted as they should.

Of course she loved her baby daughter with all a mother's passion, but in a deep crevice of her being she began to hate her too. She began to hate the tiny screaming thing who placed such small merit on all her loving efforts to comfort her.

Once or twice, after a night feed, she dropped her quite roughly in her cot; now and then, as she changed a nappy, she almost slapped the buttocks of the tiny screaming thing. Afterwards she always regretted her roughness and tried to push the memory of it far away—far into the crevice of her being where she began to hate herself... to really loathe the terrible mother of the tiny screaming thing.

"Help me O God," she cried. "Help me, my baby is always crying. I can't stand the screaming that possesses her. I no longer trust myself to hold my daughter gently and to treat her with tenderness." "Have mercy on me God," she cried, "as You see into this deep crevice of my being. Forgive this terrible mother who hurts her baby. Remember the Canaanite woman long ago? She dared to hope for your mercy, she was desperate for your help. She knew the agony of being a mother like me. Great indeed was her faith, but great also must have been her need." The tiny thing began screaming again, the terrible mother wept.

"Lord, help me," she cried, "remember the Canaanite woman, help me too."[52]

Returning to the text, I would draw attention to verse 27, in which the woman ironically turns Jesus' words and the perspective they represent upside down. So clever and so effective is her response that the reader is left to wonder if the exchange, rather than evoking the miracle worker/supplicant relationship as hinted at earlier, alternatively suggests the challenge-riposte within the honor system. The exchange between Jesus and the Canaanite woman contains all the elements of the challenge-riposte, with verse 27 being climactic.[53] In this respect, however, the text creates extraordinary

---

52. Presented by J. Frazer Cosgrove as part of a project, in her own words, "creatively appropriating the texts considered in the theological, liturgical and spiritual lives of the contemporary Christian community."

53. B. J. Malina and J. H. Neyrey ("Honor and Shame in Luke-Acts: Pivotal Values of the Mediterranean World," *The Social World of Luke-Acts: Models for Interpretation* [ed.

tension for the reader, since one significant rule has been violated in presenting the story in such a way: only equals can play. As Bruce J. Malina and Jerome H. Neyrey specify, "Thus an inferior on the ladder of social standing, power, and sexual status does not have enough honor to resent the affront of a superior. On the other side, a superior's honor is simply not committed or engaged by an inferior's affront."[54]

While the earlier reactions of Jesus represent the brushing aside of the challenge of an inferior, his response to the woman in verse 28 acknowledges and validates her challenge: "Woman, great is your faith! Let it be done for you *as you wish.*" Jesus' honor has been preserved as he remains faithful to the *basileia* vision that he preaches. The woman, however, acquires honor beyond the cultural limitations placed on her by her gender. As such, she provides a significant model not only for first-century Matthean community women but also for women today. Her preparedness to continue to stand against the system of injustice and to use its language and its structures against it to bring about transformation can prove symbolic for women today, especially as we encounter the same wall of resistance that she knew.

At this point in the interpretive process, however, I also find myself being read by the limitations of the text and its symbolics, by the limitations of our hermeneutics and rhetorics, no matter how clearly we define them. As the Matthean story has been constructed, the only discourse available to the woman is the male discourse. While she is the initiator of the action leading to the healing of her daughter, the source of that healing is within the kyriocentric system that Jesus represents. While her story stands within the Matthean story as deconstructive and while she can function for contemporary Christian women as foremother or foresister in our work of deconstruction, that is not sufficient. I am reminded here of the words of Audre Lorde, which have been used by women from so many fields of feminist labors:

> For the master's tools will never dismantle the master's house. They may allow us temporarily to beat him at his own game, but they will never enable us to bring about genuine change. And this fact is only threatening to those women who still define the master's house as their only source of support.[55]

J. H. Neyrey; Peabody, Mass.: Hendrickson, 1991] 29–32) set out three phases of this type of social interaction: challenge, perception, and reaction. They also list its typical elements as claim, challenge, riposte, and public verdict. In reading their explanation, one could see very readily how the interaction in the story of Matt 15:21-28 could well belong to this particular code of the first-century cultural world.

54. Ibid., 30.

55. A. Lorde, *Sister Outsider,* quoted in E. A. Meese, *Crossing the Double-Cross: The Practice of Feminist Criticism* (Chapel Hill: Univ. of North Carolina Press, 1986), 70.

We need, therefore, not only our old stories and our old stories remembered but also new stories, stories that will construct "woman" differently. It is here that Justa challenges me as feminist reader to leap beyond the confines of her story to claim a new discourse, new images, to dialogue with new sources of power, sources that emerge from communities of emancipatory praxis seeking to move beyond patriarchy. It is in these circles that old stories are told anew[56] and that new stories find a voice, stories that cross religious and ethnic boundaries.[57] She challenges us to come into dialogue with women working in so many other disciplines, so that together we may discover the female symbolic that has so long been denied us.[58] As her daughters, healed of the demon of patriarchy, we may tell the story or the stories that will empower us for life beyond patriarchy and androcentrism, for life that, in our present, seems but a dream.

A first step in the new discourse is the imaginative reconstruction of the Matthean community's traditioning of this story. Such a reconstruction will enable more of the voices of women—voices marginalized by our traditional reconstructions of the Matthean community—to be heard not just from the margins but at the center.[59]

Voices at the Center:
Feminist Reconstruction and Creative Appropriation

Our story takes us to the ancient city of Antioch, where we meet members of a number of house churches scattered around the same part of the city. The members and perhaps even the leaders met one another in the city square or the marketplace and at gatherings of leaders in the house of Ruth and Matthias, descendants of the founder of the community. Ruth

---

56. Within the *ekklesia* of women, as Schüssler Fiorenza describes it and as I have experienced it in exploring with others a feminist reading of the biblical text, we have undertaken the work of creative articulation that empowers us to tell old stories anew in a way that breaks them free of their bonds within the androcentric biblical text.

57. It is some of these stories that Meese (*Crossing*) analyses.

58. This is the type of dialogue that is now taking place between scholars in women's studies, biblical studies, and other disciplines, as we listen to one another's methods, theories, and insights across traditional disciplinary divides. It is the type of dialogue that was initiated at the Australian National Women's Conference (see "Is It Worthwhile for Women to Pour Their Energies into a Feminist Movement within Christianity? A Debate," *Conference Proceedings*, 204–14), but I would question whether the debate format offers the best possibilities for dialogue.

59. This reconstruction is informed not only by creative imagination but also by the careful redactional study of Matt 15:21-28 found in *Towards a Feminist Critical Reading*, 217–47, as well as the work of exploring this text among communities of emancipatory praxis. It takes account also of the social scientific, archaeological, and historical material available. I would like to acknowledge here the work of Australian theologian Christine Burke (*Through a Woman's Eyes: Encounters with Jesus* [Melbourne: Collins Dove, 1989]), whose reconstruction of the Syro-Phoenician woman's story (9–13) provoked me to give voice to the Matthean women whose stories I had come to know so intimately.

and Matthias were a focus of unity for the different communities, and hence they heard the stories of life in the various house churches in their city. Oftentimes they had welcomed Johannan, in whose home a number of Aramaic-speaking families met to celebrate a sacred meal and to tell the stories of Jesus, linking these stories with their ancient scriptures as the Jesus stories spoke into their present reality. The Roman official Justinian led the Greek-speaking community from a nearby neighborhood. They were a loose-knit group that felt free to explore new ways of leadership and of supportive companionship that were not as readily available to them in their civic contexts or in many of their prior religious contexts. While Justinian was the present leader of this group, that role had been undertaken in the past by Nympha, Sylvanus, and Julia. This community was particularly interested in those stories of Jesus that legitimated the breaking of socioreligious boundaries that limited their vision. Miriam was the leader of the community that had struggled with the most diversity. The community met in her house at present, but it was perhaps even a misnomer to call her the leader because the house church worked in a participative way, coming together to decide on matters of concern for the community. Greek- and Aramaic-speaking households were welcomed. Presiding at the celebration of the sacred meal and leading the community in worship and prayer were undertaken by those women and men whom the community elected for this role. Resources too were shared abundantly in this community.

One of the tasks that Ruth and Matthias were currently undertaking was a gathering together of the traditions that were especially significant among the various house churches in Antioch. On one particular day—according to our reconstruction—they called together Miriam, Justinian, and Johannan to discuss with them the story of a woman who came to Jesus asking healing for her daughter. They had heard this story told so differently in each of their communities and yet told so often that they felt it necessary to try to determine what its significance might be in their project of gathering the Antioch story of Jesus. Miriam was the first to speak because this story was particularly significant in her house church. She told it as the story of Justa, the woman of Tyre, whose granddaughter was now a member of their community. Justa had told and retold the story of her encounter with Jesus when he was in her region at a particular time when her young daughter had been ill for so long that many thought that she must have been demon-possessed. Justa was desperate, and so she called out for help to this itinerant Jew who had wandered into the area and who was being followed by such a close-knit group of women and men that he gave the appearance of being a holy one. How taken aback she was when she received this insulting rebuff: "It is not fair to take the children's food and throw it to the dogs." Justa's need, however, was greater than any humiliation she could receive, and so, led by some power even beyond her own consciousness, she quipped back: "Yet even the dogs eat the crumbs that fall from their masters' table." She remembered her own fear at the realization of what she had just said but also her experience of a new power that she had not known before, a power that would never again allow her to be put down in such a way. She remembered also the look of astonishment, recognition, and even shame that passed across the face of the Jewish holy man whom she later came to know as Jesus. He spontaneously held out his hand to her in welcome, drawing her up from her position of supplication, and he acclaimed her: "Woman, great is your faith!" Miriam acknowledged that their community had extended the saying of Jesus, "Let it be done for you as you wish," so as to highlight Jesus' recognition of what Justa had taught him, a recognition that linked her insight into wholeness with that of God whose way, whose dream, Jesus was to establish on earth.

At this point in Miriam's storytelling, Johannan interrupted, "You tell this story as if it were a story of Justa rather than Jesus. Our community is much more aware of the outrage that Jesus must have felt when confronted by this foreigner who was not only Syro-Phoenician, a veritable Canaanite according to our biblical tradition, but also female. We have it on good authority from those who knew Jesus' companions of that day that Jesus at first ignored the woman. Indeed, his stance was emphasized by those companions who begged him to send her away. Furthermore, in the story as we received it from our Hellenistic brothers and sisters in southern Syria, Jesus is reported as saying to the woman: 'I was sent only to the lost sheep of the house of Israel.' This is a very different picture of Jesus than that presented by Miriam. Jesus may have eventually given the woman what she wanted because she was shouting after them as the disciples suggested, but the story still preserves the integrity of his mission to Israel rather than to the Gentiles and the gender distinctions we hold as part of our tradition."

It was now Justinian's turn to intervene: "Johannan, we have had this conversation many times before, I know, but Jesus' own vision of his ministry was more universal than you say. This is one of our key stories, which illustrates the movement within Jesus during his lifetime enabling him to see his mission as one including us. This woman, whom we don't name and I am happy to learn her name, this woman Justa is indeed for us the foremother of the mission that includes us as Gentiles. Just as she won healing and wholeness for her daughter, so too she won it for us, her daughters and sons today. While she does not have a name in our story, she does, however, have a voice. She addresses Jesus as Kyrios and 'Son of David,' and she cries out in the language of prayer and liturgy: 'Have mercy on me' and 'Help me.' Indeed, for us, her voice echoes the voice of the women of our community who participate in the liturgical life of the community and in our theological reflection. I hadn't heard the conclusion to the story as Miriam has told it, but I can tell you, Ruth and Matthias, it will be significant in our house community, and we will add it to our telling of the story, so you would do well to include it also."

Such a reconstruction does not leave us in ancient Antioch. It returns us to contemporary Australian soil and challenges its readers in the "unwrapping" of "ourselves," as Pam Maitland imaged our process in her poem. I have been invited to shed the old skin of ethnic specificity in order to see my Australian sisters "glisten" in all their cultural, religious, and ethnic diversity. I have been challenged to discover "rooms never guessed at," rooms in which we will begin to see the female imaginary or the female symbolic that has been hidden from us. In such a room, Justa and her daughter will have their place. They have invited me within and have invited me beyond their story as I have sought to hear it, to read it in a new key.

Part Three _____

Readings from Europe

9

Gender Hermeneutics:
The Effective History of Consciousness
and the Use of Social Gender in the Gospels

_____ Lone Fatum ____

I should like to begin with a personal introduction describing, however briefly and superficially, the social location in which I work, think, and speak my mind.

First, Danish society is comparatively privileged: economically sound, politically stable, and with a high standard of education, social welfare, and health care.

Second, it is a largely homogeneous society in terms of ethnicity. Only recently have we begun to see serious problems emerging: the presence of many immigrants represents a new challenge, and racism, unfortunately, is beginning to show its ugly face in Denmark.

Third, Danish society is also still largely homogeneous with regard to religion and theology. About 90 percent of the population are members of the Church of Denmark, though for the most part passive members; as such, the Evangelical-Lutheran tradition represents more or less the official religion of Denmark.

Fourth, it should be noted that the Lutheran tradition characteristic of northern Europe in this century has developed a high intellectual tradition, in which I am rooted. Accordingly, my commitment to exegesis and New Testament hermeneutics is primarily intellectual, not spiritual. I would add, however, that I am an ordained minister in the Church of Denmark, that I have worked for a number of years as a parish pastor, and that since my university appointment I have occasionally had the opportunity of leading services.

Fifth, from an academic point of view, I was raised on existentialism. I have, like many other women of my generation, been influenced as well by political theology and, subsequently, feminist liberation theology. However, I have also become more and more aware of the dangers, from a hermeneutical point of view, of presenting contemporary political utopianism in the disguise of critical exegesis.

Finally, I prefer to define my present position as gender hermeneutics, by which I mean a critical endeavor on my part to work out ways of understanding the New Testament texts without letting myself be overpowered and oppressed by the literal meaning and historical effects of these texts. I believe this makes sense as a very Lutheran approach: we have no pope, no synod—just text. Thus, in every respect I am literally confronted with texts and constantly challenged by a particular text and its traditional impact. Therefore, I need to work out ways to deconstruct the texts as well as their historical effects in order to be able to defend and define myself as a product of women's history within patriarchal and androcentric Christianity.

We cannot undo history, but we can perhaps understand it. With reference to my intellectual roots, I think, therefore I am; even more importantly, I critique in order to understand, and therefore I survive. What is our theologizing all about? Should we as responsible theologians be struggling with life and not with ideas? I see this as a false alternative, for it is my sincere belief that, whether we like it or not, we struggle with life through ideas.

Gender Hermeneutics

The present essay constitutes, therefore, an argument for gender hermeneutics as a critical position of historical analysis and reflection. Five points are central to the argument: (1) the New Testament text as a literary construction within the history of consciousness; (2) the need to recognize the disparity between the New Testament text of the past and its Western, northern European interpreter of the present; (3) the hermeneutical implications of the fact that the effect of the text is able to forestall any new interpretation, even though this effect is oppressive and unacceptable to many of us; (4) the need to differentiate between the critical understanding of a text and the possible use or misuse of it; and (5) the need to apply models and methods of interpretation that will enable us to critique the use of social gender from the perspective of androcentric normativity, be it in texts of the past or in our own cultures of the present.

History or Literature?

Is the New Testament to be read from the perspective of historical criticism as source material for formative Christianity and early Jesus-history? Or is it to be read as significant literature, as a collection of religious texts characterized by a special meaning and a special purpose? Although these questions are often seen to imply an either/or answer, they ought to be recognized as calling for a both/and reply.

Obviously, the New Testament material consists of historical texts, and we cannot evade reading them historically as evidence of and for a distant past, if we want to recognize their historical contextuality. Only if we respect the texts methodologically as historical products from a world different from ours can we hope to understand them on their own historical presuppositions and not merely on ours. Nevertheless, the New Testament is also literature of a certain kind—namely, it is a historical collection of religious texts that in various ways formulate a confession of Jesus as the Christ for the purpose of committing a particular audience to this confession as well as its social and moral consequences for the life of the congregation.

Thus, the texts should be read historically as religious literature, with awareness of their contextuality and the different genres they represent. A Gospel text, for example, makes other demands on method than a Pauline letter, insofar as it uses certain specific means of rhetorical persuasion and displays characteristic forms of narrative strategy. Generally, however, we must take into methodological consideration the fact that each New Testament text not only has a purpose and a meaning but also implies an author and an audience within the pattern of a deliberate staging or presentation, structuring the text thereby as a universe of historical consciousness.

Thus, a fusion takes place between history and literature: a New Testament text is historical material, but it is also literature in the sense that it is a literary construction of historical consciousness. Whether it is a Pauline letter or a Gospel narrative, the text before us is, to begin with, a literary construction and, as such, a historical universe in its own right, based on its own presuppositions and limited by its own horizon of interpretation and identification. It is animated by its own life and its own actors, and its purpose or meaning is enacted as a narrative sequence of symbolic plausibility within its own world of shared reality.

From such a perspective, historical meaning cannot be separated from literary meaning, and historical reality is not to be found behind or below literary reality. The aim of historical interpretation is rather to understand the literary construction of the text in relation to the historical context in which it was produced and was meant to have its effect. This historical approach I would call critical deconstruction. The hermeneutical point is not to get behind or to do away with patriarchy and androcentrism by means of interpretation; on the contrary, the point is to recognize fully and with critical assessment how patriarchy works in the text and what are the implications of androcentric normativity in formative Christianity.

The Literary Jesus

A Gospel text may seem descriptive or narrative; in effect, however, it is prescriptive, as we know, and its purpose is to demonstrate to its Christian audience what it means to believe in Christ and to live the social lives of committed Christians. This implies that Jesus does not appear in the various texts as a human being or as a historical person of individual quality, but rather as the Christ of a particular congregation. Jesus as well as the people around him are actors in the reality of the text, and we know them only as such. We meet them playing their parts in the adaptation of Christian meaning that is the deliberate purpose of the text. In other words, in a particular Gospel text both Jesus and the people around him are bearers of just those symbolic values on which the universe of Christian plausibility is structured and meant to be sustained in a particular congregation. But, to be sure, an author is responsible for the literary construction as well as the deliberate staging of the actors as narrative agents, and so the author is present in the text as the structuring consciousness, as is the historical audience the author implies within the construction.

Thus, Paul is present in his letters as the implicit author addressing his congregations with the authority of his calling, and we know him only from the way in which he presents himself as an apostle. Correspondingly, however, in our interpretation of Gospel narratives, we must allow for the presence of an author who presents his universe according to his purpose, on the presuppositions and symbolic values of his context, and so we must recognize that the historical quality of a New Testament text, be it letter or Gospel, is the particular quality of the history of consciousness.

What is important is not the description but the purpose and meaning of the description that convey the symbolic interest of the construction. By the same token, what matters is not events or persons but the staging of the events and the symbolic use of personification and social stereotyping that contain the Christian interpretation and are meant to institutionalize this interpretation.

Consequently, in the history of consciousness, Christ defines and qualifies Jesus. Jesus does not exist independently of Christ, but neither does Christ exist independently of those Christians who have identified with him in the New Testament texts. While Christ authorizes the reality of a particular congregation, Jesus exemplifies this reality in the text. This implies that each Gospel has its own literary and theological program regarding how to apply the confession to Christ both as interpretation and as maintenance in the practice of congregational identity. Thus, what we meet in the various texts is not just one monolithic Christ of paradigmatic importance, exemplified by just one monolithic Jesus as the focus of identification and imitation; rather, we meet a pattern of correlations, which is characterized on every level of meaning by its contextuality.

To sum up, the purpose of the text is both to establish a particular Christian plausibility and to sustain with absolute authority this plausibility as Christian reality.[1] Accordingly, it is the aim of the author to demonstrate his interpretation and, by the same token, to commit his audience to the common responsibility of adhering to the meaning and consequences of this interpretation in order to secure for both parties its ideal quality of shared reality. And this, in effect, is what determines the text as persuasion, conveying through the form and functioning of the textual construction the particular pattern of symbolic values that is to be accepted by the audience as the authoritative assertion of Christian meaning.

Insofar as the reality and moral relevance of textual meaning depend on the effectiveness of the persuasion and the contextual compatibility of the Christian assertion implied, Christian reality may be said to depend on the means of persuasion, rhetorical and narrative, applied by an author in his exchange with an audience. Thus, textuality cannot be separated from contextuality, nor can contextual meaning be separated from the textual means of persuasion.

However, this should not lead us to the conclusion that we are to take a New Testament text at its word in order to accept it at face value. No matter how easily we may feel in correspondence with its purpose or meaning, and no matter how much we may seem able to compare our own situation to that described or implied by the text, we must recognize from the outset that we, the readers and interpreters of today, are not the author's intended audience. We are simply not included in the implied audience of the text, for no New Testament text may be said historically to have been addressed to us, and we cannot pretend, therefore, that it speaks and conveys its meaning immediately to us today. Historically, the New Testament texts belong to their own context of the past and are limited by their own horizon of comprehensibility, just as we belong to our context of the present and are limited by our horizon of comprehensibility. And yet, of course, a connection or even a fusion between these separate horizons[2] is possible, and it is realized through what is called *Wirkungsgeschichte*, or effective history.

The Implications of *Wirkungsgeschichte*

This aspect of *Wirkungsgeschichte* is, I believe, crucial in our hermeneutical discourse, insofar it serves to combine kerygmatic significance with

---

1. See P. L. Berger, *The Sacred Canopy* (New York: Anchor, 1969) 3–80; see also P. L. Berger and T. Luckmann, *The Social Construction of Reality* (New York: Penguin, 1976) 63–146.

2. See H.-G. Gadamer, *Wahrheit und Methode* (Tübingen: Mohr, 1975) 261–95, 329–82, and 415–65.

canonical status, thus emphasizing, for better or worse, the very powerful effectiveness within our history of consciousness of the New Testament literature. Thus, to speak of *Wirkungsgeschichte* means to confront the hermeneutical problem that to a Lutheran interpreter may perhaps appear as the most difficult of all: the fact that not only established textual meaning but also the traditional use of the text for traditional purposes are able to forestall or curtail any new and intentionally critical interpretation.

The correlation between the history of consciousness and the *Wirkungsgeschichte* has once and for all disposed of the ideal of objective or disinterested interpretation. But the same correlation implies a hermeneutical warning against being content with just a synchronic approach to a New Testament text. If we content ourselves with a synchronic reading and limit ourselves to the surface of the text, to the words and their immediate impact or associations, we run the risk of falling into the sentimental or affective error of reading into the text whatever we want or expect to find, either because we have committed ourselves to certain religious or theological prejudices or because—as apologetic interpreters are apt to do—we have made our interpretation conditional on the superior purpose of liberation or personal affirmation.

A synchronic approach enables us to explain a text, but a diachronic approach helps us to understand a text. Thus, synchronic reading will have to pave the way for diachronic methods, enabling us to analyze and reflect on the context of both the past and the present as well as—and this is equally important—the influence of the past on the present through *Wirkungsgeschichte*. Only by means of diachronic methods can we ask not only how the text works but also, in the critical process of deconstruction, why it works contextually the way it does. In other words, we can ask specifically and to the point these questions: Who wants what from whom in a particular text? On what presuppositions and conditions? In what interest, at what cost, and to whose benefit?

Through critical questions such as these, we can apply diachronic analysis together with ideological criticism in order to emphasize the historical subjectivity of any text of the past vis-à-vis the historical subjectivity of any interpreter of the present, and we can make allowance for the fact that we are dealing with two different contexts or universes of consciousness. We must keep the text in its place, as it were, but in the same way we must recognize our own status and role as contextually determined interpreters, with our own need to critically confront these particular texts and their effects both in our history and on our minds.

To conclude, only by means of diachronic methods can we clarify for ourselves how and to what extent the process of interpretation is a historically mediated process, taking on the form of a dialogue between two parties coming together, virtually speaking, from different worlds or continents in order to exchange questions and answers and further questions.[3] The more conspicuous it becomes that distance and disparities are separating the text of the past from its interpreter of the present, and the more conspicuously both parties are reflected in their respective historical contextuality, the greater is the possibility of ensuring intersubjectivity and dialectic interaction in the ongoing historical process of interpretation.

The Ideal of Intersubjectivity

The fact that the ideal of objectivity has lost credibility does not imply that from now on subjectivity shall reign supreme. Rather, the relationship between text and interpreter must aim at intersubjectivity, recognizing this as the only way to make sure that neither party to the dialogue has beforehand been awarded the means and the absolute power to persuade or overrule the other.[4] Obviously, this hermeneutical goal is not easily attainable, and yet it becomes even more important when the text to be interpreted is characterized by both kerygmatic significance and kerygmatic status and when interpretation is carried out within the framework of effective history, where the text is already institutionalized by tradition and traditional

3. Ibid., 344–60. See P. Ricoeur, "Qu'est-ce qu'un texte? Expliquer et comprendre," *Hermeneutik und Dialektik: Aufsätze. Hans-Georg Gadamer zum 70. Geburtstag* (2 vols.; ed. R. Bubner et al.; Tübingen: Mohr, 1970) 2:181–200; and his several contributions to *Exegese im Methodenkonflikt: Zwischen Geschichte und Struktur* (ed. X. Léon-Dufour; Munich: Kösel, 1973) 19–39, 47–68, 188–220. It is crucial for any dialogue of interpretation to acknowledge the distinctive otherness of the interlocutor. See G. A. Kennedy, *New Testament Interpretation through Rhetorical Criticism* (Chapel Hill: Univ. of North Carolina Press, 1984); and, more broadly, C. Geertz, *The Interpretation of Cultures* (New York: Basic Books, 1973).

4. This must be emphasized against the incapacitating effects of the existentialist notion of *Sprachereignis* vis-à-vis the absolute *Wahrheitsanspruch* of the New Testament kerygma, so characteristic of Protestant neoorthodoxy. See, for example, E. Fuchs, "Das Sprachereignis in der Verkündigung Jesu, in der Theologie des Paulus und im Ostergeschehen," *Zum hermeneutischen Problem in der Theologie: Gesammelte Aufsätze* (Tübingen: Mohr, 1965) 1:281–305. However, Gadamer's concept of tradition and authority makes no room for ideology critique; understanding is to him acceptance in the sense of acquisition and absorption. See also R. Bultmann, "Das Problem der Hermeneutik," *Glauben und Verstehen* (Tübingen: Mohr, 1965) 2:211–23. For a critical assessment, see D. Sölle, *Politische Theologie* (Stuttgart-Berlin: Kreuz, 1971). See also the discussion between J. Habermas and H.-G. Gadamer in *Hermeneutik und Ideologie-Kritik, Theorie-Diskussion* (ed. J. Habermas et al.; Frankfurt am Main: Suhrkamp, 1975). Also interesting in this context of political critique is M. A. Tolbert, "Defining the Problem: The Bible and Feminist Hermeneutics," *Semeia* 28 (1983) 113–26. The insistence of liberation theology on the hermeneutics of suspicion has made an important impact on feminist interpretation. See, for example, E. Schüssler Fiorenza, *Bread Not Stone: The Challenge of Feminist Biblical Interpretation* (Boston: Beacon, 1984). However, when the aim of interpretation is the affirmation of women, there is an apologetic limit to the hermeneutical suspicion; suspicion becomes the feminist token of Christian acceptance instead of the means of critical rejection. See the apologetic reconstruction of an early Christian reality positive to women in E. Schüssler Fiorenza, *In Memory of Her: A Feminist Theological Reconstruction of Christian Origins* (New York: Crossroad, 1983) 97–241.

use and where, consequently, its social and moral implications are often taken for granted.

As such, it seems to me that only by stubbornly insisting on intersubjectivity as the aim and hermeneutical criterion of the process of interpretation can we hope to sustain an open dialogue between text and interpreter in the dynamic exchange of intercontextuality. In principle, such a process is boundless because, ideally speaking, any answer induces and should induce further questions. This hermeneutical position, however, implies the important recognition that an understanding of a particular text cannot be limited in advance, say, in terms of a dogmatic interest in mere acceptance of the text. Critical interpretation does not aim at making a text useful or even relevant, and so understanding in the sense of deconstruction has nothing to do with use or usefulness of construction, let alone dogmatic reconstruction.

Rather, any understanding of a text must include the possibility of acceptance along with the possibility of rejection, that is, if the dialogue of interpretation is to be kept open and if critical analysis shall have free reign. It is crucial to uphold the view that the kerygmatic significance and canonical status of the New Testament texts do not between them imply a fixed sum of only absolute answers that should remain unchallenged. For the point is that in a dynamic process of interpretation, based on diachronic analysis, no answer whatever may exempt the interpreter from the critical obligation of asking further questions, thus expanding the dialogue in order to make room for still deeper and more varied insights and reach beyond the limitations of common prejudice as well as personal bias. I should add that not even the often-used canon-within-the-canon principle may serve as a hermeneutical excuse for not asking further and still further critical questions.

Whether the questions asked result in acceptance or rejection of the text, the interpretive dialogue with this text is never exhausted, under any circumstances. For our common *Wirkungsgeschichte* will of course continue, and the role and status of both the text of the past and the interpreter of the present will continue to be embodied in this history, and so also, within our common history of consciousness, the text will retain its kerygmatic significance as well as its canonical quality.

Gender Hermeneutics:
Models, Methods, and Examples

Among the analytical models and methods that have made significant contributions to the development of the diachronic approach during the last fifteen years, I would emphasize the insights from philosophical hermeneutics and ideological criticism[5] and, in particular, from the sociology of knowledge and cultural or social anthropology.[6] All in all, these insights represent today a fertile combination of methodological tools enabling us to work out a project of interpretation that is characterized, on the one hand, as historical criticism in continuity with historical-critical methodologies and yet, on the other hand, as consciousness criticism, focusing not on historical data and events in a referential and positivist sense but rather on the construction of Christian ideology through the literary patterns of symbolic meaning and normative social values.

Because these insights enable us to focus on historical consciousness, they also help us to grasp the far-reaching implications of symbolic meaning in any construction of social reality. And thus they help even a northern European interpreter of the present to recognize fully the interdependence, in general, between the New Testament texts and the patriarchal society of antiquity and, in particular, between the symbolic value system of formative Christianity and androcentric normativity, no less familiar to us today than to the New Testament authors of the past.

I should now like to demonstrate what the application of the tools of these hermeneutical insights to the deconstruction of a particular text entails in actual practice. I have chosen as an example the brief narrative about Peter's mother-in-law according to Mark 1:29-31 in order to emphasize the paradigmatic significance of this narrative for a full understanding of the social implications of the Markan concept of discipleship as *imitatio Christi.*

---

5. For the discussion between Gadamer and Habermas, see n. 4, above. See also K.-O. Apel, "Szientistik, Hermeneutik, Ideologiekritik: Entwurf einer Wissenschaftslehre in erkenntnisanthropologischer Sicht," *Hermeneutik und Ideologie-Kritik,* 7–44; idem, "Szientismus oder transzendentale Hermeneutik?" *Hermeneutik und Dialektik,* 1:105–44; R. Bubner, *Dialektik und Wissenschaft* (Frankfurt am Main: Suhrkamp, 1974) 89–111 and 129–74. For further critique of the paradigmatic constructions of science and knowledge, see T. S. Kuhn, *The Structure of Scientific Revolutions* (Chicago: Univ. of Chicago Press, 1970). From a feminist perspective, see E. Fox Keller, *Reflections on Gender and Science* (New Haven: Yale Univ. Press, 1985); S. Harding, *The Science Question in Feminism* (Ithaca, N.Y.: Cornell Univ. Press, 1986); idem, *Whose Science? Whose Knowledge?* (Ithaca, N.Y.: Cornell Univ. Press, 1991). See also R. Braidotti, *Patterns of Dissonance* (New York: Routledge, 1991).

6. Berger, *Sacred Canopy;* Geertz, *Interpretation.* See especially M. Douglas, *Purity and Danger* (London: Ark Paperbacks, 1988), and idem, *Natural Symbols* (New York: Vintage, 1973). See also B. J. Malina, *The New Testament World: Insights from Cultural Anthropology* (Atlanta: John Knox, 1981), and idem, *Christian Origins and Cultural Anthropology* (Atlanta: John Knox, 1986). Also important in this regard is S. B. Ortner and H. Whitehead, eds., *Sexual Meanings. The Cultural Construction of Gender and Sexuality* (Cambridge: Cambridge Univ. Press, 1988). The impact of sociology on New Testament interpretation is significant in J. G. Gager, *Kingdom and Community: The Social World of Early Christianity* (Englewood Cliffs, N.J.: Prentice-Hall, 1975); H. C. Kee, *Christian Origins in Sociological Perspective* (London: SCM, 1980); G. Theissen, *Studien zur Soziologie des Urchristentums* (Tübingen: Mohr, 1979); W. A. Meeks, *The First Urban Christians: The Social World of the Apostle Paul* (New Haven: Yale Univ. Press, 1983); idem, *The Moral World of the First Christians* (Philadelphia: Westminster, 1986).

Peter's Mother-in-Law

The meeting between Jesus and Peter's mother-in-law is quite brief. It is arranged by others, and, as soon as the sick woman is cured of her fever, she sees to her household duties—she serves (*diakonei,* v. 31). Thus, she carries on in the text just as she is expected to carry on, given what she is— a woman. At the narrative level, this characterization conveys the fact that her life as a woman continues; this is, obviously, the immediate interest of the author.

Those who go for historical probability in a positivist sense may point to the fact that Peter is described as a house owner in Capernaum, as married, and as having his mother-in-law residing with him in the house. However, this information is irrelevant to the purpose of the narrative as an account of a healing miracle and an example of a woman's service (*diakonia*).

If the narrative is read synchronically and interpreted in its literary context, the exemplary meaning is emphasized. The narrow context is represented by 1:21-34, a section that describes Jesus in the role of Christ during the course of one day. It contains those narrative elements that characterize the work of Jesus in the Gospel of Mark: his public appearance consists in authoritative teaching and demonstrative acts of superiority in confrontations with evil; his private activity consists in exhortation of the disciples. To this latter category belongs the motif of *diakonia* in verse 31 on this first paradigmatic day. The full context of the Gospel makes it evident that the motif of *diakonia* is in fact at the center of the exhortation of the disciples according to Mark. Thus, after the confession of Peter in 8:27-30, the three predictions of suffering and death form the basic structure of the demand made to the disciples to be followers of Christ on the conditions of the cross. In this way the *diakonia* of the disciples is defined throughout the exhortative section of 8:31—10:52 as a life characterized by self-resignation, debasement, and lack of power.

Thus, synchronic reading has paved the way for diachronic questions regarding the role played by the mother-in-law as an example of disciple-*diakonia*. If one's interest lies in reconstructing a Christian past positive to women by means of Mark 1:29-31, one may choose to see Peter's mother-in-law as the first woman disciple of Jesus and thus as a historical guarantee of equality between women and men in the Jesus-movement and in very early Christianity. However, when the text is used in this way for the sake of the affirmation of women, the meaning of the symbolic values of the narrative is overlooked and the historical significance of the social staging by the specific use of gender difference and femaleness is ignored.

Even though the woman of the text serves as an example because of her service, she merely does what women do within the social reality of the narrative. Thus, her exemplary value is not established in relation to other women, who already do as she does within the assigned limits of women's lives. A woman, playing the role of woman, simply cannot qualify as a special example to women; as a social representation, she is oddly circular or merely tautologous. Therefore, in order to grasp the specific meaning of the *diakonia*-motif as represented by Peter's mother-in-law, we must recognize her as a social example to men, not to women. In other words, if the *diakonia* of a woman is thrown into relief by the social reality of a man's world, the ordinary social behavior of the woman may function as an example to men, illustrating in social practice what it implies for a man to be a true disciple. And thus the very ordinariness of the woman's social act conveys to the man the extraordinary social costs of a full commitment to Christ on the terms of *imitatio*.

In sum, the *diakonia*-representation of the mother-in-law as a social example is meant to appeal to men whose social behavior was determined in antiquity by the symbolic concept of honor in contrast to the social behavior of women, which was determined and qualified in every sense by shame.[7] Thus, the status and identity of the male, according to the social code of gender values characterizing the Markan Gospel as a whole, rest on the fundamental difference between the separate worlds of social gender identities and the well-defined boundaries regarding the respective obligations and social duties attached to male versus female activity.

However, this dyadic interpretation is by no means a Markan peculiarity. Rather, it is evidence of the extent to which the Markan construction of symbolic meaning must necessarily depend on the historical contextuality of patriarchal antiquity and, in particular, on the symbolic presuppositions of androcentric reality, in order for the Markan author to throw the woman's example of *diakonia* into the starkest possible relief of social meaning. When a man's self-understanding is adjusted in every detail to the social difference between male honor and female shame, the moral emphasis on the woman's exemplary act of disciple-*diakonia* represents for men a gross reminder of the social radicality of the demands pertinent to a life in the imitation of Christ.[8] To ask a man within the society of antiquity, firmly established as a social hierarchy of patriarchal order and administered in practice as a system of androcentric alliances, to commit himself

---

7. On honor and shame as a dyadic pattern of social values and, accordingly, as a moral division of labor, see Malina, *New Testament World*, 25–93. It is important to distinguish a dyadic pattern (honor-shame, clean-unclean) from a dualistic one (mind-body, spirit-sexuality), but it is equally important to realize how both patterns depend on hierarchical classification for the purpose of social and moral discrimination. For a further discussion of the redoubled negative effect within formative Christianity when dyadic discrimination is fused with dualistic denunciation regarding the meaning of femaleness, see my book, *Kvindeteologi og arven fra Eva* (Copenhagen: Gyidendal, 1992).

8. In Mark 9:33-37 the desire for greatness is contrasted with the insignificance or social nonstatus of the small child; correspondingly, in 10:35-45 the desire for power and superiority is contrasted with the social inferiority and humility not only of *diakonia* but also of slavery. In this connection it is worth noting that male Sufi-disciples, for example, in Senegal, may still be seen as practicing humility by doing women's work in public.

as a disciple through the ways and means of life characteristic of women is nothing short of demanding his social suicide. It requires self-debasement not only in terms of renouncing his status of social identity but also in terms of actually adopting a woman's behavior in order to identify with female shame instead of with male honor.

Hence, the purpose of the narrative of Peter's mother-in-law is not to qualify women as disciples; rather, it is to teach men the social costs of true discipleship. And thus the narrative testifies to the fact that the symbolic meaning of the Markan text depends not only in a general sense on the social consciousness of patriarchal antiquity but also in a very specific sense on the plausibility of androcentric normativity, implying in effect that Christian interpretation of social existence is androcentric interpretation.

Conclusion

We may, indeed, not like the outcome of such a deconstruction of the use of social gender. Yet it seems to me to be the only practical way, if in gender hermeneutics we seriously want to know and be able to look through what, so to speak, we are up against in the administration of symbolic gender values in formative Christianity. If the text is read in such a way with critical consistency, with deference to both its literary and its historical contextuality, we may be able to ascertain not just how the text works but also to what purpose and with what implications for whom. Thereby we are able to understand the symbolic use of social gender, even though we may not be able to accept it.

Thus, the process of interpretation may continue as a dialogue between two parties, both of whom become outlined in their subjectivity and in their historical contextuality. But it should go without saying that in order to enable ourselves to interpret critically patriarchal texts, which aim at committing their audiences to a system of social and moral consequences based on androcentric gender values, it is essential to uphold the hermeneutical principle that the dialogue of understanding should be open and unending and that in this dialogue no answer should be allowed to exclude further questions. The better we become at deconstructing the workings of patriarchy and androcentricism in the universe of the New Testament texts, the better we may hope to engage in the ongoing deconstructing of patriarchy and androcentricism in the universe of our own social location.

10

In This Place:
The Center and the Margins in Theology

————————————————— Christopher Rowland ———

In this essay I want to do three things. First, I want to set out in outline something of the context in which I carry out my exegetical work. I want to reflect on the constraints of doing exegesis in a particular place as a preliminary to exploring the extent to which there can be a contribution to my particular political and religious commitments from within a traditional educational establishment. Second, I want to outline the importance of liberation theology for my exegetical work and try to relate it to my context. Third, I want to explore the historical and exegetical interests that have been at the center of my biblical study for the last twenty years and draw on the early Jewish mystical and apocalyptic tradition. In particular I want to test one of the basic convictions of liberation theology and explore whether there is in the Gospel of Matthew an apocalyptic and mystical strand that supports a hermeneutical privilege for a group of marginalized people. Finally, in the last section of the essay, having been in conversations with Itumeleng Mosala, who has been resident in Britain for the last few years, I want to enter into dialogue with his work and explore the character of our disagreement because I think that this reflects the different priorities that emerge from the places in which we do our exegesis.

Social Location as Exegete

The location in which I do my exegesis involves a variety of different and overlapping settings. It would be possible to compartmentalize life, and yet, for a number of reasons that will become apparent in this essay, I consider it important to try to inhabit these different worlds and understand and accept the tensions and constraints they place upon me. I have no illusions about the self-interest that is served in accepting the economic benefits that the higher education system offers its employees. There is space for study and research without the besetting insecurity that life lived on the fringes would involve. My work and this essay are born of a series of compromises, therefore. First and most obvious it arises in the everyday world of a prestigious university with its particular ethos and pervasive educational assumptions. Second, I am a priest of the Church of England and a husband and father of four teenage children. If there has been a price to pay for the particular options that I have made, they are the ones who have often had to bear it. Third, my theology over the last fifteen years has been influenced by acquaintance with Latin American liberation theology and experience of working with the largest development agency of the British churches, Christian Aid. For years now Christian Aid has been supporting poor people in many parts of the Third World in various practical ways and in return has been the recipient of a fund of wisdom and insight from those poor communities that are its partners. At the heart of its work is the belief that poverty is a practical concern integral to the practice of religion. It seeks to persuade the churches and the community at large of the priority of the responsibility to the poor and needy. An important ingredient of this is the theological foundation for that commitment, and it is to that I shall be endeavoring to make a contribution.

I have learned much from liberation theology, particularly the distinctive ways in which the Bible is read. I have found myself accepting much but questioning parts of what is offered. Some suppose that much exegesis in the liberationist tradition is little more than making connections between Scripture and present situations and concerns, similar in many respects to the methods of Bible study groups elsewhere in the Christian church. Perhaps the space between text and interpreter is overcome too readily; there is not enough resistance to the text and employment of those critical faculties that might enable us to understand the text as a complex expression of a conjunction of interests: religious, social, psychological, and economic. Readiness to make connections between texts and present context can lead to a naive identification with the Scriptures in which the importance of the particularity of the present experience is diminished. Critical distance from culture can help avoid theology being the ideological wrapping for a particular group. Christian theologians do well to heed Marx's assertion that Christian theology was the most pervasive form of ideology, which made it peculiarly able to serve the needs of a variety of sectional interests.

The demand that primacy be given to an honest appreciation and analysis of where we are doing our reading is crucial to the understanding of the liberationist exegesis. In many respects it is a plea for a more consistent application of historical criticism. That will involve us in attention to the context of our reading and application of Scripture, for we are all engaged in the production of meaning, which it is our duty to understand as fully as we can. Theory and practice are closely linked. The liberationist perspective contributes to the quest for the unmasking of the ideological character of all reading. The aims of reading the text simply on its own terms and getting at the plain meaning of the text uncluttered by ideology are laudable. But that is much more difficult than many exegetes allow. At least the committed reading frequently has the merit of being more clear about where it is approaching the text from. Exegetes have been somewhat coy about their own interpretive interests. Perhaps the recent trends in narrative theology may give that a much higher profile. In some narrative criticism the interaction between reader and text in the articulation of plot and theme demands a greater awareness of the complex process whereby a text is construed.

Liberation theology's overt commitment and practical involvement can make it an obvious target for criticism. Does it not seem to be the case that this means that it bypasses the careful questioning and necessary provisionality of much of our interpretation? For the liberation theologians the pursuit of understanding of God comes in the midst of practice. So for them theology is inevitably contextual and conditioned by the environment and activity in which the theologians are themselves engaged. Mine may not be the obvious struggle of South Africa or El Salvador. No doubt I have leisure and research facilities that enable me to work in a way in which many Third World theologians cannot. The opportunity to work as I do comes through support from inherited wealth from the past and government funding. Individually, I am aware of the need to justify my existence whether by meeting the criteria of an academic discipline or those of an institution. Often, there will be no obvious correlation between those meanings that we in "northern" educational institutions produce and the situations in which we live and work. But the apparent absence of partiality in our reading should not lead us to suppose that there may be no interest at stake. We need to question how much our exegesis is really detached and objective. I suspect that the character of the contexts that inform our interpretation will be many and various; in the increasingly privatized world of the capitalist culture in which we live such diversity is inevitable. There will be struggle, but it will be individualized and fragmented in a situation where a sense of community and cooperation is subordinated to the achievement of individual goals. To be part of a community of interpretation and action in the church is to be committed to values that challenge the priorities of our age. In much of its understanding of community the church has for two thousand years kept alive an antidote to that unfettered individualism that seeks to fragment and destroy.

Liberation theologians have probably drunk no deeper of "the spirit of the age" than other more ideologically complacent exegetes and may in fact be more open about their interpretive prejudices. There is a growing appreciation of the mutual benefit that dialogue between First and Third World theologians may offer. And it is here that the Oxford academic may have a contribution to make. The study of the Bible on a full stomach and without threat to life and limb offers an important opportunity that many liberation exegetes I know would want to support and encourage. There is value in having a biblical interpretation that can be attentive to that resource of human memory that the rich tradition of an institution like Oxford offers. Theology has always sought to be a formal enterprise in which the intricacies and perplexities of the life of faith have received a careful and systematic analysis. In the last two hundred years theology has had a difficult relationship with the church. A central part of theological education is the constructive dialogue between academic theology and the life of the church. Oxford provides a setting for that dialogue. The Faculty of Theology has had over the years a fruitful relationship with those training men and women for full-time ministry. It is unusual for a university to have a faculty with many members engaged in this. The exegesis of Holy Scripture that is sensitive to contemporary issues but critically aware has an indispensable contribution to make to wider theological education. That will be a Janus-like enterprise. It cannot afford to confine its interests to the ecclesiastical only. Its location in the university invites and enables it to seek a broader horizon for its task. The committed exegesis will benefit from the disciplines and resources of the university. There is a need for committed contextual theology and conventional theology to share their agendas. The importance of an environment such as that in which I work is that it is a place where profound differences can exist and advocates of opposing positions can be better enabled to see more clearly the shortcomings and strengths of the case they seek to present. The concerns of the liberation theologians with ordinary readers indicate that the scope of theological education extends far beyond the walls of university or seminary, for there is a large constituency in the churches ready to engage in continuing education in biblical studies and theology.

In Britain there is need to explore whether a response to the poor should be a central component of life rather than an optional extra. Care for our fellow human beings should need no theological rationale, yet the lack of consensus in society as well as church demands that attention be given to this. That continues to be so in the churches, where doubts are often expressed about particular forms of the practice of charity. The reason for this is not too hard to seek. Whether we like it or not texts are sites of struggle. In their production they betray the ideological conflict of their day, and in the history of their use they have served very different ends. They can enable change but may just as easily be co-opted in the service of a dominant ideology. Biblical texts in particular are tied up in a particular set of human struggles because of their authoritative status, and the careful exposition of their use is a necessary part of the interpretive enterprise.

Importance and Influence of Liberation Theology

Liberation theology's promotion of the option for the poor and outcast and their privileged epistemological perspective has met with heated criticism not only because it seems to be a thinly disguised privileging of Marx's proletariat but also because it seems to use the Bible in a way that ignores facets that do not sit easily with its program. It claims a privileged epistemological perspective for the poor and the marginalized and a divine bias to the poor. It thus has a distinctive perspective on the world and its affairs and holds that this perspective in some way reflects the point of view of God. The elites of the world almost always miss this perspective because of their position in society.[1]

An apocalyptic and mystical thread runs throughout Matthew's narrative. From the dreams of Joseph and the Magi that assist in the recognition and deliverance of the Son of God to the dream of Pilate's wife at the end of Jesus' life, insight by means of dream and revelation, familiar to us from the apocalyptic tradition, is dotted throughout the Gospel. The Transfiguration, particularly in its Matthean version, has several points of contact with ancient Jewish descriptions of theophanies and the developing traditions connected with them, but that is only the most obvious of several passages where such a background is likely. Others relate directly to the theme of the poor and outcast.

The vision of God is alluded to earlier in the Beatitudes. Jesus declares that the pure in heart will see God. Similar terminology is used in the Jewish mystical tradition in which the mystic is vouchsafed a glimpse of the divine *kabod* (glory) after the heavenly ascent. In the Jewish mystical tradition that can only come after the thorough grounding in Mishnah, Talmud, and Midrash. An ethical dimension is stressed in the passage most quoted in connection with the poor, the judgment scene at the conclusion of the eschatological discourse. Here the heavenly Son of Man sits on the throne of glory. This verse offers the closest parallel to the Similitudes of Enoch, especially *1 Enoch* 69:26, where the heavenly Son of Man sits on God's throne of glory, exercising judgment and vindication on behalf of the elect. But the eschatological appearance of the glorious heavenly Son of Man in Matthew turns out to be no remote expectation confined to an eschatological future. Not only does the story conclude with the disciples being confronted with Jesus, to whom is given this divine sovereignty (28:18), but in 25:35-40 itself we find the interpretation of the glorious theophany in the more mundane circumstances of human need. Thus, surprising as it may seem to them, the righteous learn that they have in fact met the

---

1. This takes up themes from my inaugural lecture at Oxford University, " 'Open Thy Mouth for the Dumb': A Task for the Exegete of Holy Scripture," *Biblical Interpretation* 1 (1993) 228–45, and a forthcoming article in *The Journal of Theological Studies,* "Apocalyptic, Mysticism, and the Poor in the Gospel of Matthew."

glorious eschatological Son of Man who occupies the throne of glory in the persons of the naked, the poor, the hungry, and so on. The moment of judgment is brought into the present (parallel to the developments that have often been noted in the eschatology of the Gospel of John) and its outcome determined by patterns of reaction to those who appear to be nonentities. Of course, there continues to be a debate about the identity of "the least of these my brethren." Are they disciples or all the poor and outcast? Superficially Matthew's use of "brethren" might suggest the former and so support a more exclusive reference. There are, however, other factors that need to be taken into account that suggest a more inclusive reference.

In chapter 18 the disciples ask Jesus who is the greatest in the kingdom of heaven. He answers by taking a child and instructing the disciples to become like children. It is that which enables greatness in the kingdom of heaven. In this chapter it becomes clear that the child is identified with another key term in Matthew's Gospel, "the little ones." In 18:5 Jesus is portrayed as speaking of the children as these little ones. Here too response to the child or the little one is the same as response to Jesus. Just as fulfilling the needs of the hungry and the thirsty means acting in that way to the heavenly Son of Man, so receiving a child means receiving Jesus (v. 5). A woe is pronounced on those who cause children to stumble, for they are "these little ones who believe in me" (v. 6). This phrase is found here alone in Matthew. Its narrowly Christian ring is suggested by parallel references in John and Paul. In Matthew, however, belief and confession are not confined to disciples (who are portrayed as betraying and forsaking Jesus). Children are offered as the models to those who are called to be disciples because they are the ones whose particular perspective allows them to recognize Jesus when others who should have known better fail to recognize him (21:16; see 11:25-26).

There is something special about the children, for they are given a rare privilege. Their angels have the privilege of beholding God's face. Here too we have an allusion to the mystical tradition. The climax of the heavenly ascent is the vision of God enthroned in glory. In several apocalypses that is the prelude for the revelation of a variety of secrets, particularly about the future. That was something denied to ordinary mortals and to angels too. These can be no ordinary angels, therefore. They stand in close proximity to the throne of glory and share in that destiny that is vouchsafed to the elect in the New Jerusalem (Rev 22:4) of seeing God face-to-face. These angels are linked, possibly as guardian angels, with those who in worldly terms are insignificant but from the divine perspective receive a particular privilege. The children or the little ones have heavenly representatives who are peculiarly able to have a vision of the divine. Revelatory insight is given to the truly humble and the childlike (Matt 11:25).

This emphasis on children is a particular feature of Matthew's Gospel, though it is rooted in the Synoptic tradition. Children, of course, are important in the Bible. They continue the race and are a sign of hope (and in the case of Immanuel, of judgment). But in much of the Bible their task is to continue in the tradition of the fathers: they are to be obedient; they are to be drained of immaturity and filled with adult wisdom. Thus Matthew's perspective—privileging the apparently insignificant and children, a perspective given added importance by the mystical tradition that forms part of the story Matthew tells—is surprising. It is a surprising perspective. The child moves to center stage. To place a child in the midst of the disciples is to challenge the assumption that the child has nothing of worth and is meant simply to receive another's wisdom. The ordering of things that characterizes the adult world is not the embodiment of wisdom and may in fact be a perversion of it. Here is a perspective that challenges the traditions of older generations. Identification with the child is a mark of greatness, and it is the children and those who identify with their lot who have solidarity with the humble. The position of children in the ancient world was much inferior to the more child-centered world of today. According to Matthew's narrative, for example, to be a child is to be at the mercy of the powerful (as is evidenced by Herod's action) and to be despised by the sophisticated (as is evidenced by the attempts by the ruling elite to keep the children quiet in the temple). Matthew's perspective is not meant to lead to a sentimental or nostalgic glorification of the innocence of childhood but rather reminds us that although the experience of childhood has almost always been that of receiving and having to accept another's wisdom and outlook, children do have an insight that has to be cherished, not repressed or despised.

There is, therefore, a case to be made for finding in Matthew's Gospel a perspective that gives epistemological privilege based on divine insight to a group that may include disciples but at other times is focused on the children and the disadvantaged. One may protest that it is not based at all on social status but is to be explained by reference to divine insight that might be given to anyone. Yet in Matthew that divine insight is confined to certain groups and, apparently, kept from others, if 11:25-26 is anything to go by. It is too simple to say that those who receive these insights are the "poor." "Marginal" might be more appropriate as a description of them. They are humble, both in terms of status and circumstance. There is a privilege for this group, as is evident also in the blessings pronounced at the beginning of the Sermon on the Mount. The privilege should be understood as an advantage rather than a right. The perspective of the poor is not an infallible guide to Scripture or the world. The poor too have imbibed the dominant ideology, which may turn some of their number in the crowd against Jesus. For all that, in glimpsing the significance of Jesus they have seen a way of changing their lot. Their perspective does represent a challenge to those who think that they know how to understand scripture and the world when in fact the secret is hidden from them.

At the heart of Matthew's Christology is the deliberate identification of "God-with-us" with the powerless and the weak rather than the strong. From the very start of the Gospel, Immanuel is a child who is faced with the brutal repression of the rulers in Jerusalem. As the child of God par excellence, he is concerned and identified with the lot of the downtrodden. This is brought out in the explanatory words in Matt 8:17 and 17:12 that stress Jesus' role as God's child who took on the afflictions of humanity. The poor, epitomized particularly by children, are shown solidarity by the heavenly Son of Man. Their lot is chosen by the humble Messiah. As a child he is the victim of persecution and deliberately offers himself as a humble king whose followers must espouse similar humility. The one enthroned in glory is located among the outcast and not only in heaven on the last day. The privilege of "seeing" God's glory is no longer confined to the seer or mystic, nor confined to the life after death, but occurs in the midst of contemporary circumstances. In the most unlikely persons and situations the glory of God is found in this age, hidden, mysterious, but demanding a response from those who are confronted by it.

Dialogue with Itumeleng Mosala

Liberation hermeneutics seems at times to mark a resurgence of "biblical theology" in its attempt to offer an overarching biblical theme. Its attention to the narrative and to "surface readings" is in line with wider trends in biblical hermeneutics. Such trends are not without their problems for liberation exegesis. Itumeleng Mosala has warned colleagues who prefer to concentrate on the "surface" of the text and avoid engaging with the origins and influences that contributed to its present form. In many respects his concerns echo those long part of historical scholarship.[2] His work is a reminder not to turn our backs on those tools that have enabled us to ascertain something, however partial, of the way texts are infiltrated with the dominant ideology. Mosala offers a way of reading that recognizes the diversity both religiously and politically within one text. Thus the use of a particular interpretive perspective, say the hermeneutical privilege of the poor and oppressed, must not ignore or play down the significance of those parts of the text that do not espouse that preferred perspective. Certain forms of traditio-historical analysis can ride roughshod over the text as we

---

2. See further my article "In Dialogue with Itumeleng Mosala," *Journal for the Study of the New Testament* (1993), in which bibliographical details may be found. There I discuss the approach to liberation hermeneutics taken by Mosala in his book *Biblical Hermeneutics and Black Theology in South Africa* (Grand Rapids: Eerdmans, 1989).

have it in the search for the favoured insight, the pearl of great price compared with which all else may be cast on one side. Mosala's interpretation does not ignore those parts of the tradition that do not conform to his interpretive prejudices. We do not have to jettison in order to practice a criticism that is sensitive to the social and political dimension. Texts do include the dominant ideology either by way of reaction or specific espousal alongside their witness to other less conformist traditions. A biblical interpretation that is sensitive to the ideological variety of the Bible will seek to understand its complexity and not move to outright rejection of those sections that fail to meet the criteria of acceptability. Understanding the variety is the basis of the criticism that Mosala beckons us to espouse. Even what appear to some of us to be the Bible's more difficult passages may help us understand something of our own prejudices as we glimpse something of the compromises in the texts of the past. What is more, as Frederic Jameson reminds us,[3] even what may appear to us to be the most reactionary texts may surprise us by offering what he calls a "utopian impulse." Criticism has a role in helping lay bare that impulse, but the task of retrieval is not its only, or even its main, function. All facets of texts are revealing about human striving and the compromises that attend it. We are forever destined to use old wine skins for the new wine and to risk losing both. There is no way out of that impasse, however much we may long to grasp hold of the definitive story, whether of the historical Jesus or the authentic memory of the poor. The need is for constant critical vigilance about ourselves and our reading in the same proportion to that which we devote to the texts of which we are seeking to make sense. Perhaps in this way some of the tensions that are so much part of the interpretive task can at least be recognized and be theologically productive even if they cannot be entirely overcome.

Mosala's discussion of the New Testament (the Gospel of Luke) is much shorter than the treatment of Micah in his provocative essay on biblical exegesis. In the latter he suggests ways of reading the complexity of a prophetic composition so that the various levels of social concern could be recognized. Micah is thus seen as a composite text in which the early radical critique of the oppression of the poor by the rich in Judaea becomes an inclusive text in which the elite of Judaean society themselves are presented as victims. In doing this Mosala shows the difficulty of reading a biblical book as the "literary memory of the poor" and thereby suggests reasons why the Bible does not easily function as a ready resource for those at the base of society struggling for liberation. The reason is that in its final form the traditions have been appropriated by an intellectual and social elite and their radical thrust neutralized. Only a careful analy-

---

3. F. Jameson, *The Political Unconscious: Narrative as a Socially Symbolic Act* (Ithaca, N.Y.: Cornell Univ. Press, 1981).

sis of the texts and a recognition of the extent of that process can release the radical spirit trapped in the shell of ideological justification of the interests of the elite who controlled Jewish society. He is right to remind us that one of the ways whereby Christianity sought to ensure its survival was through seeking to persuade and perhaps even placate those in power. Part of the task of Christian intellectual production in its earliest phase was to position itself over against the dominant ideology, whether it be a dominant form of Judaism or the ideologies of the wider Greco-Roman world.

Luke (among other reasons) wrote in order to present an acceptable religion that conformed to the canons of Judaism and would not completely exclude the penitent rich and mighty. The writing of the story of Jesus in this form is a product of a particular moment in Christianity when issues of identity became particularly pressing. Despite the concern to give it a conventional setting the story he tells is remarkable in its subordination of the rulers of the contemporary world to the background of rural Galilee, whose populace is confronted with good news that differs markedly from the propaganda of the imperial world.

For all its conventional opening and setting in the context of contemporary history, Luke's Gospel hardly exhibits an unambiguous attitude toward established institutions and beliefs. It is after all Luke's Gospel that portrays Jesus as predicting the destruction of city and temple in the light of their inability to understand what led to their peace. The Gospel's attitude to messianism is hardly an unquestioning assumption of the expectation of the Davidic king. The manifesto of Jesus in Luke 4 questions that assumption (looking forward to the detaching of messiahship from Davidic descent in Luke 20:41-44). In Luke the message to the rich is hardly a very palatable one. The reader of the Gospel is left in little doubt about the appropriate response to those like Lazarus. The chapters after the infancy narratives have plausibly been seen as a contrast to more militant sentiments earlier in the Gospel. Of course, this may have suited the apologetic aim of a writer who wished to portray a pacific religion. But elsewhere there is little evidence of any obsequious attitude toward Rome. Certainly it is less obvious than in the writings of Josephus, Luke's contemporary. Yet even the more obviously sycophantic Josephus enables us to catch a glimpse of another dimension to the story of Second Temple Judaism than what appears to have been the one preferred by him.

However, it seems to me important to face up to the contradictory signals that have been picked up by interpreters of Luke-Acts. On the one hand, there is the clarion call to liberation in Luke 4:16, in the uncompromising attitude toward wealth and poverty and the prominence of women in the narrative. On the other hand, there are the apparent nods in the direction of accommodation, particularly in Acts. The account of Cornelius's conversion leaves open the question of the character of life of the newly converted gentile soldier; Ananias and Sapphira's sin is deceiving the Holy Spirit rather than refusal to share their property, perhaps a tacit acceptance of the need to move away from the practice of the earliest church in Jerusalem according to Luke. The ambiguity is no more evident than in chapter 16, where the utter repudiation of Mammon and the disparagement of Dives sit uneasily with assertions that one has to use the Mammon of unrighteousness in order to gain access to heaven.

That which is considered important in the eyes of humans (wealth, privilege, and so on) is an abomination. The word *bdelugma,* which occurs in Matthew and Mark in the context of the eschatological discourse (for example, Mark 13:14) and refers to the future desecration of the temple, refers in Luke to the idolatrous practice of worship of Mammon, which detracts from worship of God. Even the strange story of the "unjust" steward can be read as an attack on the values of Mammon. The wisdom of the steward is in his recognition that human dignity (even if it is his own) transcends the strict rules of accounting and property that go with the service of Mammon. The story may suggest that there is no merit in keeping to the rules of accounting if the result is utter penury. Possessions are not the absolutes that should govern life. Despite the stark warning in 16:13, it is impossible to avoid Mammon. Nevertheless, divine service must determine one's attitude to it, thus subordinating the standards of the present age to those of God and ensuring that the unavoidable administration of Mammon is carried on according to the divine rules. Entry into the everlasting habitations, as the story of Dives and Lazarus clearly indicates, comes through use of Mammon that recognizes and meets the needs of the outcast.

We should resist seeking to resolve these tensions. Mosala's method offers us a way to explore them. They may well have been provoked by the tension between eschatological existence in Christ and the demands of the overarching political and economic order of the old aeon. All this speaks not of growing conformism, in which one may lament a lost narrative of revolution. It is more the recognition of the constraints imposed upon the practice of religion in circumstances that were hardly auspicious for its particular values. Christian historiography and theology from Luke onward manifest a greater concern to convince and perhaps even placate the influential and important rather than be mouthpieces for the oppressed. If our major interest is the story of the poor, we shall not find rich pickings in Luke or for that matter elsewhere in the Bible. But then history is rarely the memory of the poor and insignificant, which is frequently lost forever from our view. Of course, the shape of the story would be different if we sought to write it consistently from the perspective of the poor and voiceless. Its retrieval is often the task of the sympathetic voices of another culture or class. Part of the task of liberation theology has been to engage in that project. The resulting presentation of the "voice of the voiceless" is almost inevitably in an idiom at a significant remove from the story that the poor might tell.

The focus of interest in the Gospels is different from a grassroots story of popular protest. They have Christology, albeit in narrative form, at the center of their presentation, and this towers over all other concerns. Luke's mediation of the story of Jesus can never fully capture the precise character of the Galilean messianic movement, the voices of those who responded to it, why it was so important for the crowds who followed Jesus (in religious and socioeconomic terms), and the character of the liberation that was experienced. But in the process of convincing Theophilus of his version of the story of Jesus, Luke at least ensured that the story was written. It may have been subject in the process to a variety of changes but ensured the continuing interest in the memories and culture of rural Galilee. It is part of the critical task to recognize the shortcomings of all attempts to encapsulate the story, but, as the quest for the historical Jesus indicates, there must be grave reservations about the notion that there is an easy route to a privileged authentic version of events apart from the extant narrative. The writing of the tradition about Jesus was a formative moment for the way in which the story was appropriated. Whoever took that decisive step set the story in the midst of genres that largely were the prerogative of those who served the interests of the politically powerful. Luke to some extent falls into the category of a book that seeks to set down a story that might hardly merit a record in the annals of the ancient world and in so doing includes a glimpse of those poor and insignificant people who were the beneficiaries of the Gospel. Luke does not by any means present a story in which Jesus merely represents the opinions of the groups of people Luke may have been writing for. So it is hardly surprising that basic ecclesial communities in the contemporary world have frequently found in reading Luke a challenge and a voice that in some way expresses their own aspirations and hopes. Whatever its original intention and setting and the distortions that may have taken place in writing, the readers have been able to retrieve that liberative strand without the difficulty that Mosala suggests.

Mosala's frank recognition of the starting point of his exegetical work turns the spotlight on an exegesis that claims to be above the struggle of contemporary life. The time is surely past when we can any longer assert that we are engaged in an exegesis that is removed from the messy business of life that is so dominant in Mosala's reading. What is needed is a frank recognition of why we prefer to conceal the interests at work in the First World exegetical enterprise. Unmasking them will be good for our method and enable us to see more clearly what kind of exercise we are engaged in. It will make us sensitive to our context, so that the process of learning that is needed within the churches will attempt to meet people where they are and empower them to explore the illumination of contemporary life by the Scriptures. If Mosala is right about the attitude to the poor in Luke-

Acts, for example, there is a sense in which its prominent concern to get the rich to engage with the poor is peculiarly applicable to the concerns of the majority of Christians in the First World. The texts as a whole, though not the individual sayings and stories in them, are more akin to First World struggles than a repository of the cry of the oppressed.

Mosala is right to remind us that the Bible is not in any straightforward sense the literary memory of the poor. Merely collecting biblical texts ignores the fact that the Bible continues as it always has to be a site of conflict of human interests and in its final form represents the dominant ideology with all its compromises and contradictions that are so typical of such hegemonic discourses. Yet I disagree with Mosala's rejection of a narrative approach. The evidence suggests that whatever the origins of texts like Second Isaiah (and the experience of the elite in Babylon *could* be regarded as a period of opportunity of identification with the weak and vulnerable of the world), they have enormous potential for inspiring and determining debates about appropriate responses in situations of injustice. Although they are inevitably shot through with the interests and concerns of an elite in Babylon and their liberation, that does not *determine* their future use. Even if they were coined for the elite of Judaean society, were taken into exile, and evidenced little care for the majority of ordinary people left behind in Judaea and Jerusalem, their liberative message has been appropriated by others who do not share their privileged background. The exiles in Babylon learned oppression and in that temporary solidarity with the exiles and migrants glimpsed something of the vision of God for the oppressed.

While there is need for attentiveness to the text's origins, care needs to be taken with an application of the hermeneutics of suspicion that makes the ordinary reader dependent on the skills of the sophisticated interpreter to enable a reading that is ideologically aware. More important, it seems to me, than disentangling the ideological struggles in the Scriptures is the attention to the understanding of the effect of a text in a particular context and the way in which that context conditions interpretation: What is it that causes a particular effect, and what is it about the situation that conditions its reception? In this the history of interpretation will form a part, but that must be matched by the attempt to understand as much as possible the particularity of a context that conditions meaning and the reasons for the particular perspectives that emerge, whether it be the struggle for liberation or the canons of the academy.

Mosala's work is another reminder of the importance of the critique of ideology. With whatever necessary refinements, that is one of the abiding legacies of Marx. But unlike Marx we cannot be so confident that we have that superiority of vantage that can enable the forthright critique of *The German Ideology.* If I understand the German philosopher Theodor Adorno aright, capitalism confronts us like an apparently unassailable cliff. The task of the climber is to discover crevices for handholds. Similarly the critic is searching for some purchase on the overwhelming reality that surrounds and pervades us. The critique of ideology in such circumstances is a complicated task requiring patience, self-criticism, and resistance to generalization. Mosala reminds us that criticism that is a matter of only theoretical reflection is insufficient. The perspective of those who find themselves oppressed, vulnerable, and confined to the margins of our world is an essential ingredient of the articulation of the critique. If in Mosala's hands this forms the basis for an imaginative reconstruction of the prehistory of the biblical text, we should not ignore the fact that the primary purpose of his exegesis is not uncovering ancient history but the prosecution and clarification of the way of God in solidarity with the oppressed. That perspective is not found directly in the pages of Scripture. But even if the Scriptures are the production of an elite, what they produced is not the seamless robe of an all-conquering ideology. Those who produced these texts often found themselves in vulnerable positions on the margins of the dominant contemporary culture. The Scriptures are full of traditions that, particularly when illuminated by the awareness of the experience of suffering, indignity, and inhumanity, can facilitate the pursuit of criticism and action that may contribute to a theology that takes seriously the plight of those condemned to the margins of our world.

11

Working for Liberation:
A Change of Perspective in
New Testament Scholarship

Luise Schottroff

My Context

I live in West Germany. Even after the so-called joining of the former German Democratic Republic with the Federal Republic of Germany, the rift between the peoples in the two parts of Germany is still so deep that I honestly have to speak of "West Germany" as my context. The still-existing prosperity of West Germany is based on the exploitation of the Two-Thirds World and the repression of the recollection of the poor, including the poor in Germany. In my context, biblical interpretation is shaped by social and political structures. First, it is shaped by the structure of theology as it is carried on at universities and by the majority of the male leadership of the church; I will call this theology "dominant" theology. Second, it is shaped by a broad and lively tradition of Christian practice and reading of the Bible within the new social movements—the peace movement, the women's movement, the "Third World" movement, the movement of solidarity with the unemployed, and the movement working to restore the integrity of creation. I opted out of the realm of dominant theology and biblical science into the area of the peace movement and the women's movement. I deliberately took the plunge. In what follows, I will describe the experiences underlying my development. I have paid for my decision with social isolation from the academic community. My male colleagues "excommunicated" me with remarkable brutality and generally try to oppress the new social movements.

I was not alone on my way. Since 1977, I have been working together with a group, the Heidelberger study group (*Heidelberger Arbeitskreis*), from which have come many a publication. Since 1989, every issue of the journal *Junge Kirche* has included a sociohistorical interpretation of a biblical text. This is politically meaningful since this journal, which has its roots in the Confessing Church (Bekennende Kirche), identifies itself as the mouthpiece for both the peace movement and the movement for social justice. Very, very slowly a connection to the women's movement is being established as well. We, that is, my friends and I, have named our theological approach a "sociohistorical interpretation of the Bible."

Sociohistorical Interpretation of the Bible

The brief definition that follows, taken from an invitation to contribute sociohistorical interpretations to *Junge Kirche* by Willy Schottroff in 1989, is meant to serve as the basis for further explanation regarding our sociohistorical interpretation of the Bible:

> For us, exegesis has to be committed to two social contexts: the social context of the time in which the biblical texts originated and the social context of today's readers and interpreters of the Bible. We investigate as concretely as possible the living conditions of classes, races, and sexes, and the meaning of faith for the everyday life of the people in the past. The practice of faith is always reflected. Our exegesis is part of the Christian-Jewish dialogue and of feminist theology. According to its self-understanding, social-historical interpretation aims at contributing to the development of liberation theology within the European context.

The origin of *liberation theology within the German context* is closely linked with the discussions within the Program to Combat Racism of the World Council of Churches. In 1970 the executive committee of the World Council of Churches approved a special fund for humanitarian purposes within the framework of its Program to Combat Racism (two hundred thousand dollars for nineteen organizations).[1] At the time, the public discussion focused on the oppression of the black population in South Africa. The counterargument against the program raised by church leaders and theology professors to the effect that the program was supporting Communists and murderers was both untruthful and demagogic. The decision of the executive committee touched the heart of the problem by characterizing the program as a "redistribution of power." As a result, the comparatively low amount of money assigned became a question of principle. How, according to the gospel, should the rich treat the poor: by way of charity or the redistribution of power?

This discussion challenged many Christians in both parts of Germany to realize that they belonged to the rich who profited from the exploita-

---

1. For the history of the Program to Combat Racism, see especially the document "Anti-Rassismus Programm der Ökumene" *epd Dokumentation* 5 (1971).

tion of the so-called Third World. The proper consequences of this insight could only be to participate in the work of the solidarity movement and the peace movement. Such has been the situation since 1970 until the present day. The Bible has been a source of inspiration for this political work of self-organized groups (mostly on the fringes of the parishes). Above all, the biblical interpretation of the peasants of Solentiname, Nicaragua, became the school where we learned to reread the Bible.[2] "Blessed are you poor" (Luke 6:20) could not and cannot mean for us, in our context, to be satisfied with giving donations. It called and calls us to analyze economic interconnections, to name in public the acts of violence of capitalism, and to work for changes. Sociohistorical interpretation, as we and our companions[3] understand it, is closely linked to this social and political work, as is also the materialistic interpretation of the Bible based on the scientific tradition of French structuralism, with its somewhat different methodology.[4]

In the Western European context, liberation theology is supported by those who continue the urgently needed work of the peace movement, even if such work receives little public recognition. Parts of the women's movement and the ecology movement, as far as they relate in a positive way to Christian traditions, also support liberation theology and identify themselves with it. Many women relate to the Bible as a source of encouragement, as a document recording the struggles of their female ancestors, and as a document of patriarchal attempts to suppress women.[5]

At first, we used the term "sociohistorical" in order to point to a basic methodological weakness of German or Western biblical science that we wanted to rectify: dominant biblical science relies on the history of ideas and disregards the social reality behind the biblical texts as well as the social reality of the contemporary interpreters of the Bible. Many exegetes at

---

2. The first volume was published in 1976 and the second in 1978. The books were quickly reprinted several times, and they are still much in use—and rightly so; see E. Cardenal, *The Gospel in Solentiname* (4 vols.; Maryknoll, N.Y.: Orbis Books, 1976–78).

3. The reference is to the Heidelberg study group. We have documented our work continually in the Kaiser Verlag, Munich. The titles of our books indicating the path of our work are: W. Schottroff and W. Stegemann, eds., *Der Gott der kleinen Leute: Sozialgeschichtliche Auslegungen* (2 vols.; Munich: Kaiser, 1979), Eng. trans., *God of the Lowly: Socio-Historical Interpretation of the Bible* (Maryknoll, N.Y.: Orbis Books, 1984); W. Schottroff and W. Stegemann, eds., *Traditionen der Befreiung* (2 vols.; Munich: Kaiser, 1980); L. and W. Schottroff, eds., *Mitarbeiter der Schöpfung: Bibel und Arbeitswelt* (Munich: Kaiser, 1983); L. and W. Schottroff, *Wer ist unser Gott? Beiträge zu einer Befreiungstheologie im Kontext der "ersten" Welt* (Munich: Kaiser, 1986); M. Crüsemann and W. Schottroff, *Schuld und Schulden: Biblische Traditionen in gegenwärtigen Konflikten* (Munich: Kaiser, 1992).

4. See especially F. Belo, *A Materialist Reading of the Gospel of Mark* (Maryknoll, N.Y.: Orbis Books, 1978), and K. Füssel, *Drei Tage mit Jesus im Tempel: Einführung in die materialistische Lektüre der Bibel* (Münster: Liberación, 1987).

5. See 1 Tim 2:11-15; see E. Schüssler Fiorenza, *In Memory of Her: A Feminist Theological Reconstruction of Christian Origins* (New York: Crossroad, 1983).

German faculties still hold on to the claim of being objective, neutral, and, as such, "serious" and scientific. In contrast, the basic methodological demand of liberation theologians is to name and uncover one's own interests, biases, and partialities. We challenge the practitioners of dominant biblical science as not neutral and for not exposing their interests.

A further explanation of the term "sociohistorical" is necessary, given its use with regard to another method of biblical interpretation. This other approach differs a great deal from ours, first of all, because of its starting point, which is the work of Ernst Troeltsch. Troeltsch and his followers made a sharp distinction between "sect" and "church" as an institution. Consequently, within this approach the Jesus movement is presented as a movement of itinerant charismatic men who lived an elitist ethos, while local communities of "sympathizers," "normal" people, did not practice such a radical ethos but rather stayed at home with their families.[6] The latter represent the "church," which is characterized by "love-patriarchy." The latter term refers to a certain structure of church and society that legitimizes and maintains the power of the rich, the males, and the dominant. Their power and domination is softened but not called into question. The powerful are asked to exercise their power with loving-kindness but not to give it up in favor of real equality. Women, the poor, children, and slaves are admonished to be obedient. The term "love-patriarchy" itself reveals its implicit intention to disguise injustice, for it combines love and oppression within itself.

This sociological concept, with which I disagree at a fundamental level, has gained increasing acceptance not only in the exegetical field but also among the more accessible interpretations of the Bible. With its distinction between radical wandering charismatics and conformist local sympathizers, the approach neutralizes the prophetic tradition and the gospel of Jesus. According to this approach, the Sermon on the Mount is neither relevant nor obligatory for "normal" Christians.

Sociohistorical interpretation, as we understand and advocate it, challenges and criticizes this sect-versus-church concept and works with another set of questions. We call for liberating practice and search for structures and legitimations of oppression. New Testament eschatological texts as well as many other Jewish texts teach us how to understand liberation, namely, as expectation of the *basileia tou theou,* the realm of God, with all its consequences for today's life within the community of saints. It is the variety of liberation practices and liberation movements (as well as of forms of oppression) that compels us to a concrete, de-

---

6. Such is the thesis of G. Theissen (*Sociology of Early Palestinian Christianity* [Philadelphia: Fortress, 1978]). For a critical discussion of Theissen's approach, which may be seen as a cornerstone of the "new consensus" (W. A. Meeks) within Western social history of the Bible, see Schüssler Fiorenza, *Memory of Her,* and L. Schottroff, *Befreiungserfahrungen: Studien zur Sozialgeschichte des Neuen Testaments* (Munich: Kaiser, 1990) 247–56.

tailed analysis of both our present and the past of the New Testament texts. There is as yet no coherent sociological model for this work, but Karl Marx can still function as a good teacher. Biblical terminology itself is well-suited for an analysis of the two contexts, insofar as it has to do with concrete realities. Thus, for example, in the Magnificat (Luke 1:46-55) the sociological terminology of the Bible is sensitively focused and provides a methodological apparatus that concretely names liberation and oppression.

Since the oppression of women is basic to the functioning of all societies today, the positive relation of this approach to feminist theology must be more than just a polite formulation. To deny this form of oppression is to avoid a truthful insight into our context. The gospel of the poor belongs first of all to those at the bottom, to the "last" (Matt 20:16). Women and children are always the ones who have the most to fight in order to survive hunger, ecological disasters, and wars. Problems and methodological demands raised by the Christian feminist movement since the 1970s constitute a rich source for the growth of liberation theology. Attempts to destroy the feminist work are manifold and brutal, as, for example, in the case of the campaign by evangelical Christians against the recently founded women's study center of the Protestant Church in Germany. Again and again, the oppression of women through the establishment of patriarchal marriage and family is declared to be genuinely Christian, even if the biblical traditions must be perverted to fit this legitimizing purpose.

Without the essential critique of the biblical traditions coming from the women's movement and from liberation theologies within different contexts, there will be no responsible and liberative reading of the Bible. There is no doubt that the Bible is androcentric: in fact, all biblical texts are androcentric and support patriarchy, and a number of them are explicitly hostile against women, for example, 1 Cor 11:3. But this is precisely why it is necessary to criticize biblical traditions. Paul, for example, was as unable to recognize the oppression of women as many theologians of today, and yet he remains an important witness for a certain liberation practice and a witness for hope.

Biblical interpretation, especially in the German context, must proceed within the context of a theology after Auschwitz and the Jewish-Christian dialogue. This means, in part, that Jewish-Christian dialogue must include solidarity with the suffering of the Palestinian people. It means also that, at the very least, we have to unlearn Christian anti-Judaism: that is, to begin with, we must develop a theology that no longer misrepresents and disqualifies Judaism. We have to learn that Torah does not mean "law" as opposed to gospel, that Judaism is not a "legalistic" religion versus Christianity as a love religion, and that the New Testament is a Jewish book, like the so-called Old Testament. We have to call into question a Christology that declares Jesus to be the *only* Lord, who exclusively mediates salvation.

Such an understanding must be rejected as an expression of Christian imperialism that excludes Judaism and other religions from God's salvation. The
fact that Christ means life and hope for us must not lead us to disqualify
other religions. We have to be aware of the fact that Christian theological
anti-Judaism supported the German murder of millions of Jews. The critical
discussion of Christian anti-Judaism shakes the very foundations of Christian theological traditions. We will not be able to appropriate the power of
the Bible without a critical consciousness of the almost two-thousand-year-
old Christian hostility against the Jews and all its acts of brutal violence.
Scientific research into the separation between Judaism and Christianity in
New Testament times must be seen as an attempt to deny the fact that the
New Testament is a Jewish book.

The locus of our sociohistorical interpretation is the Jesus movement of
today. People who are not ready to give up—even in the face of wars, militarism, racism, women's oppression, the devastation of creation, and the
murder of human beings through poverty—reread the Bible. The biblical
texts themselves provide information regarding the social situation of the
past and can be supplemented by nonbiblical sources. From Luke 18:1-8,
for example, I can learn about the life of a woman and, then, begin the
analysis of the social context and develop further sociohistorical questions
in regard to both past and present. The starting point of the theological
enterprise lies in the experiences of the readers of the Bible, their actual
social practice, as we learn from feminist and liberation theologies. The
analytical category of "experience" refers not to arbitrary but rather to
structural experiences that can be examined within an analysis of analogous
situations.

"Different approaches to the Bible" has become a popular topic for
conferences today. In some meetings, psychoanalytical, sociohistorical, feminist, historical-critical, and biblio-dramatic approaches are juxtaposed.
Each of these approaches implies certain exegetical and theological presuppositions and decisions. The problem is that these decisions are often
uncritically taken from the point of view of dominant Western biblical
science. The result is that the dominant perspective on and the dominant
exegesis of the Bible are rendered as *the* right perspective and *the* right
exegesis. However, the fact is that one can base one's psychoanalytical interpretation *either* on dominant exegesis *or* on sociohistorical exegesis within
the framework of liberation theologies. There is a decision on method and
perspective to be made. Thus, we have to examine every approach by asking: What do "the gospel of the poor," "the option for the poor," and "the
problem of antiracism" mean concretely? Each sentence that interprets the
Bible can help to build liberation, justice, peace, and the integrity of creation—or prevent them. Thus, it is essential to make a decision regarding
one's historical method.

Talking Theologically about "the Human Being"

I continue with a comparatively harmless experience in my own scholarly work from more than fifteen years ago. Two New Testament scholars from whom I learned a great deal—Rudolph Bultmann and Herbert Braun—employ in their works the *religionsgeschichtliche* (history-of-religions) method by comparing Christian positions with other religious positions present in the "environment" (*Umwelt*) of the New Testament.[7] Bultmann, for example, explains the command to love one's neighbor by contrasting it with "Greek ethics"[8] or writes an essay comparing the understanding of the world and the human being in the New Testament and "Greek antiquity."[9] Greek philosophers, gnostic myths, and "late Judaism" (*Spätjudentum*)[10] become thereby the partners in the conversation. Braun, who also works with these juxtapositions, coined a proposition that summarizes the enterprise well: he says that if one wants to carry on a meaningful conversation between Qumran and the New Testament, one should ask, "How is the human person viewed on this side and the other?"[11]

In my own work with gnostic texts, it became clear to me that this comparative procedure was not a "conversation" at all, for it always had the same result, namely, that according to the opinion of the authors the New Testament/Christian position was the right one and the position of the others simply "the other." It also became obvious that it was impossible to draw such a clear-cut line between, for example, the Gospel of John and Gnosticism. Any sharp confrontation always treats and devalues Gnosticism in the light of the Christian dogmatic enterprise: in Gnosticism the human person was *physei sozomenos,* or saved by nature (wrong); in the New Testament she or he obtains salvation by grace (right).[12] The critique of this procedure within the *religionsgeschichtliche* approach led me to conclude that here, from a Christian perspective, the "other" religions—the "environment"—were devalued.

---

7. The following volumes are typical of this approach: H. Braun, *Gesammelte Studien zum Neuen Testament und seiner Umwelt* (2d ed.; Tübingen: Mohr, 1967); R. Bultmann, *Das Urchristentum im Rahmen der antiken Religionen* (Zurich: Artemis, 1949), Eng. trans., *Primitive Christianity and Its Contemporary Setting* (Cleveland: World, 1964).

8. R. Bultmann, "Das christliche Gebot der Nächstenliebe," *Glauben und Verstehen* (Tübingen: Mohr, 1954) 1:229–44.

9. R. Bultmann, "Das Verständnis von Welt und Mensch im Neuen Testament und im Griechentum," *Glauben und Verstehen* (Tübingen: Mohr, 1954) 2:59–78.

10. The discussion exposing the Christian anti-Judaism of this terminology was unknown at the time.

11. H. Braun, *Qumran und das Neue Testament* (Tübingen: Mohr, 1966) 2:362.

12. L. Schottroff, "Animae naturaliter salvandae: Zum Problem der himmlischen Herkunft des Gnostikers," *Christentum und Gnosis* (ed. W. Eltester; Berlin: de Gruyter, 1969) 65–97; see also my exposition of Johannine dualism in L. Schottroff, *Der Glaubende und die feindliche Welt: Beobachtungen zum gnostischen Dualismus und seiner Bedeutung für Paulus und das Johannesevangelium* (Neukirchen: Neukirchner Verlag, 1970).

As a result of the discussions of the early 1970s, it further became clear to me that "the human being" properly understood, according to Bultmann and Braun, was not only seen from the perspective of Christians but also from the perspective of the so-called First World. A few years later, through the women's movement and through my own professional experiences, I learned of the crucial importance of gender differences. Whenever today in my context someone speaks theologically about "the human being," that human being is in fact seen from the perspective of white Christian males of the First World. Behind the *religionsgeschichtliche* comparison the shapes of colonialism and its aftermath in today's world emerge. The Christian subject, the white, middle-class male of the First World, defends positions of domination by theological means, through the claim, perhaps implicit, that the best, most accurate, and deepest understanding of "the human being" is that of the New Testament or, more generally, that of Christianity. The claim is that "the human being" in question is a category beyond time that includes the reality of all humans, while in fact the human person is seen from a restricted perspective with certain "interests." For the feminist critique of the category "the human being," I refer to the critique of patriarchal hermeneutics by Elisabeth Schüssler Fiorenza;[13] for the critique of ideology, to Jürgen Habermas.[14]

Since, however, the New Testament itself, and especially Paul, uses *ho anthropos*, "Adam," or "I," with reference to all humans, the feminist critique of the ideology at work in theological discussions regarding "the human being" has a twofold consequence. First, an exact determination of the person in question and the naming of perspectives and interests have to replace current theological discourse about "the human being" as a general category. Second, the New Testament talk about "the human being" has to become sociohistorically anchored. Which humans does Paul talk about, for example, in Rom 7:24? He refers to all humans as under sin. But does the cry for liberation apply equally to the situation of women and men, equally to the situation of the poor and the rich? Even though the critique of patriarchal hermeneutics has had some impact—and I hope more so in the United States than in Germany, where much still remains to be seen—I have still not seen many results in the writings of biblical scholars in the Western context, with the exception of feminist authors. Up to this point, there has been no critique of theological generalizations and their hermeneutics of domination that would lead to a sociohistorical analysis of New Testament theologies, particularly that of Paul. Indeed, a key grounding for Christian theological self-understanding as the true and most accurate view

13. Schüssler Fiorenza, *Memory of Her*, 4–6 and passim.
14. J. Habermas, *Erkenntnis und Interesse* (Frankfurt: Suhrkamp, 1968), Eng. trans., *Knowledge and Human Interests* (Boston: Beacon, 1971).

on humans seems to be the Pauline conception of sin. A thoroughly critical rereading of this concept is very much needed.

In the future, the analysis of the context of the subjects of theology by all theologies of liberation has to take sexism seriously as class domination. Therefore, I believe, future New Testament scholarship has to be feminist: it has to analyze patriarchy in its historically changing forms; it has to serve the interest of abolishing all injustice among people, including injustice between the sexes.

The analysis of the social context in which theology is done and Christian faith practiced has to include an analysis of the structures of sexism as well. The following questions have proven helpful to me in this type of analysis: How is the role of women defined by those who dominate society? What does the daily reality of women look like? How do women who do not fit the defined role of the ideal woman (for example, the unmarried woman) live? How are women integrated into the professional world (where often women's work is not defined as "work" in the sense of male professional work)? For example, in the New Testament the admonition to be submissive addressed to the slaves is followed by the admonition to work diligently (Eph 6:6-7; Col 3:23). The admonition to the women, however, demands only submission. Women's work itself is not mentioned. Women are expected to provide their labor for the whole of their lives, but it is so much understood as *part* of their submission that it remains invisible in the parenesis. At best, the rejection of laziness (1 Tim 5:13) and the term *oikourgos* (home management) (Titus 2:5) show that the female role includes work. Quite typically, however, one can observe how in both the history of the latter text and modern translations women's labor disappears linguistically: *oikourgos* became *oikouros* (domestic); and modern translations are falsely based on the latter term.[15]

My exposition of the need to analyze the real history of women as a task of theology and biblical scholarship has concentrated so much on women's work because I regard the analysis of sexism and its interconnection with economic interests as its starting point and center. The utilization of women's labor happens so invisibly, or more precisely, so often without recognition, that the analysis of the respective forms of patriarchy should start at this point. Violence against women and children is the other side of the exploitation of women and the silence regarding their work. The New Testament scholarship that I propose will view the recognition of women's labor and domestic violence as a central *theological* task. Such scholarship will have to understand, for example, the situation of prostitutes as a problem related to the exploitation of women and as female

---

15. See, for example, W. Bauer, W. F. Arndt, and F. W. Gingrich, *A Greek-English Lexicon of the New Testament and Other Early Christian Literature* (2d ed.; ed. F. W. Gingrich and F. W. Danker; Chicago: Univ. of Chicago Press, 1979).

wage labor and stop discussing it as a moral issue (repentance from harlotry). For this it would have an important ally in Jesus (Matt 21:31; Luke 7:36-50).

From a sociohistorical perspective, it is no longer possible to speak of biblical anthropology as a unified concept. The more I know about the social context of the Yahwist or of Paul, the better I shall grasp their ideas. The Pauline concept of the sin of all humankind in its particularity mirrors the experience of powerlessness of the lowly people under the Roman Empire.[16] Paul is thinking, in effect, from the perspective of lowly males. When Eve's guilt is pondered in different religions of the Mediterranean at Paul's time, the claim emerges that the woman's sin was her sexuality.[17] In theology and New Testament scholarship, the sin of "the human being" is described as arbitrariness, striving for emancipation, hubris against God. This definition is so common that one can use commentaries on Romans at random for verification. Paul himself does not say this. The sin of lowly people, especially of lowly women, is not just hubris but the acceptance of their own powerlessness. Theological discourse pointing to arbitrariness on the part of "the human being" as the center of Christian anthropology is oppressive discourse in the interest of domination. Its message is: striving for emancipation is sin. According to this anthropology, there is no escape from sinfulness in this world and especially no escape by one's own power. This, too, is a topos that serves the conservation of domination, and it conceals the gospel of Paul, namely, that through Christ's resurrection God has broken the power of sin.

Practice of Faith and Orientation toward the Base

In my graduate studies I learned that love of enemy was a sublime idea, an unlimited expansion of the neighborly love command, the proof for the importance of Jesus for the history of humankind. However, through the discussions on nonviolence, I learned from Martin Luther King Jr. that one had to distinguish between the demand of nonviolence on the lips of church and state leaders and a nonviolent praxis of resistance.[18] Therefore, the question to be asked of New Testament texts must be: *How* did

---

16. L. Schottroff, "Die Schreckensherrschaft der Sünde und die Befreiung durch Christus nach dem Römerbrief des Paulus," *Evangelische Theologie* 39 (1979) 497–510; an abbreviated English version appeared in *Theology Digest* 28 (1980) 129–32.

17. L. Schottroff, "Evas Schuld: Die weibliche Urschuld im Judentum, Christentum und in der Gnosis in den ersten Jahrhunderten n. Chr," *Schuld und Macht: Studien zu einer feministischen Befreiungstheologie* (ed. C. Schaumberger and L. Schottroff; Munich: Kaiser, 1988).

18. For a critique of this discourse on nonviolence ("from above") in the interest of domination, see especially, "Eine Herausforderung an die Kirchen: Das KAIROS Dokument: Ein theologischer Kommentar zur politischen Krise in Südafrika," *Junge Kirche* 47 (1986).

the first Christians *practice* love of enemy? How does one do this, loving one's enemy? Who are those who love, and who exactly are the enemies in a sociohistorical sense?[19] In effect, the question raised by the history-of-religions approach—How do I prove by *religionsgeschichtliche* comparison the uniqueness of the idea of loving one's enemy?—is the wrong question because it is oriented toward domination. From liberation theologians in Latin America I have learned that the question oriented toward the practice of faith has to replace a theology that is oriented toward the history of ideas. In idealist theology, the practice of faith appears as a "deed" that ensues from the content of faith, the development of which constitutes a minor matter. If the "deeds" become the central content of faith, one speaks of justification by deeds and legalism. In the graduation requirement and other institutional structurings of theology in my context, one can see a hierarchy at work where ethics and social ethics are considered minor fields while New Testament and systematic theology are seen as major fields. New Testament scholarship itself repeats this hierarchy internally. So-called ethical lists, for example, are looked down upon as moralistic demands. Thus, with regard to Romans 6 one finds extensive treatment of the systematic grounds for Christian action and discussion of some overall ethical *demands* (love of neighbor) but hardly any research into the concrete praxis of the early Christian congregation. Similarly, the attempt to understand the beatitudes of the poor in the context of the *practice* of solidarity with the poor in the Jesus movement is disqualified as Marxism.[20]

As a result, Christian life is in fact shaped by three crucial models of action: (1) patriarchal marriage (and family); (2) the giving of alms; and (3) the acknowledgment of the political status quo. From this practice, a hermeneutics emerges that finds precisely these models of action in the New Testament. But it does not question these models theologically or historically, for the deeds of faith are but secondary if measured by the genuine tasks of theology. By separating theology and practice, "theology" and theological ethics, and faith and action, the relevance of life-practice for hermeneutics is not recognized at all, and actual practice is not analyzed with regard to society. Thus, the issue is not whether practice influences our biblical exegesis but rather which practice we have and whether we expose it to analysis and change.

The hermeneutics that emerges from a practice of liberation presupposes

---

19. I pursued this issue for the first time in 1975: L. Schottroff, "Gewaltverzicht und Feindesliebe in der urchristlichen Jesustradition," *Jesus Christus in Historie und Theologie: Festschrift für Hans Conzelmann* (ed. G. Strecker; Tübingen: Mohr, 1975) 197–221), Eng. trans., "Non-violence and the Love of One's Enemies," L. Schottroff et al., *Essays on the Love Commandment* (Philadelphia: Fortress Press, 1978) 9–39.

20. E. Lohse, "Das Evangelium für die Armen," *Zeitschrift für die Neutestamentliche Wissenschaft* 72 (1981) 51–64.

as well as initiates a dialectical process of liberation: liberating practice yields recognition of liberation history, and recognition of (early Christian) liberation history leads to further development of liberating practice. The dialogue with history initiates learning. This means that New Testament scholarship must dwell within the context of a liberating practice unless it wants to lose sight of its goal, the liberation of all humankind to a life of fullness and justice. If I cannot explain to my Christian siblings in the peace movement and in the women's movement what sense my particularly historical work makes, I will have no choice but to question this work and review its conception. This does not mean that I regard differentiated and detailed historical work, whose particularities and erroneous ways are of no notable practical interest, as superfluous. It just has to be made clear which goal and which interests are served by seemingly remote research and with which practice it is connected.

A liberating practice of faith entails participation in the work of liberation at some point, such as, in my context, solidarity work with the unemployed or the always urgently needed antimilitaristic work for peace. Such involvement results in conflicts that ultimately teach an analysis of society much more sharply than any reading of the relevant books. As long as I abstain from conflict-laden daily tasks in my context, I am able to nourish the illusion of neutral scholarship and church. This illusion is based on the drawing of lines that separate religion and daily life, faith and politics, scholarship and practice. If "wholeness" is to be more than a fancy term, this drawing of lines has to be recognized as a method of domination: by crossing these lines I find out which interests are really being served.

The foundations of a liberating practice provided by early Christianity consist of the gospel of the poor and an orientation to the will of God. I am using the formulation "orientation to the will of God" despite my awareness of the history of misuse of this and other similar phrases. Such phrases have often implied the orderly practice, well-suited for domination, that I referred to earlier (marriage, charity, authorities) or have simply functioned as "empty formulas," asseverations of required Christian behavior that were not taken seriously anyway. "Orientation to the divine will" is for me (as for Paul [for example, Rom 12:2]) the best possible way of understanding Christian practice. This formula makes it clear that concrete decisions are oriented toward a goal: the *basileia tou theou,* the new creation, the peace of God, the new heaven and earth, to quote a few New Testament images for this goal. The formulation "orientation to the will of God" makes it clear as well that concrete decisions always have to be substantiated anew by analysis regarding their content. One has to examine what the will of God is (Rom 12:2).

Hope and Partiality

Bultmann's demythologizing project of 1941 and his commentary on the Gospel of John were the decisive reasons for me, in 1951, to attend seminary. Here I found a credible theology that liberated me from all the old dogmatic junk. I could be a Christian, and I could become a theologian, without having to believe all the things that did not fit my worldview—from the virgin birth to the trumpets at the day of judgment. "One cannot use electric power and radios, in case of illness utilize modern medical and clinical means, and at the same time believe in the world of ghosts and miracles of the New Testament."[21] What a liberation Bultmann's theology meant for me and so many others of my generation! Yet when I look back today, I am startled by my past.

At the very time that Bultmann was writing these words, concentration camps were already in existence; it was wartime. Why does all this not appear in his presentation of the modern worldview? For him, the scientific worldview was a theological problem, but not so Auschwitz and the nuclear bomb. This is not a query regarding Bultmann's personal integrity, which is beyond question, but rather a query regarding his theology in its context, for which such happenings were simply not a theological problem. At a much deeper level, however, this problem is directed at myself. I was more than a generation younger than Bultmann. My childhood was marked by National Socialism, war, and the postwar times. Already during the war, my parents openly talked to their children and the church congregation about the violent regime of Hitler, the murder of the Jews, the existence of concentration camps. I had the best presuppositions to understand that Auschwitz had crucial *theological* meaning. I did not grasp it. I grasped the meaning of the first nuclear bomb in August 1945 for myself, for the world, but not for *theology*. In the following years, I suffered from fear of another war. And I studied theology with the liberating feeling that fortunately I did not have to believe in the virgin birth. Only today, when in Germany anti-Semitic tendencies are beginning to surface once again, do I grasp the dimensions of my theological failure and that of my generation. Why did the discussion of Christian anti-Judaism emerge so late and so marginally for us in Germany? Why did I spend all my years in seminary without making a theological connection between my own daily life, its historical and political dimensions, and my theological studies? It is often said today that the explanation lies in the guilt we had to repress. My problem, however, in those years was more fear than guilt. I was liberated from this fear by Bultmann's repetition of the Pauline *hōs mē* (as though): *oi klaiontes hōs mē klaiontes* (Those who mourn as though they were not

---

21. R. Bultmann, *Offenbarung und Heilsgeschehen* (Munich: Kaiser, 1941) 31.

mourning) (1 Cor 7:30).[22] "This *elpis* is the being free and open for the future, because the believer in obedience has left the care for herself or himself and thus the care for her or his future to God."[23]

From Ernst Käsemann I learned theological doubt regarding this limitation of faith to the existence of the individual. I discovered that my theological thinking lacked the cosmic dimension (the global reign of Christ) and the daily dimension ("worship in the daily life of the world").[24] "Justification of the ungodly certainly affects me concretely. But this formula is deprived of its weight if salvation for every human being and the whole world is not proclaimed through it."[25] What Käsemann did not articulate, Dorothee Sölle did: it is the human beings in the Third World, Vietnam, and Auschwitz who are meant. Since the early 1970s, collaboration with Dorothee Sölle has become crucial for my scholarly endeavors.

Because of Käsemann's insistence on "apocalypticism as the mother of Christian theology"[26] and because he taught me and others to see the global implications of Christian faith, I believe eschatology to be at the heart of the question of God. Thus, I could grasp the theological importance of Ernst Bloch.[27] The importance of an apocalyptic eschatology for the *whole* of the New Testament and for myself has become clearer and clearer to me. I want to explicate the problem by way of an example: the so-called delay of the parousia.

Since the discovery of the importance of eschatology for Jesus by Johannes Weiß, Albert Schweitzer, and others, it has been widely held that very early on—already in New Testament times—disappointment about the nonarrival of the parousia, the delay of the parousia, had played a significant role. A variety of texts, for example, in the Synoptic Gospels, have been interpreted in the light of this assumption. Statements like the demand for watchfulness (for example, Mark 13:33, 37) and corresponding parables have been understood as expressions of the delay of the parousia, and this delay of the parousia has been seen as the decisive force in the formation of early Christian congregations.[28] This hypothesis I believe to be historically incorrect. In effect, demands for watchfulness and even state-

---

22. See R. Bultmann, *Theology of the New Testament* (New York: Scribner's, 1941) §40.2 and passim.

23. Ibid., § 35.3.

24. E. Käsemann, "Gottesdienst im Alltag der Welt," *Exegetische Versuche und Besinnungen* (Göttingen: Vandenhoeck & Ruprecht, 1964) 2:198–204.

25. E. Käsemann, *Paulinische Perspektiven* (Tübingen: Mohr, 1969) 138, Eng. trans., *Perspectives on Paul* (Philadelphia: Fortress Press, 1971).

26. E. Käsemann, "Die Anfänge christlicher Theologie," *Exegetische Versuche und Besinnungen,* 2:100.

27. E. Bloch, *Atheismus im Christentum* (Frankfurt: Suhrkamp, 1968), Eng. trans., *Atheism in Christianity* (New York: Herder & Herder, 1972).

28. See E. Grässer, *Das Problem der Parusieverzögerung in den synoptischen Evangelien und in der Apostelgeschichte* (Berlin: de Gruyter, 1960).

ments in the parables that the Lord was delayed (*chronizei* [Matt 24:48 par.; 25:5]) represent expressions of expectation of an imminent parousia, utterances of a life carried by the hope that it would not be long before the realm of God arrived and that it would include heaven and earth. The delay of the parousia in New Testament times plays a role only in the mouth of the *mockers* (2 Pet 3:3-4; *1 Clem.* 23:3). Similarly, the "redactors" Mark, Matthew, and Luke—in the time after 70 CE—live by this hope of the nearness of the *basileia tou theou,* the worldwide revelation of God in action. Thus, the delay of the parousia as a model of explanation in New Testament scholarship is an invention of scholars; in effect, they see their enlightened and chronological thinking already at work in parts of the New Testament, preventing people thereby from finding their way to hope and liberating practice. This assessment of the importance of eschatology for all of Christianity during New Testament times does have consequences for the interpretation of particular passages. For example, all interpretations of the parables with respect to the conditions of the church/congregation, for example, ecclesiological interpretations, become questionable. Even Mark 4:13-20 par. (the supplementary interpretation of the parable of the sower) does not talk about church groups with different ways of behavior but about the eschatological consequences (thrive/pass away) of certain ways of behaving.

New Testament scholars often assume that expectation of an imminent parousia is the ground for ethics, meaning an interim ethics. By the same token, an ethics that shaped the world would be dependent on the willingness of the ones involved to make long-term preparations for the world. With this explanatory construct the orientation toward action of the early Christian communities is misinterpreted. On all levels of the tradition, the nearness of God, the proximity of the *basileia tou theou,* engenders an all-encompassing shaping of daily life as well as perspectives for action. Humans long for salvation, yearn for the revelation of the Human One (traditionally rendered as the "Son of Man") from the clouds of heaven (Mark 13:24ff.), and shape their lives as children and imitators of God (Matt 5:9, 45). Like the delay of the parousia, the interpretive model of interim ethics is to be explained by the distance of scholarship from the subject under consideration.

Existentially, early Christian eschatology is very important for me. My analysis of the ecological, military, and political situation of the world is very negative. Therein, I see myself in agreement with many people who politically and religiously have taken very different stances. The probability that humans will really be able to prevent a self-produced catastrophe from happening decreases from year to year. The crucial religious or Christian issue of today is whether hope is sensibly and honestly possible. Is not the insistence of faith on the nearness of God a transparent attempt to comfort oneself and close one's eyes in face of the future? Is hope but cowardice?

Many people of my class in my context have given up. For this I cannot condemn them. I hear their critique, that hope for the nearness of God is something like the singing of children in a dark basement. This critique is a more serious questioning of early Christian eschatology and of Christian faith today than the scientific worldview is. Today, I can demythologize the trumpets on the day of judgment as a mythic image of past times, as Bultmann did. In so doing, the hope for the nearness of God by which the first Christians lived is not called into question; it is only categorized in terms of concrete historical forms. It is not the temporal conceptions belonging to a specific historical situation that prove to be the problem, but hope itself. It is my experience that through participation in the struggle of resistance—even if in a very small way—hope does grow. Therefore, I can repeat all the yearning expressions of the New Testament that implore the realm of God without restrictions. I too will continue to wait and to hope.

Part Four

Readings from Latin America

Social Location and Biblical Interpretation: A Tropical Reading

_____ Tereza Cavalcanti ___

I take as my point of departure for these reflections two recent scenes from real life. These two scenes reflect a concrete social location out of which has emerged an original reading of the Bible, popular in character, a reading that I should like to analyze in this study. I shall then expand on these two scenes by describing a biblical course whose theme and participants correspond to the participants and theme present in the scenes in question. The intention of this study is not to formulate a theory, develop a theme, or interpret a specific text from the Bible. My aim rather is to raise a number of questions regarding the way in which (the method by which) individuals from the popular class read, interpret, or refer to the Bible in their everyday lives. By way of conclusion I shall offer a few brief reflections simply meant to get the discussion started.

The Location of Those Who Have No Location

First Scene

Rio de Janeiro; a Tuesday; winter of 1990. We find ourselves in a quite chic neighborhood of the city, O Jardim Botánico (Botanical Garden). It is cold. In a half-abandoned lot I witness an eviction scene involving three families.

Two well-dressed men are engaged in conversation. A truck is waiting to take away the load. Next to it, a police van and a number of police officers. The families about to be evicted are agitated. The women protest that the children are sick and have nowhere to go. I try to speak with the well-dressed men. One of them is a lawyer. He mentions a court order. The other man identifies himself as a member and representative of the family that owns the lot. He warns that the squatters are dangerous people,

This is a translation of the original manuscript, "Lugar social e interpretação bíblica: Uma leitura tropical." The translation is by Fernando F. Segovia; the assistance of Dr. Elena Olazagasti-Segovia is kindly acknowledged as well.

criminals.... When he finds out that I work for the church, he asks me to do him a favor: to arrange a place for these people to stay. In the end, that's what the church is for, isn't it? To help the poor...

The court official arrives. I speak with him in an attempt to delay the eviction. Nothing doing. The workers begin to destroy the houses. A woman, in her sixties, enters the scene. From the way she dresses, it is clear that she is a "believer" (*crente*).[1] Dona Maria—that's her name—paces up and down in anguish, saying, "God will help me! I am sure of it." But the eviction continues. The houses are torn down one by one; the furniture is taken away and tossed into the truck. The only house still standing is that of dona Maria.

It is clear that both the owner and the lawyer are troubled. The woman once again approaches the lawyer and says, "God will help me. 'Those who humble themselves will be exalted.'" The man, visibly disturbed, responds, "But I am not humbling you! I am only carrying out the law!" "Oh no, sir," answers the woman, "you are not humbling me; it is I who am humbling myself. I am begging you to let me stay here a few more days, until Sunday, so that I can arrange for another place to go! I am confident that the Lord is going to help me...."

After some conversation, the lawyer and the owner agree (they were the ones who seemed humbled, while the woman actually grew in dignity). I thought to myself: dona Maria is a teacher. I must learn to read the Bible as she does. Her Pentecostalism will not prevent me from learning from her.

Second Scene

Duque de Caxias, a "satellite" or dormitory city (*cidade satélite*) of Rio de Janeiro; summer 1988. Heavy rains have caused flooding in the Baixada Fluminense (the Fluminense Plain). Schools and churches have been converted into shelters for the thousands of people afflicted.

Rosa, a black pastoral worker about twenty-five years old, interrupts her vacation to help her community, affected by the floods. When she arrives, she finds the church full: people asking for food, homeless, wounded. The mix is great: families from the community lie next to well-known and feared criminals. Among those who had come to help there were Kardecistas (spiritualists, followers of Kardec), Methodists, Catholics, and people of other religions. Soon after, help arrives in the form of mattresses, clothing, food, and medicine. An inventory of the homeless families is made: those who have in fact lost their homes, those who are ill, children, pregnant women...

Rosa goes out to visit the neighborhoods affected. It is necessary to convince those at risk to leave their homes, but they refuse, even with water

---

1. Such is the name given to any member of a Pentecostal church.

up to their waists, afraid to lose their "possessions." The firefighters themselves bide their time: they neither have the right equipment nor wish to deal with the mud and the current. Two boys, burned by the explosion of a gas tank, cannot be removed, and no one wants to lend a hand because they are well-known outcasts. Rosa doesn't want to know whether they are outcasts or not; the fact is that they are human beings and they are in need of help. She deals with the situation—"I, who was always in mortal fear of roaches, went into all that water and mud, knowing that there must have been even snakes in there!"

After their removal, Rosa coordinates the distribution of food and mattresses for the homeless, according to the needs registered in the inventory. As she is about to cross a wooden plank, a boy comes up to her (she knows that he belongs to the gang of criminals) and demands that the goods be given over to his house. She responds that there are others who are in greater need and will be looked after first. He warns her, "If you don't hand those things over to me right away, you are going to wake up dead in that ditch, with your mouth full of ants!"

"Maybe," she answers him, "but first I am going to distribute these things as has been agreed. Let me through!"

"But the pastor says that you have enough food for all of us and that you are the one in charge. So, hand those mattresses over to me right now, because I am not joking around!"

"What pastor? That pastor doesn't know what he is talking about! The food we received is limited and not enough for so many people. We have taken inventory of the families that are homeless in order to help those who need it the most. And it is to them that I will take it!"

"Then I am going to settle accounts with that pastor."

"No, it is I who will settle accounts with him," Rosa concluded and went on her way.

Later on, she found out that the pastor in question had wanted to help with the homeless but, faced as he was with an "avalanche" of people and few recourses, panicked and told the people to go to the Catholic church.

In the end Rosa came to be respected and loved by the homeless, even by the family of outcasts. Later on, when she was recounting the story, I asked her if she had had any particular biblical passage in mind during those difficult moments.

"I often thought of the prophet Elijah. When he lay himself down beneath a tree and wanted to die, because he thought he was alone in the struggle. But he was wrong. Doesn't the text say that later on a whole multitude of prophets appeared? [She was referring to 1 Kings 19, especially v. 18.] He was not alone. I too came to see that those who know how to say beautiful things in church or in public are nowhere to be found when you need them. One feels alone. But then others who had remained hidden come forward to help in the time of need."

"I also thought of the light breeze," Rosa continued. "God passed by un-noticed. Sometimes, when one speaks with the simple people, from whom no great thoughts are expected, one finds the right word."

Developing the Question

In the light of these two scenes, I should like to raise the following ques-tions: How did the immediate situation influence the way in which the Bible was read and interpreted? What kind of relationship with the Bible did these two individuals, faced with a problem of housing, show in a situation of tension and danger?

First, there are important differences between these two interpreters of the Bible: dona Maria is defending her own rights; Rosa is defending the rights of her fellow human beings. Maria works alone and improvises; Rosa works with others (has the support of a group) and in organized fashion. Maria is a mother, about sixty years old; Rosa is single and about twenty-five years of age. Maria lives in a rich neighborhood but is poor; Rosa lives and works in the periphery. Despite such differences, there are significant similarities as well in their respective attitudes: both are faced with dan-ger and react firmly and courageously; refer to the Bible and the biblical texts; have clearly received prior instruction within the context of a reli-gious community; and reveal a consistent and mature life of faith, which comes to expression in the confidence and certainty with which they carry out their lives.

With regard to their reading of the Bible, the following should be noted:

1. They refer to the Bible in a way that is intimately connected to their everyday life. One could even say that their everyday life precedes their recourse to the Bible.

2. They quote the Bible by heart, with no need to have the text on hand. This means that the texts have not only been already read and reread but also reflected upon, allowed to mature, "ruminated" (*ruminados*) as Carlos Mesters would put it.[2]

3. Maria cites a verse from Scripture, textually, as a principle for action. Rosa refers to a biblical situation and a biblical character with whom she identifies.

With these observations in mind, I return to the questions posed at the beginning of the section: How does this process of familiarization with the Bible among individuals from the popular class take place? What is the

---

2. Carlos Mesters is a well-known biblical scholar who has devoted himself to the study of the popular reading and interpretation of the Bible. He is mostly active in Brazil, though also elsewhere in Latin America. He is the author of many works, some of which have been translated into a number of other languages.

journey traversed by these people, and how does it come about that a history and a message of two thousand years ago are transformed into living references for contemporary practices? All I wish to do in this study is to point out a few aspects of such a process, attempting to identify within it the role played by the social location and situation of the group in question. For this purpose I shall turn to a concrete experience: a course entitled "The House in the Bible" given to leaders of biblical circles and pastoral workers in the state of Rio de Janeiro, January 24–29, 1993.

Reading from a Place

The course was organized by the Ecumenical Center for Biblical Studies (Centro Ecumênico de Estudos Bíblicos [CEBI]) through its regional office in Rio de Janeiro. The CEBI has always been characterized by a concern for access on the part of the poor and the marginalized to a reading of the Bible, as a way of shedding light on life and allowing life to flower. As such, it has developed its own methodology for the reading of the Bible.[3]

Constructing a Tropical Reading

The methodology behind the biblical reading of the CEBI involves three factors: the biblical text; the present reality of the readers; and the community of faith. For an understanding of the biblical text, the method makes use of the exegetical sciences—especially historical-critical, sociological, and literary methods. For an understanding of contemporary sociopolitical and socioeconomic reality, the method has recourse to the social sciences, but always taking the lives of the readers as its point of departure. To make the community of faith come alive, the method pursues the reading of the Bible within a context of prayer, celebrations, dramatizations, dances, and so on, in an atmosphere of profound human exchange and mutual solidarity.

The Local Situation

Rio de Janeiro and the Baixada Fluminense. The state of Rio de Janeiro is located in southeastern Brazil; it is a narrow strip of land bordering the Atlantic Ocean, in a fully tropical zone. The participants in the course came from three regions of the state: (1) the mountainous region, with cities located in the Serra do Mar (the Sea Mountain Range), characterized by

---

3. See C. Mesters, *Flor sem defesa: Uma explicação da Bíblia a partir do povo* (Petrópolis: Vozes, 1983), Eng. trans., *Defenseless Flower: A New Reading of the Bible* (Maryknoll, N.Y.: Orbis Books, 1989), esp. chaps. 2 and 3. Further references to this book will follow the pagination in the English edition.

mountains that have suffered grave erosion as a result of the rains and are crisscrossed by rivers. Every summer in this region the poor are threatened by mountain slides that bury houses and streets. (2) The seaside region, where one finds a great deal of land speculation and where the capital of the state—"the marvellous city" (*cidade maravilhosa*)—is located, also famous for its *favelas* or shantytowns, where the drug trade has a powerful hold on the people.[4] (3) The Baixada Fluminense, a poor and quite hot region, where, in addition to a rural area, lie the "satellite" or dormitory cities of the people who work in the capital. Migrants from all over Brazil flock here, looking for work and a way to survive, but often find only hunger, garbage, crime, and neglect. This is the most violent region of the country, where urban services (transportation, basic sanitation, hospitals, schools, and so on) either do not work or work badly. Many times, as a result of the rains, flooding occurs, causing deaths and epidemics. The situation regarding land ownership here is quite irregular. It was in this region that the course I am about to describe was given.

Access/Ascent to the Locale for the Course. We had no street name, no number, and no telephone number to help us find the place where the course was to be given. Some instructions were given as to how to reach the *casa de encontros nosso lar* (our home retreat house); we were to take the bus and ask for directions along the way. This was the first lesson of the "facilitator" (*assessor[a]*):[5] to travel as the people of the periphery travel. I invite the reader to come with me on this journey.

At the bus-stop, opposite the train station, a spectacle of misery and sociostructural collapse. Hundreds of buses followed one upon the other, fast-moving, with people hanging out the doors, stopping only when those who were waiting for the bus signaled insistently. Children, quite young, barefoot and ragged, ran around the buses, hitchhiking on one or the other, risking their lives, kicking cans and plastic cups lying on the ground. From the garbage on the streets and pavement, it looked like the aftermath of a market day, but was actually a consequence of the snack bars that cater to workers returning home and facing several hours of transportation.

After a thirty-minute wait, a bus appears, almost full. With luck I secure a place, standing, handbag on the floor (I had to take sheets, a towel, clothes, the Bible, books, and paper). After about an hour or so, I had to get off "at the stop after the St. Martha School." Does anybody know

---

4. In 1990 there were 565 *favelas* with more than nine hundred thousand inhabitants. See *Onde Moras?* (São Paulo, 1992) 102; this is the textbook used in the Campanha da Fraternidade da CNBB (Confêrencia Nacional do Bispos do Brasil)—the Campaign for Solidarity of the National Conference of Brazilian Bishops.

5. This is the name given to those who serve as leaders in this type of popular courses. Such individuals do not lecture as such, but present themes, talk about the historical and literary context, and address the questions of the participants.

where it is? It seems nobody does. An alternative: get off at the last stop. I risk the latter.

Relief: someone had come to fetch me—such is the privilege of being a facilitator! It is Tânia, a strong dark woman, smiling, confident, a leader in the work of the CEBI in the region. After a few steps, she insisted on carrying my bag, and we went up the mild incline of a dusty road for about four hundred meters.

The retreat house is comfortable. Spacious, located at the top of a hill, and surrounded by a garden with fruit trees and a variety of flowers. Even so, there was no protection against a temperature of 42 degrees centigrade (107 degrees Fahrenheit), day and night for the entire duration of the course. The mosquitoes made sleeping quite difficult, so much so that the group preferred to go on singing and dancing until the early hours of the morning instead of sleeping. Nevertheless, a sense of humor prevailed from beginning to end. Surprise, learning, and admiration on the part of the facilitator.

Profile of the Participants

There were about forty persons in all—some older than others (four were over sixty years old), with a majority of adults and about fifteen young people. In all, thirty-one women and nine men. The group came from the popular class and included students, housewives from the lower middle class, pastoral workers, small-business owners, a professor, three seminarians, two or three religious sisters, and a German young man engaged in a sort of "theological-pastoral tourism."

The atmosphere was one of great conviviality (it was the only way of fighting the heat), with a good rapport between old and young. The hospitality extended to the beginners in the CEBI and the young German was remarkable. Similarly noteworthy was the sympathy and gratitude shown to the women from the local community who volunteered to work in the kitchen.

The Structure and Dynamics of the Course

On the first day, after a simple prayer, we had the presentation of the participants, who proceeded to describe the problem of housing in their respective regions: high rents; people having no dwellings and living in shelters; other people living under bridges, in the streets, or as squatters or land invaders;[6] lack of sanitation and infrastructure; prison seen as subhuman

---

6. *Ocupação,* or land invasion, refers to illegal possession of the land by homeless persons who take over a lot or a house in which no one resides. It is a strategy meant to force the government to carry out land reform and to pay greater attention to the pressing problem of housing.

dwelling; migrants and those who are homeless as a result of floods; the selling of huts and cement slabs for others to build on top; many not being able to afford to pay their mortgages and thus being in danger of losing their property. One exception: the German young man in whose country most of the people live well. Subsequently, a text was assigned right away for group study: Genesis 24. Many questions arose as a result of this reading.

On the second day, a number of questions from the previous day were addressed, and new texts were analyzed by groups: Gen 18:1-16 (Mamre); Gen 25:19-34 (the birth of Esau and Jacob and the buying of the birthright); Gen 27:46—28:5 and 29:1-30 (the marriage of Jacob); Genesis 16 and 21:1-20 (Hagar); Judges 4 and 5 (Deborah); Judg 6:1-24 (Gideon); Gen 47:13-26 (Joseph's land policy). The reports from the different groups were presented in a highly creative fashion, using puppets, dramatizations, songs, psalms, posters, and activities involving all participants.

The objective of these first two days was to study the theme of the "house," that is, the place or mode of residence in the tribal and patriarchal society of premonarchic Israel.

On the third day, we focused on the transition from a rural/pastoral and tribal society to an urban structure, ruled by kings and called into question by the prophets. The problem of land accumulation on the part of the more powerful with the resulting expropriation of the land of the poorer segments of society was discussed. The texts examined were 1 Kgs 21:1-16 (Naboth); Isa 5:8-10, Amos 3:15 and 5:11 (the accumulation of property); Isa 10:1-2 and Mic 3:9-12 (the corruption of justice); Jer 22:1-9, 13-19 (against the palace); Jer 7:1-15 (the temple); Hos 2:16-25 and 12:10 (the return to the tents); Hos 4:1-3 and 11:1-11 (unfaithfulness of the inhabitants of the land and the faithfulness of Yahweh); and Dt 24:1-22, especially verse 5 (laws regarding the household). On this day we had a major celebration, with a climb to a nearby hill, a gathering in an improvised tent under the trees, an exchange of testimonies,[7] prayers, and hymns.

On the fourth day, we focused on the theme of dwelling in the New Testament, with analysis of the following texts: Luke 2:1-19 and John 1:14 (the birth of Jesus); Mark 5:21-43 (the daughter of Jairus); Luke 10:38-42 (Martha and Mary); Luke 7:36-50 (a sinful woman at the feet of Jesus); Luke 19:1-10 (Zacchaeus); John 2:1-12 (Cana); Mark 14:12-15 and John 13:1-12 (preparation for the Last Supper and the washing of the feet).

The fifth day continued with the study of the New Testament, examining the role of the house in the early communities: Acts 2:1-4, 42-47 (the Jerusalem community); Acts 16:11-15, 29-31 (Lydia and the jailer); Luke 2:25-52 and Matt 21:13 (Simeon, Anna, Jesus, and the temple); Mark 2:1-

---

7. It was at this time that Rosa, the main character in the second scene, gave her testimony.

12 (the paralytic enters through the roof of the house); 2 Cor 5:1-10 (the body as a dwelling); and Acts 20:7-11 (a young man falls during Paul's preaching). We went back to a text from the Old Testament—Isa 65:17-25, especially verses 21-23—to examine the ecological and eschatological point of view. The course ended with an evaluation and a final celebration.

The predominant mode of study throughout was the group form, but there were also individual readings as well as readings in groups of two. The themes for each day were introduced by the facilitator, accompanied by a simple historical and literary explanation. Some questions were used to give direction to the task of the small groups, who then reported to the group as a whole in creative ways. Thereupon the facilitator took the lead once again: fielding, commenting upon, and responding to questions from the participants. Study time was interspersed throughout with prayers, celebrations, activities, joking around, songs, and whatever proved of help in overcoming the heat and the exhaustion.

The Influence of the Local Situation on the Reading of Texts

I list at this point only some of the questions raised by the participants, questions that arose out of their own concerns and that were projected unto the texts read. I reproduce as well a number of the forms of expression used by the participants to communicate the message discovered in the biblical reading.

Letting Go the Chains. The use of Genesis 24—the story concerning the wedding of Isaac and Rebekah—as a point of departure was a risk taken by the facilitator. The aim was to introduce the participants to the context of a society that lived in tents. Thus, the wedding ceremony consisted in an announcement to the effect that the groom was taking the bride into his tent (Gen 24:67). However, this purpose was not understood right away; it was as if something were missing in the communication between the facilitator and the participants. In the middle of the discussion, they asked about the meaning of "putting the hand under the thigh" (Gen 24:2). When it was explained that taking an oath required the subject to hold his partner's genitals as a sign of commitment to life, the group relaxed and laughter broke out. Communication "caught on" because an atmosphere of frankness and familiarity had been established both with the text and among those present. From this moment on, the course flowed.

An Avalanche of Questions on the Basis of Genesis 24. The comments and questions arising from Genesis 24 were many and varied; I reproduce but a few here: "The text suggests that at the time the people lived in tents. Were they nomads? But Abraham seemed to live in a country. Did they live in houses when the text was written?" "The narrative shows the importance of the patriarchal family and the mixture of cultures. Did Rebekah's family then acknowledge Yahweh as God? Did Abraham's servant, most probably a foreigner, worship Yahweh as God?" "In Gen 24:2 does 'house' refer to a place of dwelling? Does it mean land? What was the system of land ownership at the time?" "Did God approve of this patriarchal and slave-owning society? Is this liberating?" Questions such as these led to explanations on the part of the facilitator[8] and more comments by the participants. An unexpected comment, linking the situation of a biblical character and the people of Brazil today: "Just as Isaac was sad as a result of Sarah's death, so too are we sad on account of Lula's defeat in 1989. The meeting of Isaac with Rebekah was like the impeachment of Collor for us."[9]

Matriarchs and Feminist Prospects. With regard to the focus on patriarchal, pastoral, and tribal society (the texts of the second day), the comments had to do above all with the status of women. Let me offer a few.

- On Judges 4 and 5: "Deborah called on the people to resist during the situation of oppression. Likewise today the renewal of hope comes by way of the women. Above all with regard to the question of housing."[10]

- On patriarchal society: "A woman today is still not liberated. When a woman opens the door of the house to a stranger, he asks whether her husband is home. If the husband is not home, then he asks her to call her father or brother.... Our society is still a patriarchal society."

- Linking with the experience of the church: "The patriarchal family has influenced the church as well: there is a situation of dependency on the leaders. In celebrations many is the time when the husband begins to speak while the wife holds the microphone...."

- Comparing patriarchal society with our own society: the older women in the group expressed their disappointment with the fact that today "no one wants to have more than two or three children." They spoke, with pleasure and pride, of their own large number of children, raised among many difficulties but now educated and making progress in life. "In patriarchal times marriage had reproduction much more

---

8. The bibliography used in this regard may be found in R. de Vaux, *Ancient Israel: Its Life and Institutions* (New York: McGraw-Hill, 1961).

9. In the 1989 elections in Brazil, Lula was the worker candidate, the representative of the popular classes, supported by the parties of the left. Collor, the candidate of the elite, won the election but was removed by impeachment in 1992 on the charge of governmental corruption.

10. Women have played a leading role in the Sem Terra (without land) and Sem Teto (without a roof) movements. Homeless women, sanitation workers, prostitutes, and migrants as well as women who live in the slums or *favelas* have emerged as a most powerful element in the resistance struggle of the popular movements.

in mind; today, the young people are more interested in material possessions."

- On the power of women: the women participants observed that in patriarchal society women exercised some type of power—they chose their daughters-in-law (Hagar); showed favor to their favorite child (Rebekah); and were shrewd in the presence of male authority (Rachel deceives Laban). "Today too the woman holds power in the family. A mother worries about the marriage of her children: whether her daughter-in-law is going to take care of her husband, whether her daughter is going to get beaten up by her husband. . . . A mother does not impose herself but offers advice."

- On the financial dependency of women: "In patriarchal society women were very much dependent on men. Today, a married woman who works outside the house demands more of her husband, whether it be leisure time or a better life. However, with the economic crisis everyone is turning into a 'production machine.' "

The Emergence of Political Conscience. A socioeconomic focus also played an important role in the reading and interpretation of texts. A few examples follow.

- Concerning the nomadic way of life: "The preoccupation with tying oneself to the land existed then as much as it does today, and it is linked to both the preoccupation with the family and the historical memory of the people." "Anyone who rents is a nomad." "In the nomadic way of life camps were set up next to water. Today water remains a preoccupation. In the cities above all water is a problem, along with a number of other urban services that are lacking in the poor neighborhoods: sanitation, electricity, garbage collection, transportation, and so on."

- Concerning the tribal system: "In tribal life there is communal living. Today, building construction favors the private rather than the communal realm: those who live in apartments ignore one another, yet listen through the walls to see what is going on in their neighbors' house." "In tribal society the household was the family [*familia* = *Bet-Av* (in Hebrew) = the father's house]. It is important today to rediscover the family, not in terms of an individualism involving two or three persons but as a space for human exchange, affection, reception." "In that society much importance was placed on hospitality. The Brazilian people, hospitable by nature, are losing that characteristic as a result of the lack of adequate housing and for fear of violence (no one opens the door to a stranger)."

- At a certain moment there was a turn from the Bible to a sort of baring of the heart, based on life: "In certain neighborhoods there are days when no one can leave the house without risk of life" (a reference to the war among drug gangs). "Many people are embarrassed to give their address because they are ashamed of the place where they live." "The housing problem in Brazil is acute. Besides the homeless and those who live in the streets, the poor live in greatly reduced and inhuman quarters. There is no privacy. Unplanned marriages and financial difficulties cause many families to come together in one house: there is incest, promiscuity, conflict, with great damage inflicted above all on the children." "The home, which should be a place of wellbeing and comfort, becomes inhospitable. The people prefer to meet in bars or in the street; there is no desire to go back home. Many are thrown out of their houses on account of unemployment, pregnancy, illness, and vices."

The study of patriarchal and tribal society concluded with a strophe from the song composed by the group that had studied Judges 4–5 (see 5:31):

> Tanta luta, tanta guerra
> tanta força pra vencer
> mas Javé lhe deu a Terra
> pra ver o sol nascer.[11]

Monarchical and Urban Society. With the transition to the study of monarchical and urban society in Israel, the participants sought to link the biblical texts with contemporary reality and expressed themselves by way of jesters, imitation of television news, songs, and dramatizations. The questions revolved around the political dimensions of history, and it was evident that they had already read and studied some of the prophets beforehand. I highlight at this point the work of the group that studied Jer 7:1-15, which proceeded to reproduce the prophet's speech with contemporary reality in mind:

Listen to what Yahweh says to our people:
"Watch out with regard to your way of life! Look what you are doing! Look around you! Abandoned children; addicted children; young girls in prostitution; broken families; exploited workers—and you remain there, inside your churches, thinking that you are protected by God. If you think that God is present in those churches and that you can keep on calling on his name, you are greatly deceived. Join the

---

11. "So much struggle, so much war / so much force for conquering / but Yahweh has given the earth to them / so that they might watch the sun rise."

struggle! Go to the streets! Take care to improve this situation! Listen to the cry of the people who have no justice! Join your brothers and sisters who are suffering! Bring back that hope which is no more! "You must live out the true meaning of prayer (praying-action).[12] Build community! Seek equality! Recover dignity! Value life! Only then will Yahweh, the God of liberation, live in the midst of the people."

The Theme of the House in the Gospels. This theme aroused great interest and participation. The juxtaposition of Luke 1:5-25 (the announcement to Zechariah) and Luke 1:26-38 (the announcement to Mary) in the introduction made by the facilitator had a lot of impact. In the first episode the action takes place in the temple and has to do with the old covenant; the announcement is made to a priest (an old man), who doubts and is punished by being rendered speechless. In the second episode the action takes place in a house of the people; the announcement is made to a lay young woman; she believes and is blessed; she subsequently breaks into song (the Magnificat). The sacred space of the people of Israel, which had remained fixed on the temple throughout the entire period of the monarchy, now becomes with the new covenant the house of the people. From there we proceeded to look at the texts that show Jesus' activity in the houses of Palestine.

Once the Gospels had become more familiar, the group was able to express itself with greater freedom of interpretation, exploring the theme of dwelling in each passage read.

Thus, for example, in the light of Luke 7:36-50, a question came up regarding the rich man's house—large, spacious, and comfortable: "Is hospitality possible only within such a context? It doesn't seem that way. It was the sinful woman who served as the true hostess.[13] Today, when we visit the rich, they say, 'Please feel at home,' but they distance themselves. The poor, on the contrary, are constantly asking us if we are all right and make themselves available the whole time. Perhaps the woman in that story of Luke was not able to receive Jesus in her own home, but she did welcome him with her gestures."

In its study of John 2:1-12, the group affirmed that a "house" was more than a "place," that it was a relationship. Hospitality functioned as an important condition for the happy beginning of a marriage. With such reflections as their point of departure, the group acted out a brief scene: on the occasion of a child's birthday, the mother wants to throw a party but

---

12. The authors are playing with the form of the Portuguese word for prayer, *oração,* which they see as including both praying (*orar*) and action (*ação*).—TRANS.

13. Without any profound knowledge of the biblical commentaries, this group reached the same results as the experts. See, for example, the bibliography on Luke 7:35-50 in my "Jesus, a pecadora e o fariseu," *Estudos Bíblicos* 24 (1989) 30–40.

the father balks. The mother insists. (The group is invited to sing a refrain, "To enter José's house, one must ask and demand, again and again" ["Para entrar na casa do José, tem que bater o pé, tem que bater o pé"].) With the help of her friends, the mother makes ready for the party, despite their limited resources. The guests are many and the food runs out. A neighbor woman shows solidarity. She calls her son. He responds that that has nothing to do with him, but he ends up bringing flour and sugar. The woman bakes a cake, and everyone celebrates.

The group that was acting out the story asked for the participation of the others, to stand around the scene as if they were the walls of the house. When things went right, the "walls" would take a step forward; when things went badly, a step backward. In this way we beat back heat and exhaustion; at the same time, each participant tried to "be a house" for the others. Such bodily activity made it possible to have a moving experience as well as to identify with the theme.

Other Biblical Texts. In the final part of the course, the participants themselves suggested a number of other biblical texts, mostly taken from the New Testament, in which the theme of dwelling appears. It was important for them to take note, once again, that the house in the New Testament is where Pentecost and the Eucharist take place, where the breaking of the bread in the first Christian communities takes place. Of the texts selected for this section of the course, I mention but one, Acts 20:7-11, insofar as it brought forth a highly creative and unexpected interpretation. The reason for the choice of this text may have been its character as a narrative of popular stamp, with certain comic aspects. Our people are in need of laughter and relaxation; however, the dramatization occasioned by the text brought tears to the eyes of the group in the end. The dramatization proceeded as follows: at the sound of a drum, four individuals—representing, respectively, an abandoned child, a homeless person, a marginalized young man, and a prostitute—fell to the ground, one by one, as if dead. At the sound of the melody from "Our Father of the Martyrs," these same four individuals began to rise and break bread, offering it to the others as well. The message of the text was summarized as follows: "What remained strong was the breaking of the bread, out of which resurrection takes place" ("O que ficou forte, foi a partilha do pão, de onde surge a resurreição").

In this interpretation, therefore, the theme of dwelling was expanded to include the social problem as a whole, as manifested in these four categories of human beings who have no home.

Celebrating the End. The celebration of the end of the course was brief and quite meaningful: the group gathered into a circle and, extending their arms forward and upward, formed as it were a large tent. Underneath there was a Bible, lying on the reports for the day's journal. Without any sort of prior or explicit planning, all three angles of interpretation were present there: the Bible, social reality, and the community. We read John 1:1-14 and prayer flowed from all of us in the sense of offering ourselves to become the tent of God in the midst of our reality.

Reflections on Interpreting from Such a Location

Given such a way of reading the Bible, I should like to raise at this point a few questions and then go on to reflect upon them in the light of the contributions made by three authors who have worked with biblical hermeneutics in Latin America—Clodovis Boff, Severino Croatto, and Carlos Mesters.

Three Challenges to the Popular Reading of the Bible

The reading and interpretation of the Bible described in this study pose countless questions to exegesis, theology, and pastoral theology. Before proceeding to those matters, I want to raise three challenges that are often raised regarding the popular reading of the Bible.

1. There is recourse to a great number of texts without detailed analysis of any one text. It is a panoramic and superficial reading that does not take into account the contributions of exegesis.

2. The move from the biblical reading to the contemporary situation is quite rapid, without respect for the historical distance that exists between us today and the time of writing. One runs the risk thereby of turning out mechanical interpretations, isolated from the historical and literary contexts of the texts.

3. The Bible plays a secondary role in this type of interpretation. The references to life and contemporary practice become primary and leave the text behind. There is a danger of transforming Sacred Scripture into a simple pretext for talking about life.

Questioning Such Challenges

In a very succinct way I should like to review and respond to these challenges from the point of view of the service rendered to the poor who search in the word of God for light and strength for their lives.

1. The poor read and quote the Bible across an enormously wide range of situations. Their reading is not continuous but does preserve the continuity of faith. Like dona Maria and Rosa, the poor "pick out" texts and stories in their everyday life that they have had the chance to read and reflect upon in the course of some celebration or that they have studied as part of some course (there are also courses on a biblical book or text).

When they read a series of separate texts focused around a specific theme, the people have the chance to go beyond a limited view and develop a vision of the whole. There is great richness in the Bible, an enormous variety of perspectives with regard to the perception and interpretation of life. To read different texts, from different historical periods and contexts, is a way of revealing its plurality/diversity while at the same time safeguarding the broad unity that runs through the whole Bible as a book of faith and hope.[14]

2. In going from the biblical text to actual life and vice versa without examining the specificity of the writing (its historical and literary context), there is a real risk of making the text say whatever we want and not what the author wanted to say. However, it is good to remember that it is not only the simple people who engage in this type of interpretation. So do the magisterium of the church and the theologians, and so did the fathers of the church when they developed the "spiritual or symbolic reading." Moreover, this is a phenomenon to be found in the Scriptures themselves, when the New Testament reads the Old Testament in the light of the paschal event.

That does not absolve us, however, from maintaining a critical perspective in order to avoid detours and unfounded interpretations.[15] Clodovis Boff distinguishes between two models of interpretation:[16]

a. The first involves a correspondence in terms, as conveyed by the following equation:

$$\frac{\text{Jesus}}{\text{his context}} = \frac{\text{Christian community}}{\text{contemporary context}}$$

In this model the terms in question are compared by placing them parallel to one another and then transferring the meaning of the first fraction to the second. This model can be seen at work in the course when Deborah (Judges 4–5) was compared to the women today who organize the popular resistance. It was also the model employed by dona Maria and perhaps in part by Rosa as well in the two scenes portrayed at the beginning.

b. The second model involves a correspondence in relationships, taking into account the interpretive process itself: from the original happening to its consignment to writing, and then continuing afterwards with the relationship among the readers, the text, and the meanings that emerge from the text:

---

14. This is a favorite theme of Mesters; see, for example, *Defenseless Flower,* 12–54.

15. Such is precisely the job of the facilitator.

16. C. Boff, *Teologia e prática: Teologia do político e suas mediações* (Petrópolis: Vozes, 1978), Eng. trans., *Theology and Praxis: A Theology of the Political Realm and Its Mediations* (Maryknoll, N.Y.: Orbis Books, 1987) 143–46. All references are to the pagination in the English edition.

$$\frac{\text{Scripture}}{\text{its context}} = \frac{\text{we}}{\text{our context}}$$

This model involves a creative relationship, which comes about when the communities strive to reread the Bible using their own particular situation as a point of departure. Thus, comments C. Boff:

> We need not, then, look for formulas to "copy" or techniques to "apply" from scripture. What scripture will offer us are rather something like orientations, models, types, directives, principles, inspirations—elements permitting us to acquire, on our own initiative, a "hermeneutic competency."[17]

This type of interpretation can be seen at work in the course when one of the groups proceeded to write a prophetic speech in imitation of Jeremiah. The group captured the spirit behind the letter of the text. As such, the group was at the same time creative and faithful.[18] Similarly, in expanding the meaning of the episode concerning the young man who fell out the window (Acts 20:7-12), the group also had recourse to this second interpretive model. In a certain sense, Rosa, the main character of the second scene, employed this method of interpretation.

This method is possible because the biblical text is not closed in on itself but remains open to ever-new interpretations, provided it is read in different situations and with the "eyes of faith." In other words, Scripture possesses what Croatto calls a "reserve of meaning," a potential for a variety of interpretations, which make the text "speak" to the today of its readers.[19] Thus, for example, the reading of the story concerning the sinful woman who is forgiven (Luke 7:35-50) gave way—when the story was looked at from the perspective of dwelling—to an interpretation whereby human beings can be a "house" and shelter others by means of an affectionate and loving relationship. Such was the lesson given by Jesus to the Pharisee, who was transformed into an apprentice to the true hostess.

3. At times the Bible played a secondary role. At various points during the course, the group put the Bible aside and proceeded to vent their hearts, to comment and reflect upon contemporary life—forgetting the text, its historical context, the message of the authors, the traditional interpretation. In a sense life took the place of the Bible. But is this not the aim of the Bible? To make room for life, and "abundant life" (John 10:10)?

---

17. Boff, *Theology and Praxis*, 149.

18. Freedom and faithfulness are two characteristics that Mesters finds in the popular reading of the Bible; see his "How the Bible Is Interpreted in Some Basic Christian Communities in Brazil," *Conflicting Ways of Interpreting the Bible* (ed. H. Küng and J. Moltmann; *Concilium* 158; New York: Seabury, 1980) 41–46. [The latter study becomes the first chapter of *Defenseless Flower*, 1–11.—TRANS.]

19. S. Croatto, *Biblical Hermeneutics: Toward a Theory of Reading as the Production of Meaning* (Maryknoll, N.Y.: Orbis Books, 1987).

Such is quite clearly the position of Mesters. Using the method followed by the fathers of the church as well as by the sacred authors themselves as a basis, Mesters insists on the priority of life over Scripture, of the present over the past, and of the Spirit over the letter.[20] C. Boff takes the same position when he declares, "Priority is to be accorded to the value of the real practice of the community over that of any theoretical elaboration" in the exercise of the hermeneutical task.[21]

Thus, when the readers of our poor communities go from the Bible to life, they are operating within the center of the hermeneutical circle: they are allowing the creation of meaning to flow from the reception of meaning.[22] They are allowing hermeneutics to bloom into ethics and are thereby quite simply carrying out the aim of the Bible itself. The Scripture ceases to be a text to be read and becomes a light for the eyes to read the text of life and construct meaning from it.

Conclusion

Putting aside the tendency to idealize, it is imperative to acknowledge the fragility of every particular reading and the relativity of every historical subject in the interpretation of the Scriptures. The Bible itself is but one of the great cultural patrimonies produced by humanity, under the influence of the Spirit. Two passing scenes and a very modest course have served as the basis for these reflections. The latter are provisional and subject to many corrections, but it was my intention to contribute in some way to the discussion regarding "social location and biblical interpretation."

---

20. I have devoted a chapter of my doctoral dissertation to this question; see "O método de leitura popular da Bíblia na América Latina: A contribuição de Carlos Mesters," Ph.D. diss., Pontifícia Universidade Católica de Rio de Janeiro, 1991, chap. 5.2.

21. Boff, *Theology and Praxis*, 150.

22. Ibid., 136.

13

Exegesis of Second Isaiah from the Perspective of the Oppressed: Paths for Reflection

J. Severino Croatto

The reading of the Bible, like the reading of any text, is always carried out from a particular location. The social practices of the exegete condition his or her reading of the biblical text. This is an unquestionable fact, though not always acknowledged. There is no pure, much less objective, "academic" exegesis as such. Objectivity is relative, if not deceptive. Thus, generations of exegetes can work on a text, approaching it from many different directions and employing all the methods at their disposal, and yet fail "to see" dimensions of meaning that are *in the text*. For example, much has been written about the story concerning the Tower of Babel, but only interpreters who have experienced in their own lives the imposition of a "sole language" have been able to see in the text a sociopolitical dimension involving a project of domination (with the city and the tower as its symbols) grounded, at both an ideological and a political level, in a control of the people by means of a sole language, namely, the language of the dominant power (the central power). In the narrative of Gen 11:1-9, therefore, Yahweh's punishment does not consist so much in the multiplication of languages—which actually signifies the liberation of the oppressed through a decentralization of the power of the city—but rather in the dismantling of the project of domination as sustained by a "sole language."

Similar examples can be readily multiplied. In fact, a good *hermeneutic* reading of the biblical text consists of an exegesis that is carried out from within the situation of the interpreter. Hermeneutics has to do with the exploration of the reserve of meaning of the text, which is not "imposed" on the text but rather discovered *in the text*, even if it does not coincide with the intention of the author.[1] To undertake a reading of the Bible "from one's own place" is to do hermeneutics correctly, with all of

This is a translation of the original manuscript, "Exégesis del DeuteroIsaías desde el lugar de los oprimidos (pistas de reflexión)." The translation is by Fernando F. Segovia.

1. See J. Severino Croatto, *Biblical Hermeneutics: Toward a Theory of Reading as the Production of Meaning* (Maryknoll, N.Y.: Orbis Books, 1987) 22.

its implications. At the same time, any good exegesis, even scientific exegesis, cannot but be hermeneutics, either because the conditions for each and every reading cause it not to reproduce a past meaning but to "produce" a meaning that makes sense for the reader or because the exegete approaches the biblical text with the belief that the text has to do with him or her. Consequently, all exegesis is at the same time eisegesis, whether one likes it or not.[2]

Before turning to the main theme of this essay, I should like to foreground an important component of our *hermeneutical* reading of the Bible in Latin America. Since *liberation,* a theme that permeates large portions of the Bible, constitutes one of the central semantic axes of such a reading, the reading that we do "from our location" of oppressed and forgotten peoples leads us to rediscover the sociohistorical horizon involved in the *production of the text.* Put in contrary terms, an analysis of the social and political conditions out of which a biblical text emerges leads us to a message that is in accord with that demanded by *our* own situation.

A socioanalytical reading of the Bible, an interpretive dimension almost completely bypassed in the traditional historical-critical methods, foregrounds the rhetorical situation that gives rise to the text, a situation that may be and usually is similar to that of the reader. Such a reading, however, goes beyond simple parallelism or concordism (*concordismo*): the two situations are by no means regarded as equal; rather, the situation of the reader is seen as allowing the reader to discern in the text dimensions that prove relevant. Thus, a socioanalytical reading of the Bible represents for us an important aspect of that hermeneutical and situated reading that we wish to carry out.

In the present study I shall engage in such a reading of Second Isaiah (Isaiah 40–55). Historical-critical studies, abundant and useful as they are, do suffer from a fundamental weakness, the principle of incoherence. All such studies—whether they proceed to subdivide the text ad infinitum or place it within literary or semiotic complexes of different lengths and whether they are whole commentaries or isolated studies—"presuppose" certain untouchable truths, which are not truths at all but actually render a global interpretation of the prophetic text impossible.

One of these false "truths" is to see in Second Isaiah a universalist concern involving the conversion of other peoples. How can the urgent message of liberation from exile, however, be "combined" with this other message of conversion?

The same thing happens when those passages that seem to speak of a call on the part of Yahweh, especially the badly named "servant songs" (42:1-7; 49:1-9a; 50:4-9b, 10-11; 52:13—53:12), are associated with the prophet-author. The result is another incoherence: Why refer in the text

---

2. Croatto, *Hermeneutics,* 66–83.

to the prophet who produces the text? The text speaks of Israel and its liberation; the prophet is nowhere to be found, not even at the beginning (40:1-8 is *not* a prophetic call). In any case, at the redactional level the text is the same as that of Isaiah 1–39.

My goal, then, in this study is to carry out a coherent reading of Isaiah 40–55 as a program for the liberation and reconstitution of all Israel on its own land. It is a reading that is undertaken "from our place." In the process we shall gradually discover the results of an exegetical work—already gathered together into a full commentary of the text[3]—undertaken from our reality as peoples oppressed, disintegrated, without offers, dispersed, "unbelieving," and without utopias.

Paths for a New Reading of Second Isaiah

The Context of Second Isaiah

I should like to begin with the rhetorical situation that gives rise to the production of the text of Isaiah 40–55. Such a situation is twofold.

On the one hand, there are the captives in Babylon, from where the prophet is writing—these are the primary addressees of his message of liberation. Thus, the imperial capital is mentioned in 43:14 and 48:14, 20; the burlesque poem of 47:1-15 refers to it as well; and the oracle of 46:1-13 alludes to its tutelary god, Marduk (as well as to his son, Nabu, from the neighboring city of Borsippa). In addition, almost the entire text reflects the "theology of Marduk," the heroic protagonist of the Babylonian poem of creation (the *Enuma Elish*) and legitimator of the Chaldean Empire and its practices of domination.

On the other hand, there are groups of Judaeans (and Israelites from the north) dispersed among the nations of the empire, as a result of commercial, economic (the poverty of Judah after the Chaldean invasions of 597 and 586 BCE), or political reasons (other deportations). Texts such as 43:5-6 (the return of the exiles from the four cardinal points) and 49:12 (the return from the north, the west, and the south) as well as the language concerning the "extremes/ends of the earth," which we shall examine below, point to an imperial world extending beyond the geographical borders of Babylon.

Within this broad imperial realm—extending from Babylon all the way to the "islands" and the "ends of the earth"—the groups of Judaeans or Israelites either are prisoners, are condemned to forced labor, or have perhaps accommodated themselves to the new conditions (acculturation). In every situation imaginable, the figure of Yahweh must appear worn out,

---

3. This commentary has been written for Editora Vozes of Petrópolis, Brazil; it will be published earlier in Spanish by Editorial Verbo Divino of Quito, Ecuador.

inoperative. After having lived for so long in a new cultural and religious context, such people must have internalized the cultural realities of their new situation. Marduk, the god of the empire, and the many other gods of life must now hold the attention of the followers of Yahweh. What can Yahweh do to win them back?

It is not easy to convince Israel with regard to any proposal for liberation—an Israel that lies disintegrated, dispersed among many countries, disenchanted with its traditional God, who is responsible for such a situation. How is it possible to speak to Israel? What should be said?

These two questions show that the prophet will be able to send a valid and credible message only if he knows *what* to say and *how* to say it. In other words, the message must be coherent from beginning to end and must have recourse to all available rhetorical strategies. Such is in fact the case: Second Isaiah is not at all a disorganized collection of oracles involving a variety of literary genres.[4] Not only is it possible to identify larger narrative sections within it,[5] but also the text should be read in one sitting, insofar as it is a *literary work* with a kerygmatic and theological intention that is deployed as such rather than in terms of fragments.

The present study presupposes such previous work, that is, an analysis of the text as a whole. Such analysis reveals a remarkable sense of coherence, especially highlighted by the many literary genres employed (salvation oracles, disputations, lawsuits, hymns, a lamentation, exhortations, invitations, and so on) as well as the repetition of formulas, lexemes, titles of Yahweh and Israel, images, and so forth.

The Message of Second Isaiah

The text begins with a deliberate inversion: a reference to Jerusalem in the overture of 40:1-11 (see vv. 2, 9) that should come at the end and a con-

---

4. For such a fragmented perspective, see, for example, C. Westermann, *Sprache und Struktur der Prophetie Deuterojesajas* (Stuttgart: Calwer, 1981); R. P. Merendino, *Der Erste und der Letzte: Eine Untersuchung von Jes 40–48* (Leiden: Brill, 1981); K. Elliger and Hans-Jürgen Hermisson, *Deuterojesaja* (Neukirchen-Vluyn: Neukirchener-Verlag, 1978) vols. 1 and 2; R. N. Whybray, *Isaiah 40–66* (Grand Rapids: Eerdmans, 1981). For a more literary, and even semiotic, approach, see, for example, R. Lack, *La symbolique du livre d'Isaïe: Essai sur l'image littéraire comme element de structuration* (Rome: Biblical Institute, 1973); Y. Gitay, *Prophecy and Persuasion: A Study of Isaiah 40–48* (Bonn: Linguistica Biblica, 1981); A. Laato, "The Composition of Isaiah 40–55," *Journal of Biblical Literature* 109 (1990) 207–28; C.-W. Park, "The Triadic Pattern: A Study in the Structure of Isaiah 40–49," Ph.D. diss., Aberdeen Univ., 1984; H. C. Spykerboer, *The Structure and Composition of Deutero-Isaiah, with Special Reference to the Polemics against Idolatry* (Meppel: Krips Repro, 1976).

5. For more or less extended divisions, see Lack, *Symbolique;* P. Bonnard, *Le second Isaïe, son disciple et leurs éditeurs: Isaïe 40–66* (Études Bibliques; Paris: Gabalda, 1972); R. F. Melugin, *The Formation of Isaiah 40–55* (Berlin-New York: de Gruyter, 1976), with emphasis on the redaction of Second Isaiah; Gitay, *Prophecy,* with emphasis on rhetoric; Park, "Composition"; J. Goldingay, "The Arrangement of Is 40–45," *Vetus Testamentum* 29 (1979) 288–99.

clusion in 55:12-13 that deals with the "departure" from Babylon. In the central section, then, two major parts can be discerned: the first, 40:12—49:13, attempts to *persuade* the captives of the salvific power and will of Yahweh; the second, 49:14—54:17 or 55:11, sets out to console Zion with the hope of an imminent liberation. The result is a literary strategy whereby the two moments of the foreseen event are brought closely together: the departure from captivity and the arrival in the old capital city, from which the exiles had been taken.

This perspective is the same as that of the exodus tradition: departure from Egypt and journey to the promised land. Given the framework presented by the Pentateuch, there is *no* arrival in the land; in fact, after Num 22:1 the people move no farther. The same holds true for a prophetic text such as Second Isaiah, given its utopian dimension: there is no arrival in the land; what matters is the *hope* of arrival, not the way in which such an arrival is accomplished. Furthermore, the return of 538 BCE (the Edict of Cyrus) is not a fulfillment of this hope. Consequently, the text of Isaiah 40–55, as it presently stands, should not be seen as coming in its entirety from the time of the exile. Rather, I prefer to see it as a work that was brought to completion at a later time, given both its use and rereading of material from Second Isaiah (the message to the captives in Babylon) and its proposal for a reconstitution of the ideal "Israel" in its own land, a proposal that leads in turn to a call for the return of the people from all the corners of the world ("the ends of the earth").

I have argued in my commentary on Isaiah 1–39 that the proper horizon for the reading of this text (that is, chaps. 1–39) is that of the Persian period rather than the eighth century, since approximately 80 percent of it consists of rereadings, some of them quite close to the language of Second Isaiah.[6] A passage such as 11:10-16 is decisive in this regard. I shall return to this point later; at this time, however, I should like to analyze the proposal put forward by Isaiah 40–55.

1. The first aim of the author is to "empower" Yahweh for a liberating action. From a literary point of view, the author has to create discourses that are rhetorically effective for the addressees of the message. He has to *convince* the addressees that it is Yahweh, and no other god, who is both able and willing to save them. The task is by no means easy since the addressees believe that their God has forgotten them. The complaint of 40:27 ("Hidden from the LORD is my way; my God has forgotten my liberation")[7] is programmatic in this regard. Such is the problem that the text will seek to answer.

---

6. See J. Severino Croatto, *Isaías: A palavra profética e sua releitura hermenêutica, I:1-39: O profeta da justiça e da felicidade* (Petrópolis: Vozes, 1989) 20–25.

7. Bible quotations throughout the essay are the author's own, adapted into English by the translator.—TRANS.

The first step is to remold the figure of Yahweh in such a way as to render the God of Israel's proposal for liberation credible. In other words, given the fact that there is another great god (Marduk) who triumphs with the empire, that there are many other gods of life who "function" within the cultural context in which the exiles find themselves, and that when all is said and done Yahweh is the God of a land no longer inhabited by Yahweh's people, how can this God be seen as having a valid offer for the Israelites? How can such a line of thinking be overcome?

The prophet has recourse to an excellent device, with profound psychological effects—a description of Yahweh along the lines of Marduk, that is, bearing the attributes of Marduk. The presupposition here of course is that Marduk is known as presented in the *Enuma Elish,* where he is characterized as the wise Creator, Arranger of the Cosmos, Savior, King, Invincible Hero, and Lord of the Word. The poet carries out this transference of attributes by various means: the disputations with the other gods or with Israel (actually, all the disputations have to do with Israel); the satires against Babylon (chap. 47) and its tutelary gods (46:1-2, 5-7); the appeal to the "historical memory" of Israel; and above all the impressive list of functional titles assigned to Yahweh throughout the work. The opposition between the figure of Yahweh in Second Isaiah and the figure of Marduk in the *Enuma Elish* is remarkable and deserves close analysis.

2. All of the titles bestowed on Yahweh have to do with the proposal of liberation from captivity and oppression. For example, the title of "Savior" has nothing to do with sin or any other interior and individual dimension of human beings but rather with the situation of slavery faced by the people. A *go'el* is (*a*) a relative who intervenes in order to redeem property that has been sold (Lev 25:23-24) or a family member who has fallen into slavery (Lev 25:47-55); or (*b*) one who takes revenge for the death of a relative (Deut 19:6). In Second Isaiah the term is transferred onto a religious plane and applied to the relations between Yahweh and Israel, but its connotations are *social* and *political:* the one redeemed is the Israel of the exile and the diaspora.

As a result, the frequent designation of Israel as the "servant" of Yahweh, its owner and LORD, becomes quite important. Marduk, its present owner, shall no longer be its "Lord." The title is also programmatic. To claim that the servant is the prophet who writes constitutes an unforgivable exegetical distraction: either because the sociopolitical dimension involving an oppressed people and not an isolated individual is lost thereby or because the text explicitly designates *Israel* as the servant of Yahweh (41:8, 9; 43:10; 44:1, 2, 21 [2x]; 45:4; 48:20; 49:3, 5, 6, 7). This last text is particularly to the point, insofar as it situates the title of "servant" within a political and social context of domination: "Thus says Yahweh, the *Savior* of Israel, his chosen one, to the one despised, abhorred by all, the *servant of dominators:* 'Kings shall see and shall arise; princes, and they shall prostrate themselves.'" Can such a title refer to the prophet? Not at all; the servant of the four "songs" cannot but be Israel (see no. 7 below).

As Isa 49:7 also suggests, the title *qĕdoš Yiśra'el* should be included within this perspective as well. To translate it as "the Holy One of Israel" is to blur its meaning. If *qadoš* means "set aside, different, consecrated," then the title can be understood as "the Chosen One of Israel." In the context of Second Isaiah, however, this title is used polemically, in a *counterhegemonic* sense: it reclaims the exclusivity of Yahweh in Yahweh's dealings with Israel and denies the complicity of the other gods and their relevance for Israel. Such gods do not form part of Israel's "historical memory." Thus, many texts speak of their inability to reveal ("to point" [*nagad*, Hi.]), to make people listen (see 43:9, 12; 44:6-8), and even to "act" (for example, 41:21-24). It is not so much a case of ontological inability (because they are nothing) but its very opposite: the gods are nothing *because* they have never intervened in the history of the people *of Yahweh* (see, within the literary genre of the disputation, the above-mentioned texts as well as 41:1-5, 21-29, and 45:20-25).

Now, to be sure, the referential addressees of these disputations with the gods are neither the gods themselves nor their worshipers, but *Israel*. Therefore, the title "the Chosen One of Israel" is central (41:14, 16, 20; 43:3, 14, 15; 45:11; 47:4; 48:17; 49:7 [2x]; 54:5; 55:5) and especially highlighted given its rarity outside Isaiah (Jer 50:29; 51:5; Pss 71:22; 78:41; 89:18).

At the same time, given the fact that Marduk is the "Creator" God par excellence in the Mesopotamian tradition, it is not at all surprising that Second Isaiah should constantly transfer this title onto Yahweh, with reference to both the cosmos (40:26; 42:5; 45:7, 18 [2x]) and human reality (41:20; 45:12; 48:7; 54:16 [2x]), above all Israel (43:1, 7, 15). Marduk also controls all the corners of the universe and human history. It is imperative, therefore, to deprive him of this attribute and to show that it belongs exclusively to Yahweh. Such a transference accounts for the frequency of the verbs (in participial form when used to describe Yahweh) "to create" (*bara'*), "to make" (*'aśa*), "to fashion" (*yaṣar*) (the three together in 45:7), often in association with "to redeem" as well (43:1, 7, 14-15). These verbs are meant to awaken the historical memory of Israel, exclusively tied to Yahweh as it is.

The clearest manifestation of power is tied to the title "King," a title that in the Babylonian poem all the gods bestow on Marduk so that he may deliver them from the threat of Tiamat (symbol of the "rebellion" of the enemy). In a key passage this title is linked to the power of the word and directed toward an act of salvation:

You are the most honorable of the great gods,
Your decree is without equal, your command is Anu.

You, Marduk, are the most honorable of the great gods,
Your decree is without equal, your word is Anu. . . .
Your word will be immovable, your command beyond question. . . .
Oh, Marduk! Truly you are our vindicator.
We have bestowed on you royal power over the entire universe.
When you take your seat in the assembly, your word will be supreme.

· ·

When the gods, his parents, saw the fruit of their word,
they rendered homage with joy: Marduk is King!

(4.3-15, 27-28)

This concentration of "effective" power in Marduk finds its historical correspondence in the hegemony of the king of Babylon. The myth represents, therefore, an ideological legitimation for the Babylonian Empire and its repression of other peoples, including the people of Judah.

To be sure, the prophet could not ignore this aspect of the figure of Marduk, given the effect it could have on the captives, who no longer experienced the action of their own God. In four important passages of the oracles, Yahweh is called "King" ("King of Jacob" [41:21]; "your King" [43:15]; "King of Israel" [44:6]; "your God reigns" [52:7]). The last example represents a good tiding to Zion brought by a messenger who announces its liberation. The proclamation recalls that of the *Enuma Elish* cited above (4.28). The other three passages are just as eloquent, dealing as they do with the polemic against the other gods (41:21; 44:6) or the creative and redeeming power of Yahweh (43:15, after the reference to Babylon in v. 14). The sociopolitical connotations of the title are evident and come to the fore in a reading from the perspective of the oppressed.

3. The concrete historical focus of the prophetic text calls for comment regarding a group of words of great density that have, however, been largely misrepresented in the translations: *mišpaṭ, ṣedeq/ṣedaqa, yeša'/yešu'a*. What is the meaning of Israel's complaint in 40:27, "My 'right' is hidden from Yahweh" (see also 49:4)? What is the "right" or "judgment" that the servant of Yahweh will bring forth to the extremes of the earth, according to 42:1, 3, 4? What does it mean for Yahweh to call this same servant "according to justice" (42:6) or to raise up a liberator "whom justice shall meet at every step" (41:2)?

A term can be dense, suggestive, but not ambiguous from the point of view of the message. If a term has various semantic connotations, as in the cases cited above, the literary and referential context (rather than its etymology) bestows upon it a *univocal* meaning. What all these terms have in common is a reference to an action, an intervention on the part of Yahweh, with a plan in mind. There is a correspondence between these terms and the Sumerian *me*, the *kittu/mîšarum* of the Akkadian texts, the *dikē* of the Greeks, and the *neltiliztli* of the pre-Colombian Nahuatl of Mexico.[8] There is a transcendent order with manifestations on the divine, cosmic, social, liturgical, and ethical planes. Put in terms that are closer to the biblical worldview, Yahweh has a plan or project that is made concrete in the history of Israel by means of Yahweh's powerful interventions. Such acts are the ones expressed by means of this terminology, to which the following terms must also be added: *šalom* or *ṭobah* as result and *torah* as ideological component. Consequently, I have opted for an understanding (and translation) of these terms within the context of the plan or acts of *liberation* on the part of Yahweh. Thus,

- *mišpaṭ* = "liberation" (40:27; 42:1, 3, 4; 49:4); "salvific action" (51:4).

- *ṣedeq/ṣedaqa* = "salvation" (41:2, 10; 45:19, 23); "plan of salvation" (42:6; 45:13); "salvific action" (42:21); "acts of salvation" (45:24); "liberation" (45:8 [2x]; 46:12, 13; 51:5, 6, 7, 8).

- *yeša'/yešu'a* = "salvation"; or sometimes, "project of salvation" (46:13a).

- *šalom* refers to a state of wholeness and plenitude and is perhaps better translated as "well-being" rather than "peace" (45:7; 48:18, 22; 53:5; 54:10, 13). In 52:7 a messenger of good tidings arrives in Jerusalem announcing "well-being" (*šalom*) and "happiness" (*ṭob*), and hence "salvation." The three terms are interrelated. To translate the first as "peace" would leave a lot unsaid. The message has nothing to do with the end of a war or a conflict; rather, it concerns the beginning of a new situation, with all of its economic, social, and—to be sure—political ramifications.

One passage where all of these terms come together is 51:8. In the announcement of verses 4-8, which is modulated by the alternation of *ṣedeq/ṣedaqa* and *yeša '/yešu'a*, one finds as well a twofold occurrence of the term *torah*, the first as parallel to *mišpaṭ* and the second as parallel to *ṣedeq* (v. 7a). The message speaks of the proximity and duration of liberation. In such a context, *torah* is not the law, much less the law of Moses, but the "instruction" or teaching that Yahweh offers—an "Isaian" way of referring to the salvific plan of the God of Israel as made known by the prophet (see 2:3; 8:16, 20; in 28:9 the verb). In 42:4 and 42:21 *torah* may

---

8. For some of these concepts, see H. H. Schmid, *Gerechtigkeit als Weltordnung: Hintergrund und Geschichte der alttestamentlichen Gerechtigkeitsbegriffes* (Tübingen: Mohr, 1968); N. P. Lemche, "*Anduārum* and *mîšarum*: Comments on the Problem of Social Edicts and their Applications in the Near East," *Journal of Near Eastern Studies* 38 (1979) 11–22.

be found as parallel to *mišpaṭ* and *ṣedeq,* respectively, showing thereby the association of this term with the lexicon of liberation and salvation.[9]

In sum, I should like to emphasize that one must restore to these terms their theological and kerygmatic density rather than dilute it by means of generic equivalencies. When the text is read from a situation of oppression, these terms have a reserve of meaning that has by and large been bypassed.

4. One finds in Second Isaiah a group of passages that are usually characterized as "anti-idolatrous" (40:19-20; 41:5-7; 44:9-20; 46:1-2, 5-7 [+ 42:17; 45:16a, 20b]). It is clear, from the point of view of literary criticism, that these passages break up the normal sequence of the text. Isaiah 44:9-20 (prose) provides the best example in this regard: verses 21-23 follow much better after verses 6-8 than after verses 9-20. Likewise, the satire of 41:6-7 is regarded as a displacement from 40:19-20, with some versions relocating it in that context. At the same time, the more recent literary criticism (which pays far more attention to the actual composition of the text as a literary *work* than to the origin of its different units) has pointed to the rhetorical function of these passages *as they presently stand.*[10] There is no need to insist on this point.[11] My concern here is to determine the textual and referential addressees of these passages, and for this task a global reading of Second Isaiah is in order.

The characterization of the theme in terms of "idolatry" already represents a step in the direction of incoherence in interpretation. If the main theme has to do with the making and worship of *idol*-statues, then the situation involves the critique of a cult in which the sacred images are *divinized.* Such a critique, however, amounts to a parody of universal religiosity. The images of the gods are "symbols" of the gods, not their material nature; insofar as the gods are transcendent—otherwise, they would not be gods—they can reveal themselves only in representations of our human existence. Idolatry as such does not exist, even if the Bible itself is at the heart of such language (Pss 115:4-8; 135:15-17; Jer 10:2-5; Wis 13-15; and so on, including of course the texts from Second Isaiah).

The actual problem addressed in these passages is that of the *other gods* represented by these statues (with the statues themselves seen as specific to the various gods). When read from this perspective, the four texts men-

---

9. Only in 42:24 (and perhaps in 42:21 as well) does *torah* seem to refer to the law already known, but v. 24b does not come from the same hand as vv. 24a and 25, introducing as it does the language of confession of sins (cf. Neh 9:33; Dan 9:5-19; Ps 106:6-47) as a result of the disobedience of the law, a typical theme of the Deuteronomic "editor" (see Deut 28:63-68; 29:21-22; Josh 23:12-16; 1 Kgs 8:44-51; 2 Kgs 23:26-27). In a prophetic text such as Isaiah, however, the term can refer to disobeying Yahweh's voice as made known by the prophets.

10. See, for example, Melugin, *Formation;* and Spykerboer, *Structure.*

11. See R. J. Clifford, "The Function of the Idol Passages in Second Isaiah," *Catholic Biblical Quarterly* 42 (1980) 450–64.

tioned suddenly take on a sociopolitical dimension. Again, the problem has nothing to do with the statues as such but rather with those gods who are not Yahweh. Thus, it is necessary to disqualify them as gods, to show their emptiness and nonexistence (with the term *tohû* [41:29]; with *'ayin* [41:24; 44:6-8; 45:5, 6, 14, 18, 21, 22; 46:9; 47:15]), their inability to reveal and carry out any act of liberation (see no. 2 above).

As a result, we can now see these seemingly out-of-place texts as forming part of a literary network that reinforces their rhetorical function.

One question comes immediately to the fore: To whom is the prophet speaking? Is it to those who worship these "other" gods? But that is not the problem of Second Isaiah nor perhaps of any other biblical book (except for Rom 1:18-23, where the Christians, however, are the addressees). The alternative, "Yahweh or the other gods," is formulated from within the faith of Israel, as in Josh 24:14-24. In whom do the captives within the Babylonian Empire place their trust? Given the process of acculturation, quite long already and in all likelihood quite profound as well, they should be leaning toward other gods more effective than Yahweh, the God of their ancestors. At the same time, to be sure, the internalization of the gods associated with the oppressive empire is a process that gradually stamps out any possibility of liberation.

Thus, the prophet has recourse to many rhetorical devices in order to "convince" the exiles that Yahweh alone is God. One such device is the mockery of these other gods with respect to the making of their images (40:19-20; 44:9-20; 46:6) and the worship through such images. These gods cannot sustain themselves (40:20b; 41:7b; 46:7) but must be "carried" and sustained (46:1-2)—they are gods who *cannot save,* even when called upon to do so ("Save me, for you are my God!" [44:17b]).

The real addressees, therefore, of these "antigods" (and not "antiidolatrous") texts are the Israelites themselves, whose incredulity with regard to Yahweh is reflected in many other passages (see, in programmatic fashion, 40:12-31 and the criticism of the deaf and the blind in 42:18-20 and 43:8). The most telling proof that those who trust in other gods and worship them through their images are none other than the exiles lies in the long complaint of 48:1-11. They constitute the textual "addressees" of Yahweh's oracle (v. 1); they are the ones who forget their "historical memory" (vv. 3-5), a memory that would have kept them from calling upon the help of other gods: "For this reason I revealed these things to you a long time ago; before they came to pass, I made you listen, so that you would not say, 'My image made them; my statue and my molten image commanded them.'"

The three substantives refer to the images that function as symbols for the different gods. An introduction of the term "idols" at this point (see the common versions) serves only to muddle the clarity of the passage.

The prayer to the god "that was made" of 44:17b ("Save me, for *you* are *my* God!" with the emphatic "you" at the end) shows that the theme in question is that of liberation, that it has to do with the people of Israel and no other people.

Texts such as these are examples of countercultural resistance.

5. This problematic is directly related to another exegetical distortion, namely, the "missionary" interpretation of a number of passages from Second Isaiah. The passages in question are those that speak of "islands"/ "nations" (41:1, 5; 42:4, 10, 12; 49:1; 51:5, and so on) or "extremes/ends of the earth" (41:5, 9; 42:10; 43:6; 45:22; 48:20; 49:6; 52:10). Such passages are usually taken to point to the efficacy of Yahweh's action with regard to other peoples or as an invitation to the "pagans" to turn to the "true God." To be sure, behind such a (re)reading stands a long tradition of interpretation, already found within the New Testament itself (Acts 13:47; see Luke 2:30-32). In its time such a reading was indeed legitimate, as an interpretation "from a specific location" (the missionary concern of the earliest Christian church). However, *our* reading place is different; as oppressed peoples, we have other lenses with which "to see" the text.

Furthermore, what actually justifies a sociopolitical reading of these texts is the fact that such a reading recovers the level of their first production. The "missionary" interpretation deviates in two ways from this initial meaning. On the one hand, it sidesteps the dominant sociopolitical character of the entire book, to which I have pointed all along. On the other hand, it modifies the addressees, who turn out to be the "pagans" (an infelicitous term from the Christian tradition) rather than the *Israelites themselves,* as it should be for the sake of coherence. There is no rhetorical situation within the text itself that calls for such an interpretation. What is urgent is to save Israel, not only from captivity itself but also from its slide toward other gods who are not, at least from the point of view of its own "historical memory," liberating.

In conclusion, all these oracles that refer to "islands"/"nations" or the "extremes/ends of the earth" have to do with the world of the Chaldean Empire (or the Persian Empire, in the case of the final level of redaction). As metaphors, such expressions may be an exaggeration; however, they do testify with eloquence to the universal power of Yahweh and Yahweh's plan of salvation for the *whole* of Israel.

6. The message of Second Isaiah, then, works with two figures of Israel, in opposition to one another. One of these has to do with the present reality of a disintegrated people, dispersed throughout the world. It includes not only those captive in Babylon since 597 or 586 BCE but also those who have settled in the different countries of the empire. One must keep this twofold Israel in mind in order to understand many texts from Second Isaiah and other prophetic books. I shall return to this point below. The other figure of Israel is programmatic and clearly utopian; for the prophet, it is the figure

that should prevail and replace the other: *all* Israel must return to its land, as symbolized by Zion/Jerusalem.

Thus, the frequent designation of these addressees as Jacob/Israel (generally in that order: 40:27; 41:14; 42:24; 43:1, 22, 28; 44:1, 5, 21, 23; 45:4; 46:3; 48:1, 12; 49:5, 6; in reverse order, only in 41:8) is quite important; they are never referred to as "Judah," a term that is used only in a geographical and nontheological sense, as in 40:9 and 44:26, or derivatively, with specific reference to the "house of Jacob"/"Israel" in 48:1. It should be noted that the pair appears only in the first part of the book (40:1—49:13), with its emphasis on the liberation and recovery of this "twofold Israel," the Israel of Babylon and the Israel of the other nations.

In this first part of Second Isaiah, there are two texts that are quite explicit with regard to the salvific will of Yahweh.

The first such text is 43:5-6. Within a literary context marked by attributes of Yahweh that have to do with liberation ("Creator," "the one who fashions," "I redeemed you," "the Chosen One of Israel," "Savior"), all of which are addressed to a "you" who is none other than Jacob/Israel (vv. 1-4), verse 5 bursts out as follows:

> Do not be afraid! For I am with you.
> From the East I shall bring your offspring,
> and from the west I shall gather you together;
> I shall say to the north, "Hand them over!"
> and to the south, "Do not hold them back in prison;
> bring my sons from afar
> and my daughters from the extremes of the earth."

From the four cardinal points, and not just from Babylon, the exiles shall return in order to be "reunited" in their own land of Judah (40:9) and Jerusalem (= all their land)—the theme of the second part (49:14—55:13). The other passage in question, just as eloquent, is 49:12:

> Look, these from afar shall come,
> and look at these others from the north and the west,
> and those from the land of Syene.

Only three cardinal points are mentioned. The east is missing for a very simple reason. The oracle begins in 48:20 with an exhortation to leave Babylon. The captives in Babylon must become messengers of the good tidings "to the extremes of the earth" in order to proclaim that "Yahweh *has redeemed* his servant Jacob" (v. 20b). After the exhortation the original journey through the desert is recalled (v. 21 with verbs in *qatal*) as the model for the new journey (with verbs in *yiqtol* [49:9b-11])—prior to the insertion of the poem concerning "the servant of Yahweh" of 49:1-9a and the formula of 48:22. Then, once the presentation of this new exodus comes to an end, 49:12 proceeds to supplement it with an extension of the salvific plan of Yahweh for the other groups of exiles. The emphatic expressions of 43:6, "*my* sons"/"*my* daughters," make it very clear that the reference is to Israel and not to other peoples or to the "pagans."

A further and complementary proof that the salvific plan presented by Second Isaiah is concerned only with Israel may be found in the parallel text inserted in Isa 11:10-16, of either exilic or postexilic origin.[12] To understand the terminology one need only read verse 12:

> He shall raise a standard for the nations,
>   and shall reunite those expelled from Israel;
>   and the dispersed of Judah he will bring back together
>   from the four corners of the earth.

It is clear that "the nations" of verse 12a are not the beneficiaries of the envisioned reunion but rather the place where the exiles of Israel/Judah are to be found. The same motif reappears in 49:22 (a new parallel to Second Isaiah), as Yahweh promises to raise a standard *toward* the peoples and his hand *toward* the nations in order to bring back the sons and daughters of Zion to their land. The other peoples, their kings and princes, shall be their servants, and thus not "called" at all to become part of Israel (v. 23).

Such a focus confirms what I argued in no. 5 above, namely, that the universalist geographical expressions—"the extremes/ends of the earth," "islands"/"nations," and other such expressions—do not connote, and much less denote, a salvific ethnic universalism but rather a plan of salvation for Israel. The plan is to retrieve all Israel from all corners of the world, in order to fashion a people that belongs to Yahweh (a plan well articulated in 44:1-5; see especially v. 5).

In the light of this reading, a number of texts can be better understood. For example, one finds in 45:20 an invitation to "those who have fled among the nations" to join forces with Yahweh in a legal complaint (vv. 20-21); this is followed by an exhortation to "all the ends of the earth" to return to Yahweh in order to be saved (v. 22a). The commentaries take such allusions to refer, without much discussion, to the pagans,[13] although at times a contrary position is adopted.[14] The reference, however, is clearly to the exiles, as in the equivalent expression of 4:2b ("those of Israel who

---

12. The exile of Judah (v. 12b) and above all the diaspora throughout the world (from Elam to the east and Ethiopia to the south, to central Syria and the islands of the Mediterranean to the north and the west [v. 11b]) are presupposed. While v. 16 mentions only the exiled in Assyria (as the beginning of the list of v. 11b), the present text presupposes a broad dispersion, pointing to a late redaction.

13. See, for example, Bonnard, *Second Isaïe*, 178–79.

14. See, for example, Whybray, *Isaiah*, 111–12. Whybray, with reference to other authors,

have fled"), a late text belonging to a batch of rereadings within First Isaiah. The worshipers of other gods criticized in 45:20b are not members of other ethnic groups but the exiles themselves. They believe that they are saved by a "god who does not save," when it is only Yahweh who actually possesses a plan of liberation (vv. 15, 17, 19b, 21b, 23-24), which "all the offspring of Israel" shall experience (v. 25)—another way of referring to all the groups dispersed throughout the world. In sum, the expression "those of Israel who have fled among the nations" means "those of Israel who have fled and are among the nations."

Another such passage is 52:12b. The participle, "the one who gathers you together," is usually understood as "the one who brings up your rearguard," in contrast to the one who goes "before you" (an invocation of the imagery of Exod 14:19). In Second Isaiah as a whole, such a designation seems to be a new title for Yahweh as the "Gatherer" of the Israel dispersed among the peoples (it is the same lexeme as in 49:5 and 11:12a, and it has to do with the same theme).

7. At this point, I can turn to the mission of the "servant of Yahweh" as formulated in the so-called songs of 42:1-7; 49:1-9a; 50:4-9a, 10-11; and 52:13—53:12. Given the coherence of Second Isaiah, where *Israel* is referred to as "the servant (of Yahweh)" (41:8, 9; 42:19 [2x]; 43:10; 44:1, 2, 21 [2x]; 45:4; 48:20), these four texts also have to do with Israel and not with the prophet. The four poems "cut" a fluid and uniform text, a sure sign of their insertion at some point in the redaction of the book. As a result, the figure of the servant does resemble at times that of a king with political power (with reference to the proclamation of liberation: 42:1b, 3b, 4b; with reference to the release from prison: 42:6b-7; with reference to the gathering together of Israel: 49:5-6). However, in the book as it presently stands, the figure can only refer to Israel and not to Cyrus or the prophet (as usually affirmed above all with regard to 50:4-9a, 10b-11 and 52:13—53:12).

If the servant is Israel, however, how then can the figure serve as a "covenant of the people" (42:6b) or reunite Israel (49:5b, 6a) and suffer on its behalf (53:1-12)? This is the dilemma faced by those who wish to see Israel as the servant but come face-to-face with this incongruity. Such an incongruity vanishes, however, if one sees the servant as the Israel of the Babylonian captivity, whom the prophet addresses first and foremost and whose own liberation Israel itself must proclaim to the ends of the earth (as pointed out earlier with regard to 48:20). As such, the servant can be metaphorically assigned the mission, more proper to a king, of "proclaiming liberation to the nations" (42:1b) and entrusted with the task of "making Jacob return" (49:5a; see v. 6a) or serving as

———————————

sees the universalist interpretation as possible only in v. 22, in and of itself already a concession to incoherence.

a "light to the nations" (42:6b; 49:6b), an expression that, in keeping with 42:7, should be taken to refer to the liberation from the darkness of prisons.

The tradition looked upon those deported to Babylon by Nebuchadnezzar as the ones actually punished by Yahweh. In both the historical books (2 Kings 25) and the prophetic warnings, the exile is seen as the chastisement par excellence of Judah. Consequently, all those who had subsequently emigrated to other countries, whether as a result of necessity or for political and commercial reasons, did not carry such a load upon their shoulders. They seemed removed from the guilt of exile that lay upon those in Babylon. More likely than not, they would not have much interest in returning to their land.

However, the discourse of 53:10-12 sees them in a different light altogether, namely, as capable of solidarity with the humiliated Israel-servant.

One point should be noted: it is not the *suffering* of the servant that leads to the well-being of the "many" (vv. 5b, 11). In fact, the text never presupposes the innocence of the servant. What the confessing speakers of 53:1-10 declare should be understood in the light of what Yahweh has to say in 52:13-15 and 53:11-13, namely, that they acknowledge the value of such suffering (the exile) *because of Yahweh's liberation* ("exaltation," in the language of the text, 52:13) and redemption of the captives. A correct reading of 52:13—53:12 should, therefore, keep in mind the "good tidings" that come right before this text in 52:7-10.

Given such a context, it is very difficult to grant that the confessing group of 53:1-10 represents either "pagans" who speak of the servant-Israel or the Israel of the exile that thus refers to the prophet himself.[15] We have already seen that the pagans do not lie within the purview of the salvific plan of Second Isaiah; moreover, nothing in the text points to a conflict with the prophet, much less to the results described. In the light of Isaiah 40–55 as a whole, therefore, the presence of the twofold Israel in 52:13—53:12 satisfactorily accounts for the various components of the passage. Nevertheless, the anomalous character of the passage—like that of all the other "songs"—mentioned above should always be kept in mind, if the major differences in content vis-à-vis the rest of the work are to be properly understood.

Conclusion

In this study I have aimed at a coherent reading of the text of Second Isaiah, a reading that can recover the sociohistorical message at the time of pro-

---

15. For the first position, see Bonnard, *Second Isaïe*, 271ff.; for the second, see Whybray, *Isaiah 40–66*, 171.

duction (both with respect to the prophet and the final redactor), a reading that is made possible by the fact that it is undertaken from the location of the oppressed. This "location" of mine as exegete is neither ideal nor imaginative but real and concrete. It is like the air that I breathe, and it drives me to find in the text a profound harmony (not a simple parallelism or concordism) with reality itself. If the kerygma of Second Isaiah were antiliberationist (a position that would be in principle difficult to imagine) or purely spiritual and religious (as in the "missionary" interpretation described earlier), a clash would have occurred with the reading from the perspective of the oppressed, and the text would have been put aside as irrelevant to the situation at hand. However, the very opposite has happened: Second Isaiah engenders its message from a situation of captivity. A good exegesis must be mindful of this, especially if it pretends to be scientific.

Thus, I have considered it essential to emphasize over and over again that the level of production of the text and the level of production of our own reading in Latin America are one and the same—the sociopolitical. The prophet proposes, in effect, a project of liberation that has to do with the sociopolitical, with its economic base and its ideological legitimation in religion. The centrality of a Yahweh who is anti-Marduk and antigods is essential for such a legitimation.

By way of conclusion, I should like to reinforce these final remarks by turning to two other texts that have been usually interpreted from a spiritualist perspective but that actually possess enormous historical-political impact. The first is 41:17-20:

> The oppressed and the poor look for water,
>   but there is none....
> I shall make rivers flow in bare mountains, springs...

While the text paints a dramatic picture for the oppressed, some exegetes have advanced a metaphorical interpretation of its central theme: the oppressed as those who are in need of God and God's word (water). If the water functions as a metaphor, it is a metaphor for the social, economic, and political situation of the exiles. There is no mention whatsoever in the text of a search for the word of Yahweh.

The same happens with the invitation of 55:1-3a. Those who are invited to eat freely are the thirsty and those who have no money—those who have nothing. It is not the oppressed who live in abundance; rather, they are used to hunger and thirst. For the rich, on the other hand, good meals are the norm, and as a result this type of invitation is not needed. The text employs symbols, but it is not metaphorical. The "come to me" of verse 3a, along with the insistence on "listening" to Yahweh (vv. 2b-3a), does not imply that nourishment is to be seen in terms of the divine word or the promise that follows in verse 3b. The text remains at the economic level, and it is important to read it as such. The whole of Second Isaiah constitutes a proposal for political and social liberation and hence economic liberation as well. Why should one in the end spiritualize it?

The same applies to a number of other passages. The reading of Second Isaiah elaborated above will help us to keep the message of the prophet at its true level of meaning, to recover the hope that it has to offer, and to carry out a rereading that is relevant to our situations.

14

Reading the Bible in the Ecclesial Base Communities of Latin America: The Meaning of Social Context

_____ Paulo Fernando Carneiro de Andrade _____

The centrality of the Bible is one of the most powerful identifying elements of the Catholicism represented by the ecclesial base communities; such Catholicism can be readily distinguished thereby from other forms of Catholicism, past or present, in Latin American culture. This reality came to light as a result of the investigations carried out by the Pastoral Assessment Team of the Institute for Studies of Religion (Instituto de Estudos da Religião [ISER]) with regard to ecclesial base communities (_comunidades eclesiais de base_ [CEBs]) in a number of Catholic dioceses throughout Brazil. In these investigations, undertaken as a contribution to local processes of pastoral evaluation, a significant number of the base communities always pointed to a knowledge of the Bible as the most important element in their history.[1]

This is a translation of the original manuscript, "A leitura da Bíblia nas Comunidades Eclesiais de Base Latinoamericanas: Um debate sobre o significado do contexto social." The translation is by Fernando F. Segovia; the assistance of Dr. Elena Olazagasti-Segovia is kindly acknowledged as well.

1. Since 1984 the Pastoral Assessment Team of ISER—presently consisting of Carlos Steil, Clodovis Boff, Faustino Teixeira, Ivo Lespaubin, Pedro Ribeiro, Névio Fiorin, Solange Rodrigues, and myself—has assisted a number of dioceses undergoing such a process of pastoral evaluation. This task of assessment has involved, among other things, socioanalytical research into the pastoral profile of the diocesan base communities, from which a number of statistical and analytical findings have been taken for this study. The dioceses presently being assessed by ISER in this capacity are the following: Vitória, Crateús, Picos, São Félix do Araguaia, Conceição do Araguaia, Cametá, Bom Jesus da Lapa, São Mateus, Volta Redonda, and Bonfim.

Reading the Bible: A Novel Element
in the Catholicism of the CEBs

The first form of Catholicism in Latin America was traditional Iberian Catholicism, which arrived with the discovery and subsequent colonization. In Brazil this type of Catholicism, hegemonic until the end of the nineteenth century, may be summarized in terms of the popular saying, "Muita reza e pouca missa, muito santo e pouco padre" (Much praying and few masses; many saints and few priests). It centered on devotions and the saints and was lay in nature, its daily character and continuation depending little on the presence of a priest; indeed, the faithful, especially in the countryside, saw a priest only at the time of their fulfillment of the Easter duty or at other key moments through which the sustenance of the greater Catholic community was made possible.[2]

In the last quarter of the nineteenth century, after the end of Vatican I, this type of Catholicism was replaced—not without a struggle—by so-called Romanized Catholicism, centered on the sacraments and thus strongly clerical in character. The transformation of the one form of Catholicism into the other was as swift as it was relatively efficient, so much so that anyone who today mentions "traditional" Catholicism has in mind not the Iberian Catholicism present in Latin America for over five hundred years but rather the Romanized Catholicism first introduced in Brazil less than a century ago.[3]

In the end such a Romanization of traditional popular Catholicism gave rise, by way of reaction, to the development of a third type of Catholicism, the so-called private Catholicism, in which the cult of the saints remained central but now was no longer practiced in community but only in a private and individual fashion. A number of sacramental practices from romanized Catholicism did become part of this new Catholicism, but also in a highly private fashion and without any communitarian dimension.[4]

With Vatican II, Catholicism renewed itself in a number of directions. Among the popular social classes of Latin America, the emergence of the base communities proved to be the main innovation. This was an expression of a new form of Catholicism, centered on reading the Bible and committed to a transformation of society whereby the poor would become subjects in a new social and ecclesial reality.[5]

---

2. See P. Ribeiro de Oliveira, *Religião e dominação de classe* (Petrópolis: Vozes, 1985) 29–166.

3. Ibid., 169–337. See also R. Azzi, *O Episcopado brasileiro frente ao Catolicismo popular* (Petrópolis: Vozes, 1977), and idem, *O Catolicismo popular no Brasil* (Petrópolis: Vozes, 1978).

4. See P. Ribeiro de Oliveira, "O Catolicismo do povo," *A religião do povo* (ed. B. Beni dos Santos; São Paulo: Paulinas, 1978) 72–80.

5. See F. Couto Teixeira, *A gênese das CEBs no Brasil* (São Paulo: Paulinas, 1988).

A number of preliminary points should be made about the meaning of this novel encounter with the written text of the Bible on the part of the Catholic base communities. To begin, it should be noted that even in traditional Iberian Catholicism, centered as it was on the cult of the saints, the Scriptures were not absent. The difference is that within this first type of Catholicism the presence of the Bible made itself felt almost exclusively by way of oral narratives, passed on from parents to children. Such narratives contained the biblical facts and message practically without any contact with the Bible as a written word.[6] In romanized Catholicism a similar situation can also be observed, insofar as contact with the Bible took place primarily through the mediation of the priest, who explained the Scriptures to the faithful.

The introduction of the Bible as written word in the base communities gave rise to a principle of authority different from that of the ancestors or that of the priest.[7] Contact with the written text allowed the communities to insert themselves into the context of modernity, where the principle of authority is the written word—a document that is subject to criticism and not to the oral tradition of the ancestors. Whoever gains access to the written text is no longer subject to the exclusive meaning given by the oral narrator, whose interpretive authority is grounded in the fact that he alone knows what is being narrated. Consequently, direct access to the biblical word allows for the liberation of the different meanings of the text, making way thereby for the possibility of a plurality of interpretations; such a concept, in turn, profoundly alters the existing relationships of power and authority, even allowing for the construction of new models of being church.

The investigations carried out by the Pastoral Assessment Team of ISER in the context of diocesan pastoral evaluations show that the great majority of the leaders in the base communities read the Bible directly.[8] The novelty of this is far-reaching. There is also something essentially novel in the way the Bible is read in these communities, insofar as the different biblical programs given throughout Brazil since the late 1960s have sought to develop and promote a common reading method meant to bring faith and life together in a new way.

Such a method seeks to relate the Bible to the life of the community as well as the broader social reality.[9] For Carlos Mesters—one of the better-known biblical scholars involved in the development of this method—it is

---

6. See the excellent treatment of this theme in C. Steil, P. Ribero de Oliveira, and B. Ferraro, *Síntese Teológico-Pastoral da avaliação da Diocese de Bom Jesus da Lapa* (Rio de Janeiro: ISER), mimeograph.

7. Ibid., 8.

8. In the diocese of Bom Jesus da Lapa, for example, the number reaches 85 percent (ibid., 8); similar and even higher numbers have been found in other dioceses as well.

9. See F. Couto Teixeira, *A fé na vida: Um estudo teológico-pastoral sobre a experiencia das Comunidades Eclesiais de Base no Brasil* (São Paulo: Loyola, 1988) 135–63. See also

the triangular relationship of the Bible with the community and with social reality that allows life to shed light on the Bible and the Bible to penetrate life, giving rise thereby to the dialectic of faith and life that characterizes the biblical reading of these communities.[10] Before turning to the specific character of this dialectic, I should like to mention a number of other constitutive elements of such a reading that highlight its novel character.

First, the reading is characterized by a shared belief in the appropriation of the Bible by the people. The poor, always at the margins of power and looked upon as devoid of knowledge, take the Bible in their own hands and read it with enthusiasm, as something that belongs to them.[11] Such appropriation produces familiarity with the Bible as well as freedom of interpretation, not only making possible the discovery of a new meaning for everyday life but also giving rise to a sense of personal and social importance—God addresses the word to us. The poor find themselves in the Bible and discover in it the meaning of their lives, their struggles, their sufferings, and their hopes.[12] Such an appropriation of the Bible by the poor is justified, from a theological and hermeneutical point of view, by the following principle: since the Bible was written from within a context of oppression-captivity, its meaning can be fully attained only by means of a reading with a similar point of departure, such as that lived by the poor of Latin America.[13]

Second, the reading is further characterized by the diffusion and appropriation of the findings of the biblical sciences. By means of biblical courses, pamphlets, and primers, the findings of contemporary exegesis have been made widely available to the base communities, so that their reading of the Scriptures can bring together exegetical knowledge and research with the culture and life of the people.[14] This is a very important element of this reading, and one that is not always properly emphasized, insofar as it shows that the reading of the base communities is not just spontaneous, as indeed no reading ever is. At the same time, it cannot be said that such a reading is a mere reflection of contemporary biblical exegesis. Such exeget-

C. Mesters, *Defenseless Flower: A New Reading of the Bible* (Maryknoll, N.Y.: Orbis Books, 1989).

10. See Couto Teixeira, *Fé na vida*, 136–38; Mesters, *Defenseless Flower*, 12–54 (chap. 2); this second chapter was originally published as "A brisa leve, uma nova leitura da Bíblia," *SEDOC* 115 (1979) 733–65.

11. See the interview with W. Gruen in *Teologia da Libertação: Novos desafios* (ed. F. Couto Teixeira; São Paulo: Paulinas, 1991) 113–14. This volume contains a number of interviews with different theologians and biblical scholars of Latin America represented in the Coleção Teologia e Libertação.

12. Couto Teixeira, *Fé na vida*, 139–41.

13. See in this regard the reflections of Mesters on Matt 11:25-26 ("I bless you, Father, Lord of heaven and earth, for hiding these things from the learned and the clever and revealing them to these little ones. Yes, Father, for that is what it pleased you to do") in *Defenseless Flower*, 18–20.

14. Ibid., 19.

ical tools and results are, according to Mesters, like eyeglasses that allow the eyes to see better. The eyes—that is to say, the vision—are and must continue to be those of the people, who direct their sight and their eyes wherever they see fit.[15] It should be emphasized as well that just as so-called scientific exegesis plays a part in the reading of the base communities, so does this reading make a significant contribution to scientific exegesis insofar as it opens up new meanings and possibilities in the text.[16] What this biblical reading of the base communities does is to transcend the dichotomy, arising from time to time, between a spiritual-pastoral reading of the Bible and an exegetical reading—in and of itself an important novelty.[17]

Third, the reading is characterized as well by its communal aspect. The subject of the reading is the community, not the individual. The Bible is read not as a personal book, meant for individual piety, but as a book of the community, even when read individually.[18] In the community are to be found the criteria for reading that give unity, not uniformity, to the interpretations of the people. The community is the depository-transmitter of the greater tradition (which includes the biblical reading conducted therein) of the faith. Such a communitarian reading allows for both mutual correction and a deeper understanding of the interpretation given the text read: no one individual possesses interpretive authority; such authority belongs to all as a community.

The Emphasis on the Relationship between Faith and Life

I should begin by making it clear that it is not only within the Catholicism of the base communities that faith and life are brought together. In all religions, and thus in all forms of Catholicism and Christianity, faith and life are somehow related. In traditional popular Catholicism, when the faithful pray to the saints and ask, in return for a promise, for health and protection in the midst of any type of difficulty, they are relating their faith to their life and their everyday reality. The question is not, therefore, whether in any particular type of Catholicism there exists a relationship between faith and life, but rather what area of life is related to faith and how such a relationship is conceived.

The way in which faith and life are brought together in the Catholicism of the base communities does represent a novelty in terms of how the life of the poor as well as their political, economic, and social struggles are related

---

15. Ibid., 19–20.
16. See J. Swetnam, "Parola di Dio e Teologia Pastorale nella Chiesa contemporanea," *Vaticano II: Bilancio e prospettive vinticinque anni dopo 1962–1987* (ed. R. Latourelle; Rome: Cittadella, 1987) 324–39; Mesters, *Defenseless Flower,* 10–11.
17. See Couto Teixeira, *Fé na vida,* 139.
18. See the interview with Mesters in Couto Teixeira, *Teologia,* 114.

to Scripture. The poor discover in the Bible not just a history of earlier times but their own life, as if in a mirror.[19] For the poor who read the Bible in the base communities, there is such a connaturality between their lives and the stories narrated in the Sacred Scriptures that they recognize themselves in the Scriptures, thus allowing for their appropriation of the Bible in the manner described above.

This novelty has proved so important that it has often been taken to mean that this is the only form of Catholicism in which faith and life are brought together, as if the specific way in which these two realities are related in the base communities were the only possible or legitimate way of doing so.[20] Despite such extrapolations found in a number of interpretations, one cannot deny or underestimate the profoundly transformative and original value of this linkage of faith and life carried out in the base communities.[21]

The reading of the Bible in the base communities does not seek to address questions that arise out of personal curiosity but rather questions that emerge from the daily life of the poor, who, gathered as a community, struggle against oppressive social, political, and economic structures in such a way as to establish a relationship between the political practice of the people and faith.[22] Without such a reading of the Bible, the base communities would not possess the important political function that is so characteristic of them. Such a reading allows for the development of the political dimension of faith in the direction of social transformation, making sure that the struggle waged by the popular classes in the so-called popular movements (*movimentos populares*) does not run parallel to the religious life but finds in faith instead both a stimulus and criteria for a discernment that leads to action. As such, the struggles of the people are not only lived in profound connection with faith but also looked upon as something that cannot and must not be reduced to a purely religious sphere, thus going beyond the various other models of Christianity.[23]

Many are the testimonies of individuals from among the people, members of base communities, who speak about having discovered in the Bible the link between, on the one hand, social struggle and a liberating political course of action for the people and, on the other, faith:

- One learned that Jesus was not that distant from us. All that Jesus has to say can be found within our own reality. The daily life of a worker is but a role that he or she must play. In the course of such a life takes

---

19. Couto Teixeira, *Fé na vida*, 149–55.

20. See C. Boff, *Como trabalhar com o povo* (Petrópolis: Vozes, 1984) 106–7.

21. See Frei Betto, *O que é Comunidade Eclesial de Base* (São Paulo: Brasiliense, 1981) 29–41; D. L. Fernades, *Como se faz uma Comunidade Eclesial da Base* (Petrópolis: Vozes, 1984) 63–64.

22. See C. Mesters, *Deus, onde estás* (Belo Horizonte: Vega, 1971) 1–6.

23. See Betto, *Comunidade*, 24; Boff, *Trabalhar*, 106.

place all that is written in the words concerning the life of Jesus. His words can fall directly in our ears today. All one has to do is read or listen to them a couple of times, think about the reality of life, and apply the gospel to life: everyone understands, easily, that the gospel is there, in the midst of our way.[24]

- The cry of the people represents God's call to us. Like Moses, God sends us to work and to struggle for the liberation of the people.[25]

- As in the time of Moses (the exodus), God continues to look upon the weakness and the misery of God's people and continues to call new Moseses for liberation.[26]

- In any place the struggle is born from the word of God.[27]

- [One person said] "As I went on reading the Gospel, I came to see that God could not be happy with the suffering of the world. At that point, I went on to join the community."[28]

The biblical circles (*círculos bíblicos*) introduced the method of communal reading of the Bible in the base communities. The biblical circle, which normally consists of a not very large group of neighbors (ten to fifteen persons) belonging to a base community, has a rather simple working structure, without any significant variations. It begins in a rather general way with an exchange of ideas and experiences concerning some fact of life, such as a local experience in the struggle of the community, a problem like lack of water or sanitation in the neighborhood, or any other difficulty of everyday life.[29] At this point, the circle involves a dialogue among all the members present regarding problems with which they are personally acquainted in order to achieve a more self-conscious knowledge of these problems. In the words of Mesters:

The first phase of the biblical circles aims at discerning the problem of life. For that reason the circle begins with an exchange of ideas concerning the problems that life creates. The purpose is not to magnify the problems which already exist but to try to find a solution for them. We raise the problems in order to resolve them, with the help of

---

24. Words of a field worker cited in Couto Teixeira, *Fé na vida*, 151.
25. Final Document of the Fourth Interecclesial Encounter of CEBs, which took place in Itaici, São Paulo, in April 1981; see also Couto Teixeira, *Fé na vida*, 151.
26. Report from the communities of Bahia, presented in the Fourth Interecclesial Encounter of CEBs; Couto Teixeira, *Fé na vida*, 151.
27. Couto Teixeira, *Fé na vida*, 160.
28. Ibid., 161.
29. See in this regard *Curso bíblico para monitores: Relatório de um curso bíblico para animadores dirigido por frei Carlos Mesters em São Mateus, Espírito Santo, de 30/6 a 6/7 de 1978*, mimeograph. The text is taken from Bulletin no. 27 (1978) of the Diocese of S. Mateus.

the word of God. When an engine breaks down and does not work, the first thing to do is to see where the problem lies. When life is miserable, the first thing to do, before attempting to fix it, is to see where the problem lies. In the first phase of the circle, we attempt to do just that: to find out where the problem with the engine of life lies.[30]

In the second phase of the biblical circle, a reading from the Bible, whether from the Old or the New Testament, follows, and then the reading is commented upon both in the light of the situation just discussed in the first stage and as a source of light for such a situation. It should be pointed out, however, that the solution for the problems of life is not sought in the Bible:

> No one goes to the Bible in order to learn how to prepare a healing remedy or how to cook or till the field.... The Bible has nothing to say with respect to such things. One seeks help from individuals who have proper knowledge and can be of help in such matters. Similarly, one seeks the Bible in order to find a word of God as one orients one's life towards one's destiny. The Bible is like a map: it points the way; it shows where one must go; it reveals the value of things and persons; and it can thus indicate what is right and what is wrong with our lives.[31]

In a third phase the biblical circle seeks to elicit practical suggestions for the problems of life in the light of the entire discussion. Thus, the methodology of the biblical circle allows life to be taken to the Bible and the Bible to be brought to life, while at the same time attempting to make sure that such mutual enrichment does not become an invasion whereby the relative autonomies of what is social and what is religious are annulled. The Bible serves as a map or a guide in the search for ways to resolve the difficulties of life, not as a manual where the solutions to such problems can be found.

To assist with the analytical understanding of the problems of life so that appropriate solutions can be found, the base communities frequently offer courses in social analysis. These courses—grounded in some type of sociological apparatus, usually critical-dialectic in character—have as their aim a structural understanding of how society and the economy function, while at the same time promoting an analysis of their juncture.[32] In this way the reading of social reality offered by sociological analysis is integrated

---

30. Ibid., 2.
31. Ibid., 2.
32. See in this regard my *Fé e eficácia: O uso da sociologia na teologia da libertação* (São Paulo: Loyola, 1991) esp. 169–200, where an analysis of the relationship between the sociological apparatus employed by the CEBs, the theology of liberation, and Marxist theory can be found.

with a biblical reading that sheds light on this reality from the point of view of faith.

The Importance of "Context" for a Reading of the Bible

Latin American theologians and biblical scholars have always emphasized that the believing and oppressed people are the subject of the reading of the Bible taking place in the base communities. The twofold condition of the subject—that is, the people's faith and concrete social realities—is taken to be primarily responsible for the discovery of new meanings in the text. The biblical circle, given its specific methodology for reading, functions as a facilitator, providing the believing people with an opportunity to read the Bible and make it their own, bringing the Bible to bear on their lives and bringing their lives to bear on the Bible.[33]

It is this junction between the people's social reality and the community where the people celebrate their faith that constitutes the "location" from which the people read the Bible, giving rise in the process to "a new way of seeing": "The people are looking at the Bible, lying on the ground of life, on the dirty sacking of injustices, wearing clothes soaked in dirt and blood."[34] In this way the Bible leaves the "location of the powerful" to be placed on "the side of the oppressed," who read it with the eyes of captivity.[35]

According to Mesters, this "location" can be characterized as involving (1) a situation of captivity; (2) a practice of "walking toward and struggling for liberation"; (3) a lack of separation between faith and life; (4) a faith placed in the service of life in the process of liberation; and (5) a faith nourished by the reading of the Bible.[36] According to this interpretation, the "location" from which the biblical text is read is not constituted solely by the concrete social conditions of life but by the junction between such conditions and the community where the reading takes place. In the end, however, it is not at all unusual for the concrete social conditions of life to be emphasized as the main factor in the makeup of the "location" from which the text is read, as the following story supplied by Mesters readily shows:

> During the meeting someone described the following incident. On one occasion a worker was commenting on a particular text of the Gospel and another man said, "Hey, you've read that bit and drawn your conclusion. The other day in church I heard a priest, who's even

---

33. See Betto, *Comunidade,* 736–38.
34. Mesters, *Defenseless Flower,* 17.
35. Ibid., 15–20.
36. Ibid., 15.

taught at the university, read the same bit and draw a conclusion exactly the opposite of what you said. How can that be?" The worker replied with complete simplicity, "But I'm a worker!"[37]

One could say, therefore, that the different concrete social conditions of life represent different "locations" from which the Sacred Scriptures are read. In such a case, the "context" from which the text is read is identified with the social context, that is, with the concrete social conditions of the life of the readers; furthermore, the concrete social conditions of the oppressed-poor are further identified as a privileged "location," insofar as it is connatural with the "location" from which the Bible itself was written.[38]

At this point, a question arises: How can one explain the difference between the reading of the Bible in the base communities and the reading of the Bible by popular Pentecostals who live in the same social context? In both cases, the subject who reads is a popular and communal subject; however, the result of such readings is for the most part diverse and conflicting. This question can also be formulated as follows: How can individuals who belong to the same social context, that is, who share the same concrete social conditions of life, read Scripture in different ways, as if they were reading it from different "locations"?

A first response to this question can be found in the different methods employed in such reading: while in the biblical circles within the base communities life is taken to Scripture and Scripture is brought to life, in the biblical fundamentalism of the Pentecostals life is prevented from interacting with Scripture.[39] Such a response is unsatisfactory. First, it is not true to say that Pentecostals do not bring Scripture to life or that their lives do not enter Scripture. It is only that the process takes place in a different way, either by relating different aspects of life to Scripture or by relating the same aspect—for example, politics—in a different way. In addition, such an explanation fails to offer an adequate response to the question of why the Pentecostal reading proves to be as plausible as that of the base communities.

A second response is advanced by those who argue that such a difference in reading is due to the fact that, while the members of the base communities truly constitute a proper "location" for reading, the Pentecostals do not. Despite their concrete social conditions, the Pentecostals are said to read the Bible from the "location" of the dominant. The fundamental category at work here is that of "alienation": the members of the base communities differ from the Pentecostals insofar as they have clarified their vision, having liberated themselves from the dominant ideology in and through the base community, where the people receive anew their

---

37. Ibid., 15–16.
38. See the interview with T. Cavalcanti in Couto Teixeira, *Teologia*, 115.
39. See the interview with Mesters in ibid., 123–24.

name and their history, that is, their identity. Upon undergoing this process of disalienation, they are free to see both reality and the Scriptures from the point of view of the oppressed, that is, with their own way of seeing and not that of the other, the oppressor, constituting as a result the "location" for the reading of the poor.[40] According to this interpretation, the reading of the Pentecostals would not be a spontaneous reading, informed as it is by the ideology of those who oppress the poor, while the reading of the base communities would be the spontaneous reading of the poor, which comes about when the poor appropriate the Bible free of the dominant ideology.[41]

As formulated, this explanation seems unsatisfactory, not only because it is simplistic but also, in a certain sense, because it is accusatory: those who do not possess the same reading we do are alienated; should they remove the veil from their eyes, they shall see and read as we do. One can, however, expand on such a response by turning to an intuition present within it that has not been properly thematized: that which constitutes the "location" of reading is not the concrete social conditions of life as such, "in themselves," but the interpretation of these conditions. In other words, the life that is taken to the Scriptures is not life "as it is" but rather a life that is interpreted, that is, understood within a certain cultural framework; indeed, life "as it is" does not exist: life is always interpreted life. Thus, one could say that the "social context" that characterizes the reading of the text must be always understood as "interpreted social context." To read the Bible "with the eyes of the oppressed" means, therefore, to read the Bible from the point of view of a life that is interpreted as oppressed in social and economic terms. According to this interpretation, the relationship between the "concrete social conditions of life" and the text is no longer seen as direct but as complex: as a relationship between such conditions, the culture within which such conditions are interpreted, and the text, likewise taken as a participant in that same culture within which the conditions are interpreted. Thus, popular Pentecostals as well as members of the base communities would be reading the text from different "locations," insofar as they belong within different cultural traditions of interpretation regarding their concrete social conditions of life. The plausibility of a textual reading is thus linked to the plausibility of culturally constituted interpretations about the concrete social conditions of life.

Such an interpretation can, in a certain way, be readily integrated with that already found in Mesters, who includes the community in the formation of the "location" from which the text is read.[42] The community, however, provides not only the context of faith within which the text is

---

40. See ibid., 125–26.
41. See the interview with Richard in ibid., 125–26.
42. Mesters, *Defenseless Flower,* 13–21.

read but also the interpretive framework for the concrete social conditions of life. Thus, community and social reality are related to one another, giving birth to the "location" from which the text is read.

In this regard, the first phase of the biblical circle, in which a "fact of life" is discussed, would have the important function of allowing the participants to debate their interpretations of their concrete social conditions, since the community within which the debate takes place emerges as both carrier and producer of a cultural tradition where such conditions of life of the Latin American poor are interpreted as "oppression." Discussing the fact of life results in the socialization of such an interpretation and the reinforcement of its consensus. One should point out in this regard the fundamental importance, already noted above, of the courses in social analysis offered in the communities and dioceses where pastoral work is undertaken from the perspective of a popular pastoral program. Along with the pastoral workers and the people of the base communities, such courses carry out the important task of socializing an interpretation of reality as a reality of oppression. In turn, the reading of the biblical text from such a perspective makes possible such an interpretation, enriching it and amplifying it: such an interpretation ceases to be merely sociological and becomes instead an interpretation in which the elements of faith and the elements of rationality proper to the social sciences are brought together.

I should like to raise at this point the matter of the crisis in sociological paradigms in the base communities. It is obvious that to the extent that such paradigms are used by the base communities in interpreting the concrete social conditions of the life of the poor, such interpretations will have to be modified. Given such a modification, the "location" from which the text is read is altered as well, and one can envision as a result the possibility of a crisis in the biblical reading of the base communities or of an enriching transformation.

In fact, certain new developments can already be perceived within such a reading that seem to point toward the formation of a richer and more complex "location," resulting in the rise of new popular and communal subjects, who in turn produce different readings: women; blacks; Amerindians; the marginalized who have neither roof nor work; prostitutes; street children. The emergence of such new subjects has been made possible by the collapse of the dichotomy between oppressor and oppressed, which homogenized all the poor under the same category, and in itself makes possible a new and more complex interpretation of the concrete social conditions of life, leading to the discovery of new meanings of the biblical text and thus continuing the great movement of biblical appropriation by the poor that the Spirit has brought about in Latin America.

I conclude, then, by affirming that a deeper understanding of the given "social context" that characterizes the reading of the biblical text can be of assistance in the emergence of these new subjects, whether by serving as an aid in going beyond the crises to come in the Latin American reading of the Bible as a result of the crisis in sociological paradigms or as a means in working toward a dialogue between the members of the base communities and the popular Pentecostals, making possible thereby a better understanding of each other's readings of the Scriptures.

___ 15 _____

Apocalyptic and the Economy:
A Reading of Revelation 18 from the Experience
of Economic Exclusion

_____ Néstor Míguez ____

Contemporary biblical criticism has been enriched by the new perspectives to be found in the contributions of the "new theological subjects." Both the popular reading of the Bible and the studies undertaken from the point of view of women have made it possible to discern certain aspects of Scripture and certain conflicts in the text itself that had remained hidden from the academic erudition of the North Atlantic. The theologies that have emerged out of Africa, Asia, and the black communities of America have raised a number of fundamental questions, which have led in turn to a rereading of the texts with new critical eyes. In general, the theologies of liberation have been accompanied by hermeneutical emphases that have opened the way for a greater understanding of the biblical message, its social conditions, and its possibilities. Such developments have led to a pronounced emphasis on the social context of both texts and readers.

At the same time, the emergence of a new methodological apparatus, involving certain developments in the linguistic and social sciences and their application to the biblical text, has also had a significant impact on the discipline. The revelatory character of the texts now comes across as much more rooted in human soil. Such soil as well as the different components of it that feed the biblical texts are now studied with much greater rigor. As a result, biblical interpretation has witnessed a new spring, whereby new branches have been allowed to grow and the old sap of the biblical sciences has been renewed.

_____

This is a translation of the original manuscript, "La apocalíptica y la economía: Lectura de Ap. 18 desde la experiencia de la exclusión económica." The translation is by Fernando F. Segovia.

The Impact of the Economic Factor

All of these recent contributions have brought about a displacement of the traditional analytical focus in biblical criticism. Such a displacement, however, has not taken place in the same way in the different alternative readings. For obvious reasons, having to do with readers and contexts, priority has been assigned at one time or another to culture, social location, race, gender, or a combination of these factors. Indeed, such readings have occasionally been played off against one another as well. My primary goal in this study is to show how the new conditions at work in Latin America (and not only in Latin America) in the last few years and especially in what has already transpired of the present decade have led to a renewed emphasis on the economic factor. Such a focus was quite prominent in the early years of Latin American liberation theology and has now emerged once again, after having played a secondary role for a while, as crucial.[1]

In effect, the "present new international order," which has been established on the basis of an unchecked application of the principles of economic neoliberalism (for example, budgetary cutbacks on the part of government; privatizations; redistribution of the global market; and exclusion of the needs of the poor from administrative considerations), has generated new and more severe conditions of poverty and misery—a real exclusion of access to the fundamental goods of life; such conditions are presently affecting human life in Latin America in a decisive way, even from a biological point of view. A summary description of these conditions, based on properly documented analyses of our reality, reveals a clear accumulation of economic power, drastically sharpening thereby what was already an unequal distribution of wealth and power in our societies. This is the first visible sign of the application of extreme capitalism, highly coherent and technological from the point of view of a functionalist logic. The gulf between the rich and the poor has widened, while the middle classes tend to disappear. The ever-greater concentration of economic power in the hands of a "select minority" has created a clientele for luxury goods—generally of foreign origin—who benefit from the "free-market system." At the same time, as the internal market contracts, following the same mechanism of accumulation, a regression in economic production takes place, accompanied by a growth in unemployment and misery. The mechanism of solidarity present in the labor unions has weakened.

This is by no means a new development in our continent, or in other continents for that matter. However, in the past there has always existed a mechanism for social resistance that was able to block the most extreme

---

1. See J. M. Sung, "Economia: Um assunto central e quase ausente na teologia da Libertação: Una abordagem epistemológica," Ph.D. diss., Centro de Post-graduação em Ciencias da Religião, Instituto Metodista do Ensino Superior (São Bernardo do Campo, S.P., Brasil), 1993.

consequences of such a system. In the last few years, however, the capitalist system has been presented as the "only way" and imposed by means of the global financial networks. Such univocal dominance on the part of neoliberal capitalism has allowed it to impose new conditions at will, especially on those societies that are economically weaker. Budgetary cutbacks emerge, therefore, as the new agenda. However, such curtailment in the functions and possibilities of the state results in the exclusion of broad segments of society from basic public services, such as health and education, with an inevitable increase in social violence as well as criminal or apathetic marginalization. These developments have provided in turn an excuse for a new concern with "security," resulting in the ghettoization of enclaves for the economic aristocracy, an increase in the power of the police, and the actual repression of the marginalized sectors of society, especially the young.

As the "ideological threat" has diminished, the social threat from those who have been made hungry and those who have been excluded has increased. The sense of powerlessness generated in the sectors thus punished leads to responses along the lines of "horizontal militancy." The powerful appear so remote, so inaccessible, so beyond questioning that the explosion is unleashed in a downward direction, toward those who are weaker or those who find themselves in the same situation. There is an increase in social disintegration, in family violence (suffered for the most part by women), in the neglect of children (abandoned in the streets), in disdain for the handicapped and the elderly, in prejudice toward those who are different, who become the target of such frustration, since its real causes disappear in the anonymous nature of the system. As a result, the mechanism of victimization becomes inscribed in and remains concealed within the system.

The hermeneutical task becomes, therefore, one of unmasking. Such unmasking can be properly carried out only from the perspective of the victims—who play out and become aware of the process of victimization; who tell their story and recover their dignity through their ability to speak; and who are able to name their executioner.[2] In and through such a process the victims are able to recover their human condition and build anew hope and solidarity. It is from this perspective, the perspective of the victims of the new economic order, that I should like to approach the biblical text.

Reading from an Apocalyptic Perspective

Although a great number of biblical texts reflect the perspective of the poor, the marginalized, and the victimized, apocalyptic literature stands out as

---

2. For a more expansive exposition of these concepts, see N. Míguez, "Las víctimas en el Apocalipsis: Estudio de Apocalipsis 5 tras 500 años de incorporación de América al dominio occidental," *Revista de Interpretación Bíblica Latinoamericana* 12 (1992) 167–85.

the place par excellence for the expression of such a perspective. The reason is clear: apocalyptic sets out to locate the present within a global historical framework and to extract from historical events their transcendent dimensions. In apocalyptic, moreover, the future is read from the perspective of the victims—who refuse to give up; who continue to hope for justice; and who await the irruption of the absolute. Despite their historical impotence, the victims refuse to resign themselves to historical fatalism but make room instead within history itself for the eagerly awaited presence of that which is beyond all expectations. In contrast to all historical determinisms (whether Marxist or Hegelian, fatalist or optimistic), the victims know that human history remains open, given the revelation (and hence its name) of a justice that transcends all of the human forces that shape history. The belief in the final victory of the victims (the kingdom of the slaughtered lamb) is not a new form of determinism but rather calls into question all historical determinisms, all possibilities of a univocal history. In becoming subjects of a living faith, the victims regain their human dignity. In conceiving of themselves as participants in a new future, they become subjects of hope and, as such, subjects of a different history, a space for the construction of a different historical alternative. This triumph over determinism marks the difference between apocalypticism as ideology and apocalyptic literature as symbolic expression of hope.[3]

The economic factor is very much present in apocalyptic literature. Insofar as the economic element also represents a form of victimization, the redemption of the victims implies as well a reversal of the economic mechanisms of victimization. This insight has not escaped the biblical authors. It lies beyond the objectives of this study, however, to engage in an exhaustive analysis of apocalyptic literature, even within the New Testament itself, from the point of view of economics. I limit myself, therefore, by way of example, to Revelation 18, where the question of wealth with regard to condemned Babylon emerges as highly significant.

The Fall of Babylon: Condemnation of an Economic System

Location and Structure of Revelation 18

Chapters 17 and 18 of the book of Revelation make up one of the final visions in the section dealing with the eschatological struggle before the end and the triumph of the lamb, now depicted as the victorious equestrian warrior who finally subdues the beast (chap. 19; see 17:14). In other words, within the framework proposed by Revelation, we find ourselves

---

3. See J. Severino Croatto, "Apocalíptica y esperanza de los oprimidos (contexto socio-político y cultural del género apocalíptico)," *Revista de Interpretación Bíblica Latinoamericana* 7 (1990) 9–24.

in the realm of temporality. The judgment and fall of Babylon, announced by the angels who carry the bowls, belong to the temporal realm and constitute the necessary conditions for the irruption of eternity. That which is radically new (chap. 21) is possible only when evil no longer exists, not even as a form of condemnation (20:14-15).

Within this vision chapter 18 provides an anticipation/revision of the time of the fall. Through the successive voices that gradually disclose the imagery of the scene to the reader, a symbolic description of the cause and condition for the judgment of God on the oppressive city-system takes place. In this presentation the economic isotopy emerges as dominant, as I shall point out throughout this study. Since both the literary structure of the chapter and its actual location within the overall framework of Revelation have already been satisfactorily addressed by the scholarly literature, a detailed analysis at this point is unnecessary.[4] At the surface level I would argue for a concentric structure, with the angelic interventions, which begin and close the chapter, serving as an inclusion around both the instructions to the faithful and the successive laments on the part of the kings, the merchants, and the seafarers. Within this overall sequence, the following outline can be further distinguished:

A   Angelic intervention (v. 1) and announcement of the fall (vv. 2-3)

B   Instructions to the faithful (v. 4) and divine judgment (vv. 5-8)

C   Laments of the accomplices

     c′   Kings: description of complicity (vv. 9-10a)
        Lament of the kings (v. 10b)

     c″   Merchants: description of complicity (vv. 11, 15)

        [Excursus on trade (v. 12-13) and condemnation-lament regarding trade (v. 14)]

        Lament of the merchants (v. 16-17a)

     c‴   Seafarers: description of complicity (vv. 17-19a)
        Lament of the seafarers (v. 19b)

B′   Instructions to the faithful (v. 20a) and divine judgment (v. 20b)

A′   Angelic intervention (v. 21a) and announcement of the fall (vv. 21b-24).

---

4. See A. Yarbro Collins, "Revelation 18: Taunt-Song or Dirge?" *L'Apocalypse johannique et l'Apocalyptique dans le Nouveau Testament* (ed. J. Lambrecht; Paris-Gembloux: Éditions Duculot; Louvain: Louvain Univ. Press, 1980) 185–204, esp. 188–200; and D. Ramírez, "El juicio de Dios a las transnacionales: Apocalipsis 18," *Revista de Interpretación Bíblica Latinoamericana* 5 (1990) 55–74.

Given the goals of the present study, the importance of the excursus on trade and its accompanying condemnation-lament should be especially noted, situated as they are at the very center of the chiasm, breaking up the description regarding the complicity of the merchants. As a result, the description of the merchants' complicity is expanded and the reference to their weeping and mourning repeated.

Semiotic Codes

In order to do a semiotic analysis of this text, it is necessary to identify the dominant semantic fields as well as the various codes that structure the discourse. To begin with, a number of figurative complexes can be readily identified; these complexes gather around themselves, throughout the length of the text, a number of descriptive themes that allow us to focus in on the meaning of the text. Rather than present the entire process of analysis at this point, I limit myself to a few conclusions.

A first such complex is tied to the figures of power and greatness (*ischura, exousia; megas*): God (v. 8) and the angels are described as powerful (vv. 1, 2, 21) but so is Babylon (vv. 2, 10, 16, 18, 19, 21) and its merchants (v. 23). In this complex one must also include the figures associated with government (root: *basil*): Babylon the queen (v. 7) and the kings of the earth (vv. 3, 9). It should be noted that in this last case the figure of prostitution always appears in the immediate context. The antithesis of this complex is formed by those who have been deprived of all power: the dead (prophets and saints) and those who have been slaughtered (v. 24). We can thus identify at a semiotic level the axis, power/victim, that expresses a polarity of the text.

Not far from this first complex, another figurative complex can be found, revolving around the theme of wealth: Babylon is rich (v. 17a), and in its wake merchants (vv. 4-15) and seafarers (v. 19) have grown rich as well. The catalog of luxury goods in verses 12-13 should be included within this complex as well. The other catalog, of goods denied (vv. 22-23), can also be associated with this isotopy, but in a contrary sense. In contrast to the luxury goods, the catalog of verses 22-23 lists the pleasures of daily life. In the process the negatives are brought together: there will be nothing left; nothing will remain (vv. 14, 21, 22). Thus, a second axis, getting rich/being deprived, can be identified.

A further complex is associated with the images of judgment. In verses 8 and 20 the root *kri* is attributed to God. Rejoicing appears as a consequence of justice (v. 20). Babylon is considered unjust (v. 5: *adikos*) and brought to judgment (v. 10). Given the context of the work, the results of condemnation—the retribution brought upon Babylon (v. 6)—should be located within this complex as well: fire (vv. 8, 9, 18); plague (vv. 5, 8); torment (v. 9); desolation (v. 17, 19). Given these consequences of sin, "my people" must separate themselves from (leave behind) the sin accumulated by Babylon, if it is to share in the justice of God. This axis involves the opposition, to be just/to be unjust.

An analysis of how these semiotic axes intersect one another around the actants of the narrative reveals a number of identifications, which in turn begin to point toward the meaning of the text. A beginning classification of the actants allows for a distinction between heavenly beings (angels; voice; God) and earthly beings, in two groupings: Babylon, kings, merchants, traders, seafarers (list A); human bodies and souls, saints, apostles, prophets, all those who have been sacrificed on earth (list B). Among the earthly beings, those in list A appear as accomplices of the figure of Babylon, while those in list B have been denied by those in list A, either regarded as goods for trade (v. 13) or killed (v. 24).

The heavenly beings share in the images of power and justice, but not in those of wealth. In contrast, among the earthly beings, those in list A share in power and wealth, but not justice; those in list B lack power and wealth, but share, out of empathy, in the justice of the heavenly beings. The results can be shown in the following outline:

Heavenly beings: power   justice   no-wealth
Humans (A):   power   no-justice wealth
Humans (B):   no-power (justice)   no-wealth

We can distinguish thereby between a power that is linked to wealth and a power that is associated with justice. Thus, justice and wealth emerge as antagonistic within the circulation of the text. When transferred onto a semiotic chart, the dynamics of power emerge in figure 1.

Figure 1

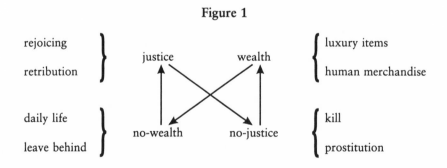

Temporal Codes

The difficulty occasioned by the seemingly arbitrary use of verbal tenses in Revelation has been duly noted in the scholarly literature. Revelation 18 in particular constitutes a good example of a certain incoherence in this regard. Rather than provide all the pertinent argumentation, I limit myself to a summary of the proposal advanced by Pierre Prigent. Prigent begins by acknowledging the difficulty in reconciling the verbal tenses in the chapter and then goes on to explain it in terms of not only a deficiency in the language of the author but also an insufficiency in all human language in the face of the irruption of the Absolute. He states:

> The eschatological future is not different in nature from the present of Christian life. The victory of Christ is a revelation which subverts as well our temporal categories. Our poor human language does not allow us to translate this certainty in a satisfactory, that is to say total, way.[5]

A number of approximations are nonetheless in order: the descriptions of the power lost by Babylon appear in the voices of others as a past event; in the first angelic intervention its fall is presented as having taken place already (v. 2: *epesen* = aorist). In the second intervention, however, the fall is anticipated by means of a prophetic gesture (v. 21: *blēthēsetai* = future). The announcement of the punishment in verses 6-8 is formulated in the future tense, but the laments of the accomplices are presented as a sudden event that has already taken place. In other words, the temporal codes of the narrative give the impression of subverting temporality through the juxtaposition of the different tenses. The future can be known now; what is going to happen has to be seen as already past. The present by no means renders eternal the conditions imposed by what exists. There is an alterity that comes from the future—the eternal, the heavenly—and reveals the past of the present. Thus, Babylon, despite its claim to reign (v. 7b), has already fallen; moreover, although its fall is announced as taking place in the future, it is proper to lament its destruction already.

The celestial is a vision as long as it is absent, although it is always present. However, although Babylon is present, it is already visualized as in the past. Babylon is not what presently is but what it is going to be. Its power is a fact of its present-past. Its present-future is its judgment and condemnation. The vision is a fact that turns the future into the present.

Spatial Codes

The topographical codes reveal two spaces: the heavens (the source of visions, voices, and actions) and the earth, with an epicenter in Babylon (the scene of the events). It should be noted that the figures tied to the isotopy of judgment come from the celestial realm, while the figures associated with

---

5. P. Prigent, *L'Apocalypse de Saint Jean* (Geneva: Labor et Fides, 1988) 265.

the isotopy of the economy are earthly. One element, however, does serve as a bridge between the two spaces: "Her sins have piled up to heaven" (v. 5a). The verb *kollaō* ("to amass" or "to pile up," but also "to join together" or "to unite") in the passive form allows for a certain interpretive playfulness: on the one hand, the sins have piled up; on the other hand, Babylon lies tied to its sins, so much so in effect that it becomes impossible to condemn the sins without condemning Babylon itself. These two spaces interact with each other: the earthly realm reaches the heavens on account of its many sins; the heavens in turn take action on earth in response to such an accumulation of sins. (Could this be an anamnesis of Genesis 11 with regard to the figure of Babylon? Was Rome able to achieve, by means of its "divine" emperors, what Nimrod could not achieve?)

It should be pointed out that within the earthly realm itself there are distances. The earth as a whole is not Babylon. "My people" are called upon to leave Babylon but are not translated to the heavenly realm. Likewise, neither the kings nor the merchants are in Babylon. Even though they have had a share in Babylon and have lived in the city, at the time of its fall they place great distance between themselves and the city in ruins. They themselves do not fall, only the source of their power or wealth. While in the heavens there is but one space, on the earth two spaces can be distinguished: the space where the wealth of Babylon is (was) stored; the space where human beings reside, be it that of "my people," to avoid having a share in Babylon's sin, or that of its accomplices, to escape from Babylon's destruction. The text does not establish the identity of these alternative spaces.

Distinctions and Identifications

All search for meaning is based on establishing identifications and distinctions. In this section I limit myself to identifications and contrasts of an intertextual nature; in the final hermeneutical synthesis that follows, I shall deal with the question of extratextual projections.

I have already highlighted the opposition, heaven/Babylon. Babylon represents all that the heavens are not. The preceding analysis of the semiotic, temporal, and spatial codes confirms this radical antithesis, evident even at the level of a surface reading of the text. All other oppositions and identifications are structured on the basis of this fundamental opposition.

At the level of the actants, corresponding identifications and oppositions are established as well, even if somewhat qualified. The heavenly beings are opposed to the accomplices of Babylon yet at the same time identified with the victims of Babylon. In this identification, however, a distinction should be noted: while the heavenly beings have power, their people on earth do not, not even after the fall of Babylon. The latter share in the judgment as a result of empathy rather than action. They are distinguished thereby from the accomplices of Babylon. They rejoice while the accomplices of Babylon lament. However, while the accomplices of Babylon did have power, wealth, and greatness, in the final inversion such attributes are not transferred onto them but destroyed.

Even among the accomplices of Babylon there are distinctions. In the first place, they make a distinction between Babylon and themselves, putting distance between them and the city at the very moment of its fall. They condemn themselves in their own lament, even though their punishment consists in no longer possessing the power and wealth they had enjoyed.[6] In the second place, they make distinctions among themselves: while the kings raise their lament because the hour of the city's judgment has arrived (v. 10; they lose the power and position that were theirs as a result of their share in corruption), the merchants weep for their luxury goods as well as the desolation of their wealth (v. 17a; they lose the source of their "greatness" [v. 23b]) and the seafarers complain both because they lose all chance of getting rich and on account of the desolation of the city (v. 19; they reveal thereby the instrumental nature of their activity).

The parallelism among the various laments establishes identifications as well as distinctions: judgment and desolation represent two facets of the same divine activity, depending on whether it is applied to the earthly power as such, which is always corrupt, or to the accumulation of goods. Such desolation represents the true visage of the city that goes on piling up goods:

Once again John prophesies the decadence of the great city, once its charm has been broken: its true corruption appears in this vision of ruins visited by demons, spirits, and repulsive birds. Such is her true face, once the makeup has been removed.[7]

There is a fundamental distinction as well between the catalog of verses 12-13 and that of verses 22-23. The first list identifies luxury goods, which can be accumulated; the second list is concerned with elements of everyday life, activities that give rise to the rejoicing and production that allow for human life. It should be noted that it is not the goods themselves but rather the activities as such—or the signs of such activity and rejoicing (which cannot be accumulated), above all the sounds and lights—that make up this catalog. While in the first list human bodies and human life (v. 13) appear as goods for trade, in the second list they constitute the very contents of the catalog. Consequently, the merchants have turned their power and possessions into a "deceiving fetish" (v. 23b), which ends up by destroying all life (v. 24). Babylon has piled up luxury goods and, in so doing,

---

6. Collins, "Revelation 18," 203.
7. C. Brütsch, *La clarté de l'Apocalypse* (Geneva: Labor et Fides, 1988) 265. This is a translation of the author's own translation of the French into Spanish.—TRANS.

has turned its back on everyday life. Such instrumental logic (accumulation of power and wealth, leading to victimization) negates a humanizing logic (justice and creative activity, leading to joy). Wherever one form of reason becomes enthroned, the other no longer exists. Finally, the lament of verse 14 shows that, within the revelatory vision, the imposition of a purely instrumental logic ends up by destroying its object. That is the very heart of the text.

It is trade, the "marketplace," that reveals the homicidal character of Babylon. The "accumulation of her sin" is revealed in the accumulation of its luxury goods, which have in the end turned life itself into a product for trade. If there is no trade, there is no life: that is the Babylonian creed. However, when trade becomes the supreme authority, the fullness of life in its creative activity can no longer come to expression. Earthly power is established on the basis of corruption and accumulation; its greatness is nothing but deceiving sorcery, a pure fetish (v. 23b). The "economic isotopy," focused on the marketplace, expanded and situated at the structural center of the text, has made it possible to distinguish between instances of life and instances of death, of victimization, within the isotopies of judgment and justice. The heavenly power is forced to take action as a result of such an accumulation of sin, commanding its people to exclude themselves from such a fetishistic logic, such a logic of death, and to rejoice instead in the life-giving logic of justice.

Hermeneutical Synthesis from the Perspective of the Victims

One could show the relevance of this vision with regard to the objective conditions that governed the life of the poor and persecuted Christians of Asia Minor within the Roman system of slavery of the first and second centuries. However, it is not my purpose in this essay to establish point-by-point identifications of an extratextual nature (Babylon = Rome; the kings = the client kingdoms; and so on); other commentators have already done so quite well. I do believe, on the other hand, that the mythopoetic language of apocalyptic and the revelatory polysemy of Scripture make it possible to read this text from the perspective of the victims of the neoliberal capitalist marketplace and its imposed instrumental logic.

It is in the victims that the true nature of the system is revealed. Behind the mask of luxury and progress lies the true visage of human destruction. The repulsive spirits of violence, racial hatred, mutilation, and exploitation roam the streets of our Babylons in Latin America (and the globe); their presence is clear once one looks beyond the glimmering lights of the neon signs. It is the accumulation of goods as such that gives birth to these spirits. The vision of John is thus "revelation" in this sense as well. The Christian saints and persecuted prophets are by no means the only victims of the corrupt power of Babylon. "All the slaughtered of the earth" have experienced the dimension of death implicit in the "Babylonian principle."[8]

Babylon is not just a city, imperial Rome, or the corrupt Jerusalem of the temple. It stands for whatever system enthrones the marketplace, elevating it to the status of a god and giving it the power to decide who lives and who dies. Babylon stands for whatever turns the human body and soul into merchandise for trade. Within such a system the only need that exists is the need of those who have the ability to pay; consequently, the basic needs of all human beings yield to the luxury markets of great merchants and traders. Wherever such luxury goods are piled up, the sounds and lights of creative activity, of the everyday life of all human beings, are excluded. This is not just a diagnosis of the future: the system itself explains as quite logical the presence of poverty, the scarcity of goods, and the lack of jobs. The productive activity of the poor is limited by the needs of the rich. Just this year, for example, the laws of the marketplace have driven fruit growers in the south of Argentina to let their fruit rot on the trees, while at the very same time child malnutrition continues to grow in the country as a whole. Such examples could be multiplied infinitely... all the way to the heavens, showing how the accumulation of riches and power leads to an accumulation of the sin that destroys human life and awakening the memory of the God of justice.

There is a direct link between the logic of the marketplace and official corruption. Examples along these lines can be easily multiplied as well: Fernando Collor de Melo in Brazil and Carlos Andrés Pérez in Venezuela represent but the tip of the iceberg within a system of political corruption that embraces all of Latin America and goes hand in hand with the system of the marketplace wherever it is imposed. As the laments reproduced by John show, both the marketplace and its attendant corruption rely on the same logic, are accomplices in the same sin, and will lament on account of the same decadence.

The imposition of economic logic excludes the logic of justice. The power generated by the marketplace (the power of *hoi emporoi*) is antithetical to the justice affirmed in the God of life. The spell of this deceitful power lies in concealing the very possibility of an alternative:

The economic fetish, as idolatrous object, has captured the nations and kings of the earth. The holy apostles and prophets (vv. 21, 24) did not succumb to this spell and suffered persecution and death as a result.[9]

---

8. For the "Babylonian principle" as the principle of exploitative accumulation, see E. Dussel, *Ética comunitaria* (Buenos Aires: Paulinas, 1986) passim, esp. 37–47, Eng. trans., *Ethics and Community* (Maryknoll, N.Y.: Orbis Books, 1988).

9. Ramírez, "Juicio de Dios," 70.

As in the case of John, the system condemns those who expose the fetishistic nature of the marketplace. Its claim to uniformity, its constant presentation of itself as the only way, its conviction that any other alternative is bound to fail also form part of this logic of death. In the end, such logic also includes self-destruction. To affirm its logic of exclusion, the system must demonize the enemy, the other, those who are different. In so doing it engenders and institutionalizes alongside itself a victimizing violence. The system cannot live, therefore, without killing its own children, without destroying what it generates. "It is the victims and only the victims who can put an end to this violence without end."[10]

The system creates a victimizing exclusion whereby it deprives of life those for whom it has no need. The system also destroys, however, the lives of its own accomplices. The system can produce only false imitations, deceiving fetishes of true life. All expressions of life are reduced thereby to the value of the marketplace, are "inertialized" as products. According to the apocalyptic text, however, the accumulation of goods does not ensure life but rather leads to death. All those who set out to make us believe that Babylon is the only reality, that with the system of accumulation humanity has reached its fullness and history its end, that all ideologies are now dead and with them all alternatives, will someday have to lament the fall of Babylon, even if some of them, while continuing to share in the logic of Babylon, begin, as a result of their own doubts regarding the system, to put distance between themselves and Babylon by way of conferences and encyclicals.

For those of us who nourish an apocalyptic faith (a faith that trusts in the power of revelation to unmask and the power of the God of justice), the earth is more than Babylon. The celestial voice invites the people to exclude themselves from such logic. Alterity is not only possible but also necessary, so as not to be confused by the homicidal dynamics of the marketplace. A life with music, craftsmanship, production, light, and family lies not within the system but outside the system. From the perspective of no-power, it is possible to imagine and project a different future, a different logic, the reverse of history. The power of Babylon is finite, temporal. The hope in the justice of God is infinite, eternal. Thus, a concept of dignity is constructed that rests not on having but on trusting, not on accumulating but on rejoicing, not on the corrupt power that enslaves but on a celebration of everyday life.

---

10. F. Hinkelammert, *Sacrificios humanos y sociedad occidental* (San José: DEI, 1991) 194.

16

The Hermeneutics of Liberation:
A Hermeneutics of the Spirit

Pablo Richard

My point of departure for this study shall be the colonial conquest of the Third World and its consequences for spirituality and hermeneutics. I shall then go on to examine how resistance against colonial domination in Latin America has succeeded in the reconstruction of a new spirituality within a hermeneutics of liberation. Western colonial Christianity imposed the domination of the Spaniard over the Indian, the male over the female, and the human being over nature; in so doing, it laid the foundations for a spirituality that was, at one and the same time, ethnocentric, patriarchal and anti-body. However, in the course of five hundred years of resistance against Western domination, a new consciousness and a new experience of the Spirit have come to life—a new spirituality informing above all the liberation movements on behalf of native peoples, blacks, women, the young, the body, and nature. I shall show how this subversion of the Spirit has a direct influence on how the Bible is read and interpreted. I am particularly interested in showing how, in the last few years, the hermeneutics of liberation has gradually turned into a hermeneutics of the Spirit in Latin America.

The study will cover five major subjects: (1) the spirit of Western colonial domination; (2) the five hundred years of spiritual resistance against Western colonialism; (3) the reconstruction of the Spirit against Western Christianity; (4) the Bible: conquest and resistance; and (5) a hermeneutics of the Spirit.

The Spirit of Western Colonial Domination

Christianity came to Africa, Asia, and Latin America with the conquest and expansion of Western colonialism. This is a historical fact, objective and

This is a translation of the original manuscript, "Hermenéutica de la Liberación: Hermenéutica del Espíritu." The translation is by Fernando F. Segovia.

global, that does not deny either the individual positive deeds or the generosity and good intentions of the missionaries. The original inhabitants of these three continents suffered the arrival of Christianity as an imposition on behalf of a Western and colonial system of domination. From the sixteenth century until the present day, this process of domination has continued, whether by way of its Catholic or Protestant version. This historical fact represents a profound spiritual and hermeneutical perversion at the very core of Christianity. I should like to illustrate such a judgment with a concrete example. I turn to that one author of the sixteenth century who best captures the spirit of the Western colonial conquest, Juan Ginés de Sepúlveda, and use as reference his fundamental work entitled, *Tratado sobre las justas causas de la guerra contra los indios* (Treatise on the just causes of the war against the Indians).[1]

Texts

It is not my intention here to deal with the complex character of this work as a whole or to enter into the discussion of this theme in the sixteenth century.[2] I simply wish to examine a few texts where the author sets forth his fundamental argument regarding the justification of the war against the native peoples. The argument proceeds as follows:

> It is just and natural for men who are judicious, upright and humane to rule over those who are not.... [For that reason] it is perfectly right for the Spaniard to rule over these barbarians of the New World and adjacent islands, who are as inferior to the Spaniards in prudence, intelligence, virtue, and humaneness as *children* are to *adults* and *women* to *men,* with as much difference between them as there is between *savage and cruel peoples* and *most merciful peoples,* between the wildly *intemperate* and the *temperate and moderate,* as well as—I am tempted to say—between *monkeys* and *men.*[3]

The war of the Spaniards against the Indians is declared just on the following grounds:

> Since barbarians are by nature slaves, uncivilized and inhuman, they refuse to acknowledge the rule of those who are more prudent, powerful, and perfect than they—a rule that would bring them enormous advantages and a rule that is also just, since it is a law of nature that

---

1. Juan Ginés de Sepúlveda, *Tratado sobre las justas causas de la guerra contra los indios* (Mexico City: Fondo de Cultura Económica, 1979). This is a bilingual edition containing the original Latin text as well as a Spanish translation.

2. See in this regard F. Mires, *En nombre de la cruz: Discusiones teológicas y políticas frente al holocausto de los indios (período de conquista)* (San José: DEI, 1986).

3. Sepúlveda, *Tratado,* 101; emphasis added.

matter be subject to *form,* the *body* to the *soul, passion* to *reason, animals* to *men,* the *female* to the *male, children* to the *father,* the *imperfect* to the *perfect, what is worse* to *what is better,* for the universal well-being of all things.[4]

Elsewhere he adds:

What could have been more convenient and salutary for these barbarians than to be made subject to the rule of those whose prudence, virtue, and religion will convert them from *barbarians,* so much so that they hardly deserve the name of human beings, into *civilized men,* as far as that is possible; from being *slow-witted* and *lustful,* into *upright* and *honorable men;* from being *ungodly* and *slaves to demons,* into *Christians* and *worshipers of the true God?*[5]

All this argumentation is used to justify a global domination:

It is natural and just for the *soul* to rule over the *body,* for *reason* to govern over *passion.* . . . For that reason, *wild beasts* are domesticated and made subject to the rule of *man.* For that reason the *male* rules over the *female,* the *adult* over the *child,* the *father* over his *children,* that is to say, those who are *more powerful* and *more perfect* over those who are *weaker* and *imperfect.*[6]

The thought of Juan Ginés de Sepúlveda represents the attitude and thinking of the entire enterprise of conquest and colonization of Abia Yala.[7] This author brings to expression what the majority of the conquistadores and evangelizers felt, thought, and did. He is thus by no means a marginal author but rather a typical representative of the entire colonial transformation of society and Christianity.[8]

Global Character of Domination

I shall begin by examining the binomial *Spanish/Indian* as indicative of the relationship of colonial domination. The Spaniards are said to be most merciful; superior in prudence, intelligence, and virtue; more powerful and

---

4. Ibid., 153; emphasis added.
5. Ibid., 133; emphasis added.
6. Ibid., 85; emphasis added.
7. "Abia Yala" is the name given by the Kuna Indians of Panama to Latin America. For us "Latin America" is a colonial and meaningless designation. In the Kuna language "Abia Yala" signifies "Mature Earth," "Great Mother Earth," "the Earth of Blood"; see A. Wagua, "Present Consequences of the European Invasion of America," *1492–1992: The Voice of the Victims* (ed. L. Boff and V. Elizondo; *Concilium* 232; London: SCM; Philadelphia: Trinity, 1990) 47–56.
8. See P. Richard, "1492: The Violence of God and the Future of Christianity," *1492–1992,* 59–67.

perfect. In contrast, the Indians are described as barbarians, uncivilized, intemperate; a savage and cruel people. The Spaniard is humane, represents humanity. The Indian is inhumane, hardly deserves to be called human, behaves like a monkey. Sepúlveda constantly refers to them as "little men" or hominoids (*hombrecillos;* in Latin, *homunculi*).[9] Salvation can come to the Indians only by way of a subjection that transforms them from barbarians into civilized men; from slow-witted and lustful into upright and honorable men; from ungodly men and slaves to demons into Christians and worshipers of the true God. The binomial *Spanish/Indian* is replicated in these other binomials as well: *male/female, adult/child, father/son.* Finally, it is also likened to the relationship *human being/animal.* We thus have the following coordinates:

Spanish	Male	Adult	Father	Human Being
Indian	Female	Child	Son	Animal

The Spaniard is like the male, the adult, the father, the human being; the Indian is like the female, the child, the son, the animal. The relationship that obtains between the two is one of domination: "Wild beasts are domesticated and made subject to the rule of man. . . . The male rules over the female."

As a result, the inherent relationship among colonial domination (Spanish/Indian), gender domination (male/female), generational domination (adult/child), and natural domination (human being/animal) becomes evident. Colonial domination is global in character and encompasses all dimensions of both the human being and nature.

Metaphysical, Necessary, and Natural Character of Domination

The relationship of colonial domination is identified with the relationship of domination of form over matter, soul over body, and reason over passion.[10] The Spaniard is to the Indian as the soul is to the body. The same applies to the relationship of domination over the female, the child, and nature. The relationship of domination is further presented in terms of the relationship of the powerful over the weak, the perfect over the imperfect, and what is better over what is worse. Sepúlveda goes on to add, "This is the natural order which, as mandated by the divine and eternal law, is to

---

9. Sepúlveda (*Tratado*, 105) declares, "Now compare these qualities of prudence, intelligence, magnanimity, temperance, humaneness, and religion [of the Spaniards] with those possessed by those *hombrecillos* among whom you will scarcely find any vestiges of humanity (homunculos illos in quibus vix reperies humanitatis vestigia)."

10. See n. 4 above. I reproduce here the Latin text in order to show the exact terminology employed: "justum est eo jure naturae, quo materia formae, corpus animae, appetitus rationi, hominibus animalia bruta, viris mulieres, patribus filii, imperfecta, scilecet, perfectis, deteriora potioribus, debent, ut utrisque bene sit, obtemperare."

be observed at all times."[11] Everything is proved with certainty by calling upon the authority of Aristotle, Saint Augustine, and Saint Thomas, all of whom are quoted abundantly.[12]

Given its identification with the rule of form over matter, the soul over the body, and reason over passion, domination takes on a spiritual, metaphysical, rational, natural, and necessary character. The conquistador (as well as the male, the adult, and the human being) is the one who creates order, who is spiritual, who imposes rationality. The Indian (like the woman, the child, and nature) is matter, body, passion; as a result, the Indian is not human, has no soul, is like a wild beast, like a monkey. Just as the soul must exercise violence against the body, above all when the body rebels against it, so too the conqueror may and must exercise violence against the Indian—the male against the female, the adult against the child, the human being against nature. It goes against natural and divine law for the Indian to rule over the Spaniard, the female over the male, the animal over the human being; it would amount to the triumph of passion over reason and matter over spirit.

Five Hundred Years of Spiritual Resistance against Western Colonialism

The colonial thinking exemplified by the work of Juan Ginés de Sepúlveda represents the theoretical expression of the conquest and its entire human, ecological, economic, political, social, cultural, and religious destruction. The sixteenth century witnessed the genocide of sixty million Indians as well as twenty million blacks brought from Africa—the greatest genocide in the history of humanity, entirely perpetrated within the context of Western Christianity.[13]

Resistance to the colonial conquest and domination followed a number of different paths. To begin with, there was prophetic resistance to be found among the Spaniards themselves, with Fray Bartolomé de Las Casas as its most famous exponent.[14] Besides him one also finds a whole generation of prophetic bishops, religious, and theologians in the sixteenth century who defended the Indian and made possible a liberating evangelization. Just as the dominant position of the church was indeed one of collaboration

---

11. Sepúlveda, *Tratado*, 153 ("Hic est enim ordo naturalis, quam divina et aeterna lex ubique servari jubet").

12. The influence of Aristotle on Sepúlveda is decisive and omnipresent, especially in terms of the *Politics* (see 1.3). The Bible is seldom cited and then only in a literal and accommodating way.

13. For the concept of "Western Christianity" or "Christendom," see P. Richard, *Death of Christendoms, Birth of the Church* (Maryknoll, N.Y.: Orbis Books, 1987).

14. See G. Gutiérrez, *Las Casas: In Search of the Poor of Christ* (Maryknoll, N.Y.: Orbis Books, 1993).

with and legitimation of the colonial power, so there was also, despite such domination and in direct reaction to it, an authentic evangelization ("Evangelization itself constitutes a type of indictment against those responsible for such abuses").[15]

Besides such prophetic resistance on the part of a number of missionaries, there was also native resistance. This type of resistance developed along two main lines: an Indian resistance that maintained its identity in silence, clandestinely, in the mountains and jungles; and an Indian resistance that preserved its identity in dialogue with the Christian religion itself. Out of these two types of native resistance emerged what are now known as Indian-Indian theology and Indian-Christian theology.[16] Later on, a similar process of resistance took place among the black slaves brought over from Africa, eventually giving rise to an African American theology, quite developed and important today.

Within this Indian and African American resistance of five hundred years, one finds the most profound and significant historical roots for resistance against Western colonial domination as well as for the construction of other alternatives to such domination. In effect, Latin America will be able to reconstruct its life, its identity, and its autonomy only if these native and African American roots of resistance are adopted as a point of departure. The struggle of Indians and blacks for their lives, their cultures, and their religions constitutes the only perspective radical enough to allow for a critical consciousness regarding Western colonial domination and a theological, hermeneutical, and spiritual reflection that is truly liberating and that can serve as an alternative to Western domination.

The struggle of the Indians for their lives, their culture, and their religion integrated from the start the reality of woman as well as the reality of nature. In all the native cultural traditions of Abia Yala, from one end of the continent to the other, one finds from the beginning the unity of female and male and the identification of both with nature. God is always female and male; nature likewise is always female and male. The earth is Mother Earth, and in it resides the fullness of God. If colonial domination rests on the domination of the male over the female and human beings over nature, native resistance finds its grounding and strength in the equality of female and male and nature and humanity. It was this native dimension of gender and nature that served as the millenarian grounding for its confrontation with Western domination.

---

15. See the final document of the Fourth General Conference of Latin American Bishops held in Santo Domingo, October 1992, no. 18.

16. Contemporary literature on Indian theology is rich, available for the most part only in mimeograph form or by way of occasional pamphlets; as such, it can still be considered as a form of oral culture. Important publications in this regard include: *Teología India: Primer encuentro taller Latinoamericano* (Mexico City: Cenami; Quito: Abya Yala, 1991) and an issue of the journal *Christus* (7 [1991]) devoted entirely to the theme of Indian theology.

Today, resistance to colonial domination—domination in the contemporary form of a "new international order"—reveals the same original expression found in the deep roots of our identity. Contemporary resistance takes the shape of a critical consciousness with regard to the unity that exists among the different dimensions of *culture* (Indian; black; mestizo), *gender* (women), and *nature* (the earth, the body, the cosmos, and the environment). Most recently, the dimension of *generation,* with reference to the young, who not only constitute a majority in Latin America but also wish to be real and authentic historical subjects (not just the "hope of tomorrow"), has been mentioned as well.

Such critical consciousness—a consciousness that brings together culture, gender, generation, and nature—is differentiated and multiple, though profoundly united in resistance against the present colonial domination. This historical awareness has been assigned the symbolic name of Sur (South), given the emergence of the confrontation between North and South as dominant after the end of the cold war and its confrontation between East and West.[17] This new consciousness coming to life in the South—where the unification of culture, gender, generation, and nature is taking place—calls as well for a *hermeneutics of the South,* a hermeneutics that will guide and inform a new biblical interpretation in the face of the dominant Western colonial consciousness (represented by the imposition of the Spaniard over the Indian, the male over the female, the adult over the child, the human being over nature; and metaphysically grounded on the rule—on the basis of "natural law"—of soul over body, reason over passion, and form over matter).

The Reconstruction of the Spirit against Western Christianity

The fundamental axis of the thought of Juan Ginés de Sepúlveda, and perhaps of all Greek-Latin-Western thought, is the duality soul/body. The new element encountered in the colonial conquest is the identification of this relationship of soul/body with that of Spanish/Indian. The Spaniard is identified with Christianity and the worship of the true God; the Indian is savage (barbarian/pagan) and a worshiper of demons. The Spanish is to the Indian as the soul is to the body, God to demons, and grace to sin. The Spaniard, like the soul, is the expression of the spiritual and the divine; the Indian, like the body, is the expression of the material and the demonic. The soul is the realm where one encounters God; the body is the domain of the demon and sin. Salvation takes place when the soul rules the body, when the body is repressed, and ultimately when the soul is freed from

---

17. See P. Richard, "El Sur existe y tiene su teología," *Envío* 137 (1993) 28–41. This journal is published in Nicaragua.

the body. Similarly, the Indian attains salvation by leaving behind identity, culture, and religion and becoming a Christian. If the Indian resists, it is legitimate to use violence for the sake of salvation, just as the individual uses violence against the body for the sake of salvation. This entire framework is reinforced by Sepúlveda when, following Aristotelian tradition, he identifies the relationship soul/body with those of form/matter and reason/passion. The Spaniard, identified with the Spirit and God, becomes thereby the incarnation of reason. What is rational is European, white, Western. The Indian is passion, irrationality; for that reason the Indian is characterized as libidinous, stupid, animal-like, savage, barely human, monkey-like.

The same framework is used for domination over the female, the child, and nature. The male is identified with the soul; consequently, he is spiritual and rational. The female is body, carnal desire, irrationality. The male is close to God; the female is identified with sin and often with the devil (witches). Likewise, vis-à-vis the adult, the child is seen as unformed matter and irrational being. The very same framework—soul/body, reason/passion, form/matter—is applied to the domination of man over nature. The spiritual man rules and exercises violence over both material nature and his body. The destruction of nature and the body, like the destruction of the Indian or the female, is not important for the spiritual identity of the West. In this tradition what is essential and what is ultimately saved is not the body or nature but the soul; the decisive and definitive encounter with God takes place not in the body or nature but in the soul.

The colonial expansion of Western Christianity in Abia Yala—given its identification of the spiritual and the rational with the rule of the Spaniard over the Indian, the male over the female, the adult over the child, and the human being over nature—brought about the profound annihilation of the spiritual dimension present in the Indian, the female, the child, nature, and the body. The conquest of the West imposed both a rationality and a spirituality that were ethnocentric, patriarchal, authoritarian, antinature, and anti-body in character. In so doing the West sought to delegitimize and destroy the cultural, religious, and spiritual experience of the Indian peoples. The Indian possesses a culture that is profoundly religious and spiritual. The Indian, male as well as female, experiences God, male and female, in nature and above all in Mother Earth. In Indian religion there is a profound identification among female, nature, and God. In all the religious traditions of Abia Yala, God and the Spirit are always present in the community (culture), the human person (male/female), nature, and the earth. In the conquest a radical confrontation took place between the spirituality of Western Christianity and the spirituality of the Indian peoples. The West denied the presence of the Spirit in the life of the Indian. These five hundred years of native resistance have been five hundred years of *spiritual resistance* against Western colonialism.

The same can be said of that critical consciousness coming to the fore today in civil society and the social movements of the South. I have already mentioned the identification of culture, gender, nature, and generation. For us today that identification is also the privileged space of the spiritual, the rational, the presence and revelation of God. The liberation movement of the oppressed—the sum total of the movements involving the native peoples, African Americans, workers and peasants; the women's liberation movements; ecological movements; movements on behalf of children and young people; movements of national liberation—is a movement for life in all of its diversity as well as being spiritual. Today the liberation of the oppressed is rescuing the sense of the spiritual in history. Western thinking, given its framework of soul/body, denigrated the body, the Indian, the black, the female, the child, and nature; today, the consciousness taking shape in the South values as spiritual and rational the liberation of the body, the Indian, the black, the female, the child, and nature. The liberation movement radically rescues the Spirit in that space where domination rules it out. The movement of liberation is thus fundamentally a *spiritual movement*. The South is poor in terms of wealth, technology, and armaments; it is rich, however, in Spirit, humanity, and culture. In the South the power of God becomes manifest not in terms of arms and wealth but rather in terms of the spiritual strength of Indians, blacks, peasants, young people, women, the earth, and nature. The hermeneutics of liberation is a hermeneutics of the South, a hermeneutics of the Spirit, a hermeneutics characterized by the theology of the cross (see 1 Corinthians 1–2).

The Bible: Conquest and Resistance

The Bible and the Conquest

The Western framework for domination—grounded in the distinction soul/ body and used as a social paradigm to justify the rule of the conquistador over the Indian, the male over the female, and the human being over nature—amounted to a profound perversion of the biblical tradition. The Bible was read and interpreted from a colonial and Western hermeneutics of domination. Up to the present day the native peoples of Abia Yala have been traumatized by the Bible. The Bible as a whole was interpreted in opposition to the spiritual experience of the Indian peoples. For example, the biblical framework of Joshua's conquest over the Canaanites was applied to the Indian peoples. Similarly, the Indian religions were approached in terms of the prophetic tradition against idols. Moreover, the New Testament was read from the point of view of an imperialist Christology and a patriarchal ecclesiology. The spiritual realm was identified with Western culture, with the rule of the male over the female and the human being over nature.

This spiritual perversion, perpetrated by the Greek-Latin-Western tradition, placed the Bible at the service of colonial domination. The Jewish-Christian tradition was inverted and transformed into its very opposite. It thus became possible for Juan Ginés de Sepúlveda to use both the Bible and Western Christian thinking to justify the most horrendous genocide in the history of Christianity.

The Bible and Resistance

Biblical anthropology is fundamentally defined by the opposition life/death. The Spirit (*pneuma*) represents the tendency of the human being (in body and soul) toward life; its opposite is the flesh (*sarx*), the tendency of every human being (in body and soul) toward death. So, for example, Rom 8:6: "The flesh tends toward death; the Spirit, however, toward life and peace."[18] The carnal man or woman is that man or woman whose orientation, in body and soul, is toward death; the spiritual man or woman is that man or woman whose orientation, in body and soul, is toward life. The spiritual is defined by the triumph of life over death. Salvation consists in overcoming death, in body and soul. The Holy Spirit brings the tendency toward life to fulfillment, beyond death itself, in the resurrection; the opposite is sin, which reinforces in our body and soul the tendency toward death. Thus Paul can say, "The rule of the Spirit of life has liberated you from the rule of sin and death" (Rom 8:1-2).[19]

Despite the conquest and Western Christianity, the Indian peoples began to read the Bible in a different way. Today there already exists an *Indian hermeneutics* or an *Indian reading of the Bible*.[20] Such a hermeneutics values the "seeds of the word" present in Indian religion prior to the coming of Christianity. The Indian cosmos, culture, and religion are looked upon as the first "book" of God. The Bible becomes the second book of God for the discernment of the presence and revelation of God in the first book. The Indians themselves, within their own culture and religion, wish to be the subjects of this Indian reading of the Bible.

There exists today as well in Abia Yala a movement known as the *popular reading of the Bible,* which also goes by the name of a pastoral reading of the Bible or a communal reading of the Bible.[21] The most important el-

---

18. Bible quotations throughout the essay are the author's own, adapted into English by the translator.—TRANS.

19. See P. Richard, "Espiritualidad para tiempos de revolución: Teología espiritual a la luz de San Pablo," *Espiritualidad y liberación en América Latina* (ed. E. Bonnín; San José: DEI, 1982) 87–102.

20. See P. Richard, "Hermenéutica Bíblica India," *Revista de Interpretación Bíblica Latinoamericana* 11 (1992) 9–24.

21. See C. Mesters, *Defenseless Flower: A New Reading of the Bible* (New York: Orbis Books, 1989). See also the first issue of the *Revista de Interpretación Bíblica Latinoamericana* (1988), which was devoted to this theme and entitled *Lectura popular de la*

ement of such a reading is the fact that the Bible is read and interpreted by the poor in the ecclesial base communities, in an atmosphere of prayer and commitment. These communities have flourished above all among Indians, blacks, peasants, and in general among the most oppressed, excluded, and marginalized segments of society. The ecclesial communities are "base" communities insofar as they are deeply inscribed in civil society and social movements. Through these communities the Bible is read by the oppressed from within the social movements themselves, giving rise thereby to a spiritual movement in the very midst of the people. The Bible is read and interpreted from within the bosom of Indian and African American movements, worker and peasant movements, women's liberation movements, ecological movements, and movements of the young. The word of God is read from the point of view of that Spirit that makes itself manifest and active in these movements that have to do with the body, culture, the female, nature, and the young. The experience of the Spirit does not take place in the soul vis-à-vis the body but rather in the affirmation of life in the face of death. Life is clearly affirmed as the full life of the body, the poor, the Indian, the black, the female, the young, and nature. The realm of the Spirit is the world defined by the relationship body/culture/gender/ generation. An interpretation of the Bible from the point of view of the body, culture, the female, and nature is demanded by the Spirit. In the popular reading of the Bible, the experience of the Spirit finds a new social location in history.

Both the Indian reading of the Bible and the popular reading of the Bible are rescuing the authentic meaning of the Spirit in the biblical tradition. As argued above, the Spirit is not identified with the soul but with the tendency of the entire human being, body and soul, toward life. The Bible as a whole is now interpreted in terms of the life/death opposition rather than the soul/ body opposition. An interpretation of the Bible from the perspective of the Indian, the female, and the body is thus a spiritual interpretation carried out under the same Spirit with which the Bible was written. The Western and colonial reading of the Bible—carried out against the Indian, the female, the body—is an interpretation that perverts the spiritual meaning of the Bible. The Bible was not written with a colonial, patriarchal, and antibody spirit but with the Spirit of the poor and the oppressed. Thus, only a hermeneutics of liberation can be a hermeneutics of the Spirit, which is the hermeneutics with which the Bible itself was composed.

Biblia en América Latina: Una hermenéutica de la liberación (The popular reading of the Bible in Latin America: A hermeneutics of liberation); see especially the articles by N. Velez ("La lectura bíblica en las CEB's," 8–29) and P. Richard ("Lectura popular de la Biblia en América Latina: Hermenéutica de la liberación," 30–48).

A Hermeneutics of the Spirit

The importance of the Holy Spirit for hermeneutics may be highlighted by the following remarks of Patriarch Athenagoras, who out of his own oriental perspective writes:

> Without the Holy Spirit
> God is far away,
> Christ remains in the past,
> the gospel becomes a dead letter,
> the church is a mere organization,
> authority is power,
> mission is propaganda,
> worship is an archaism,
> and the moral life a life of slaves.[22]

St. Paul refers to the Spirit in terms of life/death (2 Cor 3:5-6): "Our power comes from God, who gave us the power to become ministers of a new covenant, not of the letter but of the Spirit. For the letter kills, but the Spirit gives life."

The importance of the Spirit for hermeneutics is not simply a matter of believing or not believing in the Spirit but is defined rather in terms of *where* the Spirit is to be found. The problem is not the existence of the Spirit as such but its *presence* or social location in history. We affirm of the Spirit what we affirm of God in general: the problem is not whether we believe in God but in which God we believe. The problem is not believing that God exists but discerning where God lies in our history. It is not the existence of God but rather the liberating presence of God that is fundamental in the world. Such a new approach to God and the Spirit of God is especially important and significant in the world of the oppressed, in the Third World or the world of the South. The challenge to our faith comes not from secularization or atheism but from idolatry. Historically speaking, the mortal threat to our faith came from the colonial conquest of Western Christianity and the holocaust of the black slaves carried out by Western Christianity; today, that threat still continues, as the powerful, the bankers, and the dictators proceed to call themselves Christians. Such developments give rise to that spiritual perversion that we call idolatry. Thus, much more important than a hermeneutics of the existence of God is a hermeneutics of the God of the poor—the God of Indians, blacks, women, and the young; the God of life who liberates the body as well as nature. Hermeneutics must render an effective and concrete account of the *social location* of God and the Spirit of God in history.

---

22. Cited by V. Manucci, *La Biblia como Palabra de Dios* (Bilbao: Desclée, 1988) 318.

I have already referred to the place assigned to the Spirit in the foundational theology of the colonial conquest in the sixteenth century. It is clear from the texts of Juan Ginés de Sepúlveda cited above that the rule of the Spaniard over the Indian—along with the rule of the male over the female, the adult over the child, and the human being over nature—finds its metaphysical grounding in the rule of the soul over the body, form over matter, reason over passion, and ultimately in the rule of God over demons and grace over sin. Within such a framework the Spirit is reduced to the colonial, patriarchal, and anti-body spirit of the Western conquest. This spirit was imposed as a law or letter that kills; in fact, it killed eighty million Indians and blacks in Abia Yala. In Western colonial Christianity the Bible was interpreted from the perspective of this spirit of the conquest: against Indians, blacks, women, the body, and nature. The Spirit of life was replaced by the system of the law, sin, and death. Hermeneutics, lacking in Spirit, was placed at the service of death.

In the course of the last five hundred years, such a Western colonial hermeneutics was further amplified and reinforced every time the Bible was interpreted from a theology that legitimized the death of the poor, the oppressed, the native peoples, the peasants, women, youth, and nature. Western theology continues to be fundamentally ethnocentric and racist, patriarchal and authoritarian, anti-body and destructive of nature. It is a theology that kills and a hermeneutics without Spirit, bearing in itself all those elements denounced by Athenagoras in the text cited at the beginning of the section.

To be sure, the exegesis of the last one hundred years has produced works of enormous importance and relevance; many exegetes, both women and men, have emerged as authentic teachers of the faith and prophets. However, the dominant *spirit* of this exegesis has been, without a doubt, the spirit of modernity—marked by positivism, rationalism, liberalism, individualism, and existentialism. Exegesis normally takes place in closed academies, where the search for power and prestige has been informed by the spirit of competition and the economy of the marketplace.

In the Third World—in Abia Yala, Africa, and Asia—we have no problems with exegetical methods; our problem lies with the *spirit* behind such methods. The methods are useful and effective, but the spirit underlying such methods continues to be the ethnocentrism, patriarchalism, and authoritarianism of the Western world, ancient and modern. A Third World exegete has given sharp expression to such dissatisfaction: "The more I study the biblical commentaries, the less I understand the Bible; the more I study the Bible, the less I understand the biblical commentaries." There are thousands of exegetical works that have no Spirit, that are born solely as products in the modern marketplace of science, at the service of money, prestige, and power. Of course, there are exceptions, but in general Western exegesis and hermeneutics suffer from a *crisis of the Spirit,* a crisis evident to us since the time of the colonial conquest.

For the hermeneutics of liberation, born in the South, in the Third World, and among the oppressed of the earth, a *rescue of the Spirit* is fundamental. The hermeneutics of liberation aims to be a hermeneutics of the Spirit and with Spirit. However, as noted above, it is not enough to believe in the Spirit; one needs to discern in *which* Spirit to believe and *where* to find it. It is not a question of any spirit but rather of the Spirit of the God of life, as revealed in the poor, the oppressed, the female, the cultural and religious traditions of peoples, and nature. It is the same Spirit with which the Bible was written. In the beautiful words of the Dogmatic Constitution on Divine Revelation (*Dei Verbum*) from the Vatican II: "Holy Scripture must be read and interpreted according to the same Spirit by whom it was written" (*DV* 12).[23]

I shall now proceed to show how a hermeneutics of liberation rescues the Spirit and becomes a hermeneutics of the Spirit. I shall do so by summarizing in five points our biblical experience and hermeneutics in Abia Yala.

Social Movements of Liberation as Privileged Spaces for the Experience of Spirit in History

What I have in mind here above all are those movements involving native peoples and African Americans; the liberation movements of women and the young; ecological movements; and all those movements tied to the earth, labor, human rights, and solidarity. Such movements take on special importance in the Third World, insofar as it is in them that is born the alternative of a new power and from them that emerge the new subjects who seek to build a different society. Faced with the impossibility of assuming power and the inability of the dominant groups to build a new society, the alternative of a new power arises, with new subjects for the construction of a different world where there is life for all. It is in such a context that a new critical consciousness is arising, bringing together all the different dimensions of power: labor; culture (native; black; mestizo; popular suburban; and peasant); gender (women); generation (the young); and nature (body; earth; the environment). All of these different dimensions establish links with one another, in different ways but with a *single consciousness,* whose common option is a fundamental option for life. Within this historical movement and this new consciousness on behalf of life, faith lives and discerns the experience of the Spirit. The hermeneutics of liberation seeks to

---

23. Citations from the Dogmatic Constitution on Divine Revelation are taken from the English translation found in W. M. Abbott, S.J., ed., *The Documents of Vatican II* (New York: Herder and Herder and Association Press, 1966).

interpret the Bible with the Spirit made manifest in these movements and in this consciousness. Such discernment is carried out in radical confrontation with the theology of conquest and Western Christianity.

The Ecclesial Base Communities as Privileged Space for the Reading and Interpretation of the Bible

The ecclesial base communities are deeply rooted in the social movements mentioned above and constitute that space where the experience of the Spirit encountered in these movements is centered and makes itself manifest. In effect, all believers who form part of these social movements take part in the base communities. The base communities function as a space for participation, solidarity, prayer, and commitment. The reading and interpretation of the Bible in the base communities yield a special presence of the Spirit—that Spirit present in the liberation movements as discerned by the community through the interpretation of the Bible; that Spirit which makes available to the community that same reading and interpretation of the Bible.

In the last few years great strides have been made in the formation of pastoral agents in the biblical sciences. Popular exegetes have gone forth to work with the base communities. The result has been a *convergence of exegesis and Spirit* at the heart of the *community*. Such a communitarian, pastoral or popular reading of the Bible, in which biblical science is directly linked with the Spirit of the communities, functions as the fundamental reference for those of us who have dedicated ourselves to exegesis at a professional level. Our exegesis finds a point of departure in this encounter between science and Spirit in the ecclesial base communities. It is the community rather than the academy that sustains and enriches our work as exegetes. Our exegetical work is also at the service of the community rather than the academy, the marketplace for the interchange of exegetical goods for the sake of profit, prestige, and power. The Spirit of the base communities liberates us from the spirit of the marketplace.

The Spiritual Meaning of the Bible in the Hermeneutics of Liberation

The following threefold distinction of biblical meaning is well-known: the *literal meaning,* or the meaning of the text as text, in terms of its words, literary structures, and intertextuality; the *historical meaning,* or the meaning of the text in terms of the history behind the text, the history of the text, and the history created by the text; and the *spiritual meaning,* or the meaning acquired by the text as we discern the presence and revelation of God in our own present history. It is this last meaning that privileges the hermeneutics of liberation as a hermeneutics of the Spirit (without abandoning the literal and historical meanings). The biblical text reveals the word of

God, but it also reveals where and how God is revealed in our own history today. We discover the literal and historical meanings of the text when we read the text itself; we discover its spiritual meaning when the biblical text reads us or reads our present historical reality. To be sure, the text itself—in its literal and historical meanings—can reveal the word of God, but the text is also able to discern the word of God in our present history. When such a discernment is carried out by the text, a production of meaning takes place in the text itself: this is what we call the spiritual meaning of the biblical text. It is a reading that is radically opposed to biblical fundamentalism, with its reduction of the word of God to a purely literal meaning, as well as biblical historicism, with its reduction of the word of God to a purely historical meaning.

The following text from St. Augustine illustrates quite well this spiritual meaning of the Bible:

> The Bible, the second book of God, was written in order to help us decipher the world, to give back to us the vision of faith and contemplation, and to transform all reality into a great revelation of God.[24]

The hermeneutics of liberation, as a hermeneutics of the Spirit, seeks to give back to the church that vision of faith and contemplation, so as to transform our entire reality, especially the reality of the poor and the oppressed, into a great revelation of God.

Tradition as the Theophany of the Holy Spirit in History

The Holy Spirit is active not only in the text of the Bible but also in the historical tradition out of which the Bible emerges and within which the Bible itself makes history. Contemporary exegesis does place value on the presence and revelation of God in history, especially in the history of the poor and the oppressed. The Protestant Reformation placed special emphasis on the Bible as the word of God (*sola scriptura*), a very positive development in its own right; however, the exclusive identification of the word of God with the Bible has also given rise to biblical fundamentalism. The contemporary biblical movement places proper value on all three meanings of Holy Scripture—the literal, the historical, and the spiritual.

We also seek today to restore legitimate value to sacred tradition, that is, the historical tradition within which the Spirit is also present and in which the word of God also reveals itself. In the words of a theologian from the

---

24. Cited by C. Mesters, *Flor sin Defensa* (Bogotá: CLAR, 1984) 28. The reference here is to the Spanish edition because the quotation is not in the English edition of Mesters's work. In effect, the English edition leaves out the very first chapter of the book—entitled "What You Must Know in Order to Read the Bible Profitably"—where this reference occurs.— TRANS.

Eastern Church, "Tradition is the epiclesis of salvation history, that is, the theophany of the Spirit, without which the history of the world becomes incomprehensible and Sacred Scripture remains a dead letter."[25] The Dogmatic Constitution on Divine Revelation of Vatican II made an important attempt to recover this sacred tradition in a positive and liberating way (see esp. *DV* 7–9).[26] That is also what the hermeneutics of liberation attempts to do today by rescuing what we call the book of life: the revelation of the word of God in nature, in the religious traditions of the native peoples, and in the traditions of the people of God and the first Christian communities. Just as we undertake a popular reading of the Bible, so should we also undertake a *popular reading of tradition,* that is, a rereading of the tradition from the spiritual experience of the people of God, especially the poor and the oppressed. Tradition is often identified with the magisterium, but such an equation is incorrect. As *DV* 10 affirms, the magisterium is not superior to the word of God but at its service. The pronouncements of the magisterium are neither revealed nor inspired; not even when taken as a whole can they reproduce in full the word of God, for the latter is the living and personal word of God—transcendent, inexhaustible, and inscrutable.[27] Tradition has the people of God as its subject; tradition also contains, transmits, and deepens the word of God. The word of God is the only source of revelation, contained in Sacred Scripture and handed on by sacred tradition. This word of God, insofar as it is of God and insofar as God is present in creation and since creation in all peoples, transcends the apostolic tradition and is present in the oral and written tradition of all peoples. In this tradition, therefore, we can include the revelation of God in the native religions of Abia Yala before 1492.

Inculturated Evangelization as the Work of the Spirit

The inculturation of evangelization served as the master theme of the Fourth General Conference of the Latin American Bishops held in 1992 in Santo Domingo. In all likelihood such evangelization will prove to be the fundamental challenge to all churches, especially in the Third World. In this encounter between culture and gospel, the hermeneutics of liberation is

---

25. These are the words of Monsignor Edelby, archbishop of Edessa, as cited by Manucci, *Biblia,* 303.

26. "The words of the holy Fathers witness to the living presence of this tradition, whose wealth is poured into the practice and life of the believing and praying Church. Through the same tradition the full canon of the sacred books becomes known to the Church, and the sacred writings themselves are more profoundly understood and unceasingly made active in her; and thus God, who spoke of old, uninterruptedly converses with the Bride of his beloved Son; and the Holy Spirit, through whom the living voice of the gospel resounds in the Church, and through her, in the world, leads unto all truth those who believe and makes the word of Christ dwell abundantly in them (cf. Col. 3:16)."

27. For the notion of the magisterium of the church at the service of the word of God, see Manucci, *Biblia,* 36.

transformed into a hermeneutics of Spirit. The native peoples of Abia Yala are not only poor and oppressed peasants but also subjects with an ancient culture and religion. In fact, their culture and religion have allowed them to survive these last five hundred years, despite the conquest of Western Christianity. Culture represents the most profound factor of identity among the Indian peoples, turning them into subjects of their own history. This identity is completely religious in character. An inculturated evangelization is possible only when native culture and religion, within which the presence and revelation of God are found from before the colonial conquest, are taken as the point of departure. A hermeneutics of the Spirit is opposed to a hermeneutics of power. Evangelization from the point of view of culture demands that the church lay aside the power of its Western colonial culture and take on a renewed faithfulness to the demands of the Spirit. As long as the church possessed power, it was unable to evangelize. Only a poor church, ecumenical and full of the power of the Spirit, can evangelize from the point of view of oppressed and marginalized cultures. The foundational mystery of an incultured evangelization is Pentecost, insofar as it allowed all peoples to listen to the gospel in their own tongues and cultures (Acts 2:11).

Part Five

Readings from North America

17

The Personification of Cities
as Female in the Hebrew Bible:
The Thesis of Aloysius Fitzgerald, F.S.C.

Peggy L. Day

The personification of cities as female in the Hebrew Bible has received quite a bit of scholarly attention recently.[1] The biblical depictions of cities as females comprise diverse status designations such as [btwlt] bt,[2] "[ado-

---

1. For example: M. E. Biddle, "The Figure of Lady Jerusalem: Identification, Deification and Personification of Cities in the Ancient Near East," *The Biblical Canon in Comparative Perspective* (ed. K. L. Younger Jr.; Lewiston, N.Y.: Mellen, 1991) 173–94; D. Bourguet, *Des métaphores de Jérémie* (Paris: Gabalda, 1987) 477–510; M. Callaway, *Sing, O Barren One: A Study in Comparative Midrash* (Atlanta: Scholars Press, 1986) 62–72; F. W. Dobbs-Allsopp, *Weep, O Daughter of Zion: A Study of City-Lament Genre in the Hebrew Bible* (Rome: Pontifical Biblical Institute, 1993), and idem, "An Interpretation of *bat-GN* in the Hebrew Bible" (paper presented at the 1992 SBL meeting in San Francisco: a revised version of this paper is forthcoming in *Catholic Biblical Quarterly*); K. Engelken, *Frauen im Alten Israel* (Stuttgart: Kohlhammer, 1990) esp. 42–43; E. R. Follis, "The Holy City as Daughter," *Directions in Biblical Hebrew Poetry* (Sheffield: JSOT, 1987) 173-84; T. Frymer-Kensky, *In the Wake of the Goddesses* (New York: Free Press, 1992) 168–78 and notes; J. Galambush, *Jerusalem in the Book of Ezekiel: The City as Yahweh's Wife* (Atlanta: Scholars Press, 1992); B. Bakke Kaiser, "Poet as 'Female Impersonator': The Image of Daughter Zion as Speaker in Biblical Poems of Suffering," *Journal of Religion* 67 (1987) 164–82; J. J. Schmitt, "The Motherhood of God and Zion as Mother," *Revue biblique* 92 (1985) 557–69, and idem, "The Virgin of Israel: Referent and Use of the Phrase in Amos and Jeremiah," *Catholic Biblical Quarterly* 53 (1991) 365–87; O. H. Steck, "Zion als Gelände und Gestalt: Überlegungen zur Wahrnehmung Jerusalems als Stadt und Frau im Alten Testament," *Zeitschrift für Theologie und Kirche* 86 (1989) 261–81.
2. The term *bĕtûlâ* is often translated "virgin," but both comparative Near Eastern and inner-biblical evidence suggests that the term denoted a female who had begun to menstruate and was therefore marriageable. See B. Landsberger, "Jungfräulichkeit: ein Beitrag zum Thema Beilager und Eheschliessung," *Symbolae Iuridicae et Historicae Martino David Dedicatae* (ed. J. A. Ankum et al.; Leiden: Brill, 1968) 57–58; M. Tsevat, *"bĕthûlāh; bĕthûlîm,"* *Theological Dictionary of the Old Testament*, 338–43; G. J. Wenham, "*bĕtûlāh*: 'A Girl of Marriageable Age,'" *Vetus Testamentum* 22 (1972) 326–48; P. L. Day, "From the Child Is Born the Woman: The Story of Jephthah's Daughter," *Gender and Difference in Ancient Israel* (ed. P. L. Day; Minneapolis: Fortress Press, 1989) 58–60. The available evidence is not conclusive but suggests that a woman was a *bĕtûlâ* until the birth of her first child. Texts such as Gen 24:16; Judg 21:12; and Esther 2 suggest that a woman who had had intercourse could still be called a *bĕtûlâ*, and Joel 1:8 seems to indicate that a married woman

283

lescent] daughter"; *'m,* "mother" (Isa 50:1);[3] *'lmnh,* "widow" (Isa 47:8-9, 54:4; cf. Lam 1:1);[4] *rbbty,* "mistress/powerful woman" (Lam 1:1);[5] *śrty,* "princess/ruler" (Lam 1:1);[6] *šbyyh,* "captive" (Isa 52:2); and *ms,* "corvée laborer" (Lam 1:1, in a simile). In addition to these explicit status designations, personified Jerusalem (Ezek 16:8; 23:37) and Samaria (Ezek 23:37) are clearly represented as Yahweh's wives, and Zion is portrayed as his ex-wife (Isa 50:1). Cities personified as women in the Hebrew Bible are also typically represented as lasciviously promiscuous or adulterous (for example, Isa 23:15-17; Ezekiel 16 and 23).

What is the origin of the Hebrew Bible's personification of cities as women? The recent discussions that I have cited above (excepting Barbara Kaiser, who does not address the question) view the phenomenon of cities personified as female as a Yahwistic adaptation of language and concepts that were applied elsewhere in the ancient Near East to goddesses.[7] More specifically, most of these recent discussions cite one or both of two articles written by Aloysius Fitzgerald, F.S.C.,[8] as proof that the biblical personifi-

---

might still be a *bĕtûlâ.* Given that entry into the status of *bĕtûlâ* is marked by menarche, the potential to bear children, and given that the termination point of the status is neither first intercourse nor marriage, the next "normal" change in a female's social status was motherhood. Note also that there was a word meaning "woman bearing her first child" (*mabkîrâ* [Jer 4:31]). Collections of the numerous biblical references are provided by Aloysius Fitzgerald (*"BTWLT* and *BT* as Titles for Capital Cities," *Catholic Biblical Quarterly* 37 [1975] 168 n. 2) and Follis ("Holy City," nn. 1, 5, and 6).

3. It is also common to encounter a personified city's inhabitants described as her sons and daughters (for example, Isa 47:8-9; 54:13; Ezek 16:20; Lam 1:5, 16) and for villages to be called daughters of particular cities (for example, Judg 1:27). In 2 Sam 20:19 the city Abel is called a mother, but this metaphor is not further personified. A. Malamat (*"Ummatum* in Old Babylonian Texts and Its Ugaritic and Biblical Counterparts," *Ugarit-Forschungen* 11 [1979] 535-36) has argued unconvincingly that *'m* in 2 Sam 20:19 should be translated "clan."

4. It is clear that in Israelite culture, *'almānâ,* usually translated "widow," did not refer simply to a woman whose husband had died. C. Cohen ("The 'Widowed' City," *Journal of Ancient Near Eastern Society of Columbia University* 5 [1973] 75-78) has argued that *'almānâ* means "a once married woman who has no means of financial support and who is thus in need of special legal protection" (77), and P. S. Hiebert (" 'Whence Shall Help Come to Me?' The Biblical Widow," *Gender and Difference,* 125-41) has concluded that an *'almānâ* was a woman whose husband and father-in-law were both dead, and who had no sons.

5. Evidence for this translation is collected and discussed by T. F. McDaniel ("Philological Studies in Lamentations. I," *Biblica* 49 [1968] 29-31). McDaniel's argument for translating the second occurrence of *rbbty* in Lam 1:1 is convincing, though because of the parallelism the first occurrence is better understood (as traditionally it has been) as a different word, meaning "full (of people)," thus creating a wordplay.

6. Reinforcing this royal imagery are several references to enthroned (for example, Jer 48:18), sovereign (Mic 4:8), or crowned (for example, Ezek 16:2) cities personified as females. See Dobbs-Allsopp, *"bat-GN,"* 19-20; Biddle, "Lady Jerusalem," 182-85.

7. Dobbs-Allsopp, *"bat-GN,"* passim, with reference (27 n. 1) to materials distributed throughout chaps. 2 and 3 of *Weep;* Follis, "Holy Daughter," passim; Frymer-Kensky, *Wake,* 170; and the references cited in n. 10 below.

8. A. Fitzgerald, "The Mythological Background for the Presentation of Jerusalem as a Queen and False Worship as Adultery in the OT," *Catholic Biblical Quarterly* 34

cation of cities as women is rooted in an alleged West Semitic notion that capital cities were understood to be goddesses who were married to the patron god of their respective cities.[9] The pervasiveness of the acceptance of Fitzgerald's thesis in the most up-to-date scholarship on the topic provides good reason (or at least a defensible excuse) for scrutinizing Fitzgerald's data and arguments. I am not interested simply in proving Fitzgerald's thesis wrong, although I will expend considerable effort demonstrating exactly on what points and why I think Fitzgerald is in error. In the process of proving Fitzgerald wrong, I want to draw particular attention along the way to the assumptions that he makes.

Fitzgerald's Thesis: Evaluation

The task that Fitzgerald sets for himself in the earlier of his two articles is

> to explain why in the OT capital cities should be presented as royal female figures and why the prophets should use adultery as an image for Israelite disloyalty to Yahweh, participation in non-Yahwist cult, or political alliances with non-Yahwists.[10]

Fitzgerald contends that these two phenomena are "closely related" and that "they can only be understood in the light of each other and against the background of a pattern of West Semitic (= WS) mythological thought into which they both fit and out of which they both stem" (404). Fitzgerald's thesis is that "in the WS area capital cities were regarded as goddesses who were married to the patron god of the city" (405). He then claims that documentary evidence establishes that "the phenomenon of viewing capital cities as goddesses can be traced back to the mid-second millennium BCE and, if the evidence from West Semitic city names is accepted, to the beginnings of urbanization in the area" (405).

(1972) 403–16; idem, "Titles for Capital Cities," 167–83. In the former article, Fitzgerald frequently acknowledges his indebtedness to J. Lewy ("The Old West Semitic Sun God Ḥammu," *Hebrew Union College Annual* 18 [1944] 429–88, esp. 436–43). I will be focusing on Fitzgerald's work rather than Lewy's because the aforementioned recent discussions cite Fitzgerald's work rather than Lewy's as authoritative.

9. Biddle, "Lady Jerusalem," 179-81; Bourguet, *Des métaphores,* 481–84; Callaway, *Sing,* 65; Engelken, *Frauen,* 42; Galambush, *Jerusalem,* 20; Schmitt, "Motherhood," 568; Steck, "Zion," 275. Dobbs-Allsopp (*Weep,* 87) and Frymer-Kensky (*Wake,* 269 n. 3) flatly reject Fitzgerald's thesis but neither engage nor refute any of his arguments. Follis ("Holy Daughter") does not indicate that she is aware of Fitzgerald's work on her topic.

10. Fitzgerald, "Mythological Background," 403.

I

Fitzgerald's first category of evidence in support of his thesis is "Evidence from Phoenician Coins."[11] Fitzgerald notes that numerous coins of Phoenician cities of the Hellenistic period depict a woman wearing a walled or turreted crown. Fitzgerald asserts that this woman, the *Tychē poleōs* (deified Fortune), is the personified and deified city. To prove this interpretation, he cites various inscriptions that appear on some of the coins:[12]

> *Sidōnos tēs hieras kai asylou* ([coin] of holy and inviolate Sidon); *Sidōnos theas; Sidōnos hieras; Sidōnos theas hieras kai asylou kai nauarchidos; lṣr 'm ṣdnm; ll'dk' 'm bkn'n; lṣdnm 'm kmb 'p' kt ṣr* ([coin] of [the city of] the Sidonians, the mother of Cambe, Hippo, Citium [and] Tyre); *lgbl qdšt*.[13]

Fitzgerald claims on the basis of this numismatic evidence that "important Phoenician cities were considered goddesses, royal figures, mothers of their inhabitants, and daughter cities."[14]

First, it should be noted that, as Fitzgerald points out, all of the Levantine *Tychē poleōs* coins are Hellenistic at the earliest and thus significantly postdate the biblical material that Fitzgerald is attempting to explain. More specifically, all of the inscribed coins that Fitzgerald cites are dated by Hill, Fitzgerald's authority on the coins, to the second century BCE and later.[15] Second, Fitzgerald is not explicit about precisely how the inscriptions *prove* that the crowned woman should be interpreted as the personified and deified city. If the inscriptions per se truly proved Fitzgerald's interpretation, then why do other authorities dispute this interpretation?[16] Third, it should be noted that only the *Greek* inscriptions of Sidonian coins cited by Fitzgerald read *theas*: no other city is so described.[17] Thus for Fitzgerald to say

---

11. Ibid., 406–7.

12. The coins, as cited by Fitzgerald, were published by G. F. Hill, *Catalogue of the Greek Coins of Phoenicia* (London: British Museum, 1910). See Fitzgerald, "Mythological Background," 406 nn. 11–20 for specific citations. The Phoenician inscriptions untranslated by Fitzgerald read "[coin] of Tyre, mother of the Sidonians," "[coin] of Laodicea, a mother in Canaan," and "[coin] of holy Byblos."

13. Fitzgerald, "Mythological Background," 406.

14. Ibid., 406–7.

15. Hill, *Catalogue*, lxix, cvi–cvii, cxxxiii, 1, 52, 98, 155, 158, 164, 174, 175.

16. For example, F. Allègre, *Étude sur la déesse grecque Tyché* (Paris: Leroux, 1889) 184–95; M. P. Nilsson, *A History of Greek Religion* (2d ed.; Oxford: Clarendon, 1952) 285; L. Kadman, *The Coins of Caesarea Maritima* (Tel Aviv: Schocken, 1957) 51, and idem, *The Coins of Aelia Capitolina* (Jerusalem: Universitas, 1956) 36; R. Mellor, ΘΕΑ ΡΩΜΗ: *The Worship of the Goddess Roma in the Greek World* (Göttingen: Vandenhoeck und Ruprecht, 1975) 20; P. Grimal, *The Dictionary of Classical Mythology* (Oxford: Blackwell, 1986) 460.

17. On the coins cited by Fitzgerald, Sidon is also referred to as "holy" and "inviolate." These adjectives refer to certain privileges granted to Sidon and therefore are not relevant to

that the coins prove that Phoenician *cities* (plural) were regarded as goddesses goes beyond the evidence he provides. In addition, it should be noted that none of these Sidonian coins have a corresponding *Phoenician* inscription that refers to Sidon as a goddess. Rather, when there is a legible Phoenician inscription, it simply reads either *lṣdnm* ("[coin] of the Sidonians") or *lṣdn* ("[coin] of Sidon"). Thus to use these coins as evidence that the deification of cities was a *West Semitic* phenomenon seems dubious. Fourth, the coins with Phoenician inscriptions that refer to cities as mothers[18] do not refer to the cities as goddesses: Fitzgerald seems simply to assume that they are relevant to proving that cities were understood to be goddesses. But given the lack of inscriptional confirmation of the equation of city and goddess, these coins would be relevant to a discussion of cities as goddesses only if the crowned woman portrayed on these coins was, without a doubt, the deified city. Since these coins are themselves supposed to be evidence that the crowned woman is the deified city, the reasoning is circular, and therefore the evidence is inadmissible. Finally, contrary to Fitzgerald's claim, none of the coins says that the cities in question are mothers of their respective inhabitants.

Thus far, Fitzgerald's evidence from "Phoenician" coins has been intended to show that important Phoenician cities were thought of as goddesses; while I am not convinced that Fitzgerald has proven his point, he has at least attempted to rally evidence. Demonstrating that Phoenicians regarded their cities as goddesses, however, is only one step toward proving his thesis that deified cities in the West Semitic worldview were understood to be married to the patron god of their respective cities. Immediately following the last sentence I quoted above (p. 286) to the effect that Phoenician cities were considered goddesses and mothers, Fitzgerald states:

> It is hardly likely that parthenogenesis is in the picture. The husbands of these Phoenician cities are not mentioned, but they were certainly gods, and it is hardly to be expected that they were any other than the patron gods of the particular city.[19]

As the reader can plainly see, Fitzgerald offers no tangible evidence whatsoever to justify the leap from city as goddess to city as mother god-

---

the issue of Sidon's alleged deification (W. Griffith, *Hellenistic Civilization* [3d ed.; London: Edward Arnold, 1952]; 82–83; J. Teixidor, *The Pagan God: Popular Religion in the Greco-Roman Near East* [Princeton, N.J.: Princeton Univ. Press, 1977] 51).

18. It should be noted that in the second of the Phoenician inscriptions that Fitzgerald cites, the reading *'m*, "mother," is uncertain. See Hill, *Catalogue*, 52, no. 5. Fitzgerald's reconstruction is not grammatically objectionable (cf. 2 Sam 20:19), but the reading "Laodicea which ['š] is in Canaan" is also a viable possibility. This latter reading would serve to distinguish the Laodicea indicated by this coin from cities in Asia Minor with the same name (G. A. Cooke, *A Text-Book of North-Semitic Inscriptions* [Oxford: Clarendon, 1903] 46, 349–50).

19. Fitzgerald, "Mythological Background," 407. Cf. Lewy, "Ḥammu," 440–41.

dess married to patron god. First, it is worth repeating that the coins that refer to certain cities as mothers do not refer to those same cities as goddesses. Second, we are asked to assume that the references to cities as mothers were understood literally by the Phoenicians as presupposing intercourse. Fitzgerald does not even entertain the possibility that these references are metaphorical[20] and therefore need not imply sexual relations. Third, we are expected to assume that the alleged intercourse leads logically to the conclusion that the city as goddess was married to a divine sexual partner. And fourth, we need to assume that each Phoenician city had one principal deity, a male patron god, in relation to whom the city/ goddess simply played the role of reproductive spouse. I will discuss each of these assumptions in turn.

One basis for Fitzgerald's first assumption is clear from some comments he makes at the beginning of the article. Fitzgerald there characterizes Canaanite (= early Phoenician) religion as a promiscuous fertility religion that included the practice of (so-called) sacred prostitution,[21] the alleged ritual/cultic reenactment of sexual intercourse between a god and a goddess.[22] Robert A. Oden has recently dealt a devastating blow to this reconstruction of Canaanite religion by demonstrating that it is almost entirely based upon biblical evaluations of Canaanite religious practice and that it is unsubstantiated by contemporary Canaanite texts.[23] Oden notes that an important part of building group identity and solidarity is the vilification of rival groups and that this vilification involves a false characterization of the sexual practices of rival groups. Hence it is methodologically unsound to accept as accurate the Hebrew Bible's characterization of its rival religion as involving the illicit and disgusting practice of ritual prostitution, particularly in light of the dearth of corroborating evidence from Canaanite sources. Like Oden, Phyllis Bird rejects the scholarly characterization of Canaanite religion as a sex-based fertility cult, arguing that scholars who subscribe to this reconstruction of Canaanite religion have confused promiscuity as biblical metaphor for apostasy with actual Canaanite religious practice.[24]

Jo Ann Hackett notes the problems raised by both Oden and Bird and interrelates them by viewing the biblical metaphor of apostasy as promiscu-

---

20. See F. C. Eiselen, *Sidon: A Study in Oriental History* (New York: Columbia Univ. Press, 1907) 25.

21. Fitzgerald, "Mythological Background," 404 and n. 5.

22. For further background to Fitzgerald's understanding of Canaanite religion, see J. A. Hackett's collection of typical scholarly descriptions of the sexually based nature of Canaanite religion and the practice of "sacred prostitution" ("Can a Sexist Model Liberate Us? Ancient Near Eastern 'Fertility' Goddesses," *Journal of Feminist Studies in Religion* 5 [1989] 71–73).

23. R. Oden, "Religious Identity and the Sacred Prostitution Accusation," *The Bible without Theology* (San Francisco: Harper and Row, 1987) 131–53.

24. P. Bird, "'To Play the Harlot': An Inquiry into an Old Testament Metaphor," *Gender and Difference*, 75–94.

ity as a powerful tool for disparaging Canaanite religion.[25] Hackett further notes that the metaphor works well because, contrary to the official Israelite cult, women were cult personnel in Canaanite religion. Hackett also points out that the absence of women in official cultic roles characterized not only ancient Israel but also the religious groups with which the modern scholars responsible for reconstructing Canaanite religion as at base a sex cult were affiliated. In Hackett's view, the "coincidence" between the lack of female cultic personnel both in official Israelite religion and in the religious groups to which the scholars themselves belonged was a contributing factor to their failure to question the extent of disjuncture between metaphorical expression and historical reality. In other words, Hackett sees the social location of the scholars responsible for the reconstruction—in this case, religious groups in which women have no role in the official cult—as itself a source of the unsubstantiated reconstruction.

Fitzgerald's second assumption was that sexual intercourse, at least between West Semitic deities, presumes marriage. This assumption is crucial to his contention that there is a necessary relationship between the biblical personification of cities as female and the prophets' use of adultery as an "image"[26] for Israelite disloyalty to Yahweh, and that this relationship has its origin in non-Israelite religion. In other words, if the deities were not thought of as married in West Semitic thought, then, for example, Ezekiel's portrayal of Yahweh and Jerusalem as married[27] and producing children (Ezekiel 16) would have to be acknowledged to be a product of Israelite religious thought. The notion that Israelite religion could be capable of generating such a blatantly sexual "image" is clearly anathema to Fitzgerald, who views Israelite religion as distinct from the indigenous[28] "nature religions" by virtue of its "revolutionary notion of a transcendent God who is not part of nature."[29] What the Israelites did was accommodate the mythology of the indigenous nature religions to their notion of a transcendent God. In Fitzgerald's words:

> Absolutely amazing about this process is its mode of adaptation—the sureness with which the canonical Israelite poets and theologians adapted concepts from mythological thought quite foreign to their own idea of God for their own purposes and without compromising their own purposes. For example, God conceptualized as "father" is a conceptualization derived from older nature religion in which the particular god is conceived of as having a divine consort with whom he

---

25. Hackett, "Sexist Model," 73–74.
26. "Image" is the term that Fitzgerald consistently uses. "Metaphor" would be a more accurate description.
27. Fitzgerald refers to this portrayal in "Titles for Capital Cities," 178.
28. For Fitzgerald, the Israelites were originally desert nomads and not indigenous to the settled areas of Canaan ("Mythological Background," 415).
29. Ibid.

begets sons and daughters. Israelite theologians are, nonetheless, capable of using the concept "father" in talking about their God while eliminating any idea of Yahweh having a consort, while presenting Yahweh as beyond the human, beyond the sexual.... Just so Israelite theologians and poets are able to use the Canaanite notion of capital cities as wives of the patron deity of the city.[30]

Clearly, Ezekiel's depiction of Yahweh as married to personified Jerusalem (chaps. 16 and 23) and fathering her children (16:20; 23:4) presents a significant challenge to Fitzgerald's understanding of the distinctness and superiority of Yahwistic religion unless this "image" of Yahweh as a married, sexually active, and reproductive male deity can be provided with a non-Israelite origin.

As the above paragraph illustrates, when Israelite religion is juxtaposed with other West Semitic religions, Fitzgerald attributes the notion of marriage in the divine sphere to West Semitic mythology. But what was Fitzgerald's understanding of this marriage of divinities in the context of West Semitic mythology? The following quote is instructive:

[The city as goddess] is the origin of the presentation of capital cities as royal females, as queens, in the OT writings. In a polytheistic society worship of other gods in addition to the patron god of a city was completely acceptable. In Yahwist circles the only possible way to view this, within a framework of thought that regarded a capital city as the wife of the patron deity, was as the equivalent of adultery.[31]

In order to follow Fitzgerald's reasoning, we have to equate the religious behavior of the city's polytheistic inhabitants (that is, worship of deities other than the city's patron god) with the sexual behavior of the city/goddess (that is, intercourse with deities other than the patron god of the city), and because the former is acceptable, the latter must also be acceptable. In what sense, then, is the city/goddess in West Semitic thought understood to be married to the city's patron god if, by analogy to her polytheistic residents, she is permitted to have multiple sexual partners? If the city/goddess was indeed understood to be married exclusively to the patron god, as Fitzgerald's thesis postulates, then would not additional sexual relations constitute adultery? Why, then, is the adultery accusation logically possible only within a Yahwistic (that is, for Fitzgerald, monotheistic) context? The problem with Fitzgerald's reasoning is that he seems to be equating polytheism, which is a way of viewing the divine sphere, with polyandry, which is a social system in which women have more than one husband.[32] But polytheistic societies need not be polyandrous. Indeed, we

---

30. Ibid., 416.
31. Ibid., 405.
32. Galambush, *Jerusalem*, 26 n. 4.

know that in the polytheistic societies of the ancient Near East women were permitted to have only one husband, and adultery was severely punished.[33] Clearly, then, in Fitzgerald's mind, polytheism is (incorrectly) linked with polygamy or, more specifically, with females having multiple sexual partners. Though incorrect, this linkage illustrates that, for Fitzgerald, marriage in a West Semitic context did not imply fidelity to a single partner and so could not generate the "image" of adultery.

Fitzgerald's third assumption was that each Phoenician city had one principal deity, a male, patron god, in relation to whom the city/goddess simply played the role of reproductive spouse. Remember, Fitzgerald cites no evidence for this and indeed maintains it in spite of explicitly recognizing that none of the inscriptions that he cites mentions a patron deity/husband of the city/goddess. I would first point out that Fitzgerald's assumption conforms to a phenomenon documented by Hackett.[34] Hackett notes the propensity of secondary, scholarly literature to attribute "fertility" (that is, reproductive) functions to goddesses while describing male deities in nonreproductive language such as "storm god" and "chief god," even though those same scholars acknowledge the male deities' role in reproduction. In Hackett's view, this attribution of reproductive functions asymmetrically to goddesses is one manifestation of the sexist tendency to describe women solely in terms of bodily/sexual functions.[35]

Do the inscriptions from Byblos, Sidon, and Tyre support Fitzgerald's assumption of the priority of a male, "chief" god partnered by a city/goddess whose sole responsibility is reproductive? YHWMLK, a king of Byblos, stated that it was "the Lady, the Mistress of Byblos" (*hrbt b'lt gbl*), who made him king of Byblos. He also asked this goddess to prolong his life and ensure that both the gods and his people treat him graciously.[36] If "the Lady" *is* the city of Byblos, as Fitzgerald would have to maintain, she is surely revered for reasons other than her reproductive capabilities. If she is not the deified city, then her importance surely belies Fitzgerald's notion that a single divine couple presided over each city. The sarcophagus inscription of King TBNT of Sidon described him as a priest of Astarte as was his father before him, and stated that to disturb his body would be an abomination to Astarte.[37] Another king of Sidon was named BD'ŠTRT,[38] which means "in/by the power of Astarte." In these Sidonian inscriptions the goddess Astarte is (independently) mentioned as a goddess to whom the

---

33. W. L. Moran, "The Scandal of the 'Great Sin' at Ugarit," *Journal of Near Eastern Studies* 18 (1959) 280-81; J. J. Rabinowitz, "The Great Sin in Ancient Egyptian Marriage Contracts," *Journal of Near Eastern Studies* 18 (1959) 73; R. Westbrook, "Adultery in Ancient Near Eastern Law," *Revue biblique* 97 (1990) 542-80.
34. Hackett, "Sexist Model," 71-74.
35. Ibid., 65-66.
36. *Kanaanäische und aramäische Inschriften* 10.
37. *Kanaanäische und aramäische Inschriften* 13.
38. For example, *Corpus inscriptionum semiticarum* 1.4.

Sidonian royal family[39] gives cult, and it is Astarte who would be offended if the king's body were to be disturbed. Again, there is no overt mention of the reproductive powers of the goddess, nor is Astarte identified with the city itself. From Tyre, to my knowledge, there is no relevant Phoenician inscriptional data.[40] Thus the available evidence does not support assuming a dominant, male patron god partnered by a reproductive city/goddess.[41]

II

Fitzgerald's second category of evidence is entitled "Similar Titles for Capital Cities and Goddesses," in which he proposes that *rbt* (mistress), *btwlt/bt* (virgin [*sic*]/daughter), *'m* (mother), and *qdšh* (holy) are all titles used of both goddesses and capital cities.[42] Frequently in his assembly of the evidence, however, Fitzgerald includes examples where the alleged title is not, in fact, clearly a title. For example, in *špš rbt* and *thwm rbh* the second word is in the position of an attributive adjective, not of a substantive/title. In the subsection on *'m*, Fitzgerald cites the proper name *'m 'štrt* ("Astarte is [my] mother") as an example of "mother" as a title applied to a goddess, and *lṣr 'm ṣdnm* ("belonging to Tyre, mother of the Sidonians") as an example applying to a city. Surely neither of these examples is transparently titular. In the subsection on *qdšh* he cites *'l gbl qdšm*, which he translates as "the holy gods of Byblos," as an instance of *qdšh* used as a goddess's title! And finally, Fitzgerald cites no examples of goddesses who have the title *bt* (daughter), nor any extrabiblical examples of either *btwlt* or *bt* as city titles. Another troubling problem in this section is that none of the four "titles" that Fitzgerald treats are applied *only* to goddesses and to cities.[43] For example, to use, as Fitzgerald does, the fact that *'m* (mother) can describe both cities and goddesses as evidence that cities were regarded as goddesses

---

39. See *Kanaanäische und aramäische Inschriften* 14.14–15, in which the king's mother is called a priestess of Astarte.

40. B. Peckham ("Phoenicia and the Religion of Israel: The Epigraphic Evidence," *Ancient Israelite Religion* [ed. P. D. Miller et al.; Philadelphia: Fortress, 1987] 80–81) discusses inscriptions from the environs and dependencies of Tyre. None is relevant.

41. In a paper delivered on November 20, 1993, at the SBL meeting in Washington, entitled "Phoenician and Punic Goddesses," J. A. Hackett concluded that Phoenician and Punic inscriptional data do not support making gender distinctions between the roles and functions of gods and those of goddesses. Hackett's conclusion is consistent with the above analysis of Byblian and Sidonian inscriptions.

42. Fitzgerald, "Mythological Background," 407–10.

43. Bourguet (*Des métaphores*, 484) recognizes the importance of establishing that a title be attributed only to cities and goddesses in order to prove that cities were considered to be divine. However, Bourguet errs when he states that such is the case for *rbt* at Ugarit. See Fitzgerald ("Mythological Background," 407, I.c.1) and J. Greenfield ("The Epithets *rbt/trrt* in the KRT Epic," *Perspectives on Language and Text* [ed. E. W. Conrad and E. G. Newing; Winona Lake, Ind.: Eisenbrauns, 1987] 36).

ignores the very obvious fact that human females can be mothers too. Likewise, *qdš* (holy) not only is an attribute of cities and goddesses but can also be used of a people (Exod 19:6; Deut 26:19) or an individual (2 Kgs 4:9). In short, I find this section unsatisfactory because it fails to distinguish titular from other uses and does not establish the existence of an exclusive and unambiguous common pool of titles applied to both goddesses and cities.

III

Fitzgerald's third category of proof is entitled "City Names Derived from Divine Names."[44] Here again we move into the realm of assumption when Fitzgerald attempts to prove that cities were believed to be goddesses who were married to patron gods. The first part of the argument is as follows:

In all the pantheons of the ancient Near East gods are paired off with goddesses. In some cases they are clearly regarded as husband and wife. In some cases (for example, *'n/'nt*) the marriage relation is not so clear. But by analogy it can be argued that some place along the line such pairs were regarded as married to each other. If what has been suggested is true in only several of the cases listed below, that is sufficient for the argument.

ES	WS
Enlil/Ninlil	'l/'lt (ilt='ṭrt; UT, 49:I:12)
An/Antum	'ṭtr/'ṭtrt
Bel/Beltum	'n/'nt
Aššur/Aššuritu	lbu/lbit[45]

Note that no references to specific pantheon lists are cited, nor does Fitzgerald provide any evidence that the alleged ubiquitous pairing of gods and goddesses was explicitly understood to be a marriage relationship. Yet "by analogy" to this unproven assertion that allegedly paired deities were married we are asked to accept, in cases where Fitzgerald himself has doubts (for example, *'n/'nt*),[46] that "some place along the line," that is, at some point prior to available historical documentation, the alleged pairs were

---

44. Fitzgerald, "Jerusalem as Queen," 410–12. In n. 37 Fitzgerald acknowledges Lewy's ("Ḥammu," 441–42) treatment of this topic.

45. Ibid., 410–11.

46. Fitzgerald's doubt here is based on his acceptance that "at Ugarit, 'Anat is apparently Baal's wife" ("Mythological Background," 410 n. 38). According to my reading of the evidence, Ugariti Anat is neither a sexually active nor a married deity (P. L. Day, "Why Is Anat a Warrior and Hunter?" *The Bible and the Politics of Exegesis* [ed. D. Jobling et al.; Cleveland: Pilgrim, 1991] 141–46, 329–32; so also N. H. Walls, *The Goddess Anat in Ugaritic Myth* [Atlanta: Scholars Press, 1992] passim).

understood to be married couples. Having implicitly insisted on paired couples being married as a rule, Fitzgerald then inexplicably shifts ground and states that the proposition need not be true for all of the pairs that he is about to list. And then when he does list the pairs, he cites no references to ancient texts in which any of the listed deities are actually paired![47] Moreover, the basis upon which these particular alleged pairs have been selected is not explained, though it can be noted for the Semitic pairs that the common factor seems to be "male divine name plus feminine ending -t equals female divine name."

Directly after the list of alleged divine pairs, Fitzgerald approvingly states that "on this basis Lewy has explained many West Semitic place-names which he regards simply as the feminine counterpart of masculine names or titles."[48] Then follows another list in which geographical names are juxtaposed with the names or titles of male deities. This list is composed of nine geographical and six divine names, and so for the sake of expediency I will provide examples rather than reproduce the entire list. The first listing juxtaposes the geographical names *b'lwt* (Josh 15:24) and *b'lh* (Josh 15:9) with the divine name Baal, and the second juxtaposes the geographical names *'ntwt* (Josh 21:18) and *'nt* (Judg 3:31)[49] with the divine name 'An. In light of Fitzgerald's favorable reference to J. Lewy's explanation of the place-names simply as feminine counterparts of masculine divine names or titles, it becomes clear that what Fitzgerald is asking us to accept is that the listed cities are uniformly named after male divinities, that is, that a city such as (for example) Anat is not named after the goddess Anat but rather the city name is "a *feminine formation* from the name of the [male] patron deity."[50] It should be noted that Fitzgerald makes this proposal in

---

47. I would also note that the first two pairs in the East Semitic list are Sumerian (that is, not Semitic) deities and that in the case of *Ibu/Ibit* the lack of textual citation puts the onus on the reader to determine where, if anywhere, *Ibu* is the proper name of a divinity.

48. Fitzgerald, "Mythological Background," 411, referring to J. Lewy, "Ḥammu" (see 436–43). In Lewy's words, the place-names "consist[] in . . . the feminine form of a name or epithet of a god" (442).

49. Fitzgerald here follows M. Noth's assessment that *'nt* in the name *šmgr bn 'nt* "may be a toponym" ("Mythological Background," 411 n. 41). For a contrary view based upon evidence unavailable to Noth, see F. M. Cross ("Newly Found Inscriptions in Old Canaanite and Early Phoenician Scripts," *Bulletin of the American Schools of Oriental Research* 44 [1980] 4, 6–7) and N. Avigad ("Two Seals of Women and Other Hebrew Seals," *Eretz Israel* 20 [1989] 95 [Hebrew] 197). As for Fitzgerald's comment ("Mythological Background," 411 n. 41) that the *'nt* of *šmgr bn 'nt* should be compared with the Mari place-name *dḤa-na-at^{ki}*, which he uses as further evidence that "Anat is at once a city and a goddess," Fitzgerald neglects to mention that the city in question is also referred to in the Mari archives as *Bīt dḤa-na-at^{ki}* (for example, *Archives royales de Mari* 8:85.48). The latter designation implies that the former is simply an abbreviated way of referring to the place. Note also that while *'nt* in the name *šmgr bn 'nt* is not likely to be a place-name, *byt 'nt* (Josh 19:38; Judg 1:33), "house/place of Anat," is certainly a city name.

50. Fitzgerald, "Mythological Background," 411 n. 42; emphasis added. On the following page, Fitzgerald cites MT's *qryt b'l* (Josh 15:60) as another name for *b'lh* on the basis that both are equated with *qryt y'rym*. BH³ considers *qryt b'l* in Josh 15:60 to be an addition

spite of acknowledging that An was not an important deity in any West Semitic pantheon known to him.[51] His response to this problem is to assert that pantheons differed according to era and area, and so "if what has been suggested up to this point is correct, it just has to be assumed" that when the town Anat was named, An was an important West Semitic deity. Once again the argument retreats into the impenetrable mists of prehistory.[52]

Considering the two lists together, what Fitzgerald is apparently asking us to believe is that goddesses "came into being" when cities named after male deities (by adding a grammatically feminine -t ending) were themselves deified. This understanding of the burden of Fitzgerald's argument is corroborated by remarks that he makes in the concluding section of the article.[53] As Fitzgerald sees the development of "religious thought," "before history" man [sic] divinized natural forces by personifying them as "supermen." Then,

once urbanization takes place and the city itself becomes powerful—the most powerful force in urban man's life—it was natural enough that the city itself should be divinized. This again takes place in the prehistorical period.... In the WS area, which has been the prime

---

and directs the reader's attention to Josh 18:14, the only other instance of *qryt b'l* in MT, where MT reads *qryt b'l hy' qryt y'rym*. I would resolve the problem by positing haplography and reading *qryt b'l[h] hy' qryt y'rym*.

51. Fitzgerald, "Mythological Background," 411 n. 42. I would point out that Fitzgerald offers no evidence that An was indeed ever a member, even an *unimportant* member, of any West Semitic pantheon.

52. Fitzgerald does not acknowledge or discuss the problem that this theory of the origin of the names of capital cities poses when viewed alongside his assertion that cities such as Byblos and Tyre were goddesses. These city names have no "feminine endings," and so how does the theory apply to them? As I have said, Fitzgerald does not address this problem, but Lewy ("Ḥammu," 441–42) does:

If the names of the Phoenician, Mesopotamian and Assyrian cities the divineness of which is directly attested by ["evidence" from the Hellenistic coins and personal names] are not provided with the feminine ending found in the names of the towns [Astarte, Baalah, etc.], this divergency can not prevent us from concluding that the latter towns, too, were regarded as goddesses, married to the gods [Astar, Baal, etc.] in the same way as the goddesses Antum and Bêltî were thought to be the wives of the gods Anum and Bêl; for the grammatical difference just mentioned obviously results from the fact that when those towns were founded and named in honor of the gods supposed to own them and to dwell therein, the Western Semites made but very limited use of the so-called feminine ending -*at* or other affixes in order to indicate the inferior status or the dependency in which, according to Semitic conception, a town, as well as other property, finds itself in relation to its owner.

I find it very difficult to entirely make sense of Lewy's comments, but what I think he is saying in part is that when Sidon, Byblos, and so on, were founded the feminine ending was not consistently in use in the Semitic languages. He offers no evidence that such a stage existed in the development of the Semitic languages. Thus Lewy, like Fitzgerald, appeals to the prehistoric and unverifiable to "prove" his thesis. I note but shall not remark on Lewy's characterization of the grammatically feminine ending as denoting inferiority or dependence.

53. Fitzgerald, "Mythological Background," 414–15.

concern here, once the city (fem.) becomes a goddess, the marriage connection with the patron god of the city would immediately suggest itself.[54]

Note that in Fitzgerald's reconstruction the first deities are all male ("supermen") and that, in the West Semitic realm at least, goddesses come onto the divine scene only when cities are divinized. Conveniently, this entire process takes place "before history," and hence no documentary evidence need be adduced to support the reconstruction. In my opinion, Fitzgerald's description of this "time before time" is essentially modern mythology. The "truth" expressed in the myth is that Fitzgerald believes in the priority of males and the derivativeness of females. Much like the myth of Eve born from Adam, Fitzgerald's goddesses are born from their eventual spouses.

IV

Fitzgerald's next section is entitled "Evidence from New Assyrian Personal Names."[55] In this brief section, Fitzgerald cites two neo-Assyrian personal names comprised of a city name plus the noun *šarratu* (queen) in the predicate state. He claims that the city names are theophoric elements in the two personal names, but in neither case is the city name preceded by a determinative to indicate divinity. In any event, this evidence is East rather than West Semitic[56] and confirms nothing about the alleged spousal status of city/goddess and male patron god.[57]

V

Fitzgerald's next section returns to the topic of the *Tychē poleōs* and Hellenistic coins.[58] Fitzgerald reasserts his interpretation that the *Tychē poleōs* is the personified and deified city, an interpretation that, as I have already noted, is a contentious one. He then qualifies his interpretation with the following statements:

> This is not to say that the city is a goddess distinct from the principal patron goddess of the city. Just as Atargatis, a combination of

---

54. Ibid., 415.
55. Ibid., 412. Fitzgerald acknowledges his indebtedness to Lewy in n. 44.
56. Fitzgerald, following Lewy, claims (ibid.) that Western Semites were influential in the neo-Assyrian period and then attributes the personal names in question to West Semitic influence. He cites no evidence in support of either proposition, and neither does Lewy.
57. Biddle ("Lady Jerusalem," 179–81), who accepts Fitzgerald's overall thesis and reproduces the bulk of his evidence, questions whether the city names are theophoric and then deletes Fitzgerald's section on neo-Assyrian personal names.
58. Fitzgerald, "Mythological Background," 413–14.

'Aštart and 'Anat, is the chief goddess of north Syria in the Hellenistic period, so too the city itself as a goddess is a combination of the
divine city and its divine patroness. The discoveries at Dura-Europos
help illustrate the point. In one of the temple frescoes portraying a
Roman tribune named Julius Terentius offering sacrifice are represented two female figures wearing walled crowns and identified as
Tychē Palmyrōn and Tychē Douras. The Tychē Palmyrōn is accompanied by a lion, the symbol of Atargatis, which is a clear sign that
Atargatis and Tychē Palmyrōn are one and the same.[59]

First of all, granting for the sake of argument that the lion is the exclusive
symbol of Atargatis, the Dura-Europos fresco demonstrates that Atargatis
is also the personified city only if we presume that the Tychē Palmyrōn is
the city personified as a goddess, which condition remains unsubstantiated.
Since the fresco is the only evidence cited to support the claim that the
city as goddess is one and the same as the city's patroness goddess, I would
maintain that Fitzgerald has not proven his claim. Second, Fitzgerald asserts
that the alleged merging of divine city and patroness goddess into a single
identity is analogous to Anat and Astarte merging to become Atargatis. Yet
Fitzgerald cites no evidence (and to my knowledge there is no conclusive
evidence)[60] to demonstrate that Atargatis subsumes Astarte and Anat, and
so his "model" is itself hypothetical.

VI

In his follow-up article, Fitzgerald focuses on two specific designations used
in the Hebrew Bible in conjunction with city names. These are btwlh (which
he translates as "virgin")[61] and bt (daughter). I will not be commenting on
the overall thesis of Fitzgerald's second article but rather will confine my
comments to points that are directly relevant to the thesis of his first article.
    In the follow-up article, Fitzgerald reiterates his thesis that the person-
ification of cities as females in the Hebrew Bible derives from the West

---

59. Ibid.
60. The argument rests on accepting that the name 'tr'th etymologically is composed
of two parts, 'tr and 'th, and that the former component is derived from the name 'ttrt
while the latter derives from the name 'nt. Among the problems with this hypothesis is the
"disappearance" of both the final t of the former name and the supposedly assimilated n of
the latter name. Cf. W. F. Albright, "The Evolution of the West Semitic Divinity 'An-'Anat-
'Attâ" American Journal of Semitic Languages and Literature 41 (1925) 88; S. Ronzevalle,
"Les monnaies de la dynastie de Abd-Hadad et les cultes de Hiérapolis-Bambycé," Mélanges
de l'université Saint-Jospeh 23 (1940) 32–33; R. Oden, Studies in Lucian's "De Dea Syria"
(Missoula, Mont.: Scholars Press, 1977) 64 n. 88.
61. Fitzgerald, "Titles for Capital Cities," 171, 178. btwlt, with t rather than h, is the
form in which the word appears when it is in apposition with a geographical name, or
with bt plus a geographical name. As I have already indicated, in my opinion "virgin" is a
mistranslation.

Semitic belief that capital cities were goddesses married to the patron god of the city. He then states:

> Thus, when an Israelite poet like Isaiah refers to Jerusalem as "daughter Zion" (*bt ṣywn,* 1:8), though there have been fundamental changes (Zion, for example, is clearly no goddess for Isaiah), it is basically upon this pattern [of regarding capital cities to be goddesses] that he is drawing for the language he uses.[62]

Fitzgerald further states that "one of the most prominent reflections of this typically West Semitic thought pattern in the OT is the use of *btwlt* and *bt* as titles for capital cities."[63] Fitzgerald later states that the use of *btwlt* and *bt* to denote capital cities in the Hebrew Bible "fits perfectly into the pattern out of which it developed."[64] On the basis of this last statement it can be concluded that Fitzgerald considers that neither *btwlt* nor *bt* falls into his category of "fundamental changes" that occurred when the pattern was "drawn upon" by Israelite poets. But if the city in West Semitic thought was regarded as a married goddess who, as we "know" from the first article, had intercourse with her husband and produced children, then why does it perfectly fit the pattern to call the personified city a daughter and, according to Fitzgerald's translation of *btwlh,* a virgin? Yet it is quite clear that Fitzgerald sees no contradiction:

> In the Canaanite area, capital cities were regarded as goddesses married to the patron god of the city. *For this reason* capital cities could be given the titles *bt* or *btwlt.*[65]

As far as I can determine, Fitzgerald never explicitly addresses the question of why the allegedly married and maternal city/goddess should nevertheless routinely be referred to as "daughter." We do, however, learn from a footnote in the first article that

> cities can be designated as "virgins" though mothers of their inhabitants and daughter cities in the same way that Anat though wife of Baal is a *btlt* [that is, the Ugaritic equivalent of Hebrew *btwlh*]. The term is used to suggest the everlasting youth, beauty and fecundity of the city as goddess.[66]

As I have demonstrated at length elsewhere,[67] there is no evidence to indicate that Anat is a sexually active and reproductive goddess, either as Baal's

---

62. Ibid., 167.
63. Ibid., 171, 178.
64. Ibid., 171.
65. Ibid., 182; emphasis added.
66. Ibid., 409 n. 30.
67. Day, "Why Is Anat," passim; idem, "Anat: Ugarit's 'Mistress of Animals,'" *Journal of Near Eastern Studies* 51 (1992) 181-90; idem, "Anat," *Dictionary of Deities and Demons in the Bible* (ed. K. van der Torn et al.; Leiden: Brill, forthcoming); cf. Walls, *Goddess Anat.*

wife or as the partner of any other deity. Rather, Anat is primarily a goddess of war and of the hunt, and she is active in these culturally masculine spheres precisely because she is an adolescent female (*btlt*) who has not joined the adult female world of marriage and childbearing. Given that the analogy of Anat does not support his point, Fitzgerald is left without evidence that one and the same goddess can be both virgin and mother. That said, we are still left with the fact that Fitzgerald somehow thought it possible for a goddess to be both virginal and reproductive. Is this simply an example of sexist scholarship's propensity to blur female identities[68] or has the Christian dogma of Jesus' virgin mother Mary made this impossible combination seem plausible?[69]

Fitzgerald's rationale for claiming a foreign origin for the Hebrew Bible's use of *bt* and *btwlt* as titles for capital cities runs as follows.[70] He first groups the occurrences of *bt* and *btwlt* plus a geographical or national[71] name according to the biblical books in which the combinations are used. Two of his observations about usage are that the combinations appear almost exclusively in poetry and in biblical books that were authored in Jerusalem and/or had a significant interest in that city. Fitzgerald then states:

> Now it is perfectly clear, especially from a comparison with the poetry of Ugarit, that Israel did not create an independent poetic tradition, but rather adopted an already existing one for its own purposes. It is further clear that when Israel adopts the prior Canaanite tradition, this not only involves form, but content as well; and that Jebusite Jerusalem become Israelite is a prime center where this assimilation of Canaanite traditions took place. Against this background, *granted the fact that the use of these titles is pre-Israelite,* it is possible to guess with a certain degree of probability that it was principally in Jerusalem at the very beginning of the Israelite monarchy that these titles became Israelite.[72]

As the reader can plainly see, in a discussion ostensibly aimed at demonstrating the foreign origin of the titles, Fitzgerald nonetheless explicitly

---

68. Hackett, "Sexist Metaphor," 65–66, 71–72, 75.

69. That Fitzgerald understood some connection between city/goddess and Mary is evident ("Mythological Background," 416): "It is interesting to note that this West Semitic notion of the city as a queen has survived in the West down to our own time. Numerous statues of the Virgin Mary still present her wearing the turreted crown of the *tychē poleōs.*"

70. Fitzgerald, "Titles of the Capital Cities," 168–70.

71. *bt* and *btwlt* are used in the Hebrew Bible as titles in conjunction with the names of countries, such as Judah, Egypt, and Chaldea, as well as with *'my,* "my people." The overall thesis that Fitzgerald is attempting to prove is that when the titles are applied to countries or a people, this use is secondary and derivative.

72. Fitzgerald, "Titles of Capital Cities," 169; emphasis added.

presupposes their foreign origin rather than proving it. His characterization of the biblical books in which the titles appear as Jerusalemite and/or greatly interested in Jerusalem is so broadly applicable to the Hebrew Bible canon as to be virtually meaningless. He includes primarily sixth century BCE works such Isaiah 40–55, Jeremiah, Lamentations, Ezekiel, and Zechariah in this category—indeed, these books provide fifty-five of the seventy-seven instances of the use of the titles—yet ultimately uses these sixth-century works to arrive at the conclusion that the titles were borrowed from pre-Israelite, premonarchic inhabitants of Jerusalem. The conclusion that the titles are of foreign origin because all but four instances of their use in the Hebrew Bible are in poetry relies upon a model of the relationship between Hebrew and Ugaritic poetry that presumes borrowing and adaptation on the part of the biblical writers rather than, for example, "evolution" from a common source, and Fitzgerald makes no attempt to demonstrate why his model is the correct one. And finally, I would note that in the first article Fitzgerald was unable to provide even one example of *bt* used as a title for either a city or a goddess outside of the Hebrew Bible, and not one example of *btwlt* as a title for a city outside the Hebrew Bible.

The second component of Fitzgerald's argument for demonstrating the foreign origin of the titles begins with the observation that the titles are used twenty-six times (*bt* twenty-three times, *btwlt bt* three times) in combination with *ṣywn* (Zion).[73] Concerning this datum, Fitzgerald makes two statements:

> The titles as used here are certainly pre-Israelite. The name *ṣywn* is generally regarded as pre-Israelite. And this could be interpreted to mean that the combination is pre-Israelite.

> What ultimately is being argued here is the probability that the titles *btwlt* and *bt* tied precisely to the word "Zion" are borrowed by the OT writers from the mythological and linguistic tradition of their Canaanite predecessors. The writer is just beginning to notice how often similar borrowings appear in a context where Zion is mentioned. . . . It is not possible here to investigate this preliminary hypothesis, but it may be suspected that such an investigation would offer some confirmation of the point being argued.[74]

Again, as the first quote indicates, Fitzgerald is simply asserting the veracity of that which he is supposed to be proving to be true. His assertion in turn is based on the "fact" that scholars generally regard the name Zion to be pre-Israelite, but his footnote in support of this "fact" reads in part,

---

73. Fitzgerald (ibid.) adds to his count six instances where the titles are used with "Jerusalem," but as will become obvious from his argument, this datum is irrelevant.

74. Ibid., 170 and 170 n. 7, respectively.

"The evidence for this is not overwhelming, but *ṣywn* is generally conceded to be pre-Israelite. The OT says it is."[75] Fitzgerald does not cite a single reference to anyone who holds the view that Zion is a pre-Israelite designation, nor does he reproduce any arguments in support of it. His only evidence from what "the OT says" is that a biblical description of David's conquest of Jerusalem states that "David captured the stronghold of Zion, which is [now] the city of David" (2 Sam 5:7 = 1 Chr 11:5). So the "fact" upon which the assertion is premised is, by Fitzgerald's own admission, conjectural. Thus what we end up with is an assertion based upon a conjecture that affords the interpretation that *bt ṣywn* and *btwlt bt ṣywn* were titles for pre-Israelite "Jerusalem." What the second quote adds is that Fitzgerald links the probability of the correctness of his interpretation to a preliminary hypothesis that he has not yet fully investigated.

VII

Having reviewed Fitzgerald's arguments at some length, we are now in a position to evaluate the thesis. First, Fitzgerald has failed to prove that there was an ancient mythological tradition in the West Semitic world that understood important capital cities to be goddesses. While it is true that Greek inscriptions on Hellenistic coins seem to refer to the city of Sidon as a goddess, this evidence significantly postdates the biblical phenomenon of personifying cities as females (which is what Fitzgerald is trying to explain), and, given that the Phoenician inscriptions on these coins do not reiterate Sidon's divinity, it is questionable whether the coins should be used as evidence of a *West Semitic* mythological tradition. Fitzgerald's evidence from "similar titles for capital cities and goddesses" is unconvincing on three counts: not all of the data rallied are demonstrably titular; no alleged title is used exclusively of cities and goddesses; and with regard to the two titles most commonly used of personified cities in the Hebrew Bible, that is, *bt* and *btwlt,* the former is found nowhere outside the Hebrew Bible as a title of either a city or a goddess, and the latter is found nowhere outside the Hebrew Bible as a title for a city. Fitzgerald's evidence from neo-Assyrian personal names is unconvincing because he neither demonstrates that the city names are theophoric elements in the only two personal names he cites nor proves that the names are West Semitic and therefore relevant.

Second, proving a city's divinity is only one step toward proving the thesis that a city as goddess was understood in West Semitic tradition to be married to a patron god. As we have seen, Fitzgerald *never* cites textual or iconographic evidence in support of this thesis but rather presents us repeatedly with unproven assumptions that he typically shrouds behind the

75. Ibid., 169 n. 5.

misty veils of prehistory, especially when these assumptions seem in danger of being contradicted by actual textual evidence.

Third, Fitzgerald's thesis that, in West Semitic mythology, the city was understood to be a goddess married to the city's patron god was intended to demonstrate an intrinsic connection in the Hebrew Bible between the personification of cities as female and the prophets' use of adultery as an "image" for Israelite disloyalty to Yahweh. The explanation that Fitzgerald offers to account for why the two phenomena must be both of foreign origin and intrinsically connected founders on his confusing polytheism with polyandry.

Conclusion

In conclusion, I should like to make a few observations about Fitzgerald's assumptions. First, Fitzgerald's thinking is characterized by a sharp dichotomy between what is biblical and what is West Semitic. Biblical thinking is theological, while West Semitic thought is mythological. West Semitic deities are nature deities, but the biblical deity transcends nature. West Semitic religion is characterized by sexuality, while the biblical god is "beyond the sexual." West Semitic polytheism is equated with females having multiple sexual partners, while biblical monotheism is responsible for introducing properly sanctioned female monogamy. West Semitic references to deities as fathers and mothers are to be taken literally, but references to the biblical god as father are not. Second, Fitzgerald's thinking is also characterized by a dichotomy between that which is associated with the male and that which is associated with the female. This dichotomy is projected onto West Semitic male and female deities. The first deities are all male. Goddesses are secondary, the result of the divination of the gods' property. Gods are the dominant patrons of cities. Their divine spouses are subordinate, and their responsibilities/powers are limited to the reproductive sphere. Third, Fitzgerald attributes mutually exclusive or inconsistent physical and social statuses to his goddesses. They are at the same time both sexually active mothers and virgin daughters, married yet permitted multiple sexual liaisons. As I have demonstrated, these assumptions have no basis in the ancient northwest Semitic "evidence" rallied by Fitzgerald.

18

Toward Intercultural Criticism: A Reading Strategy from the Diaspora

Fernando F. Segovia

I have argued that contemporary biblical criticism consists of four competing paradigms or umbrella models of interpretation and that the emergence and development of these critical paradigms reveal a process of liberation and decolonization at work in the discipline: from the long and unquestioned hegemony of traditional historical criticism; to its swift displacement by literary criticism and cultural criticism, with their corresponding and extensive diversity in the methodological and theoretical realm; to the more recent emergence of cultural studies, with its full and explicit inclusion of real readers within the optic of criticism and its corresponding diversity in the sociohistorical and sociocultural realm.[1]

I have also argued that with cultural studies the discipline begins to leave behind its thoroughly Western origins and character: away from the informed and universal reader-construct of historical criticism; beyond the largely formalist reader-constructs of both literary and cultural criticism, similarly objective and neutral in nature; to the very different construct of flesh-and-blood readers, in the fullness of their sociohistorical and sociocultural diversity. In so doing, biblical criticism—by which I understand the full range of studies dealing not only with the canonical texts as such but also with the whole of Jewish and Christian antiquity—begins to shift away from the fundamental *mythos* or narrative of the modern world, the myth of universalism and objectivity, toward the fundamental *mythos* or narrative of the postmodern world, the myth of diversity and pluralism.[2] In

---

1. See F. F. Segovia, "'And They Began to Speak in Other Tongues': Competing Modes of Discourse in Contemporary Biblical Criticism," *Reading from This Place,* vol. 1, *Social Location and Biblical Interpretation in the United States* (ed. F. F. Segovia and M. A. Tolbert; Minneapolis: Fortress Press, 1994) 1–32; and the introduction to this volume.

2. For a sharp contrast of these myths in an attempt to argue for an Asian reading of the Bible, see G. M. Soares-Prabhu, "Two Mission Commands: An Interpretation of Matthew 28:16-20 in the Light of a Buddhist Text," *Asian Biblical Hermeneutics* (ed. R. S. Sugirtharajah), special issue of *Biblical Interpretation* 3 (1994) 264–82. For the historiographical background of both myths, see J. Appleby, L. Hunt, and M. Jacob, *Telling the Truth about History* (New York-London: Norton, 1993), esp. chaps. 1, 2, and 6.

303

so doing, furthermore, biblical criticism joins the path of one of the most fundamental sociopolitical and sociocultural movements of the twentieth century: the global process and agenda of decolonization on the part of the colonized peoples and nations of the world from their respective colonial powers and masters.

As an adherent to cultural studies, I have further argued that the time has come to introduce the real reader fully and explicitly into the discourse and practice of criticism.[3] In effect, as the title for the present study indicates, I see myself as reading, interpreting, and theologizing from the diaspora, a social location whose meaning is highly complex and multidimensional and that I would specifically circumscribe as follows in my own case: first and more broadly, in terms of the massive dispersion of the children of the colonized, the children of the Third World, in the world of the colonizers, the children of the First World; second and more concretely, in terms of the rapidly growing contingent of Hispanophone Latin America in the United States, the Hispanic Americans, presently constituting over 9 percent of the country's population and the equivalent of the fifth most populous nation of Latin America.[4]

I am, of course, keenly aware of the fact that the preceding description of the diaspora has been formulated, as my use of the terms "Third World" and "First World" readily shows, from the point of view of the ideological conflict between East and West, the state-controlled societies of Communism and the liberal democracies of capitalism, that gripped the world from 1914 through 1989.[5] As such, a different description is now in order. I am persuaded and helped in this regard by the recent argument of Samuel

---

3. See F. F. Segovia, "Toward a Hermeneutics of the Diaspora: A Hermeneutics of Otherness and Engagement," *Reading from This Place,* 1:57–74.

4. See Segovia, "Hermeneutics of the Diaspora." To be sure, within the Latin American diaspora in the United States, one also finds a Lusophone (for example, Brazilian) as well as a Francophone (for example, Haitian) presence; however, to the best of my knowledge, no theological voice has yet begun to emerge from these groups. When it does, it will be necessary to begin speaking of a Latino-American voice. I should also note in this regard that there does exist a large and growing Caribbean diaspora in the United States from the Anglophone islands and nations of the Caribbean, which is thus impossible to qualify as part of the *Latin* American diaspora. At this point, a new term is obviously needed that would comprehend both diasporas, the coining of which is made exceedingly difficult by the single-handed appropriation of the terms "America" and "Americans" on the part of the United States (non-Western American diaspora?).

5. Within the context of the cold war, it should be pointed out, there was no similar dispersion of the children of the Third World in the Second World, the world of Communism, even though the latter very much constituted and functioned as an imperial network, with the Union of Soviet Socialist Republics at the center of the empire and Russia at the very nucleus of the center. To be sure, "intellectual" as well as "manual" workers from the colonies were sent to the center for periods of varying lengths and purposes; however, such a presence cannot really be described in terms of a massive migration or exodus. Indeed, since the collapse of the Soviet Empire, a very different sort of massive dispersion may be seen at work within Europe itself, as the former children of the Second World, the inhabitants of Eastern Europe, seek a better life among the children of the First World, in Western Europe. Such a diaspora, however, is quite different from the diaspora to which I belong

Huntington to the effect that with the end of the Cold War the primary source of conflict in the world is no longer a clash between competing ideologies but rather a clash among civilizations, involving at one level seven different civilizations organized around cultural fault lines and at another level, given not only the undisputed primacy of Western civilization but also its protracted history of imperialism and colonialism, the West and the rest.[6] From this point of view, the phenomenon of the diaspora mentioned above may be rephrased as follows: Western civilization, properly subdivided into European and North American "subcivilizations," finds a significant, expanding, and increasingly unwelcome presence of other civilizations within its own bosom—by and large, the children of civilizations formerly controlled by the West during its long process of colonial expansionism and imperialism in the world at large.[7] From the point of view of the United States in particular, such a presence involves African civilization, Confucian civilization, and Latin American civilization. It is to the diaspora constituted by this latter contingent that I belong, and it is from this diaspora that I read, interpret, and theologize.[8]

---

and which I have in mind; in fact, the whole framework and dynamics of colonization are largely missing from such an intra-European diaspora.

    6. See S. Huntington, "The Clash of Civilizations?" *Foreign Affairs* 72 (summer 1993) 22–49, and idem, "If Not Civilizations, What? Paradigms of the Post-Cold War World," *Foreign Affairs* 72 (November/December 1993) 186–94. Huntington, Eaton Professor of the Science of Government and Director of the John M. Olin Institute for Strategic Studies at Harvard University, argues that conflict in the modern political world has been the result of conflict within Western civilization, with all other non-Western peoples and governments as objects of history, and that such conflict has followed a threefold development: (*a*) for a century and a half after the Peace of Westphalia (1648-1789), in terms of princes; (*b*) beginning with the French Revolution through the nineteenth century (1798–1918), in terms of nation-states; and (*c*) from the end of World War I until the end of the cold war (1918–1989), in terms of ideology. With the end of the cold war, however, Huntington sees international politics as moving beyond its Western phase, non-Western peoples and governments becoming movers and shapers of history, and conflict emerging in terms of civilization, in the interaction between the West and non-Western civilizations, identified as follows: Confucian, Japanese, Islamic, Hindu, Slavic-Orthodox, Latin American, and African.

    7. Huntington ("Clash," 23–24) defines "civilization" as a cultural entity—"the highest cultural grouping of people and the broadest level of cultural identity people have short of that which distinguishes humans from other species." As such, the concept includes such common elements as language, religion, customs, institutions, and subjective self-identification. A "subcivilization" would be the next highest level of cultural grouping and cultural identity.

    8. With regard to Hispanic Americans, the term "diaspora" can be used in both a metaphorical and a literal sense. By *literal* diaspora I mean those Hispanic Americans who have found their way into the United States by way of immigration—those who know both the country of birth and the country of adoption. By *metaphorical* diaspora I mean those Hispanic Americans who were either born in the country as children or descendants of immigrants or those whose lands and ancestors were acquired by the United States in its long process of territorial expansion, which lasted through most of the nineteenth century and culminated in the early twentieth century. In other words, there are many Hispanic Americans who are not immigrants to the country, but there are also many who are. It is to this latter sense of the diaspora that I belong. For a beginning formulation of a diaspora theology, see F. F. Segovia, "In the World but Not of It: Exile as Locus for a Theology of

Hispanic American Hermeneutics

In recent years the theological voice of Hispanic Americans, among both Catholics and Protestants, has begun to emerge in the U.S. scene, and with it their hermeneutical voice as well, as theologians, historians, and critics have turned to the Bible for reflection, inspiration, and argumentation.[9] In an earlier study I pursued a critical analysis of the reading strategies and underlying theoretical models adopted with regard to the Bible in the work of several Hispanic American theologians (Justo L. González; Virgil Elizondo; Ada María Isasi-Díaz; Harold J. Recinos), none of whom was a biblical critic by training.[10] In the present study and by way of introduction to my own proposal, I should like to expand this analysis by turning to the work of three individuals whose area of specialization is biblical criticism and whose reflections have come to light since that time (C. Gilbert Romero; Jean-Pierre Ruiz; Francisco García-Treto). Before doing so, however, I should like to begin with a brief recapitulation of the findings of that earlier study.

Early Approaches to the Bible in Hispanic American Theology

The analysis of reading strategies and theoretical models at work in the first four theologians mentioned above revealed an overriding commitment to a hermeneutics of liberation in their reading and interpretation of the Bible, with the Bible emerging throughout as both an "effective weapon" in the struggle against marginalization and discrimination and a "faithful ally" in the struggle for liberation. In effect, all four individuals adopted variations of a basic model of liberation hermeneutics involving a formal analogy between past and present, between the relationship of the Bible to its social context and the relationship of Hispanic Americans to their social context, with a basic correspondence posited between Hispanic Americans today and the people of God in the Bible. The variations in question could be readily traced to the different positions adopted regarding a number of fundamental issues of interpretation: (1) perceived affinity with the text; (2) proposed locus of liberation in the text; (3) specific point of entry

---

the Diaspora," *Aliens in the Promised Land: Towards a Hispanic American Theology* (ed. A. M. Isasi-Díaz and F. F. Segovia; Minneapolis: Fortress Press, forthcoming [1996]).

9. On the development and growth of Hispanic American theology, see J. D. Rodríguez, "De 'apuntes' a 'esbozo': diez años de reflexión," *Apuntes* 10 (1990) 75–83; F. F. Segovia, "A New Manifest Destiny: The Emerging Theological Voice of Hispanic Americans," *Religious Studies Review* 17/2 (April 1991) 102–9; A. J. Bañuelas, "U.S. Hispanic Theology," *Missiology* (April 1992) 275–300; A. Figueroa Deck, "Latino Theology: The Year of the 'Boom,'" *Journal of Hispanic/Latino Theology* 1 (1994) 51–63.

10. F. F. Segovia, "Hispanic American Theology and the Bible: Effective Weapon and Faithful Ally," *We Are a People! Initiatives in Hispanic American Theology* (ed. R. S. Goizueta; Minneapolis: Fortress Press, 1992) 21–49.

into the text; (4) validity in interpretation; and (5) perceived agenda of liberation in the text.

1. *Affinity with the Text.* From the point of view of perceived affinity with the text, that is to say, of kinship with ancient texts on the part of present-day readers coming from a very different sociocultural and socio-historical context, the emphasis was clearly—despite a certain theoretical need expressed for analysis of the text within its own context, the precise nature of which remained largely undeveloped and unspecified—on ready access to and identification with the Bible. In other words, the life and struggle of the people of God in the Bible were seen as anticipating the life and struggle of Hispanic Americans today; as such, it was argued, Hispanic Americans could readily identify with the Bible and its message of libera-tion.[11] As a result, the historical and cultural distance between the ancient world of the Hebrew and Greco-Roman Mediterranean and the contempo-rary world of North American Western civilization gave way by and large in the light of the similar reality and experience posited for the two groups in question: the people of God and Hispanic Americans.

2. *Locus of Liberation.* While all agreed on the Bible as a liberating text, two major positions could be observed with respect to the proposed locus of such a message of liberation in the Bible: on the one hand, the concept of a canon within the canon; on the other hand, the notion of a unified and consistent text. In the former case, two variations could be distinguished: a focus on the historical Jesus as faithfully conveyed by the Gospels (Eli-zondo); a focus on texts judged as liberating by the experience of Hispanic American women (Isasi-Díaz). Thus, the message of liberation was traced either to the message of Jesus himself or to texts selected according to the higher canon of women's experience. In the case of the second position, two variations could again be discerned: the whole Bible as liberating in a simple, straightforward way (Recinos) or a roundabout, noninnocent way (González).[12] As such, the message of liberation was seen as present in the Bible from beginning to end but was regarded as either unequivocal, in terms of a God who sides with the poor and oppressed, or convoluted, unfolding in questionable venues and involving recurrent failures. Conse-quently, while all agreed that the Bible was a liberating text and looked

---

11. Of the four A. M. Isasi-Díaz proved to be the most cautious by far in this regard. While she did argue for the women of the Bible as anticipating the life and struggles of Hispanic American women, she also saw the Bible as both liberating and oppressive for women and thus called for a measure of critical distance, of suspicion. For further develop-ment of this position, see her "La Palabra de Dios en nosotras—the Word of God in Us," *Searching the Scriptures,* vol. 1, *A Feminist Introduction* (ed. E. Schüssler Fiorenza; New York: Crossroad, 1993) 86–100, and " 'By the Rivers of Babylon': Exile as a Way of Life," *Reading from This Place,* 149–63.

12. For a more recent articulation of Recinos's position, see his *Jesus Weeps: Global Encounters on Our Doorstep* (Nashville: Abingdon, 1992) as well as his "The *Barrio* as the Locus of a New Church," *Aliens in the Promised Land,* forthcoming.

upon it as normative and authoritative, disagreement did surface regarding the proposed locus for such a message of liberation (restricted or universal, self-evident or unexpected) and hence varying conceptions of biblical authority and normativity as well.

3. *Entrée into the Text.* From the point of view of entry into the text, all four argued for an experience of marginalization and oppression as the key to the liberating message of the Bible. However, different emphases were posited with regard to such an experience and, as a result, different conceptions advanced of the God of liberation to be found in the Bible: (*a*) racial-gender oppression or the experience of Hispanic American women, leading to the God of peace and justice present in the popular religiosity of women (Isasi-Díaz); (*b*) socioeconomic oppression or the experience of the barrio, resulting in a God of the poor (Recinos); (*c*) sociocultural rejection or the experience of *mestizaje,* giving rise to the God of the new universalism (Elizondo); and (*d*) the sociohistorical situation or the experience of exile, leading to the God of the alien and the powerless (González). Thus, while affinity with the Bible was readily granted by all, the precise nature of this affinity as well as the resulting characterization of the God of liberation in the Bible varied according to the specific experience of oppression advanced.

4. *Validity in Interpretation.* Regarding the question of validity in interpretation, that is to say, the question of proper/correct and improper/incorrect readings, all authors called for a specific way of reading the Bible: a reading of resistance characterized as in itself biblical and differentiated from other reading strategies associated with power and privilege. Such a strategy likewise received a variety of emphases: (*a*) a reading in favor of the values present in the popular religiosity of Hispanic American women (Isasi-Díaz); (*b*) a reading from the perspective of the poor and the oppressed (Recinos); (*c*) a reading faithful to the message of universal inclusion (Elizondo); and (*d*) a reading "in Spanish" with a focus on issues of power and powerlessness (González). In other words, as in the case of the liberating God identified in the Bible, the reading strategy adopted corresponded closely as well with the experience of oppression advanced as key to the liberating message of the Bible and its God.

5. *Agenda of Liberation.* From the point of view of the perceived agenda of liberation in the text, all argued for a highly utopian and subversive vision of liberation, according to which the present order of the world is radically called into question on the basis of a new order of God already at work. At the same time, within this common emphasis on the radical eschatological dimensions of liberation, different views of the new order envisioned came to the fore: (*a*) a world where women no longer suffer from sexism and racism (Isasi-Díaz); (*b*) a world where the poor and the oppressed regain a sense of dignity (Recinos); (*c*) a world where diversity is celebrated (Elizondo); and (*d*) a world where a new reformation involving

social transformation, radical ecumenism, and active participation of all is undertaken (González). Yet again, therefore, the new order envisioned was also in close correspondence with the experience of oppression presented as fundamental for a proper and correct reading of the Bible.

In sum, these first appropriations of the Bible by Hispanic American theologians yielded: (1) a text regarded as neither distant nor strange—a text readily accessible to Hispanic Americans; (2) a fundamental message of liberation—a God not at all removed or foreign, rather a God who works for the liberation of Hispanic Americans; (3) a people of God with whom Hispanic Americans could readily identify—two peoples joined in oppression, suffering, and pilgrimage; (4) a proper and correct way of reading and interpreting—a resistant, biblical reading from an experience of oppression; and (5) a utopian, eschatological vision of liberation—a vision that called into question the present order of the world in the light of an alternative world order. For all such readings the Bible became, in various ways, an effective weapon and faithful ally indeed.

Recent Approaches to the Bible in Hispanic American Theology

What follows is a critical analysis of the reading strategies and theoretical models operative in the recent work of three Hispanic American biblical critics, all of whom have addressed themselves to the question of Hispanic American hermeneutics, a self-conscious reading and interpretation of the Bible from the context of the Hispanic American reality and experience. While the first two, C. Gilbert Romero and Jean-Pierre Ruiz, are Roman Catholic priests, the third, Francisco García-Treto, is an ordained minister in the Presbyterian Church (U.S.A.).

C. Gilbert Romero: Popular Religiosity and the Bible. Two main concerns characterize Romero's work: a primary one, the world of popular devotions or socioreligious practices among Hispanics, and a secondary one, the biblical roots of such practices in the Hebrew Scriptures; both are highly interrelated and equally important for his work.[13] Thus, Romero's aim is not to provide a way of reading and interpreting the Bible as such, but he does so nonetheless, although always within the context and parameters of these two concerns. In other words, the reading strategy advanced is specifically developed and employed within the basic framework of popular religiosity or devotional piety, as he prefers to call the world of such practices. Consequently, how the Bible or the ancient world of Judaism and

---

13. C. G. Romero, *Hispanic Devotional Piety: Tracing the Biblical Roots* (Faith and Cultures Series; Maryknoll, N.Y.: Orbis Books, 1991); for a synthesis of the project, see idem, "Tradition and Symbol as Biblical Keys for a U.S. Hispanic Theology," *Frontiers of Hispanic Theology in the United States* (ed. Allan Figueroa Deck; Maryknoll, N.Y.: Orbis Books, 1992) 41–61.

Christianity is to be read outside of that framework, outside the world of popular devotions, is not at all addressed or pursued in the project.

The work reveals a complex point of departure. First, it involves popular culture in the form of the socioreligious practices or "faith-expressions" of Hispanic devotional piety found in his cultural and religious roots in New Mexico, which he describes as a mixture of official belief of European origin and unofficial belief of local color. Second, it has to do with church authority (mostly Anglo-Irish, though partly French as well) in terms of its long-standing attitude of suspicion regarding all such devotions, given not only the nature of the mixture itself (the presence of "normative" as well as "nonconformist" elements) but also the authorities' persistent questioning of whether such practices are to be seen as legitimate faith-expressions or aberrations of the faith. Finally, it also involves interecclesial conflict by way of the challenges brought against such practices on the basis of biblical authority by Protestant churches of the strongly missionizing type, such as evangelical, fundamentalist, and Pentecostal churches.

Against this background, Romero sets out to show, first of all, that such devotional practices do constitute a legitimate expression of faith. This he does in two steps: first, by positing a biblical grounding in the Hebrew Scriptures for such devotions—a fundamental correspondence between the ancient socioreligious practices of the Hebrews and the contemporary devotional practices of Hispanics in the Southwest;[14] second, by arguing for such devotional piety as a locus of revelation—a valid foundation for theological reflection and a genuine basis for spirituality. In so doing, Romero also seeks to provide a solid foundation and sanction for the popular culture of his people—and ultimately of all Hispanics[15]—in the face of persistent questions and attacks from both the institutional Catholic Church and the evangelizing Protestant churches.[16] Such practices, he counters, are

---

14. Actually, the correspondence posited is much more far-reaching (see *Devotional Piety,* 19–20): first, Hispanics are said to feel a strong attraction toward the Bible insofar as they see their own experience of poverty and struggle reflected in the sacred literature; second, Hispanics are also said to have a religious world not unlike that of the ancient Hebrews, especially with regard to the use of symbols and language. For Romero, therefore, the correspondence ultimately involves not just socioreligious practices, the main focus of the work, but also the socioreligious universe as a whole as well as socioeconomic status. I should point out that Romero favors the use of the term "Hispanics" for the group on the grounds that it is the least problematic (p. 17).

15. Although the argument is particularly concerned with popular devotions of New Mexico, its implications are seen as directly applicable to similar practices on the part of Hispanics elsewhere, whether in the Southwest, the rest of the United States, or Latin America. Within the context of New Mexico itself, Romero confines himself to an analysis of four faith-expressions: (*a*) the observance of Ash Wednesday—a penitential ceremony; (*b*) the *quinceañera,* or celebration of a young woman's fifteenth birthday—a rite of passage; (*c*) the home altar—a household shrine; and (*d*) the *penitentes,* or a brotherhood of laymen with a special devotion to the sufferings and death of Jesus—a penitential ritual.

16. Romero's agenda bears a strong ecclesiastical stamp throughout: what he seeks is affirmation of such practices on the part of an official church not only marked by traditional

profoundly biblical; hence genuine and valid faith-expressions; and thus rich in possibilities for evangelization, as the correspondence between such devotions and their biblical counterparts or "analogues" is further explored and brought to the fore. Consequently, there is no need for Hispanics to search elsewhere for a legitimate theological locus; such a locus is already provided for them by their own popular culture. Their task rather is to become aware of this invaluable resource and to use it to the full, so that they can come to see their own fundamental relationship with the people of God in the Bible. Such practices, therefore, constitute neither aberrations of the faith nor idolatrous superstition but rather have much in common with the worldview, symbolism, and imagery of the Hebrew Scriptures.

With regard to the first task of biblical grounding, Romero offers a reading strategy, applicable to both the text of the Hebrew Scriptures and the "text" of popular devotions, in dialogue with various strands of contemporary biblical criticism. This strategy is threefold, involving a basic movement from practice to text to practice. First, the devotional practice is described in terms of origins, dynamics, and meaning. Second, analogues for such practices are sought in the biblical texts and approached from the point of view of historical criticism, yielding thereby a description of these ancient practices in terms of origins, meaning, and dynamics as presented in the texts. Third, once the analogues have been set forth, there is a further analysis of the devotional practice in the light of the various themes and motifs uncovered in the exposition of the analogues. This re-

---

neglect of Hispanics but also controlled by a dominant Anglo-Irish component with deep suspicions toward minority groups. The work may thus be in part described as in search of church-sanction for the sake of church-change. Nowhere is this more apparent than in the second chapter (*Devotional Piety*, 5–14), where he goes out of his way to show how recent church documents from Rome, Latin America, and the United States argue for the value of popular religiosity and the need to dialogue with local religious traditions. In so doing, Romero strategically positions himself within the mainstream of recent official Catholic thought on the relationship between popular religiosity and church doctrine. Further, given his interpretation of this official call for dialogue as a way of preserving a healthy balance between center and local traditions, in the church, he further presents his work thereby as very much in line with such a goal: attentive to local color but also within the context of the strong structures and symbols of unity provided by church documentation. A result of such a strong ecclesiastical imprint is that the dialogue envisioned approaches the issue of critique in a mostly one-way fashion, from the point of view of official doctrine toward the local traditions, resulting in the end in a very hegemonic concept of the official church. See especially in this regard pp. 17–19, where devotional piety is described as having both an "alpha" range, containing the ambiguities and impurities of the faith, and an "omega" range, wherein are to be found the mature and liberative elements of the faith, explicitly identified with normative Catholic doctrine; consequently, devotional piety must be constantly nudged toward the "omega" pole by way of critique from official doctrine. Again, the result can only be a very condescending type of dialogue. At the same time, such nudging is present in his own work only in theory and not in praxis, given his argument to the effect that the practices in question are biblical and revelatory, that is, within the "omega" range. As such, what Romero is actually after is for normative Catholic doctrine—foreign and prejudiced as it is—to recognize these popular practices as lying fully within the "omega" range of the faith.

turn, which involves a further and much more expansive comparison of the practices and their biblical analogues, ultimately provides greater confirmation for the correspondence posited between the present-day devotions and the ancient practices as well as further illumination of each on the basis of the other. As a result, the practitioners of devotional piety are able to mine this underlying relationship for their own theological and spiritual development.

Within this last step, Romero has recourse to recent developments in biblical criticism, in terms of both cultural criticism, with special emphasis on cultural anthropology, and literary criticism, by way of structuralism and reader response. In effect, once the relationship between Hispanic devotional piety and the Hebrew Scriptures has been set forth, these various methods of interpretation are called upon to shed further light on such findings. Their application is largely sequential, with no real sense of the whole, the theoretical cohesion of the approach as such, or its parts, the theoretical relationship among the various approaches, given. What one finds instead is a listing of insights regarding the findings on the basis of cultural anthropology, structuralism, and reader response.[17]

With regard to the second task of theological validation, Romero proceeds to look at each practice, once the fundamental correspondence with the Bible has been established, as a locus of divine revelation and thus as a valid faith-expression, and then at the pastoral implications of each practice in terms of its rich possibilities for evangelization, theology, and spirituality. First, following a fundamental distinction between primary revelation (the deposit of faith) and dependent revelation (tradition and the magisterium), Romero classifies devotional piety as an example of dependent revelation. Then, in keeping with another basic distinction between authentic dependent revelation and superstition in terms of relationship to both Bible and tradition, Romero further describes devotional piety as authentic depen-

---

17. On the one hand, cultural anthropology is said to furnish a much clearer view of popular religiosity and its relationship to the Bible in terms of culture, as the faith-expression of a particular ethnic group with roots in the Bible. Quite helpful in this regard, he argues, are the following insights derived from anthropological approaches to the biblical texts and applicable, given the correspondence posited, to the "text" of popular devotions as well: the concept of God as supracultural, above all cultures and yet perceived by each culture according to its own norms; the symbolic approach, whereby human interactions are seen as symbolic interactions; the notion of the corporate personality, involving strong ties between individuals and group; a perception of the limited good, where horizontal relationships are given priority for meeting group needs; and patterns of kinship and marriage, strong in character for the sake of mutual support and affirmation. On the other hand, both structuralism and reader response are said to provide excellent tools for a study of the affective dimensions of the texts and thus of the role of the reader/hearer in interpretation, applicable as well to the "text" of popular religiosity in the light of the given correspondence. While structuralism is seen as of particular help in dealing with the deep structures of narrative and myth, reader response is regarded as specially helpful in coming to terms with feelings and attitudes in encounters with texts. On the value of these approaches, see *Devotional Piety*, 21–32.

dent revelation, given the basic relationship established between it and the Bible.[18] In other words, devotional piety constitutes an authentic, albeit intuitive, expression of the faith.[19] As such, it can serve as an excellent point of departure for evangelization, the main task of which is to bring to light this underlying relationship between the popular religiosity of the Hebrew Scriptures and the popular religiosity of Hispanics, and hence as an excellent pastoral venue for theological and spiritual development.

For Romero, therefore, a reading of the Bible turns out to be as important as a "reading" of Hispanic popular devotions, given their socioreligious, sociocultural, and socioeconomic correspondence. The two "texts" are to be read alongside each other, with the same critical methods of interpretation employed in both cases and for the sake of mutual illumination. Such a joint reading confirms the nature of the devotions as legitimate and revelatory faith-expressions and allows them to become an ideal vehicle for evangelization—a valid point of departure for a Hispanic theology and a genuine basis for Hispanic spirituality. In the process, Hispanic popular culture of the Southwest is not only defended and affirmed but also sanctioned and canonized. In the end, this proposed reading strategy is presented as both ecumenical and liberative: ecumenical, insofar as it allows all Hispanics, Catholics and Protestants alike, to come to terms with their respective forms of dependent revelation in the light of the Bible;[20] liberative, insofar as it makes for new meaning and understanding in the present as a result of the rereading and reinterpretation of the biblical analogues.[21]

---

18. Romero (*Devotional Piety*, 41–53) approaches the concept of revelation in terms of nature and function. From the point of view of nature, revelation is seen as encompassing tradition (a dynamic, reciprocal, ongoing interaction between Yahweh and Yahweh's people), history (external events plus the process of interpretation and appropriation), and symbol (process of involvement, influence on values, transformation, and opening up further horizons). From the point of view of function, it is seen in terms of faith-discourse, divine communication with a capability for multidimensional interpretation. Insofar as popular religiosity, like the Bible, is both a cultural phenomenon with elements of tradition, history, and symbol and a faith-discourse of polysemous character, it too constitutes an authentic locus of divine revelation.

19. Indeed, Romero (*Devotional Piety*, 40) makes the claim that devoted practitioners of popular religiosity, illiterate and unsophisticated as they often are, are able to offer insights into a biblical text that would be the envy of any professional exegete. Such intuitive insight he regards as further confirmation of the character of devotional piety as dependent revelation and explains in terms of the people's possession of innate elements of structuralism and reader response.

20. In this regard Romero finds J. González's reading "in Spanish" and its accompanying "grammar" to be fully in accord with his own reading strategy (*Devotional Piety*, 113–16): both place greater emphasis on readers or hearers than on texts; argue for a communitarian stance; grant validity to "simple" readings; see texts as interpreting readers; and focus on questions of power and powerlessness. However, how that "grammar" is to be integrated with his own "grammar"—complex as it is, given the various interpretive approaches invoked—is not at all clear. While the reading strategies may be compatible in theory, how they are compatible in application remains to be worked out.

21. The strategy is also described as liberative insofar as it proceeds from a situation of

Jean-Pierre Ruiz: Beginning to Read in Spanish. Ruiz's work has a twofold point of departure: on the one hand, the presence of Hispanic Americans within the "biblical audience" of the United States, that is, as actual and potential readers of the Bible; on the other hand, the implications of this presence for academic theology as well as pastoral ministry.[22] In effect, Ruiz points out how Hispanic American theologians and critics have begun to deal with this presence by listening to the people and asking what it means to read the Bible in and from such a context, raising thereby the very important question of social location in biblical interpretation and contextual theology. As a result, he argues, a particular style of theological discourse—a *teología de conjunto,* or "joint theologizing" involving a model of collaborative process—has come to the fore whereby the people and theologians are seen as organically related to one another, with the former explicitly integrated thereby into the very process of theological reflection.

In the light of such developments, Ruiz describes his own work as an assessment of these efforts on the part of Hispanic American theologians and critics from the point of view of contemporary biblical studies—a critical evaluation, in the spirit of a *teología de conjunto,* of the contextual hermeneutics emerging out of the Hispanic American theological discussion.[23] The exercise itself involves two steps. To begin with, he addresses the question of the hermeneutical framework operative in such a proposed contextual reading of the Bible—the reading "in Spanish"; then, he turns to two areas of concern to theologians and pastoral agents alike within such a reading, namely, the issue of the missionizing Protestant churches and the question of popular devotions in Catholicism. Given his commitment to collaborative theological reflection, Ruiz has particular dialogue partners in mind throughout: with regard to hermeneutical framework, Justo González; in the case of the evangelical/fundamentalist phenomenon, Allan Figueroa Deck;[24] with reference to popular religiosity, C. Gilbert Romero. In the end, Ruiz describes the aim behind such an exercise on his part as

---

oppression and represents a challenge to the structures of oppression. Such characterization is in keeping with his earlier position to the effect that the correspondence posited between ancient practices and modern devotions involves a socioeconomic dimension as well (see n. 14 above), since popular devotions represent, like their biblical counterparts, a strategy for survival in the midst of oppression. This, however, is a line of argumentation that remains largely undeveloped in the work.

22. J. P. Ruiz, "Beginning to Read the Bible in Spanish: An Initial Assessment," *Journal of Latino/Hispanic Theology* 1 (1994) 28–50. Although the overall context of the work deals with the Hispanic American reality as a whole, its specific frame of reference is that of Hispanic Americans in the Catholic Church.

23. Ruiz explicitly describes his work as a continuation of my own work in critical analysis of the use of the Bible in Hispanic American theology (see Segovia, "Hispanic American Theology," 30–31), especially in the light of my concluding remarks in that study to the effect that such readings of the Bible need to become more self-conscious and self-critical.

24. A. Figueroa Deck, *The Challenge of Evangelical/Pentecostal Christianity,* Cushwa

that of showing how biblical interpretation functions as a point of convergence, whether by way of meeting ground or battleground, for key theological and pastoral issues affecting Hispanic Americans.

First, with regard to hermeneutical framework, Ruiz follows González's project for reading the Bible "in Spanish," a project that involves a number of distinctive hermeneutical signposts: rejection of any approach with claims to objectivity in interpretation, such as that of liberal biblical scholarship; emphasis on the noninnocent character of both the Bible and history; high regard for the Hebrew Scriptures; and a fourfold "grammar" for reading "in Spanish," revolving around the issue of power and powerlessness—its very first principle. Such a project he sees as in line with the recent critique brought to bear against traditional methods of interpretation within biblical criticism itself. As such, Ruiz clearly opts for a hermeneutics of engagement. Second, with respect to the problem posed by the missionizing Protestant churches, Ruiz follows Figueroa Deck in arguing for both a fundamentalist threat and an evangelical challenge: while the threat consists in the fundamentalist rejection of all mediation except for the Bible, the challenge comes from the evangelical stress on personalism, including the principle regarding the accessibility of the Bible to ordinary believers. Such a challenge, he argues, must be taken quite seriously since it is in fundamental accord with a number of theoretical currents at work in biblical criticism itself, such as the shift in focus from text to reader, the resurgence of interest in metaphor and the dynamics of symbolism, and the redefinition of the concept of text. Finally, with regard to popular religiosity, Ruiz follows Romero's argument to the effect that Hispanic popular devotions are biblically rooted and represent an appropriate context from which to read the Bible, pointing out Romero's recourse to such newer methodologies as cultural anthropology, structuralism, and reader response; all he would add is the use of the lectionary as a further and ideal recourse for the process of biblical grounding.

In all of these recent developments within Hispanic American theology, therefore, Ruiz finds much that is in common with recent methodological and theoretical developments in the discipline. In other words, a basic correspondence is established thereby between what is going on in Hispanic American theology and what is going on within biblical criticism itself: a sharp argument to the effect that the proposed reading "in Spanish" is by no means off-base or misguided. In the end, while subscribing to and valuing much of what lies at the heart of this contextual hermeneutics, especially its stance of engagement and its commitment to dialogue with the people at large, Ruiz does point to a number of problematic issues that he sees as in need of serious attention and discussion: first, the question

Center for the Study of American Catholicism, Working Paper Series 24/1 (Notre Dame, Ind.: Univ. of Notre Dame Press, 1992).

of validity in interpretation, with a serious need for self-critical mechanisms; second, the diversity present among Hispanic Americans, ultimately leading to a diversity of readings within the group itself; and, third, the distinction between appropriation of a text and enslavement of a text. Such issues lie, to be sure, at the core of all contemporary criticism today, and thus Ruiz is in fact calling for Hispanic American theology and hermeneutics to take them to heart as well, even though he immediately minimizes their risk within the latter discussion on account of its explicit ecclesial and communitarian character.

To conclude, Ruiz's work is more evaluative than programmatic. He is not out to develop a strategy for reading and interpreting the Bible, not at this point anyway, but rather to weigh the pros and cons of the overall strategy he sees emerging from the ongoing theological discussion among Hispanic Americans, a strategy with two fundamental principles at heart, engagement and dialogue, and a strategy that he himself values and adopts. His reservations at the end, incisive and to the point, clearly prepare the way for a constructive proposal on his part in the future.

Francisco García-Treto: A Dialogic Reading of the Bible. Of the three proposals under consideration, García-Treto's is the one most directly involved with the text as such, setting forth a strategy for reading the Bible in the light of oppression and with liberation in mind.[25] The work presents two main points of departure: first, the long and widespread use of the Bible itself—whether at the hands of Spanish conquistadores, North American Puritans, proponents of apartheid, or white supremacists—to oppress "the other," the countenance of whom changes according to the circumstances; second, the reality and experience of oppression by such "others," with Latin Americans and Hispanics particularly in mind, and their attempt to read the Bible in a different way, with liberation in mind.

On the one hand, therefore, García-Treto points out how the Bible has been used repeatedly to foster xenophobia, justify oppression and persecution of "the other," and promote genocide. The problem, he adds, is not just one of usage but also one of content: within the Bible itself and alongside passages that promote the ideology of a common humanity in the image of God, there are passages that put forward the obliteration of "the other" as a divine command under the ideology of "the chosen people of God." In other words, the use of the Bible on behalf of xenophobic oppression is not at all a misreading of the Bible but rather a reading in accord with a central tradition of the Bible, whereby some bestow upon themselves the mantle of "the chosen people of God" while saddling others with the epithet of "Canaanites." On the other hand, García-Treto also

---

25. F. García-Treto, "The Lesson of the Gibeonites: A Proposal for Dialogic Attention as a Strategy for Reading the Bible," *Aliens in the Promised Land.*

points to recent attempts to read the Bible in a liberating way, with inclusiveness rather than exclusion in mind, on the part of readers who find themselves at the crossroads of oppression, as is the case with both Latin Americans, whose roots lie in the European (Iberian) conquest of the Americas, or U.S. Hispanics, as a marginalized people. In other words, given the nature and usage of the Bible, the question becomes how texts in which oppression of the highest order is presented as a divine imperative can be read as liberative by the children of oppression. In effect, García-Treto argues for a reading of such texts that is against the grain, a reading that provides healing for all and is ultimately grounded in the text itself.[26]

For such a reading he turns to the work of the Russian critic Mikhail Bakhtin and focuses on a particularly egregious example of such xenophobia in the Hebrew Bible, the command of God in Joshua 9 to exterminate all the inhabitants of the land.[27] Thus, from a theoretical point of view, García-Treto follows Bakhtin in arguing for heteroglossia or polyphony in these texts, for an awareness of the different voices present within them; for an analysis of such voices, both in terms of the dominant voice and dissenting voices; and hence for a dialogic rather than monologic reading of such texts, a reading that pays attention to the voices of dissent and uses such voices to subvert the dominant voice, the voice of xenophobia.[28] For practical application of such a reading, García-Treto turns to a narrative unit in which the dominant voice is unquestionably that of xenophobia to the point of genocide: Joshua 9 with its report of the divine "ban" placed on the entire Canaanite population of Israel, a text identified as reflecting postexilic Deuteronomistic theology and its ideology of intense nationalism. Such a passage, he argues, also offers a clear voice of dissent as well, that of the Gibeonites.[29]

---

26. It is clear, therefore, that García-Treto is not proposing a reading strategy for the Bible as a whole but rather for a certain type of texts within the Bible, whether in the Hebrew Scriptures or in the Christian Scriptures, namely, texts that embrace and promote xenophobia. It is a strategy that chooses neither to bypass or ignore such texts (a strategy of silence) nor to offset or judge them in the light of other, universalistic texts (a canon within the canon strategy), but rather to confront and subvert them from within (a strategy of open resistance).

27. With regard to Bakhtin, a representative of late Russian formalism who sought to combine in his work the principles of formalism and Marxism, García-Treto has recourse in particular to his *The Dialogic Imagination: Four Essays* (ed. M. Holquist; Austin: Univ. of Texas Press, 1981).

28. A fundamental question in this regard, and one that he does not address, is whether the same approach should be used with regard to universalistic texts, where the ideology of a common humanity in the image of God comes across as the dominant voice or ideology, and if not, why not. In other words, is heteroglossia a distinguishing characteristic of oppressive texts only? Is dialogic analysis to be applied only to texts considered oppressive and not to other texts? In other words, why is a dialogic reading to be used only in certain circumstances and not in others?

29. By way of conclusion to the study, García-Treto provides an example of dialogic analysis applied to the Christian Scriptures, the story of Jesus and the Syrophoenician woman in Mark (7:24-30). At the beginning of the story, Jesus represents the dominant voice of

In effect, Joshua 9 describes how the Canaanite inhabitants of Gibeon, faced as they were by imminent extermination on the part of the Israelites, carried out a successful subversion of the ban by means of sheer deception; in other words, via trickery and wiliness the Gibeonites managed to secure their physical survival, though they did end up as slaves to the Israelites. For García-Treto this dialogizing voice of the Gibeonites ultimately subverts the oppressive monologic discourse of the text, the voice of exclusive covenant and genocidal ethnic-cleansing, as they become subjects of their own history and succeed, even if partially, in moving that discourse away from despotism and inhumanity toward a more inclusive vision. Such a dissenting voice, moreover, fits the classic pattern of "the trickster," that character of folklore who, as an outsider, manages to bring about change through wily deception and thus survive but who never quite achieves control of the situation, remaining in the end always an outsider.

The moral is clear: for outsiders, for the oppressed and marginalized peoples, the role of the Gibeonites, and ultimately the role of the trickster, is indispensable for survival. It is a role that calls for craftiness, wiliness, astuteness. It provides a dialogic voice of dissent in the face of an oppressive monologue and as such both resistance to and subversion of, no matter how circumscribed, the prevailing monologue. Indeed, García-Treto sees such dissent and subversion as including a reading of the Bible, of those texts that foster xenophobia and genocide, that is against the grain, insofar as it looks beyond the dominant voice of oppression to underlying voices of dissent and uses the latter to displace the former. In the end, to be sure, for García-Treto the aim is not deception in and of itself but rather the need for the marginalized to become subjects of their own history and the production of a reading on their part that is healing and liberative for all, for dominant and marginalized alike.

Contrast of Early and Recent Approaches

While the preceding analysis of reading strategies and theoretical models at work in these critics shows a continued adherence to a hermeneutics of liberation in their reading and interpretation of the Bible, one also finds, on the whole, a more guarded picture of the Bible as an "effective weapon" and "faithful ally" in the struggle for liberation. With the help of the five basic issues of interpretation invoked above, I should like to summarize these findings and compare them with the earlier uses of the Bible in Hispanic American theological circles.

---

xenophobia and exclusion, while the woman craftily advances her claim by appealing to a common humanity out of her own position of marginalization. By the end of the story, the woman's skillful rejection of Jesus' monologue and pursuit of dialogue not only leads him to a position of inclusiveness with regard to the "children" but also serves to alleviate her own status of oppression and marginalization.

1. *Affinity with the Text.* From the point of view of perceived affinity with the text, the strong consensus on correspondence between the people of God and Hispanic Americans gives way to a broader spectrum of opinion. At one end of the spectrum, one still finds ready access to and identification with the people of God in the Bible. Such is the stance of Romero, given the close correspondence posited between the socioreligious practices of the ancient Hebrews and the popular devotions of modern-day Hispanics. At the other end of the spectrum, one finds instead outright warning against and rejection of such identification. That is the position of García-Treto, who looks upon the tradition of the chosen people of God in the Bible as having highly dangerous xenophobic connotations and ramifications. Insofar as he accepts González's project for reading "in Spanish" as well as Romero's argument for correspondence in popular religious practices, Ruiz lies much closer to Romero than to García-Treto in the spectrum; at the same time, however, he does issue an explicit warning regarding the danger of enslaving the text. The overall result is a more circumspect approach to the question of distance and kinship vis-à-vis the Bible.

2. *Locus of Liberation.* The consensus on the Bible as a liberating text continues, although again a variety of positions can be observed regarding the precise locus of such liberation. To begin with, without any recourse at all to the notion of a canon within the canon, Romero highlights the popular religion reflected in the Hebrew Bible as a source of liberation. By way of contrast, García-Treto looks upon the Bible as a source of both liberation and oppression, while going on to argue that even the texts that embody and promote oppression can ultimately lead to liberation as well. Finally, given his espousal of González's hermeneutical signposts, Ruiz seemingly adheres to the notion of a unified and consistent text, with a message of liberation that is present in a roundabout and noninnocent way (a God who sides with the oppressed yet does so by way of repeated failures and questionable venues); at the same time, his warning regarding the danger of enslaving rather than appropriating the text is very much to the point in this regard. As such, disagreement is in evidence with regard to not only the locus of revelation, as before, but also its mode, with very different notions of biblical authority and normativity at work.

3. *Entrée into the Text.* With regard to entry into the text, the consensus holds as well, insofar as all agree that an experience of marginalization and oppression provides the key to the liberating message of the Bible. A variety of emphases is again evident. For Romero, it is a question of socioreligious oppression in the form of disdain for or rejection of popular culture—the experience of the people, by and large poor and uneducated, engaged in devotional piety. For García-Treto, it has to do with sociocultural oppression as "the other"—the experience of xenophobia and exclusion on the part of those cast into the role of "Canaanites." For Ruiz, insofar as he fol-

lows González, it involves sociohistorical oppression directed at the alien and the powerless—the experience of exile, literal or metaphorical; however, insofar as he does warn of the need to keep in mind the diversity present among Hispanic Americans, it is clear that he also wishes to avoid any type of facile generalization or reductionism in this regard. In conclusion, a close correspondence can be noted once again between the position taken regarding affinity with the Bible and the key posited to the liberating message of the Bible.[30]

4. *Validity in Interpretation.* From the point of view of validity in interpretation, the consensus continues with all authors again calling for a specific way of reading the Bible—a reading of resistance similarly characterized as biblical and distinguished from other readings associated with power and privilege. Different emphases may be observed: for Romero, a reading in tune with socioreligious conventions and practices; for García-Treto, a reading that is conscious of the different voices present in the text, especially in terms of dominant and dissenting; for Ruiz, a reading that remains focused on issues of power and powerlessness, with a special warning attached regarding the need for self-criticism in this regard.[31] To be sure, the reading strategy advanced corresponds closely with the experience of oppression posited as the key to the liberating message of the Bible.

5. *Agenda of Liberation.* With regard to the perceived agenda of liberation in the text, the consensus regarding a highly utopian and subversive vision of liberation holds, with the following variations in evidence: a world where the socioreligious world, symbols, and practices of the people are accepted as a valid faith-expression (Romero); a world where the ideal of a common humanity in the image of God is chosen over against that of an ethnocentric and xenophobic God (García-Treto); and a world where both a *teología de conjunto* and a reading "in Spanish" are at work, with their highly ecclesial and communitarian dimensions (Ruiz). Once again, the new order envisioned is in close correspondence with the experience of oppression and marginalization deemed fundamental for a proper and correct reading of the Bible.

In sum, these more recent approaches to the Bible by Hispanic American critics reveal continuity, especially in the case of Romero, as well as discontinuity, above all in the case of García-Treto though also in the case of

---

30. Although not emphasized as such, certain corresponding images of God readily come to the fore as well: the God of popular religiosity (Romero); the God of common humanity (García-Treto); and the God of the alien and the powerless (Ruiz).

31. In all three cases, furthermore, the proposed reading is related to the world of contemporary theory in biblical criticism: Romero has recourse to structuralist, reader-response, and anthropological criticisms; García-Treto opts for the dialogic analysis of Bakhtin and late Russian formalism, with its socioliterary concerns; while Ruiz points to a wide variety of theoretical developments in contemporary biblical studies.

Ruiz, with the earlier approaches. On the one hand, a summary of the continuity would follow rather closely the summary of the earlier approaches: (1) a text that is neither distant nor strange—a text readily accessible to Hispanic Americans; (2) a fundamental message of liberation—a God for whom popular religiosity is a locus of revelation; (3) a people of God with whom Hispanic Americans can readily identify—two peoples joined in oppression and socioreligious practices; (4) a proper and correct way of reading and interpreting—a reading that correlates ancient and contemporary religious practices; and (5) an utopian vision of liberation—a world in which popular religious culture is seen as valid and revelatory.

On the other hand, a summary of the discontinuity would proceed as follows: (1) a more distant and strange text—a text whose accessibility to Hispanic Americans becomes problematic; (2) a more ambiguous message of liberation—a God who may actually work against the liberation of Hispanic Americans or a message that can fall subject to captivity; (3) a more difficult identification with the people of God on the part of Hispanic Americans—either because of the former's engagement in xenophobic oppression or because of differences among the latter; (4) a more complex proper and correct way of reading and interpreting—a reading that must subvert from within a central tradition of the Bible or a reading that is in need of constant self-revision; and (5) a more subtle utopian vision of liberation—a vision of a world where one biblical ideology prevails in place of another or where theological and hermeneutical dialogue is imperative. To conclude, while for all these readings the Bible remains without question an "effective weapon" and "faithful ally," for García-Treto and Ruiz such faithfulness and effectivity are subject to a high degree of caution and sophistication.

Intercultural Criticism

I have already delineated, within the parameters of cultural studies in biblical criticism, a first mapping of a hermeneutics of the diaspora, a hermeneutics that I presented as grounded in and addressing my own reality and experience of the diaspora and that I described in terms of otherness and engagement.[32] Such a hermeneutics calls for a corresponding reading strategy, which I would describe in terms of intercultural criticism. In what follows, I begin by recapitulating the map of diaspora hermeneutics, continue with a first mapping of the proposed strategy of intercultural criticism, and conclude by locating myself within the unfolding theological and hermeneutical discussion of the Hispanic American diaspora.

---

32. See Segovia, "Hermeneutics of the Diaspora."

The Map of Diaspora Hermeneutics

At the core of diaspora hermeneutics, I have placed the concepts of *otherness* and *engagement*.

The first concept is grounded in and reflects the reality and experience of otherness on the part of individuals from non-Western civilizations who reside on a permanent basis in the West, the children of the colonized who live among the children of the colonizers, as seen through the eyes of someone born and raised in Latin America and now a denizen of the United States and a part of Hispanic America. It is a concept with a negative side, specifically conveyed by its placement in quotation marks ("otherness"). Such "otherness" implies a biculturalism with no home, no voice, and no face: as the ones who left, we are no longer accepted where we came from, and, as the ones who do not fit, we are not accepted in our present home; similarly, within our present home, we find a script for us to play and a mask for us to wear. From this point of view, we find ourselves, following the dynamics of colonial discourse and practice, in the position of permanent aliens and strangers in the world: as imposed and defined "others," home-less as well as face-less (masked) and voice-less (silent and silenced).[33]

The second concept, that of engagement, is similarly grounded in the reality and experience of the non-Western immigrant or refugee in the West. Such a concept may be seen as the positive side of otherness, otherness without quotation marks. Such otherness embraces biculturalism as its very home, voice, and face: instead of no home, no voice, and no face, it argues for two homes, two voices, and two faces. Such otherness also holds that all reality—all homes, all voices, and all faces—is construction and, as such, has both contextuality and perspective; that there are many such realities or worlds; and that these worlds or realities, as constructions, can be critically analyzed, questioned, and altered. From this point of view, we find ourselves, following the dynamics of decolonization and liberation, in a position of critical engagement in the world, with regard to both ourselves and others: as self-affirming and self-defining others, not only creating our own home, voice, and face in the light of our own reality and experience but also engaged in critical dialogue with all other voices and faces.[34]

---

33. For a description of this life of ethnic minorities in theological education and scholarship, see F. F. Segovia, "Theological Education and Scholarship as Struggle: The Life of Racial/Ethnic Minorities in the Profession," *Journal of Hispanic/Latino Theology* 2 (November 1994) 5–25. I would describe the dynamics of colonialism as involving a series of binary oppositions, with the fundamental opposition of center/margins engendering such others as civilized/savage and advanced/primitive.

34. I would describe the dynamics of liberation and decolonization as involving self-affirmation as subjects in history, along with a self-conscious determination to let all voices speak and all faces be seen, to let all subjects construct themselves (even those most pernicious to us), as well as self-criticism, radical and continuous, along with a commitment to engage all voices critically (especially those most dangerous to us).

On the basis of this twofold reality and experience at the core of my diaspora, I have argued for an approach to the texts of early Christianity and ancient Judaism as *others* rather than "others"—as realities to be acknowledged, respected, and engaged in their very otherness rather than overwhelmed or overridden. As such, diaspora hermeneutics is committed not to do unto others as others have done unto us. To be sure, the task envisioned is not at all an easy one. Indeed, if in contemporary life, *as we well know*, it is negative "otherness" that prevails, even as such others struggle to defend and define themselves, how can positive otherness be expected in a situation where the others in question lie long silent and can no longer define and defend themselves?

In fact, it is a highly utopian task in which one has to resist at all times, against incredible odds, a reading of others as "others" in the light of one's reality and experience, social location and interests, contextualization and perspective. It is precisely with such a formidable task in mind, therefore, that I present intercultural criticism as a reading strategy.

Mapping Intercultural Criticism

Like diaspora hermeneutics, its theoretical matrix, intercultural criticism insists on contextualization and perspective and thus focuses on texts as well as readers and readings of texts as a way of emphasizing otherness and engagement. Its reading strategy I see as involving three movements, all thoroughly interrelated and interdependent but not necessarily carried out at the same time or to the same extent.

1. Intercultural criticism looks upon the ancient texts of Christianity and Judaism (or any other texts, for that matter), whether canonical or non-canonical, as literary or artistic products, rhetorical or strategic products, and cultural or ideological products.[35] First, a text is seen as constructing a poetic reality, whether coherent or diffuse, by means of its artistic architecture and texture. Second, a text is also seen as constructing such a reality with a number of specific strategic concerns and aims in mind, both dom-

---

35. For intercultural criticism the question of canon proves both important and irrelevant. It is irrelevant insofar as within each religious tradition many different realities are seen at work, both synchronically and diachronically, all worthy of attention and analysis; it is important insofar as some of these realities emerged as dominant or hegemonic over others, for whatever reason or reasons. In other words, many such realities or worlds are posited both within and outside the canon, so to speak, and each one of them is regarded as worth analyzing and engaging on its own and vis-à-vis the others. For intercultural criticism, therefore, the diversity that is seen as fundamental to the contemporary theological and hermeneutical world is also seen as central to the ancient theological and hermeneutical world. At the same time, the inescapable phenomenon of certain controlling and overpowering realities—certain sets of belief and conduct, discourse and practices—is neither ignored nor bypassed, whether in the contemporary or ancient world. For intercultural criticism, in the end, the entire panorama or spectrum of such realities proves as interesting and attractive as the emergence and hegemony of certain sets of belief and conduct within them.

inant and subordinate, yielding in the process a rhetorical reality as well. Third, a text is further seen as constructing, by means of such literary and rhetorical features, an ideological reality, a view of the world with immediate and broad implications for life in that world. Such realities are regarded as neither juxtaposed nor contiguous but rather as thoroughly imbricated or intertwined—different facets of the same reality, as it were.

Given the nature of these texts, moreover, the worldview in question, again whether concordant or cacophonous, has prominent socioreligious as well as sociocultural overtones. It is highly socioreligious, on the one hand, insofar as it involves the otherworld of suprahuman beings, the this-world of human beings, and the relationship or interchange between such worlds. On the other hand, it is also profoundly sociocultural, insofar as it involves, consciously or unconsciously, a variety of positions having to do with the whole range of factors constitutive of social location and human identity in this-world. It is a worldview concerned, therefore, not only with questions of an otherworld, of gods and spirits and their relationship to human beings, but also with questions central to the human world as such—questions of socioeconomic class and sociopolitical status, gender and race, social structures and cultural conventions, and so forth.

For the first movement of the method, therefore, a combination of formalist, practical, and cultural approaches is in order to analyze texts and unpack or dis-cover their reality as others, their provenance from a very different social and historical context. A number of comments are in order in this regard.

First, the text itself is seen not as an imitation of reality as such, recording and organizing data and facts as they occur in the world, but as a construction of reality, a construction involving a poetics, a rhetoric, and an ideology—all with a particular perspective or point of view and an underlying social location.[36]

Second, with regard to authorship, the notion of "implied" author, the image of the author put together from the totality of the text and its features, becomes more important than that of the "real" author, the flesh-and-blood author. This is so not only because of the almost complete lack of information regarding the real authors of these texts but also, and primarily, because of the importance attached to rhetorical stance—that is, the position adopted by a "real" author for whatever purpose in any particular

---

36. Such a position places intercultural criticism within a postmodernist matrix, with its myth or fundamental narrative of diversity and pluralism: the position that there is no *reality* as such, common and universal, but rather a multitude of "realities"; no omniscient narrator or observer, no universal or objective perspective, but rather a host of contextualized perspectives. "Reality" emerges thereby as fluid, polyvalent, polyglot; ultimately and inextricably related to the various constitutive factors of social location and human identity; not at all a set of data or "facts" to be apprehended and described by an impartial "self," but a construction involving interaction between "facts" and "self."

work—in any concept of authorship. A gap, then, always exists between these two notions of authorship.

Third, with regard to audience, the notion of "implied" reader, the image of the reader pieced together on the basis of the text and its features, is likewise more important than that of the "real" reader, the flesh-and-blood reader. Again, not only is there an almost total lack of information regarding both the identity of the "intended" audience and the early reception of the text, but also, and more importantly, there is a great deal of importance attached to the author's own view of such an "intended" audience.

Finally, such attempts to dis-cover and unpack the otherness of the text are undertaken not for the sake of historical or antiquarian interest—a questionable proposition in and of itself within any view of historical research as inextricably contextualized and interested—but for the purpose of critical engagement with the text. The operative position is not one of reverence for the text, even the biblical texts, but rather one of dialogue and struggle with the text in the light of one's own reality and experience.

2. Intercultural criticism also deals with readings of ancient texts, insofar as it looks upon meaning not as something that is present in the text as such and retrieved from it by way of specific reading strategies but rather as the result of interaction between texts and readers, indeed between texts that are socially and historically conditioned and readers who are socially and historically conditioned.[37] For intercultural criticism, therefore, a text is always a "text": read and interpreted in a certain way by a certain reader or group of readers at a certain time in a certain place. As such, it looks upon all readings, all "texts," as literary or artistic products, rhetorical or strategic products, and ideological or cultural products. Readings of texts are thus approached in the same way as the texts themselves: as artistic constructions, with a poetics of their own; as strategic constructions, with a rhetoric of their own; and as cultural constructions, with an ideology of their own—all with a particular contextualization and perspective, social location and agenda, of their own.

For this second movement of the method, then, an analysis of other readings of the text in question is imperative and calls for a similar combination of formalist, practical, and cultural approaches. On the one hand, such analysis is of further help in unpacking and dis-covering the reality

---

37. Such a position places intercultural criticism within the matrix of reader-response criticism in literary theory, with its broad interpretive spectrum ranging from a predominance of the text over the reader, whereby meaning is seen as coming primarily from the text by way of its own features or constraints, to a predominance of the reader over the text, whereby meaning is posited as deriving primarily from the reader, either as an individual or a social reader. Given its position to the effect that meaning is the result of an interchange between a historically and socially conditioned text and a historically and socially conditioned reader, with the latter as an inescapable filter in the reading and interpretation of such a text, intercultural criticism leans heavily toward the reader-dominant pole.

of the text as an other in the light of one's own reading of the text, one's own production of a "text." On the other hand, such analysis also serves to unpack and dis-cover as well the reality of these "texts" as others, their provenance from different social and historical contexts, vis-à-vis one's own reading. In other words, given its understanding of meaning as the result of an interchange between text and reader, heavily weighted in favor of the latter, intercultural criticism seeks to prevent an overriding or overwhelming of texts on the part of readers, any reader, by foregrounding how other readings of the text have read and interpreted such a text and, in so doing, immediately placing any one reading and interpretation, including one's own, within a spectrum of opinion and committing such an interpretation and reading to critical engagement with such other "texts."

The point of such a comparative exercise in interpretation, of unpacking and dis-covering the otherness of "texts," is not to establish the reality of the text, its one and true meaning, or, much less, the reality behind the text, but to see reading itself as the construction of a "text." In the end, therefore, intercultural criticism sees all readings of texts—all reading strategies; all reconstructions of authors and readers, implied or real; all identifications of rhetorical concerns and aims; all reconstructions of history and culture; in fact, the entire process of unpacking and dis-covering the otherness of texts—as constructions on the part of readers. As such, this resolve to take into account the reception of texts is carried out for the sake of critical engagement with such "texts," not only with respect to the text in question but also with respect to the very "texts" themselves. Again, the operative attitude is not one of ancestral obeisance or search-and-destroy demolition but rather one of critical dialogue and struggle in the light of one's reality and experience.

3. Intercultural criticism deals as well with readers of ancient texts, the authors behind the readings or "texts," given its position to the effect that all "texts" are the result of interaction between socially and historically conditioned texts and socially and historically conditioned readers. In so doing, it looks upon all readers as "texts" in and of themselves, that is to say, as literary or artistic products, strategic or rhetorical products, and cultural or ideological products. In other words, intercultural criticism looks upon all readers as constantly engaged in a process of "self"-construction and approaches such "selves" in the same way it approaches the ancient texts and the readings of such texts: as artistic, strategic, and cultural constructions.[38]

---

38. Such a position situates intercultural criticism within the overall matrix of constructive theology and cultural studies, with its belief (*a*) that all conceptions of the otherworld of suprahuman beings, the this-world of human beings, and the relationship between these two worlds are grounded in, reflect, and address cultural realities and historical experiences; (*b*) that praxis and belief, discourse and practice, go hand in hand at all times, shaping and informing one another in a continuous process of affirmation, development, and revision;

For this third movement of the method, therefore, an analysis of readers is also in order and requires once again a similar combination of formalist, practical, and cultural approaches to unpack and dis-cover the reality of such "selves" or human "texts" as others, their provenance from different social and historical contexts. Such analysis yields a view of the "self" as a literary reality, a "self" fashioned in terms of a poetics involving artistic architecture and texture; a rhetorical reality, a "self" so fashioned in terms of a rhetoric with certain strategic concerns and aims in mind; and a cultural reality, a "self" fashioned in terms of an ideology involving a view of the world and life in that world—all with a perspective and contextualization, an agenda and social location, of its own.

Moreover, by foregrounding the otherness of readers themselves, such analysis further serves to unpack and dis-cover both the otherness of texts and the otherness of "texts": if the readers themselves constitute others, how much more so their readings of texts and the texts they so read!

For intercultural criticism, then, it is not only the readers of "texts" as they reveal themselves in their own readings of texts that prove to be of interest but also the readers as they proceed to read themselves as "texts" or "selves." Indeed, for intercultural criticism the complex relationship between such constructions of the "self" on the part of readers and their corresponding readings and interpretations of texts is of profound interest as well. In other words, intercultural criticism is interested not only in the "implied" authors of "texts" but also in the "real" authors behind such "texts," in the flesh-and-blood "selves."

The point of such a comparative exercise in cultural and theological studies is not to establish the real character of the self, its one and true personality, or, much less, to look for meaning in authorial intention, but rather to see readers them-"selves" as "textual" constructions. Once again, this determination to deal with flesh-and-blood readers is undertaken for the sake of critical engagement with such "selves," similarly engaged in the reading of ancient texts and the production of "texts." As such, the operative stance taken is not one of gentle and irenic encounters but rather one of critical dialogue and struggle in the light of one's own reality and experience, one's own "self."

Locating Intercultural Criticism

This mapping of intercultural criticism as a reading strategy reveals a continued commitment on my part to a hermeneutics of liberation in the reading and interpretation of not only biblical but also nonbiblical texts. At the same time, however, I find myself arguing for an even more cautious

---

and (c) that such contextualized construction is at the very heart of all social reality and theological activity.

view of the Bible as "effective weapon" and "faithful ally" in the struggle for liberation, as the following comments based on the same fundamental issues of interpretation employed above make quite clear.

1. *Affinity with the Text.* With regard to perceived affinity or kinship with the text, I would argue for a view of the text as other, culturally and historically removed, and hence for a keen sense of distance from the text on the part of all contemporary readers, including Hispanic Americans, with a corresponding attitude of distantiation in order to discern and safeguard the otherness of the text. I would argue as well for critical dialogue with such otherness, once established, allowing thereby for the possibility of identification, to be sure, but also for the possibility of resistance. Instead of ready access to and identification with the people of God in the Bible, I would much prefer to argue for a process of distantiation and engagement, the outcome of which is never predictable and may range from appropriation to rejection.

2. *Locus of Liberation.* I would argue that the Bible may or may not be a liberating text and that the proposed locus of liberation has to be worked out by a process of engagement and struggle with the text and may lie in different places for different readers at different times, thus calling for critical dialogue with such other proposed loci of liberation as well. I would further argue that one should look beyond the canonical boundaries of the Bible to the whole panorama of Jewish and Christian antiquity. In the end, such a position amounts to a variation of the higher canon approach, in the light of which all canonical as well as noncanonical texts are analyzed, evaluated, and used; such a canon is a modern canon—the canon of human dignity, diversity, and liberation emerging from the reality and experience of the diaspora. Such a model, needless to say, operates with a very different conception of biblical authority and normativity.

3. *Entrée into the Text.* From the point of view of entry into the text, I would argue that no one experience represents the key to the liberating message of the Bible, not even an experience of marginalization and oppression. I have argued that all readings of the text are "texts," and thus I find it impossible to argue that any one "text" constitutes the key to the text, retrieving and establishing the reality or meaning of that text as such. Indeed, how could such a position be established except by those who claim to have the key themselves? I would argue rather for a plurality of readers and a plurality of readings or "texts." I would also argue, however, that an experience of oppression and marginalization does construct a reading of the text that is impossible from outside this experience and, as such, calls into question readings from an experience of power and privilege, giving rise thereby to an inevitable situation of critical engagement. In the end, such a position also has a corresponding characterization of God: the God of the diaspora, the God of human diversity and pluralism.

4. *Validity in Interpretation.* With regard to the question of validity in interpretation, of proper/correct and improper/incorrect readings, I would argue for a reading strategy that has texts, readings of texts, and readers of texts in mind and that involves a combination of formalist, practical, and cultural approaches in all three regards. Such a strategy, however, is in itself not hard and fast, but open to any number of creative combinations and applications; such a strategy, moreover, is not presented as the only proper and correct way to read and interpret, but as a strategy with its own poetics, its own rhetoric, and its own ideology in the light of the diaspora as a social location. In the end, this reading strategy may also be described as a reading of resistance, insofar as it calls for critical dialogue and engagement at all times.

5. *Agenda of Liberation.* From the point of view of the perceived agenda of liberation in the text, I would argue for a variety of such agendas in both the canonical and noncanonical texts of ancient Judaism and early Christianity. Above all, however, I would argue for the proposed reading strategy as in itself a highly utopian and subversive agenda of liberation, insofar as it allows for a multiplicity of reading strategies, readers, and readings; calls for dialogue among such readers and readings; and seeks to acknowledge, respect, and value the otherness of texts, "texts," and readers of texts. It is a world where diversity and pluralism are not only accepted as a given but also called to account.

Such an approach, I am afraid, reveals far more discontinuity than continuity with the ongoing Hispanic American theological and hermeneutical discussion: (1) a distant and strange text—a text not readily accessible to any contemporary reader, including Hispanic Americans; (2) a convoluted message of liberation—a multifaceted God who may or may not work for the liberation of Hispanic Americans and a message that may be understood in different ways by different readers; (3) a problematic identification with the people of God on the part of Hispanic Americans—based on the possibility of resistance and rejection, the call to go beyond canonical boundaries, and the diversity of readers and readings among Hispanic Americans themselves; (4) no correct and proper way of reading and interpreting as such—a reading strategy that need not be followed, that is open to variation if followed, and that is committed to conversation with other strategies; and (5) a complex vision of liberation—where a multiplicity of readers and readings is accepted as the norm and where such readers and readings are called upon to engage one another. From this point of view, the Bible is not necessarily an "effective weapon" and "faithful ally" but, along with the noncanonical texts of early Christianity and ancient Judaism, a part of our historical and religious tradition that must be dealt with and engaged critically, if only because of their importance in the society where we, as Hispanic Americans, attempt to make our "home," lift our "voice," and display our "face."

Concluding Comments

Intercultural criticism entails an analysis of texts, of "texts" or readings of texts, and of "selves" or readers of texts. As such, it is a reading strategy that calls upon its practitioner to deal with issues of interpretation, hermeneutics, and culture/ideology. Consequently, it is a reading strategy that finds its home within the fourth paradigm at work in contemporary biblical studies, cultural studies or ideological criticism. It is also a reading strategy that sees itself not as *the* one, sole, and definitive reading strategy but as a reading strategy among many, grounded in and addressing the reality and experience of the diaspora, my diaspora, and committed to the values of otherness and engagement.

19

When Resistance Becomes Repression:
Mark 13:9-27 and the Poetics of Location

_____ Mary Ann Tolbert ___

The Politics and Poetics of Location

In a 1984 essay on the possible influence of the poet in a sexist and racist society, Adrienne Rich suggested that every human being is situated in world society by "the facts of blood and bread."[1] The "facts of blood" delineate one's social, personal, and familial alignments while the "facts of bread" include one's economic, political, and national setting. One is "located" in relation to the rest of world society at any one moment by all of these complex elements together. I have adopted her metaphors of "blood" and "bread" to describe a politics of location that both affirms the "essential" ties of "blood"—like race, gender, ethnicity, sexual orientation, and physical integrity—and also reflects the complexity and fluidity of lived experience in a particular economic, political, and national setting, as symbolized by the "facts of bread."[2]

Since the "facts of blood" delineate all the deeply interrelated aspects of personal and social formation, which individually have often formed the basis of definitions of "essence" and the grounds for developing a politics of identity, they constitute the fluid and complex "identity" of the one who speaks. The "facts of bread," on the other hand, situate where one speaks, the conventional grounds of authority, the specific national and institutional framework, the economic and educational standing that contextualize each word I speak and determine who will listen to what I say and who will not. Together the "facts of blood and bread" locate each of us socially and politically at any given moment in relation to our access to

---

1. A. Rich, "Blood, Bread, and Poetry: The Location of the Poet," _Blood, Bread, and Poetry: Selected Prose 1979–1985_ (New York: Norton, 1986) 171.
2. For a full development of these metaphors as a "politics of location," see my article "Afterwords: The Politics and Poetics of Location," _Reading from This Place_, vol. 1, _Social Location and Biblical Interpretation in the United States_ (ed. F. F. Segovia and M. A. Tolbert; Minneapolis: Fortress Press, 1995) 311–17.

power, our relative freedom from oppressive treatment, and our assurance of our own human dignity, integrity, and worth.

Consequently, a politics of location not only requires one to analyze carefully the shared circumstances and political options facing those marginalized by their association with socially devalued categories of gender, race, ethnicity, sexual orientation, and the like, as well as the complex interrelations among those traits. But it also requires that the whole configuration of "identity" issues be thoroughly contextualized and historicized within the particular economic, institutional, and national setting in which it occurs in order to be fully understood. It makes an immense difference, after all, whether an Asian American lesbian works as a maid or as a college dean, or whether she lives in the twentieth century or lived in the eighteenth, or, if we identify her only as an Asian lesbian, whether she lives in the United States or in Korea. To understand her location in relation to world society, what options she has for her life, what access to power or goods she can actualize, the particularities of her various "identities" must themselves be particularized within a specific economic, historical, and cultural context. Moreover, a politics of location has at least the potential of dispelling the myopia often found in the identity politics of some First World liberation movements, which, as Gayatri Chakravorty Spivak points out about U.S. feminists, tend to suffer from "a blindness to the *multi*national theater" in which national practices and ideologies get worked out.[3]

Given this brief sketch of a politics of location, how would one informed by such a political stance conceptualize the reflective task of reading and interpreting texts; in other words, what would a *poetics* of location be like? I am, of course, assuming that all interpretation is politically aligned, whether self-consciously so or not; all interpretation is "interested," that is, it carries with it an agenda of one kind or another. The self-conscious employment of one's political stance and the honest admission of one's advocacies are preferential values in feminism and other liberation movements, and values I embrace fully.

Since a politics of location insists on the complexity, multiplicity, and contextuality of each person's "identity," a poetics of location needs to recognize the legitimacy of self-consciously adopting different perspectives on a text at different times. Thus, such a poetics quite obviously eschews claims for universal readings in favor of local readings that are careful to indicate their context and limits. The historical particularity of the text must be illuminated, including the history of its production, its material, social, and political base. In the case of the Bible, such rarely asked questions as

---

3. For a chilling example of how blind First World feminists can be to the effects of U.S. policy in the Two-Thirds World, see G. C. Spivak, "Feminism and Critical Theory," *In Other Worlds: Essays in Cultural Politics* (New York: Routledge, 1988) 91–92.

the following ought to be raised: How was writing done in the ancient world? What conditions of leisure and education were necessary? How was writing supported economically or viewed socially and politically as well as religiously? And similar questions would surround the reader's production of an interpretation. In addition, a poetics of location also encourages modern readers, who are conventionally trained to be "pleromatists," Frank Kermode's term for completion-seekers,[4] to shed their assumptions of totality in reading both interpretations and the texts they are based upon in favor of adopting a more particular, historical perspective. Consequently, by insisting on the importance of the cultural, social, and political setting of the text, the interpreter, and the audience, a poetics of location always seeks to be "a more historicized poetics."[5]

Moreover, a poetics of location openly acknowledges its allegiance to the postmodern claim that language is constitutive of reality, rather than simply reflective of it. One primary way this allegiance can be signaled is by understanding interpretation as *rhetoric* rather than hermeneutics. As rhetoric, finally and perhaps most importantly, a poetics of location comprehends that its ultimate accountability, its "truth," is primarily a matter of ethical judgment, rather than solely one of historical, literary, or theoretical evaluation. For a poetics of location, any interpretation of a text, especially a text as traditionally powerful as the Bible, must be assessed not only on whatever its literary or historical merits may be but also on its theological and ethical impact on the integrity and dignity of God's creation.

Using this very short description of a poetics of location as an introduction to its concerns, I would now like to explore some of the problematics of biblical interpretation that this stance toward texts discloses. To begin this investigation, I want to compare the resulting interpretations of two different historical contextualizations of Mark 13:9-27, a section of the Apocalyptic Discourse in the Gospel of Mark. Since I am a female biblical scholar in a profession that is not only dominated by males but often overtly misogynous, in academic contexts I am usually constantly aware of my tenuous legitimacy, especially when raising issues regarding the role and status of women in early Christianity, the Bible, or contemporary religious life. However, I am also a First World biblical scholar with all the privileges, economic power, and sanctioned ignorances which that national standing grants me. This economic, national, and political aspect of my "identity" locates me in relation to other biblical scholars throughout the world, and indeed to the authors and first audiences of all of the biblical documents, in a very different way than does my gender. Simply by rec-

---

4. A term coined by Kermode to describe the "fulfillment"- and "closure"-seeking nature of modern readers; see F. Kermode, *The Genesis of Secrecy: On the Interpretation of Narrative* (Cambridge, Mass.: Harvard Univ. Press, 1979) 64–65.

' 5. N. K. Miller, *Subject to Change: Reading Feminist Writing* (New York: Columbia Univ. Press, 1988) 4.

ognizing these two different contextualities, I have uncovered, at the very least, two quite different perspectives from which I may read texts. For this particular comparison of interpretations of Mark 13:9-27, I want to investigate how both my marginalized identity and my national, economic, political, and institutional status, or the status of the communities I inhabit, might affect my understanding and appropriation of a biblical text. I will pursue this concern by comparing the political situation of two reading sites for Mark 13:9-27, that of the probable first-century audience for which Mark was written, as I reconstruct it in relation to marginality, and that of a twentieth-century, conservative, Protestant, First World audience, like the one in which I was reared.

Mark 13 in an Ancient Context: Literature of Resistance

Chapter 13 of the Gospel of Mark is often called the "little apocalypse" because it presents Jesus' speech about the coming of the Son of Man on the clouds of glory and the destruction of the present world that will pre- cede that glorious coming. Verses 9-27 warn the followers of Jesus of the persecutions they will face at the hands of their enemies until this expected end occurs, describe the horrors that will accompany the end, and promise those who endure that they will be saved by God's gracious intervention on behalf of the elect. While the speech is presented as an answer to questions from four disciples (v. 3), its import for the listening audience of the Gospel is rather blatantly signaled several times in the text itself. Mark 13:14 contains the famous "wink" to the reader of the Gospel, "Let the reader understand," which interrupts not only Jesus' voice but that of the narra- tor as well to address the Gospel audience directly, underlining the fictional nature of the entire setting and narration. Further, Jesus closes the discourse with a direct allusion to the intended audience, "What I say to you I say to all" (v. 37). Whatever the narrative value of this speech for the four disci- ples, it is also clearly designed to apply explicitly to the experiences of the audience for whom the Gospel was written. The audience is invited by the rhetoric of the speech to recognize themselves as the persecuted followers of Jesus, the elect, who will be saved from destruction by the coming of the Son of Man.

But who was the audience for whom the Gospel was written? My short answer to that question is that I do not know with any certainty, and the striking contradictions found in recent scholarly attempts to unearth Mark's audience have convinced me, at least, that no one else knows with any certainty either.[6] Nevertheless, there are some clues in the text we are

---

6. For a sampling of opinions, see D. Senior, " 'With Swords and Clubs...'—the Setting of Mark's Community and His Critique of Abusive Power," *Biblical Theology Bulletin* 17

investigating itself about what the author believed the political affinities of the earliest audience of the Gospel might be. In 13:9-13, the enemies of the followers of Jesus, like the enemies of Jesus himself and John the Baptist (Mark 6:14-29), are presented as those in political and religious authority, "councils," "governors," and "kings" (13:9), and as members of one's own family (13:12). Indeed, throughout Mark, those associated with political or religious power, from Herod, Herodias, and Pilate to the Pharisees, scribes, Sadducees, and chief priests, reject Jesus' message and join actively in persecuting him, his followers, or his predecessors (see Mark 12:1-12) almost without exception.[7]

The sharp demarcation between Jesus and those embodying the culturally sanctioned roles of political power and religious authority in the Gospel is further strengthened by Jesus' repeated disapproval of desires for power (for example, 9:38-40; 10:13-16), of yearning for wealth (for example, 10:23-27; 12:41-44), of lording it over others (for example, 10:42-43), of aspiring to be first (for example, 10:44-45) or greatest (for example, 9:34-35; 10:43), or of ostentatious piety (for example, 12:38-40). In fact, taken as a whole, the Gospel of Mark presents what amounts to a sustained polemic against traditional social, religious, and political leadership groups by insisting on their consistently evil exercise of authority. Moreover, by drawing an audience into agreement with Jesus and the narrator, the rhetoric of the Gospel compels the intended audience to be in sympathy with these views. The audience is clearly to be aligned politically, socially, and religiously with Jesus and therefore opposed to his enemies, those dominant groups in society presently occupying leadership roles in these realms. For such a polemic to be persuasive, the author of the Gospel must have believed that his imagined audience would respond positively to this rhetoric. Consequently, whatever their specific situation may have been, the intended audience was very likely composed of those from marginal groups in antiquity who were excluded from access to social, economic, political, and religious power and, in addition, if 13:9-13 paints anything like an accurate picture, who were in constant danger of concrete persecution and repression by those presently holding that power.

Furthermore, since all of the possible sites for the writing of the Gospel of Mark suggested by church tradition or modern scholarship would have been under the control of the Roman Empire, either directly or through a local aristocracy, it seems justifiable to consider this marginalized audience

---

(1987): 10–20; M. A. Beavis, *Mark's Audience: The Literary and Social Setting of Mark 4:11-12* (Sheffield: JSOT, 1989); G. Theissen, *The Gospels in Context: Social and Political History in the Synoptic Tradition* (Minneapolis: Fortress Press, 1991), 238–39; J. Marcus, "The Jewish War and the Sitz im Leben of Mark," *Journal of Biblical Literature* 111 (1992): 441–62; and R. Rohrbaugh, "The Social Location of the Markan Audience," *Interpretation* 47 (1993) 380–95.

7. The two exceptions are Jairus, the synagogue ruler in 5:22, and Joseph of Arimathea, the respected council member in 16:43.

as, additionally, a colonized people under the thumb of an imperial power, though in making that assertion we must recognize that colonization itself is a very complex and multifaceted phenomenon with quite particular historical manifestations. However, seen in this light, the Gospel itself might be understood as an example of colonial literature or, better (given the polemic against political and religious authorities), as anticolonial literature. As in many more recent examples of anticolonial literature, the most blistering denunciations in Mark are leveled, not at imperial representatives themselves, but at local leaders, the Pharisees, chief priests, and Jerusalem authorities. The Second Gospel actually seems to make some attempt to rescue Herod and Pilate, the figures directly related to Rome, from major blame for their murderous actions by scapegoating Herodias, in the case of John the Baptist, and the Jerusalem Jewish leaders, in the case of Jesus. This ambivalence toward Rome, which may relate to early Christian hopes of winning Roman converts, can also be seen as another indication of the colonial situation: one avoids offending too greatly those with real power to harm.

If this reconstruction of the earliest audience's political situation has merit, how would such a group have appropriated the warnings and promises in 13:9-27? Clearly, the enemies they face are the present political and religious leaders, who hate them and wish to persecute them for their beliefs. Mark 13:9-27 serves primarily as an encouragement to the faithful to resist all the terrors thrown at them by the colonial powers. If they resist the political and religious authorities and endure the inevitable suffering such resistance entails, they are assured of their ultimate vindication and salvation at the coming of the Son of Man. For Mark's audience, suffering is not an end in itself and certainly not a good to be desired (see 14:34-42); it is instead a condition required by the evil opposition of those in power and willingly tolerated only for this brief period before the end of the present world. Moreover, the promises made to the elect who endure to the end are not only that they will be saved by the Son of Man but also that all their enemies, those evil power-mongers of the religious establishment and the imperial government, will finally be themselves destroyed. This is not a benign text but rather a thoroughly vindictive one.

For the earliest audience of Mark's Gospel, I submit, 13:9-27 would have functioned as resistance literature against the colonial powers who controlled their economic, religious, and political destiny. And their resistance would end in victory when those councils, governors, and kings who now persecuted them were in their turn destroyed by an even more powerful ruler, God. For a marginal, colonized, powerless group, the appropriation and application of this text is fairly straightforward. Moreover, for a modern woman like myself, marginalized in a male-dominated world, this historical construction can empower me to resist the oppression, hatred, and violence used today to keep women frightened and silent and to

↳ *But uses language of violence/oppression*

hope for a different, better world tomorrow. However, what happens when the text is read, not by the marginalized but by the oppressor, not by the colonized, but by the colonizer?

Mark 13 in a Modern Context: Literature of Repression

I was reared in a very conservative, U.S. Protestant denomination that claimed the Bible as its primary source of revelation, truth, and knowledge about the present and future and that was in addition situated in the politically conservative South, where the "American way" of capitalism, patriotism, imperialism, and also, of course, racism and sexism were idealized as our manifest destiny. America was understood to be the premier Christian nation, living under God's will and benefiting from God's favor. Since God was on our side, we were in return responsible for sending missionaries out to all the heathen countries of the world, from Europe to Asia to Africa to South America, to preach the will of God and teach the blessings of the "American way." This inflated self-definition, which unfortunately still thrives in the rhetoric of the religious right and less blatantly in the hearts of many Americans, is none other than an imperialist agenda of world colonization.

In a political, social, and religious situation in which Christians are the ones in power, in which they control the councils, are the governors and presidents, judges and lawyers, in which Christians are the ruling "colonizers," how is a text like Mark 13:9-27 to be read? In light of the vast incommensurability between the political and religious situation of my American Protestant community and the earliest audiences of the Gospel, one option certainly would be to dismiss the passage as no longer applicable to the lives of today's American followers of Jesus. However, in the community in which I was reared that option was never considered, since the Bible was believed to transcend cultural boundaries and historical ages; it was eternally relevant and true.[8] In reading Mark, we were shaped by the same rhetoric that aroused its earliest hearers to identify with Jesus and against anyone who opposed him. As followers of Jesus, we too believed that we could expect to experience persecution at the hands of those enemies who hate us, just as earlier followers had.

Our problem, of course, was identifying who those enemies were. The "councils," "governors," and "kings" were all now Christians—at least nominally so. One strategy of my community, still very commonly employed, was to suspect that all those who called themselves Christians really

---

8. For other analyses of the use of the Bible in fundamentalist circles, see, for example, K. Boone, *For the Bible Tells Them So: The Discourse of Protestant Fundamentalism* (Albany: State Univ. of New York Press, 1989); and J. Barr, *Fundamentalism* (2d ed.; London: SCM, 1981).

were not, especially if they did not agree exactly with us. Thus, many Christians continue to get caught up in an internal battle of naming just who the "true" Christians are and who they are not. Nevertheless, for the most part, we had to acknowledge that Christians were, indeed, in control of our world. Who, then, are these powerful enemies who hate us and intend to make us suffer? In the religious community of my childhood, and in many conservative Christian communities today, we identified our enemies, not as those presently in control, but as those whom we believed *wanted* to be in control. Anyone who opposed "American values" or who criticized our particular view of Christianity was fantasized to be out for world conquest in order to be able to persecute us in the future. The former Soviet Union was a favorite candidate for this role, and with its demise, other groups have been designated as the future persecutors of Christians, most notably recently, if you listen to Jerry Falwell, gay men and lesbians with their "agenda" of world sexual conquest. Mark 13:9-27 and other texts like it are often read in the ruling communities of the colonizers as *proleptic texts,* predicting what will happen to Christians, if they lose their dominance in local or world affairs. Such texts ultimately operate as calls to paranoia, for everyone who is not with us is our enemy and, moreover, is plotting to release their hatred in active harassment and persecution as soon as they are in a position of power. Furthermore, imagining ourselves as the future victims of evil non-Christian authorities becomes a vital justification for instituting all kinds of repressive measures against those we believe or fantasize are possible future enemies. Any who dissent from our specific construction of Christianity, any who criticize the actions or motivations of the United States, any who reject the benefits of capitalism or who rage angrily against the injustices of their colonized status should be repressed by whatever means necessary, not so much because of their present attitudes but because of their hidden desire, their terrible secret "agenda," to control the world in order to victimize us, the true followers of Jesus, in the future, as revealed proleptically to us in Scripture.

Mark 13:9-27 may be a literature of resistance for the marginal, powerless outsiders who made up the earliest Christian groups, but it becomes a literature of repression for the dominant, powerful insiders of some of today's American Christian communities. The shift in the political contextualization of the reader of the text produces profound differences in how the text is appropriated and understood, in how followers of Jesus believe they are being called to act in their particular social, cultural, and historical contexts. Are we to be heroically enduring martyrs or frighteningly paranoid oppressors? A poetics of location reveals *both* of these radically divergent interpretations as possible appropriations of this text. Should we just stop at this point and praise pluralism? Surely not, for these two interpretations have the power to affect the way people treat each other and the world. But how are we to evaluate or to adjudicate these two strikingly different interpretations? Can we claim one as "right" or "legitimate" and the other as "wrong" and on what bases? Is one of my "locations" within world society right and the other wrong? Or are both contextualizations legitimate and equally valid understandings of this text? And what do we mean by "right," "legitimate," and "valid" in the context of biblical interpretation?

Adjudicating Biblical Interpretations

In its two hundred year history, modern Anglo-European biblical scholarship has consistently faced the problem of adjudicating among competing interpretations of a biblical text, as have church councils throughout the centuries. Although all text-based discourses generate multiple interpretations of the same text—simply because of the inherent ambiguity of language, if for no other reasons—this inevitable phenomenon becomes deeply problematic for texts designated as morally, legally, or religiously authoritative. Fortunately, not many documents fall into this lofty category. Although some Freudian psychoanalysts may place Freud's writings in this category (though Freud himself rather clearly did not) and members of various cults or secret societies may designate their founder's writings as authoritative, cultures as a whole generally posit only two types of such authoritative texts: legal or political codes and major religious documents.

Multiple interpretations derived from legal or political texts have regularly generated elaborate bodies of arbitration. Thus, the authoritative status given to national constitutions and the legislative decrees that grow out of them is generally fully mediated by a whole system of legal and legislative groups explicitly designed to negotiate and decide matters of interpretation (for example, a judicial system or supreme court) or to amend the founding documents, when that action seems advisable for the society as a whole. Although actually altering major religious texts is not usually an option, such texts have often been treated similarly to legal and political texts, as church councils or specially designated religious leaders have determined the single "correct" interpretation for all believers to follow. Such practices can be found, for example, in Islam, in Orthodox Judaism, and throughout the history of the Christian church.

Nevertheless, for religious texts, the modern period, initiated in the Anglo-European Enlightenment of the seventeenth and eighteenth centuries, which was accompanied by the rise to dominance of reason, science, and capitalism and the increasing secularization of cultures across the globe, considerably weakened the traditional respect accorded ecclesiastical institutions and their leaders, who were charged with determining "correct" religious practice. The worldwide growth of fundamentalism during the last century can be seen as a strong backlash to that weakening in the form of ever more autocratic assertions of authority from unquestioning acceptance to "infallibility."[9] Indeed, the turn to fundamentalism and even fundamentalism itself are unintelligible outside of the context of modernity. Moreover, Anglo-European biblical scholarship with its foundations in Enlightenment reason and history can be seen as another, quite different response to the same modern milieu, and for people unimpressed with the fundamentalist agenda, it has taken on the mantle of adjudicating biblical interpretation and proper religious practice earlier ages left solely in the hands of church authorities. Professional biblical scholarship has gained this status in part by aligning its strategies and methods with some of the dominant beliefs of modernism: the priority of reason, the valorizing of history, and the assertion of objectivity. Consequently, its development, like that of fundamentalism, is unintelligible outside of Anglo-European modernity.

Johann Philipp Gabler, in his 1787 inaugural address at Altdorf, Germany, is usually credited with signaling the definitive break between "biblical theology," the new "science" of biblical study, and the dogmatic concerns of the church.[10] Gabler's "biblical theology" in its basic movement was to be true only to the religion expressed in the texts of the Bible themselves and to be unaffected by the ecclesiastical, dogmatic, or moral issues facing the church. To be fair to Gabler, he also argued for other distinctive and important levels of theological analysis, using the results of "true biblical theology," which were to take seriously the ecclesiastical and dogmatic needs of the church, but his enduring legacy is the clear delineation of a discipline divorced—at least in theory—from church influence and wedded to reason, historical research, and objectivity, a discipline thoroughly molded to the dominant emphases of Enlightenment thinking. This new biblical discipline, as it developed in the work of later German scholars like Ferdinand Christian Baur and especially William Wrede, evaluated the adequacy of any interpretation of the Bible by its closeness to the original historical situation and context. The "right" interpretation was the most historically probable one, as argued through the reason-based premises of historical criticism and as judged by one's scholarly peers; "true" and "historically original" became steadfastly linked.

Although much has changed in biblical scholarship since Gabler—there are new methods of research, much more refined understandings of history, archaeology, ancient literature, and hermeneutical theory, and even many

---

9. For thorough documentation and discussion of fundamentalism as a response to modernity, see M. E. Marty and R. S. Appleby, eds., *Accounting for Fundamentalisms: The Dynamic Character of Movements* (Chicago: Univ. of Chicago Press, 1994); and N. T. Ammerman, "North American Protestant Fundamentalism," *Fundamentalism Observed* (ed. M. Marty and R. S. Appleby; Chicago: Univ. of Chicago Press, 1991) 1–65.

10. For a brief but useful discussion of Gabler's importance to modern biblical scholarship, see H. Boers, *What Is New Testament Theology? The Rise of Criticism and the Problem of a Theology of the New Testament* (Philadelphia: Fortress Press, 1979) 23–38.

new and different voices participating in the discussion—the evaluative criterion of closeness to a proposed historical original has remained at the center of biblical study. For a biblical interpretation to be deemed "valid" (the modern, softened version of the old claims of "right" and "true") by the contemporary scholarly establishment, it must still argue persuasively its closeness to the original historical situation of the text or the original meanings the text might have had. I am not suggesting or implying that there is anything at all wrong with reconstructing history or attempting to assess a text within the context of its original historical production. Indeed, historical study of ancient texts is essential to understanding their distinctive nature, viewpoints, and conventions and to recognizing the fundamentally different social relations, cultural perspectives, ideologies, and beliefs of their authors and audiences from those of *any* reader or interpreter in the present. The acknowledgment of historical distance and difference is one of the enduring contributions of modernism. Nevertheless, the assumption that "valid," "legitimate," "right," or "true" interpretations are determined solely or even mainly by their closeness to a supposed original meaning or situation seems to me to be both an inadequate evaluative stance for a poetics of location and also a dangerous ideological and political assertion.

Logically, after all, to say that one or a few interpretations are likely to be closer to the original meanings than other interpretations is only to make a claim about history. The real question is why a claim about history in this society is accorded the added valuation of "validity," "correctness," "legitimacy," and "truth." Another way to put the issue is to ask what stands behind the valorization of history in modern, especially Western, society. While this is clearly a topic for a full book, a few concerns might be helpfully raised here. The growth of science since the Enlightenment and the success of its technological by-products have tended to make the observable (and theoretical) "facts" of scientific research our modern equivalent of "truth." That other cultures, including the Greco-Roman world in which Christianity was born, would regard this equating of fact with truth incredibly reductionistic is generally ignored in modern society—as is the constant empirical evidence that different people have great difficulty agreeing on what the observable "facts" are. Historical-critical research has quite self-consciously modeled its methods and procedures after those of the sciences; consequently, the historical "product," the reconstruction (or construction) of the past that grows out of the use of these methods, claims this same status of "fact," although since historical inquiry always works in probabilities, only "probable facts" are produced. Still, in our scientific system of faith, even probable facts manifest the aura of truth.

Perhaps even more influential than the scientific claims regarding the historical-critical method, which, after all, have been profoundly shaken by postmodernity, is the persistent *mythos* of much of Western society that the best times, the purest times, are always in the past. I call this staunch romanticism of the past the "Garden of Eden" syndrome: at some point in the past, human life was pure, simple, whole, existing in perfect harmony and wisdom with the world, and then we fell and have kept falling until the present with all its problems. For the "Garden of Eden" syndrome, solving our problems always amounts to seeking guidance and correction from that perfect past or trying to return to "the way we were."[11] Depending upon the arena of discourse involved, that perfect past moment might be the time of the Founding Fathers of the American Constitution or the time before women got the vote or the time before the foreign colonizers arrived or the time of Jesus himself.

Christianity, and especially Protestant Christianity, has certainly fueled the flame of historical valorization by claiming a special purity or power to the time of the writing of the New Testament documents or of the ministry of Jesus (and Paul). If, as Christians claim, Jesus is the special revelation of God and Jesus was born into a particular temporal and geographical moment of history, on first glance it might seem justifiable to grant that moment a unique status. However, does the belief that Jesus is the special revelation of God really make Roman Palestine, rural or urban, a purer or more perfect cultural or geographical location than all others? Or does the fact that Paul was a remarkably creative and influential early interpreter of Jesus' death and resurrection really make the social and cultural values of urban Hellenism of the early imperial period, which Paul so fully embodied, particularly pristine, simple, and exemplary? In other words, does the fact that Jesus and Paul worked and taught in a particular historical period make that period of history purer or more perfect than any other for Christians? Put as bluntly as that, few biblical scholars or other Christians would assent to this claim. Yet the undisputed status of historical originality in adjudicating "valid" biblical interpretations, I would assert, implicitly, if not explicitly, grants such heightened value to the historical time, place, and culture of the biblical documents. The real problem, of course, is that the historical Jesus, God's revelation in human form, and the teachings of the early Christians who first believed in him are irrevocably imbricated in the social, cultural, and historical life of the first-century eastern Mediterranean world. And all attempts to sort the enduring theological wheat from the transitory historical chaff, beginning as early as Gabler's "pure biblical theology" (the next step up from his "true biblical theology") through Rudolph Bultmann's "demythologizing" program, have ultimately proved to be failures: social and cultural conditioning cannot be shed like garments; they form, instead, the living material of human existence. Per-

---

11. The romantic illusion of a perfect past in the recent "family values" debates in the political arena is clearly demonstrated in the excellent study by S. Coontz, *The Way We Never Were: American Families and the Nostalgia Trap* (New York: Basic Books, 1992).

haps the deeper meaning of the incarnation for the modern period is being revealed in these failures: God in human form is God in historical, social, and cultural *limitation*.

The Ethics of Interpretation

Whatever our theological response to the profound historicity of the Christian message, the use of historical originality as the sole criterion of "validity," "truth," or "correctness" for an interpretation of the Bible remains an inadequate ground for evaluation in a poetics of location. In the first place, as I argued above, historical originality gives a kind of exemplary status to the historical period of the biblical documents. In our earlier examples from Mark 13:9-27 that status might initially seem beneficial, since it would clearly prefer the interpretation formed out of the reconstruction of the ancient reading site for the Gospel. Thus, the "correct" interpretation of Mark 13:9-27 is as a message of resistance for those marginalized against their more powerful oppressors. The direct appropriation of the text by those today (or at any time) who are not marginalized and powerless but powerful and dominant is not a "valid" reading.[12] However, two problems arise with this judgment.

Since a poetics of location acknowledges the constitutive nature of language, the "reconstruction" of an ancient reading site must be seen as a construction, a probable fiction, based on modern insights and methods, whose relationship to whatever the actual ancient situation was is never direct or unproblematic. In this case, of course, the construction of a marginalized ancient audience, while arguably probable from a historical standpoint, is clearly related to my own marginalized experience of gender identity. Obviously, the present social, religious, and cultural experience of the real interpreter is as constant and important a factor in historical constructions as it is in all other types of interpretation. The different effect of historical work arises from the fact that historical construction—because it purports to deal with the past rather than the present—hides the shaping influence of the critic more securely than other types of interpretation do. Hence the conception of "historical originality" in biblical scholarship

---

12. Insisting on the centrality of historical distance has been one of the ways biblical scholarship has challenged the more direct kind of textual appropriation often found in fundamentalist readings (although fundamentalism has its own intensely hypothetical and thoroughly rationalistic reading methods, like dispensationalism, that should not be overlooked in these "more direct" appropriations). The importance of asserting the claims of historical distance stand behind Elisabeth Schüssler Fiorenza's call for an "ethics of historical reading" in her very important early article on ethics and biblical scholarship, "The Ethics of Interpretation: De-centering Biblical Scholarship," *Journal of Biblical Literature* 107 (March 1988) 3–17.

itself is deeply dependent on the perspective of the interpreter and the interpreter's scholarly peer group, and always subject to debate and revisioning. It is a very slippery criterion to use for adjudicating interpretations. Of even greater concern is the enhancement given to this particular constructed moment in ancient Mediterranean history. By designating the ancient reading of Mark 13:9-27 as the more "valid" interpretation, am I sanctioning the views it presents? The apocalyptic vision described in Mark 13 calls for the utter destruction of the world and *everyone* in it who is not among the elect. Under what extreme circumstances is such a vengeful, bloodthirsty, and pitiless view of one's enemies morally justified? Should any group who see themselves as marginalized and powerless be encouraged to appropriate this passionate hope for the divine annihilation of their oppressors? Is the historically "valid" interpretation of this text "true" for today or "correct"? How do we evaluate the historical original? How do we call its assumptions and views into question? While the modern reading site I constructed for Mark 13 produced an interpretation of frightening paranoia, it could certainly be argued that the hatred and fear of one's enemies spurring that paranoia are indispensable to ancient apocalyptic thought as a whole. Preferring the interpretation closest to the historical original does not eradicate hatred and fear. I suppose one might counter that only those who are powerless to help themselves are justified in harboring such vengeful visions, while people with the power to act are held to a different standard. The difficulty with such reasoning is that, like the early Christians, a group's relationship to power often changes while their feelings about their enemies do not.

Apocalyptic thought, with its assumption of a vengeful divine providence that will destroy the enemies of the elect, is very probably a part of the original historical situation of the Gospel of Mark.[13] Moreover, other common views of ancient society that are morally problematic in the present, like slavery and the subordination of women, are an assumed and accepted part of biblical documents. In addition, some early Christians taught moral positions, often related to their sectarian or apocalyptic views, that many today

---

13. The most recent quest of the historical Jesus argues for a nonapocalyptic Jesus, thus removing this extremely problematic and bloodthirsty belief from Jesus himself. The author of Mark among others is credited with foisting apocalyptic thought on Christianity, making the writing of the Gospels a "fall" from the perfect time of Jesus himself. See, for example, J. D. Crossan, *The Historical Jesus: The Life of a Mediterranean Jewish Peasant* (New York: HarperSanFrancisco, 1991), and M. Borg, *Jesus, a New Vision: Spirit, Culture, and the Life of Discipleship* (San Francisco: Harper and Row, 1987), and also Borg's *Jesus in Contemporary Scholarship* (Valley Forge, Pa.: Trinity, 1994). As our modern moral sense becomes more refined, the past time of true perfection seems to become shorter and shorter, but the desire to have such a perfect time in the past continues unabated. The quest for the historical Jesus is an ideal vehicle for this nostalgia since the evidence available is so small and the need for imaginative construction so great. I think of these present-day questers as modern Gospel writers, doing for today what the authors of Mark or Matthew were trying to do for their own time.

find socially, historically, or scientifically unjustified, like, for example, divorce leading to adultery, envious Jewish leaders as responsible for Jesus' death, same-sex relations as unnatural, children as the obedient slaves of adults, wives as the obedient slaves of husbands, and so on. Although it is certainly not impossible for historical criticism to raise critical questions about the theological, moral, and political worth of the social and cultural values embedded in the texts of the Bible, the dominant tendency is to stop at the historical construction itself, explicitly or more often implicitly permitting its enhancement of the past as a better or more important time than the present to stand unexamined.

Besides its enhancement of the past, using historical originality as the main criterion for evaluating biblical interpretations is, in the second place, inadequate for a poetics of location because it legitimizes only one location for reading the Bible: the scholarly development of an ancient situation. Only specialized experts trained in the primarily Anglo-European tradition of biblical scholarship are allowed to do creditable biblical interpretation. This position utterly ignores the fact that for a large percentage of the world's population, the Bible is a living text of the present. The failure to address this dominant context of the Bible today may well be one of the reasons why professional biblical scholarship has had so little effect on public perceptions of the Bible. Yet even some biblical scholars—especially liberation scholars—admit that the use of the Bible in, for example, Latin or South American base communities is both insightful and theologically creative. However, these same scholars would be much less likely to approve of the use of the Bible in the conservative religious community of my youth. How is one modern community's appropriation of the Bible commendable and another's not? Since the main criterion for establishing a "valid" interpretation is closeness to the original historical situation, there are no established guidelines for adjudicating among interpretations that make no attempt to deal with historical distance. For a poetics of location, all interpretations, whether historical or contemporary, are rhetorical assertions attempting to persuade their audiences to accept certain values and roles over other values and roles. For a poetics of location, such a situation demands the development of an ethics of interpretation.

To call for an ethics of interpretation is to recognize the power of the Bible in the public and private lives of people around the world today and to acknowledge both the good and the evil that power has done and continues to do. I do not believe that such an ethics can be derived from the Bible alone, for to do so is simply to raise the problems of cultural imbrication all over again.[14] Thus, drawing on the best that theology, moral

---

14. This insight is at least as old as Origen, who argued that the Bible could never be taken to mean anything "unworthy of God." Origen's initial theological perception of what was and was not worthy of God then controlled his interpretation of Scripture and his use of allegory.

discourse, philosophical thought, science, and history can provide, Christians and non-Christians whose lives are affected by the Bible must—in their own individual and particular contexts—develop sets of criteria for evaluating biblical interpretations in each situation, recognizing that these criteria may be different in different locations. My own theological stance in discussing such an ethics in my particular context begins with the conviction, drawn from the Christian affirmation of a Creator God of love, that *no human creation of God should be treated as less than human*, as an object to be owned, abused, used, or ignored at will, nor should the integrity of creation as a whole be jeopardized by its human component's greed, lust for control, and domination. Interpretations of the Bible that run counter to that conviction are the ones whose "truth," "validity," "legitimacy," or "correctness" need to be questioned severely, whether or not they are historically defensible. In my two readings of Mark 13, *both* ancient and modern interpretations of the passage champion unacceptable ethical positions: neither divine vengeance nor human paranoia is a "valid" appropriation of Scripture for Christians today. For a poetics of location, the historical situation of the first Christians and the original intended meanings of the biblical texts, no matter how probably constructed, do not in themselves constitute "legitimate," "true," or "normative" readings of the Bible. The Bible's "truth" for today must be evaluated on the basis of its ethical impact, its blessing or its curse, on God's creation as a whole.

__ Afterwords

Christianity, Imperialism, and the Decentering of Privilege

_____ Mary Ann Tolbert ___

> My heart is moved by all I cannot save:
> so much has been destroyed
>
> I have to cast my lot with those
> who age after age, perversely,
>
> with no extraordinary power,
> reconstitute the world.
>
> —Adrienne Rich, "Natural Resources"

In October 1993, all of the scholars whose essays appear in this volume joined together in an international conference at Vanderbilt University. Two scholars, Itumeleng Mosala and M. L. Weli Mazamisa of South Africa, whose papers were subsequently unavailable for publication, were also among the group of presenters at the Vanderbilt conference. The conference participants were convened in discussion sessions by two specially invited observers, Mark Kline Taylor of Princeton Theological Seminary and R. S. Sugirtharajah of Selly Oak Colleges, England. While a number of the papers were originally prepared in languages other than English, they were translated for the conference itself (and this volume). Consequently, the entire conference was conducted in English with a translator present only at a couple of sessions to assist the participants. This total reliance on English, a helpful boon for the crowds who attended the sessions, is also a clear indication of the orientation of the conference toward a First World audience. Whatever the participants might wish to say to their own national or regional constituencies, at the Vanderbilt conference they were clearly speaking to the First World in one of its main languages.

In these "afterwords" I want to reflect on my personal experience of the conference and the vital issues it raised for me as a First World biblical scholar and Christian. However, I am not unaware of the irony of having a U.S.-born descendant of English and Dutch Protestant colonists to North

America compose the closing reflections on an international gathering on the Bible. Indeed, such irony is ubiquitous in international scholarship today, as well as in international relations more broadly. The economic power of the First World and its assumption of privileged status permeate most "international" scenes, producing seeming anomalies like the exclusive use of English at an international meeting. In addition, although the explicit subject of the Vanderbilt conference was the effect of social location on reading the Bible in countries around the globe, since all the participants were scholars and teachers or pastors, implicitly it also introduced difficult questions concerning the continuing Western hegemony over, for example, the location and ethos of professional training, the methods of research appropriate for diverse contexts, the shape of scholarly discourse, the granting of academic status, and the economics of research and publication. When the economic, linguistic, and cultural extent of current Western neocolonialism, that insinuating successor to actual physical colonial occupation, is recognized, the truly multinational character of any dialogue that is funded by, located in, and controlled by the First World must be open to doubt. Yet, even given the First World context, at the Vanderbilt conference the vitality of postcolonial thought and the many faces of postcolonial struggle were still readily apparent.[1]

As a First World biblical scholar at such an international gathering, I found it impossible to avoid the realization of the devastation and misery brought to most of the inhabited world by the imperialist expansion of European nations into the lands and cultures of Africa, Asia, and the Americas during the fifteenth to the nineteenth centuries. Much of this expansion was justified by and indeed fueled by calls to "spread the gospel to the nations." What this "godly pilgrimage" left in its wake was the devastation of rich and influential cultures, complete restructurings of traditional land allocations, and the deaths of millions of generally peaceful, cooperative people. Moreover, European hegemony was not attained, as we Euro-American descendants often romantically imagine, through cultural supremacy or exceptional military strategy but most often by the perniciousness of our ancestors' viruses. It has been estimated, for example, that

---

1. The relation of conference participants to both the First World/Third World division and the formerly colonized/colonizer category is quite complex. Among the First World participants, those from North America and Australia were mainly descendants of European colonial settlers, while those from Europe itself came from countries with former colonial interests. Among the Two-Thirds World participants, those from Asia and Africa were primarily members of indigenous groups whose lands had at one point or another been colonized by European settlers, while those from Latin and South America were predominantly descendants of Spanish or Portuguese colonizers. In this colonized/colonizer division, the place of Japan is an interesting one: although it is not usually considered part of the "First World," it has never been colonized in its entire history; instead, it has been one of the major colonial "oppressors" of other Asian countries. It is important to remember that the "First World"/"Third World" designation does not have its roots in the colonial period but rather in the economic and "cold war" divisions of the post–World War II era.

90 percent of the Native American population was wiped out by contact with European diseases like diphtheria, smallpox, and syphilis, for which they had no natural immunity. Contrary to popular lore, the North American West and much of the so-called New World was "won," not by the mighty gun, but by the mighty germ. How great the suffering, how great the destruction of God's good creation have been wrought in the name of Christian piety and biblical authority.

Throughout the conference, Adrienne Rich's evocative words "My heart is moved by all I cannot save: / so much has been destroyed" played in my mind. Unfortunately, too often the knowledge of this destruction of indigenous cultures in the name of financial gain and religious fervor and the profound anger it has generated toward Western Europe and the United States comes as a surprise to many in the First World because the deeply negative impact of the colonial period and the continuing corrosiveness of neocolonialism generally remain a sanctioned ignorance in Anglo-European education. Since capitalism and Western culture are presented as an unquestioned good, the development of quasi-capitalism and the infiltration of Western culture into the countries of the Two-Thirds World[2] are taken as imitation of the West rather than as intimidation by the West in its driving need to locate cheap manufacturing pools or to create new consumer markets.

When knowledge of the human and environmental costs of Western imperialism is forcefully introduced, as it was on numerous occasions at the conference, one common reaction of reasonably sensitive First World audiences is to break into lamentation, *mea culpa*s, and, of course, guilt, that most useless of all emotions. Although some of this reaction is most certainly justified, since the quest for the ever higher standard of living in the U.S. depends on the continued economic plundering of other countries, part of it may also derive from a sense of helplessness to alter the vast interwoven patterns of systemic exploitation fundamental to a modern, postindustrial global market economy. Thus, weeping is all we in the First World can do, or, perhaps more honestly, it is all enough of us are willing to do in a situation in which our own comfort and status are at war with our sense of justice. But remorse alone is an inexcusably passive response to the continued imperialism of the Western neocolonial invasion of the Two-Thirds World. Andrienne Rich's poem suggests that knowledge of the destruction of life may result in something quite different from passivity; it may, instead, ground a commitment to work in coalition with others who seek "perversely, with no extraordinary power," to "reconstitute the world." For me, possibly the most important result of the international

---

2. I prefer the phrase "Two-Thirds World" to the more common "Third World" because it is a constant reminder that the *majority* of the world's peoples and land belong in this category.

conference was a profound sense of recommitment to such acts of "re-constitution," personally, politically, and professionally. Although there are undoubtedly many ways a First World scholar may participate in acts of reconstitution, *appropriate* participation, as distinct from the more common response of *patronizing* participation, seems to me to require at least three discrete steps: listening, reflecting/analyzing, and acting. I wish to use these steps to develop my own First World response to some of the issues generated by the Vanderbilt conference.

Listening: The Legacy of Imperialism

Listening is the critical first step in constructing appropriate forms of cooperation with those whose oppressive treatment falls in some way, no matter how distantly, under one's own charge or with those whose marginalization is somehow symbiotically linked to one's own dominant position. And it is a remarkably difficult step for many to accomplish. In part it is difficult because in order to recognize the need to listen to others one must first admit one's own ignorance, and the denial of that ignorance is an essential part of the ideology of dominance. Ignorance may be denied either actively, by assuming, for instance, that one already knows all one needs to know about the experience of others (sexist and racist prejudice within a society often demand this form of denial), or passively, by the ideological bias involved in a society's production of knowledge itself. Educational systems promote an ideology of dominance or centrality through their selection of what counts as knowledge and thus, by default, what stands as sanctioned ignorance.

As an example, when I took "world" history, both in high school and in college, what was studied in detail was *European* history; Africa, South America, Asia, or practically any other spot was only mentioned when it became the object of European exploration. The history of North America or of other continents prior to European colonization or "discovery," as it is usually called, was (and mostly still is) an acceptable or sanctioned ignorance for educated Americans. Consequently, most Americans, educated in state-run school systems (and private school systems, especially the recent "Christian" ones, because of their planned homogeneity, can be even worse), are likely to know much more about the current and ancient history of England, thousands of miles across the Atlantic Ocean, than about Canada and Mexico, which are right at our borders, or Native American culture, which is right in our midst. When non-European cultures or histories are studied at all, it is usually under the rubric of an anthropological analysis of "primitive" societies. Why the fourteenth- and fifteenth-century Aztec culture of central Mexico should be regarded as more "primitive" than that of feudal Europe is intelligible only from a certain perspective of dominance. The ideological message of European hegemony in this selection of what must be known to be considered an "educated" person and what can be disregarded is obvious and shocking.[3]

Once the extent of one's "educated" ignorance is acknowledged, the need to *listen* as carefully and as thoroughly as possible to the perceptions, experiences, and viewpoints of those marginalized or traditionally silenced *before* attempting to act with them or on their behalf is indisputable. Acting without first listening, no matter how apparently well intentioned, reveals an underlying arrogance and assumption of superiority, founded upon chauvinistic ignorance. Careful listening, however, does not necessarily imply complete agreement or uncritical acceptance. All viewpoints contain their biases and perspectival limitations, and thus all viewpoints must be subject to critical evaluation and debate. During the Vanderbilt conference, for instance, several occasions arose in which European or North American women scholars questioned some of the male scholars of the Two-Thirds World about the absence of any reflection on women in their work or even the potentially negative impact of their proposals on women in their own countries. Such critiques may have validity, but they also need to be carefully nuanced. While few feminists would agree that the concerns of feminism are only Western, many would agree that gender construction and gender oppression take particular cultural forms and only women within the cultures in question really know what impacts them negatively and what does not. The same kind of issue developed at the conference in regard to the status and treatment of indigenous peoples. Given the abominable treatment of Native Americans within the United States, U.S. audiences open themselves to appreciable pillorying if they criticize the exclusionary actions of other countries toward their native populations. Yet the very recognition of the ways in which Native Americans have been and are being oppressed and of the many rationalizations that have been manufactured to support that oppression sometimes makes U.S. audiences more sensitive to those issues and justifiably more suspicious of those arguments coming from other countries. That one has oneself committed evil acts does not necessarily disqualify one from naming evil in the acts of another when one sees it—but it certainly should make one more humble and cautious about doing so. At the very least, one should be in the process of removing the log from one's own eye before criticizing one's neighbor for the mote (or log) in his/hers. It is this lack of caution and humility, more than anything else, that makes even justified critiques stimulate more anger than reflection. Thoughtful and critical listening—and some sincere repentance—needs to precede and inform any critique those in

---

3. My primary and secondary education took place in the state of Virginia. During those thirteen years of study, I had *four full years* of Virginia history, *one year* of U.S. history, and *one semester* of world history. The ideological shaping of this course of study is extremely hard to miss!

dominant locations wish to make about the activities of those who reside in marginalized locations.

In listening to speakers from other parts of the world at the Vanderbilt conference, I was struck by the highly contextual nature of the issues raised. While economics was an underlying theme of many discussions, the types of economic conditions depicted and the types of actions recommended varied greatly. Those from Europe or parts of Asia and Africa spoke of religious communities stressed by economic recessions or challenged by the influx of immigrants coupled with a lack of jobs or disrupted by the dissolution of cold war boundaries or vexed by the clash of traditional values with capitalist aspirations. For Hong Kong the looming merger with China, and the flight of people and capital to other parts of the world in advance of that unification, forms a central dynamic. Alternatively, those from Latin America and South America suffer under economies crushed by debt and controlled to a great extent by the policies of foreign banks and the International Monetary Fund rather than elected local or national officials. Their countries are not only debtor nations but are often forced to become beggar nations, a situation of helplessness that breeds both profound poverty and profound hatred. In this conference, the mutability of economics in social locations was constantly accented. Economics as a lens through which the Bible is read in religious communities may generate a wide range of possible issues. Poverty versus wealth, the primary economic theme explored by most U.S. biblical scholars, is on the world scene only one of many possible economic themes to be examined; forgiveness of debts, hospitality, taxation, almsgiving, possession of the land, labor, sharing of resources, triumph over imperialism, and exile are all important additional concerns in the diverse contexts of world economics.

Besides economics, another important aspect of location affecting the way the Bible is read is the self-understanding of Christianity in the midst of other dominant and ancient religious traditions. In Africa, Asia, and the Middle East, Christianity is a minority belief in most areas. In reintroducing Christianity to these locations,[4] the Western missionaries of the colonial period and later often denigrated the beliefs of traditional religions, which were quite ancient and well established, in their quest for converts to Christianity. Some Christian nationals in these areas today are struggling to reverse this pattern of disrespect for others and enter into mutually supportive ways of living. Conference participants differed, sometimes strongly, on how that mutuality might best be achieved. Some felt that the traditional missionary emphasis on conversion and Christian distinctiveness continued to be essential in establishing Christianity as an equal dialogue partner with

---

4. Judaism and Christianity began as West Asian and North African religions. When the Anglo-European and North American missionaries came to these areas, they were inserting Christianity into the region from which it originated and had never really disappeared.

its neighboring religions. Others argued the necessity of examining the exclusivistic claims of Christian theology in light of the spirituality of other major religions like Hinduism, Buddhism, and Islam. They thought that as a minority religion, Christianity has to recognize the serious and legitimate claims other religions make on people and that interpretations of the Bible and indeed the status of the Bible itself must be reconsidered in light of a full acceptance of religious diversity.

The political situation of readers of the Bible, which can vary radically from country to country even within the same region or from group to group within the same country, is yet a third aspect of social location that affects how people hear the Bible and what they take it to mean for their lives. Because people live in Western Europe or North America does not necessarily mean that they always read from the side of oppressive power relations, just as people living in Two-Thirds World countries do not always represent interpretations concerned with liberation. The political location of readers, their access to power in their societies, is simply too complex for such simple divisions to be accurate or even useful. Since all of the participants at the Vanderbilt conference were scholars, they were all among the more educated and thus generally more affluent classes in their societies. Yet they had all been invited because of public records of work against oppression and for liberation in their own particular situations. Hence, while concrete political affiliations or experiences were quite diverse, the educational, class, and reform orientation of the participants tended to construct a broad political common ground. Even though cultural, religious, and economic liberation for some participants would disrupt the economies and status of others, most of the conference participants, regardless of their national identification, agreed on the central importance of seeking that liberation.

As the conference progressed, I realized that my presuppositions about the areas in which participants would agree and would disagree were often wrong, and the complexity and diversity of the particular situations and experiences of participants were greater than I had anticipated. Nevertheless, in listening to this variety of conditions and circumstances, two recurrent themes kept surfacing even from the most culturally and geographically distinct locations: the profound difficulties occasioned by the colonial symbiosis of Christianity and Westernization and the remarkable energy, vigor, and theological creativity now emerging from Two-Thirds World locations.

Since Christianity and colonial occupation arrived together in most parts of the Two-Thirds World, many native Christians find themselves in the uncomfortable position of representing a belief that supported the destruction of their cultures and families. Moreover, the Western neocolonialism still pressuring many countries in the postcolonial period continues to reinforce the identification of "Christian values" with "Western values." The challenge for many Christians in the Two-Thirds World is not only to convince their neighbors that Christianity and Western capitalism are *not* the same but also to forge new, independent ways of worship, theological reflection, and religious education that employ their own distinctive cultural traditions and values. This important and creative effort to "indigenize" Christianity (in much the same way Western Europe originally blended its local customs into an eastern Mediterranean religion) has met with very mixed reactions from Western denominational or religious headquarters. The status of Christianity as a *Western* religion appears to be so crucial to some First World Christians that they view these movements toward local indigenous forms of Christianity as lapses into paganism, heresy, or worse. Like Paul, they are convinced that they alone have the "true gospel" and only by imitating them will others be "truly Christian." The effect of such anti-indigenous reactions has often been to wed Christianity ever more intimately to contemporary Western neocolonialism and thus to exacerbate the original problem. In a postcolonial world notable for the rise of nationalism, the political and theological significance of indigenization for the survival and growth of Christianity ought to be obvious. At the Vanderbilt conference the message was clear: to continue as a major religion, Christianity must truly become a *world* religion and not solely a *Western* religion.

Whether or not those of us in the First World support it, indigenous theological reflection is well under way throughout the Two-Thirds World, as represented by many of the essays in this volume. Indeed, in my opinion the theological pendulum is even now swinging away from the First World and toward the rest of the world. The variety of issues discussed, the vitality and creativity of the discussions, the sophisticated merging of critical reflection and praxis found in Two-Thirds World contexts already surpass most of what can be found in the dominant theological scholarship of the First World. Although some First World scholars may be hesitant to admit this shift publicly, two prominent features of First World behavior implicitly acknowledge it: the growth in "theological tourism" to the Two-Thirds World and the increasing reliance on liberation perspectives from Two-Thirds World writers in the publications of First World theologians. Greater and greater numbers of professional theologians and lay Christians are traveling to other parts of the globe to experience the vitality of Christianity in, for example, the base communities of Latin or South America or the indigenous churches of Africa. This "theological tourism," as many participants at the conference called it, witnesses both to the spirit of Christianity in Two-Thirds World settings and perhaps to the diminishment of that spirit in many First World locations. Similarly, the dominant theological discourse of the First World is progressively indebted to liberation perspectives developed elsewhere. The creativity of this scholarship from the margins broaches the further question of the appropriate venue for theological study. Do First World universities, divinity schools, and

seminaries, previously the unchallenged authorities in theological education and biblical scholarship, still deserve that status? While their economic
resources generally remain greater than those of most Two-Thirds World
schools, the quality and adequacy of their curricula, teaching, and research
are now increasingly open to debate. If the Two-Thirds World is becoming the more likely setting for creative, original, and engaged scholarship,
then may it not soon also be the locus for the most innovative institutional
developments in theological education?

Reflecting/Analyzing: The Status of Privilege

In reflecting upon the variety and vitality of issues raised by the conference
participants, I was forced to recognize that two of the responses most common to First World scholars in international contexts, and all too obviously
present at the Vanderbilt conference, are undoubtedly more patronizing
than appropriate. First, the general tendency of First World scholars to
seek metatheories, which purport to define the boundaries of truth for all
people everywhere or which attempt to delineate universally applicable criteria for determining correct action in all situations, generates a discourse
that denies difference as a significant category of experience. Because of
the seriousness with which difference must be taken in order to respect the
variety of opinions and concerns arising in Two-Thirds World situations,
the positing of universals or the developing of metatheories often demonstrates a basic refusal to listen, rendering the distinctive perspectives of the
marginalized invisible—again. For First World scholars who wish to respect
the insights of those from other perspectives, the desires to "fit" everyone
into one encompassing scheme, or to effect closure, or to dismiss ambiguity
must be strenuously resisted.

Second, because of the complexity and cultural specificity of each different context, the strong analytic emphasis of much First World scholarship
seems ill placed and imperious when it is focused solely on the locations or experiences of the Two-Thirds World. Are we in the First World
really the best suited to tell those in other locations how to view their
experiences? Or might people actually situated in marginalized settings be
the best qualified to observe and analyze their own circumstances? Moreover, it is remarkably presumptuous to assume that those schooled in the
methods and perspectives of Anglo-European scholarship have the skill or
perspicuity to reflect upon and analyze all contexts everywhere and determine what is needed to improve circumstances. Methods are no less
ideologically shaped than any other cultural tools. To employ Western
theoretical perspectives, developed out of the experiences of Western hierarchical power arrangements, hegemonic goals, and privileges, to analyze
Two-Thirds World contexts may very well serve mainly to replicate West-

ern structures, exclusions, and marginalities.[5] Indeed, for me it is a relevant question to ask whether or not the very use of the traditional androcentric form of the Anglo-European historical-critical method by some Two-Thirds World liberation theologians may itself account for a large part of the invisibility of women in their biblical scholarship. Perhaps in recognition of these tendencies, the richest streams of liberation theology are increasingly more indebted to native traditions than Western methods of research,[6] just as indigenous forms of Christianity around the world are primarily invigorated by local customs, beliefs, and practices.

If the experience of the Two-Thirds World itself is not the most appropriate focus for First World reflection in international gatherings, what better, more essential subject can be found? I think that the principal subject for reflection and analysis by First World scholars needs to be *their own* contexts and circumstances in light of the inequalities revealed in dialogue with those from the Two-Thirds World. It is, of course, much easier to analyze someone else's location than it is to examine one's own, but without reflection and analysis on what it means intellectually, economically, and ethically to live in the First World, whether one is a fully enfranchised member of that world or not, it is virtually impossible to speak with integrity or to act with probity.

Although categories like "First World/Two-Thirds World" or "Western" (the contrast to which is actually "global," not "Eastern"), which I have been using throughout this essay, are admittedly crude and rough generalizations about immensely multifaceted and complex phenomena, they do serve the purpose of indicating that more people living in the areas of the world designated by "First World" or "Western" are socially, politically, economically, and physically *privileged* as compared to those living in areas designated as "Two-Thirds World" or "global." The analysis of what it means to live as a more *privileged* person in relation to other people in the world is in general strikingly absent from most First World scholarship.[7] Besides the fact that it is always less painful, and thus easier, to analyze someone else's situation rather than one's own, privilege is an especially difficult experience to analyze because in terms of social location it can be defined as that which one does *not* feel. If I do not feel discriminated

[margin note: One may need to leave one's own location to analyze it.]

---

5. This is precisely the argument made by A. Lorde in her provocative essay "The Master's Tools Will Never Dismantle the Master's House," *Sister Outsider: Essays and Speeches* (Trumansburg, N.Y.: Crossing Press, 1984) 110–13.

6. See, for example, many of the essays in R. S. Sugirtharajah, ed., *Voices from the Margins: Interpreting the Bible in the Third World* (Maryknoll, N.Y.: Orbis Books, 1991), or in Sugirtharajah, ed., *Asian Faces of Jesus* (Maryknoll, N.Y.: Orbis Books, 1993).

7. Much the same point could be made by feminists in this country about most male scholarship. Even men who wish to be allied with feminist goals are all too often more concerned to analyze the situation of women and tell them what they need to do than to analyze their own relation of privilege to most women and reflect on what it means ethically for their actions.

against because of my class or race, it is because I am associated with a privileged class or race. If I do not feel poverty, it is because I am economically privileged. Privilege occurs in those social areas in which I fit the hegemonic norm of my society, for privilege is the other side of marginality. Privilege exists in those contexts in which I feel "normal" and think life is as it should be. Consequently, without external pressure from those marginalized, my privileges would remain hidden to me since they seem "natural" and attract no special attention. If I am especially sheltered in my privileges, I may actually think everyone lives as I do and their complaints of mistreatment are only so much whining or special pleading. Since it is only by comparison with others that I know that I am privileged, privilege is both deeply relational and always contextual. In moving through the changing relations of their lives, some people experience situations of both privilege and marginality but generally tend to notice only the marginal experiences because, after all, they are the ones that are unjust.[8]

The benefits of privilege are many. Those who are socially privileged have the freedom to acknowledge injustice or to ignore it. When one's existence is threatened by the prejudices of the society in which one lives or of the world in which one lives, one has no option but to face those issues daily. However, those whom these prejudices favor may choose to see the injustice of the situation or, more likely since it accrues to their benefit, to "naturalize" the inequality as just the way things are or should be. Those who are privileged are granted the power to name themselves and others. They do the speaking, so they can manage how they are depicted and how the marginalized are portrayed, allowing multiple opportunities for further "naturalizing" of their privileged status. Most importantly, they can control who gets into the privileged group or who even gets a hearing from the group and who does not and on what grounds those boons will be sanctioned. Nevertheless, privilege does have a downside. The difficulty with privilege is that it can only exist over against restriction, and in order for it to be really beneficial, those privileged must be a much smaller group than those who are restricted. This larger marginalized group, if sufficiently angry and sufficiently organized, has the potential to overturn the ordering of society as a whole, as revolutions and civil wars throughout history demonstrate. On the other hand, privileged people, as either their desire for ever greater privileges or their sense of beleaguerment by "the masses" grows, often tend to exercise increasingly repressive measures toward the larger restricted segments of the social order below them, serving to destabilize situations and precipitate major social crises. Privilege is thus inherently unstable, whether in a national or international arena.

---

8. See my fuller discussion of this position in "Reading for Liberation," *Reading from This Place,* vol. 1, *Social Location and Biblical Interpretation in the United States* (ed. F. F. Segovia and M. A. Tolbert; Minneapolis: Fortress Press, 1995) 263–68.

Social privilege is most commonly found in hierarchical societies, for such societies are explicitly constructed to privilege some and marginalize others. Who is privileged and who is marginalized and on what primary bases those distinctions revolve may differ widely; social status, land owning, and native birth, as in ancient Rome, or wealth, race, and gender, as in the modern United States, are only two possible configurations. However, regardless of the determining criteria, it is extremely important to realize that social privilege or social marginalization of this kind is not earned by an individual or group as much as it is *ascribed* or *bestowed* by the "facts of blood and bread"[9] over which the individual has little or no control. In some religious traditions, the injustice of this culturally constructed inequality has led to the formation of explanatory concepts like "fate" or "karma," the inescapable destiny that shapes my present "birthright." Since even the most privileged situation often requires some expenditure of effort to advance and fully employ this "birthright," it is easy to posit that effort as in effect "earning" the privileges I enjoy. One of my favorite lines about confusing privilege with effort is former Texas governor Ann Richards's quip about former president George Bush: George Bush was born on third base and all his life he has acted like he hit a triple. As this baseball analogy suggests, it is easy in the course of one's life to forget how far ahead of the game one started by accident of birth into the "right" (that is, privileged) gender, race, class, sexual orientation, family, religion, region, country, and so on.

Although I am clearly not in the main responsible for the "facts of blood and bread" in which I find myself, that lack of culpability does not mean that my social location entails no accountability. In fact, the very fortuitous or accidental construction of privilege raises for me its most compelling ethical obligations from a Christian perspective, for as the Lukan Jesus says to Peter, "Everyone to whom much is given, will much be required" (Luke 12:48). Privileged social location is a gift of birth, not an earned right, and the present gratuitous inequality of such "gifting" constructs a world order that is profoundly unjust. If, as a Christian, I believe that God wishes justice—indeed even mercy—for creation, I am obliged to work for the establishment of a new order, even though it means that I must lose the privileges I currently hold. I am willing to lose those privileges because I trust that in a world where there is justice for all, there will also be justice for me. In the context of the dialogue between First World scholars and Two-Thirds World scholars, I believe the establishment of justice calls for those who are privileged to work consciously to decenter the hegemony of current Western neocolonialism.

---

9. For a discussion of the use of these terms to describe social location, see pp. 331–32.

Acting: Decentering and Empowering

First World biblical scholars have one possible model for decentering their privileged status in the New Testament depiction of John the Baptist, as found especially in the Gospel of John. In the Gospel of John, John the Baptist, whose own importance is indicated by the arrival of Levites and priests from Jerusalem to interrogate him, uses his centrality to witness to the greater vitality of someone else (John 1:19-34). He then further divests himself of power, not by simply walking away from the situation, but by actually pointing out to his disciples another, better teacher (John 1:35-40). In both of these cases, John the Baptist uses the power he controls to promote the influence and value of someone else. Moreover, he explicitly announces this action as an intentional plan in John 3:25-36, where he makes the striking assertion, "It is necessary for him to increase but for me to decrease" (v. 30). Regardless of the possible historical conflict between the John the Baptist sect and the early Christians, which this polemically shaped portrayal may indicate, the narrative role John is given to play is of a powerful, central figure using his influence to advance someone else, an action that will inevitably entail his own loss of centrality. Although in the Gospel of John, John the Baptist seems convinced of Jesus' greater role from the moment he sees him, in the "Q" account of John the Baptist's relationship to Jesus, John continues to raise questions and seek evidence to prove that Jesus is who he seems to be (Luke 7:18-35/Matt 11:2-19), demonstrating that uncritical acceptance need not be the only response one makes to a new, powerful leader.

For the context of First World scholars, several aspects of this narrative portrait are valuable. First, John the Baptist does not simply disappear from the narrative as soon as Jesus appears; he continues to witness to what he has seen, and in "Q" he continues to press his own issues and concerns. One possible response of First World representatives in a potentially conflictual dialogue is simply to remain quiet or just walk away. Such disengagement is, of course, another indication of privilege, for those who can choose to leave the table when discussions are difficult are those who are secure in their own power, knowing that the decisions made after they leave will not affect them. It may be that one of the most important ethical commitments First World scholars can make for a more just world is the decision to stay engaged, to continue the dialogue, to care about the results. Second, in the "Q" account particularly, John seeks additional information about Jesus' activities and views. Although they are often called upon to perform this task, it is not the responsibility of Two-Thirds World scholars to reverse the tradition of sanctioned ignorance about global concerns endemic to First World scholarship; that effort is for First World scholars themselves to undertake. Educating myself about the traditions, conflicts, values, and methods of Two-Thirds World scholarship is another necessary and appropriate action I can take. In that education, I am, however, not required to agree with all I find nor to accept everything I hear uncritically; a respectful, justice-seeking dialogue avoids both extremes of unquestioning enthusiasm and pedantic posturing.

Third, John the Baptist uses the power he has to empower another. First World scholars have power; at the very least, they have economic power, like that which funded the Vanderbilt conference; publishing power, like that which stands behind the production of this volume and others like it; and knowledge-producing and knowledge-disseminating power, like that employed by introducing Two-Thirds World scholarship into curricula, course assignments, degree programs, or determining the boundaries of "legitimate" methods of analysis or subjects of research. To what ends and to whose benefit that power is used is another, vital area of ethical responsibility for those in the First World. Ignoring one's power or pretending it does not exist fools no one, least of all people much too familiar with the disguises of neocolonialism. Giving up power, whatever one might mean by that phrase, in this present world of power politics mainly risks having one's position and influence taken over by others less concerned with constructing a just world. In contrast, employing the power one has, however limited one may believe it to be, to level the playing field of world society in search of a more just social order is an action of profound importance. The analogy of John the Baptist and Jesus breaks down at this point because the goal of decentering is not to replace one center with another, to mow down one hill on the playing field only to pile up another one, but instead, the goal is to destabilize the whole center-margins structure, to level the field for everyone. In order to alter the present injustices in power relations, those who have power in this current order must begin to wield it to empower others.

Fourth, John the Baptist knows who he is; he knows who Jesus is; and he knows that they are different. In the Gospel of John, he is constantly reminding everyone from his Jerusalem inquisitors to his own disciples that he is "not the Christ" (John 1:20; 3:28) but a voice crying in the wilderness (1:23) or the one sent out ahead (3:28). The social locations of First World biblical scholars and Two-Thirds World scholars are not the same. The pressures, exigencies, hopes, exclusions, challenges, and so on, they face are varied and quite different. Taking those differences seriously at this moment in world history requires, among other things, that calls for unity must cease. Most calls for unity in contexts of real difference are actually thinly disguised appeals to follow one group's or person's views and dismiss the claims of others, for unity, after all, means marching under one banner rather than many. This authoritarian drive behind pleas for unity can be easily recognized in Paul's letters to the Corinthians, for example, where he is as deeply concerned that they acknowledge his influence over them as he is that they reject factionalism. Instead of calling for unity, the present situation of difference demands the willingness to confront competing constructions of what constitutes proper method, excellence in research, and perhaps even scholarship itself; to negotiate new networks of power arrangements; and to work through the inevitable conflicts such discussions will incite.

Nevertheless, while John the Baptist and Jesus were extremely different figures, they shared a similar grounding of faith and hope for the future. First World biblical scholars and Two-Thirds World biblical scholars, like First World Christians or Jews and Two-Thirds World Christians or Jews, also share common ground where bridges of understanding may be built. That common ground is the Bible itself, its stories, metaphors, images, and characters. In our very particular contexts and strikingly different locations, the biblical texts provide a shared narrative language, a mythology that can fund our discussions and undergird our negotiations. By really hearing the varieties of meanings other people out of their own social locations create in the Bible, we might actually come to understand who those others are in their differences and who we are in ours considerably better than we do now. Furthermore, because I believe that explicit attention to the particularity of others is the basis of love and that whatever truth there is in this world is not forged in me or in another but somewhere between us, I find in this process of dialogue a tiny glimpse, a faint hint of that long-awaited messianic banquet. Yet inviting all the world to sit at table together and share the great feast is a risk because, you know, they just might come.

But is it the same Bible for everyone?

Index of Names